MARKETING

FOR

SPORT BUSINESS

SUCCESS

OWNERS, TRAINERS AND PRESS ONLY

HOT DOGS · BALLPARK SNACKS & BEVERAGES

Phillies

Kendall Hunt
publishing company

Bonnie L. **Parkhouse** | Brian A. **Turner** | Kimberly S. **Miloch**

Book Team

Chairman and Chief Executive Officer   Mark C. Falb
President and Chief Operating Officer   Chad M. Chandlee
Vice President, Higher Education   David L. Tart
Director of Publishing Partnerships   Paul B. Carty
Editorial Manager   Georgia Botsford
Developmental Editor   Melissa M. Tittle
Vice President, Operations   Timothy J. Beitzel
Assistant Vice President, Production Services   Christine E. O'Brien
Senior Production Editor   Mary Melloy
Senior Permissions Editor   Caroline Kieler
Cover Designer   Marilyn Kuperschmidt
Web Project Editor   Jade Sprecher

Cover images:
Background— © Shutterstock Inc.
Top l to r— © Shutterstock Inc. © Shutterstock Inc. Used with permission of *Philadelphia Inquirer*; Michael Bryant. Copyright © 2011.
Center l to r— © Shutterstock Inc. © Shutterstock Inc. Courtesy of Brian Turner.
Bottom l to r— © The Phillies 2010. Courtesy of Mark Nagel.

Kendall Hunt
publishing company

www.kendallhunt.com
Send all inquiries to:
4050 Westmark Drive
Dubuque, IA 52004-1840

Printed in the United States of America
10 9 8 7 6 5 4 3 2

Dedication

Many thanks to Judith Switzer who was there for me through the darkness of recovering from cancer and gave me the encouragement to again celebrate life as I accepted total responsibility for this challenging project. Judy was on 1st, Melissa Tittle (Developmental Editor) on 2nd, and Paul Carty on 3rd as I went up to bat. You, the reader, gets to decide the score.

- Bonnie Parkhouse

My contributions to this book would not have been possible without the love and support of my family. Thanks to Gretchen for being my best friend, Briana for sharing my love of sports, and Alex for teaching me to see the world in a different way.

- Brian Turner

A tremendous thanks to my husband and daughter for your support, encouragement, and guidance throughout this project.

- Kimberly Miloch

Brief Contents

Contents

CHAPTER 3   UNDERSTANDING SPORT CONSUMER BEHAVIOR   55
B. Christine Green and Matthew T. Bowers

CHAPTER 4   MARKETING INFORMATION   83
Chad Seifried and Todd Hall

Preface

In the spring of 2008, Paul Carty from Kendall Hunt Publishing Company called my office at Temple University asking if I would be interested in writing a textbook on sport marketing for them. Since I was in the process of retiring and enjoyed teaching this subject to undergraduate, master's, and doctoral students, "Yes" was my immediate response. I presented him with my vision of how this could be effectively achieved. Since the field of sport marketing has become so specialized, it is necessary to call upon a number of experts in various areas so a textbook of this nature is as comprehensive as necessary to meet the job-related needs of a growing, challenging, and competitive industry. This includes state-of-the-art marketing strategies applied to the business of sport. The three co-editors and 23 contributors made this possible.

The nature and scope of sport marketing are addressed in detail; discussion of the uniqueness of sport marketing is the most comprehensive ever published on this topic. The chapter on sport consumer behavior discusses how aspects of social responsibility have emerged as a new way for sport marketers to add "secondary value" to their brands beyond the traditional "on-field" sport product. Situations are presented where marketers can strategically capitalize on their ability to foster reputational, relational, and partnership assets through social responsibility, social responsiveness, corporate citizenship, and cause–marketing efforts.

A sound understanding of segmentation and its implications for the sport industry is addressed. Following the discussion of the challenges facing sport organizations, the chapter outlines the specific implementations of segmentation as they relate to various elements of sport marketing. Included in the chapter is a structure to provide a sound understanding of marketing segmentation and how it can improve interactions with consumers. The chapter on the marketing mix explains each element in detail and provides real-world examples from a variety of sport organizations.

A ticket to a sporting event features competition on the field of play and an entertainment or fan experience featuring all elements of the *sportscape* (i.e., all components surrounding the product of sport and the design through which fans experience the product). The sport product and pricing strategies chapter explores the nature of sport products, highlights the unique characteristics of these products, and outlines the dynamics of *pricing* sport products.

The chapter on technology addresses ways to creatively use technology to produce a superior product and service to generate revenue streams and enhance the consumer's experience and entertainment value. Use of the Internet and such innovations as virtual and mobile technology are presented. As sport marketers, strategy is probably more familiar than it may be to the general populace as most individuals have a passion for playing and/or watching sport that is driven by competitive strategy. Sport marketers strive to outmaneuver their competition in the battle for consumer discretionary income. Sport business is an industrial war for market share, which requires a strategic sport marketing approach addressed in this text.

The sponsorship and endorsement chapter outlines the key concepts specific to sport sponsorship and athlete endorsement. The evolving nature of the sport industry offers unique and challenging opportunities to build lasting impressions and relationships. The focus of the chapter on brand management is to strategically craft an identity in the marketplace, create valuable emotional connections through experiences, and determine characteristics that attract loyal consumers.

The legal chapter can be easily understood by those unfamiliar with such legal concepts as: Ambush marketing, intellectual property, contracts and torts, and league licensing rights in brand advertisement. "...the legal and business sides of sports marketing are very much married to its glamour. As with all things in life, the law lives where you least expect it." The careers chapter provides hands-on, practical career insight and tools to effectively aid in the job search process (e.g., cover letter and resume construction, interview, networking, salary negotiation strategies, and portfolio development).

 In addition, a fully integrated student and instructor website for this text is available. The web access code is included on the inside front cover of this textbook. Look for the web icons in the text's margin to direct you to various interactive tools to enhance your learning experience. The site includes:

- Instructor Resource Manual

- Test Bank

- PowerPoint® slides

- Study Guide

- Poll Questions

- Glossary of Key Terms

The focus of this text is to provide a comprehensive introduction to the field of sport marketing; equally important, it presents an effective foundation from which sport marketing students are well-prepared to pursue more advanced coursework as they progress through their academic program.

Bonnie L. Parkhouse

List of Contributors

Matt Bowers, University of Texas at Austin

Christopher J. Cabbott, Esq.

Galen Clavio, Ph.D., Indiana University

Coyte Cooper, Ph.D., University of North Carolina, Chapel Hill

Sal DeAngelis, Philadelphia Phillies

Steve Dittmore, Ph.D., University of Arkansas

Andrea Eagleman, Ph.D., Indiana University, Purdue
    University, Indianapolis

Amanda Glenn, Texas Woman's University

B. Christine Green, Ph.D., University of Texas at Austin

Chris Greenwell, Ph.D., University of Louisville

Todd Hall, Ph.D., Georgia Southern University

Jason W. Lee, Ph.D., University of North Florida

Heidi Parker, University of Southern Maine

Lloyd Z. Remick, Esq.

Ryan Rodenberg, J.D., Ph.D., Florida State University

Amy Rundio, University of Texas at Austin

David Rylander, Ph.D., Texas Woman's University

Chad Seifried, Ph.D., Louisiana State University

Dustin Thorn, Ph.D., Coastal Carolina University

Matt Walker, University of Southern Mississippi

Laci Wallace, MS, East Texas Baptist University

Erianne Weight, Ph.D., University of North Carolina, Chapel Hill

Jacquelyn Wilson, MBA, Texas Woman's University

About the Authors

Bonnie L. Parkhouse received a Ph.D. in Administration from the University of Minnesota. She retired in 2008 from Temple University in the School of Tourism and Hospitality Management. Other previous faculty appointments include the University of Southern California and California State University, Fullerton. Twenty of her studies have been published in distinguished referred research journals. Numerous articles she has written have appeared in trade and commercial publications. She is the senior author of previous books and the editor of four editions of *The Management of Sport: Its Foundation and Application.*

Dr. Parkhouse is a former member of the editorial boards for the *Journal of Sport Management, Quest,* and the *International Journal of Sport Management.* She was a member of the committee that wrote the Sport Management Curriculum Standards (first published in 1993) and one of the original seven members of the Sport Management Program Review Council (SMPRC). On invitation, she has served as a consultant in sport management curricular matters at numerous institutions in the United States, Australia, Canada, the Caribbean, and England. She is recognized as a progenitor of sport management curricula and theory; her publications are frequently cited by other authors. Professor Parkhouse received an outstanding alumnae award from the University of Minnesota in 2002 and a distinguished achievement award from the North American Society for Sport Management (NASSM) and the National Association for Sport and Physical Education (NASPE) in 2007 in recognition of her contribution to the sport management discipline.

Brian A. Turner is an Associate Professor and coordinator of the Sport Management program at The Ohio State University. He earned his bachelor of science degree in secondary education from Baylor University and his masters of education degree in physical education from Tarleton State University. He received his Ph.D. in Sport Management from Ohio State in 2001. Prior to his current position, Dr. Turner served three years as the Director of Sport Management and as Assistant Professor at DeSales University and one year as a Visiting Assistant Professor at the University of Oklahoma. His research has appeared in such publications as the *Journal of Sport Management, Applied Research in Coaching & Athletics Annual, Internal Journal of Sport Management, Journal of ICHPER-SD, Journal for the Study of Sports and Athletes in Education,* the *Journal of Academic Ethics,* and *Sport Marketing Quarterly.* He is currently a co-editor of the *Journal of Issues in Intercollegiate Athletics.* In 2007, Dr. Turner was named a North American Society for Sport Management (NASSM) Research Fellow.

Dr. Turner resides in Hilliard, Ohio, with his wife Gretchen (a high school guidance counselor) and children, Briana and Alex.

You can follow Dr. Turner on Twitter at @drturner.

Kimberly S. Miloch currently serves as Associate Professor and Graduate Sport Management Coordinator in the Department of Kinesiology at Texas Woman's University. She earned her Ph.D. in sport management from Florida State University in 2002. She holds a master of science in sport management from Baylor University, and a bachelor of arts in mass communication, public relations from Texas State University. Prior to Texas Woman's University, Dr. Miloch was a member of the sport management faculty at Indiana University and Northern Illinois University.

Dr. Miloch's research focuses on factors influencing sport consumption specific to sport communication and public relations, sport brand management, sport sponsorship, and social media usage in sport. She has presented her research at over 30 professional conferences and published more than 20 peer reviewed national or international journals including the *International Journal of Sport Communication, International Journal of Sport Management, International Journal of Sport Management & Marketing,* and *Sport Marketing Quarterly.* She has co-authored *Strategic Sport Communication,* and has authored or co-authored more than nine textbook chapters.

She currently serves as the Vice President of Academic Affairs for the Sport Marketing Association and on the editorial review boards of *Sport Marketing Quarterly* and the *International Journal of Sport Communication.* Prior to entering academia, Dr. Miloch worked in marketing, sponsorship, and public relations in minor league hockey and for the United States Tennis Association Texas Section. She teaches courses in sport marketing, sport sales, sport sponsorship, and sport communication.

She lives in Denton, Texas where she enjoys playing competitive tennis, cooking, and spending time with her husband and daughter.

You can follow Dr. Miloch on Twitter at @KimberlyMiloch.

Courtesy of Brian Turner

CHAPTER 1

Sport Marketing: Definition, Evolution, Uniqueness, and Importance

Bonnie L. Parkhouse
Brian A. Turner Ohio State University

The competition in the job market today calls for being as well-prepared as possible. You must prepare for your future, and that key is education.

Paul "Bear" Bryant

CHAPTER OBJECTIVES

After completing the chapter, the reader should be able to:

- Define marketing and sport marketing.
- Explain the special nature of sport marketing.
- Identify the unique aspects of sport.
- Understand the importance of marketing at all levels of sport.
- Discuss the current state of revenue generation at the professional, intercollegiate, interscholastic, and youth levels.

Definition

Marketing, as defined by Kotler (2003), is the activity focusing on satisfying needs and wants through exchange processes (which will be referred to as traditional marketing throughout this text). Although specific definitions for the concept and practice of sport marketing have been entertained and developed since 1994, the term **sport marketing** was coined by *Advertising Age* in 1978 to define the activities of product and service marketers using sport as a promotional vehicle or sponsorship platform (Gray & McEvoy, 2005). The article noted that using sport to reach the masses was best characterized as *marketing through sport*, and emphasized that a reference to the *marketing of sport* was lacking. Since 1978, sport marketing has evolved into a well established academic discipline and a legitimate and effective platform for positioning and promoting both sport and non-sport products. According to Fullerton (2010), sport marketing has developed two major focuses: marketing sport products and services directly to sport consumers and marketing non-sport products and services through the use of sport promotions.

For the purpose of this textbook, sport marketing includes creating a demand for spectator and participant sports and sports equipment (marketing of sport) as well as marketing traditional or non-sport products and services using a sport platform (marketing through sport). The tremendous growth of the sport industry and the use of sport to position and heavily promote non-sport products and services have resulted in an ever increasing need for well-educated and highly trained sport marketing personnel. Based on these needs, this textbook focuses heavily on the marketing of sport while also devoting several chapters to marketing through sport. In this chapter, you will be introduced to key foundational concepts of sport marketing and learn how the marketing of sport and marketing through sport can be both challenging and unique compared to marketing traditional products and services.

The Evolution of Sport Marketing

Sport and non-sport products can be used in the above settings. For example, sport apparel and shoes are commonly used for comfort. A pair of Reebok shoes designed for jogging may be worn by a commuter who has her high heel shoes for the office in a backpack. Although hot dogs are sold at sporting venues, they are non-sport products, as are hamburgers and any other type of sandwich.

Industry Evolution

Although marketing of sport is the focus of this textbook, the concept of marketing through sport needs further clarification. In 1921, Babe Ruth endorsed Jockey underwear. In the early 1930's, marketers of Wheaties cereal used athletes and sports themes to sell their product. The Wheaties box is still marketed as "the Breakfast of Champions." Quarterback Joe Namath (Broadway Joe), who played for the New York Jets in the 60's and 70's, was featured in a TV commercial wearing L'eggs pantyhose. The above are examples of using a sport platform, such as athlete endorsements or sport themes to market non-sport or traditional products. Sport

Courtesy of Brian Turner.

events and venues also are used in this endeavor. Companies have notoriously paid significant sums to name sport venues. Some examples include AT&T Park in San Francisco, FedEx Field in Washington, DC, American Airlines Center in Dallas, Ford Field in Detroit, Heinz Field in Pittsburgh, and Lucas Oil Stadium in Indianapolis. Budweiser often uses the backdrops of sports stadiums in its advertisements as part of its overall marketing strategy, and some of the most well known companies in the world have used sport events as the platform to expand their brands and services in North America and globally. For example, FedEx has North American partnerships with FedEx Racing, National Football League (NFL), National Basketball Association (NBA), and FedEx Cup. Home Depot engages in partnerships with NFL, National Association for Stock Car Auto Racing (NASCAR), and Entertainment and Sports Programming Network (ESPN). One of its best known partnerships includes building the set for *ESPN's College Game Day*. Globally, McDonald's and Coca-Cola both capitalize on their respective association with the Olympic Games and both build and leverage their brands and products in doing so. Coca-Cola has used the Olympics as a marketing platform since shipping the beverage to United States athletes for the 1928 Games in Amsterdam. For the 2008 Beijing Games, the company highlighted its "Live Olympic on the Coke Side of Life" campaign. As part of this campaign, the company developed a series of collective cans encouraging repeat consumption of the product by utilizing the slogan "Bring Home the World" (Zmuda, 2008). Similar to that of Coca-Cola, McDonald's first associated itself with the Olympics when it flew hamburgers to US Olympians at the 1968 Olympics in Grenoble, France (Lefton, 2005). For the 2008 Games in Beijing, the fast food giant implemented its Olympic Champion Crew program which featured an elite team of employees representing all regions of the world. This elite team traveled to Beijing to act as brand ambassadors for the company and to serve McDonald's food to athletes, coaches, media, and Olympic personnel (Skinner, 2007).

© L. Scott Mann/Icon SMI/Corbis.

Marketers of traditional products use sport as a tool to increase consumer awareness, create new markets, and market new products:

- **Increase consumer awareness.** In the 70's and 80's, Hertz Rent-A-Car hired O.J. Simpson to endorse their product in commercials showing the dapper Simpson running through airports to catch a rental car. The Hertz strategy was to reinforce its number one position in the car rental industry by associating with a football player with similar credentials—a Heisman Trophy winner, the highest individual award in college football, and the first player to run for 2,000 yards in an NFL season. Other classic examples include the Miller Lite commercials using retired, masculine, professional athletes in the 1970's to convince the major beer-drinking demographic that Lite beer is not a diet, therefore un-macho brew. Rather, it has a "Great Taste ... Less filling!" As a result, Miller Lite's long running advertising campaign was ranked by *Advertising Age* magazine as the 8th best in history. Miller's successful creation of this low-calorie market can be compared to the highly successful rise of Xerox in the photocopier industry using sport as a setting to market its products.

- **Create new markets.** Sport also is used to attract new consumer markets. Dr. Scholl's products have long been marketed to individuals with foot problems exacerbated from aging (e.g., bunions, corns, and calluses). In 1988, Julius "Dr. J." Erving became the spokesperson for a new line of Dr. Scholl's products for the physically active, saying, "New Tritin scores the first three-point play against athlete's foot." Today, active consumers can purchase a variety of foot products including sport shoe inserts, Band-Aid type adhesive strips for blisters, and gelled, tube-like wraps to cushion sore toes.

- **Market new products.** Several years ago, Xerox introduced its new copying machines using a montage of distance runners in a marathon to highlight "a running machine" designed to withstand the greatest tests of stamina and endurance.

Academic Evolution

In the United States, although the first sport management programs were established between the 1940's and 1970's, a significant proliferation in curriculum development did not occur until the mid-1980's. In fact, by 1988, only 10 percent of the 109 programs had been in existence for more than five years. Unlike the United States, the number of Canadian academic programs has not changed significantly and is much smaller in nature.

Unfortunately, sport management programs during this early period merely repackaged existing physical education curriculum, adding catchy course titles. Such a practice lacked credibility. Parkhouse reported that a significant number of these programs included subject matter that was questionable in meeting the educational and job-related needs of this industry. Further, a significant number of these programs were "more on paper than in practice" (Parkhouse, 2005).

Sport marketing as a specialization area was initially incorporated into sport management courses taught primarily in such programs as leisure studies, physical education, recreation, exercise physiology, and kinesiology. A principles of marketing course may have included some sport examples.

Mahony and Pitts (1998) called for increased attention to developing areas of specialization in sport management. They emphasized that specialization is critical for developing a unique body of knowledge. In 1989, the North American Society for Sport Management (NASSM) and the National Association for Sport and Physical Education (NASPE) formed a joint task force to establish the first sport management curriculum standards at the undergraduate, masters, and doctoral levels. Marketing in sport was identified as a content area at the baccalaureate level and marketing in sport and public relations in sport at the masters level. Sport marketing was also a specialization option at the doctoral level. Each content area included a body of knowledge needed to meet job-related needs in the sport management industry. Today, the Sport Marketing Association (SMA) hosts an annual conference and publishes the *Sport Marketing Quarterly* (SMQ).

The international community has looked at North America, particularly the United States, as a paradigm or model for curriculum development, research, journals, and conferences in sport management-related fields. In the past decade, colleges and universities have developed degree programs in sport management around the world, including: China, Czech Republic, Finland, France, Germany, Greece, Hong Kong, India, Ireland, Italy, Japan, Korea, Malaysia, Netherlands, Norway, Scotland, Singapore, South Africa, Spain, Sweden, Taiwan, and United Kingdom.

Japan has undergone a significant change in academic program focus. Since the Japanese physical education curriculum has decreased in demand, a growing need for personnel in the commercial sector has surfaced, particularly in the driving range industry. More than 100 million people use driving range facilities each year.

The Asian Association for Sport Management, the European Association for Sport Management, the Latin American Organization in Sport Management, the Sport Management Association of Australia and New Zealand, and the Korean Association for Sport Management are among those sport management organizations worldwide.

The Special Nature of Sport Marketing

Sport is a "special" experience and, because of the unique nature of the business of sport, marketers must approach it differently than they do traditional products (Mullin, Hardy and Sutton, 2007). As Peter Bavasi of the Cleveland Indians once said, "Marketing baseball isn't the same as selling soap or bread. You're selling a memory, an illusion." Following are several unique sport characteristics important in marketing sport.

Sport Pervades All Elements of Life

Sport is a mirror of society. Tom Boswell's (1982) *How Life Imitates the World Series* suggests that sport (specifically, baseball) imitates life (or the reverse!). Sport has been called the leveler of social class. Above the logotype and name of most daily newspapers are sport scores. Sport also has its own section in the newspaper. The 10 and 11 o'clock evening news was created to primarily announce sport scores since most other news of the day was reported before sporting events began.

Following are components of this phenomenon:

- ***Food and Drink.*** Eating and drinking are very much a part of the spectator experience in the stadium or arena, as is tailgating, or watching the event on television at home or in a sports bar. Tailgating at college football games in the United States starts before dawn, even for night games! Drinking alcohol, especially beer, is definitely associated with watching sporting events.

  Although hot dogs, peanuts, soda, and beer are no longer acceptable limits for ballpark concession fare, eating hot dogs is a major part of the ballpark ritual. Where does a hot dog taste better than at a ballgame? And, food is a part of the home-field advantage. It must be a Chicago dog (celery salt, tomato, cucumber, bright-green relish, yellow mustard, chopped onion, and a seeded bun) at Wrigley Field. In Los Angeles, it's a Dodger Dog (grilled, never boiled). In Detroit,

Courtesy of Sal DeAngelis.

it's Coney Islands (chilidogs). The New York Yankees offer kosher hot dogs and the Colorado Rockies have buffalo dogs.

Noshing on local specialties has become a ballpark experience: New England clam chowder at Fenway Park, potato and cheese dumplings in Cleveland, chili in Cincinnati, bratwurst in Milwaukee, the fish sandwich in Pittsburgh at PNC Park, and fish tacos in San Diego. What has baseball become when you're able to purchase butternut squash soup and a pear salad at a game in cheese-steak-country, South Philly?

Vicarious Experiences. Sport is one of various aspects of life that is experienced vicariously. People have been modeling their lives after films for years according to film critic Renata Adler (1969). A classic example of living vicariously through the story is the 1976 film *Rocky*. It was a box office smash (and won the Academy Award for Best Picture) about a young man from the slums of Philadelphia who dreamed of becoming a boxing champion. An intense portrayal of the American dream, it shows Rocky running up the steps of the Philadelphia Art Museum in early morning workouts. A statue of Rocky has been erected at the bottom of those steps; everyday, tourists imitate that run and have their pictures taken with the statue.

Sports fans wear replica jerseys and identify with winning teams (basking in a team's victory and glory) and the legacy of athletes who, often as underdogs, surfaced from unlikely places to reach the pinnacle of athletic excellence: Michael Jordan, Muhammad Ali, Billie Jean King, Jesse Owens, Babe Ruth, and Jack Nicklaus, for example. Tennis greats Venus and Serena Williams are role models for young, Black youth who also are growing up in an economically disadvantaged environment. Golf prodigy Tiger Woods has also been a role model, although a recent marital infidelity scandal may seriously blemish his image as a clean-cut, family ambassador.

Lance Armstrong, winner of the Tour de France seven consecutive years from 1999 to 2005 and a cancer survivor, has established a foundation to combat this deadly disease. This foundation's registered trademark is a yellow rubber wristband labeled LIVESTRONG which is worn by thousands of supporters of this effort.

Some parents live vicariously through their children's athletic potential for success. A recent commercial by an investment firm shows a four year old daughter holding a racket one-half her size in both hands while her father on the other side of the net working the ball machine yells, "Emily, hit the ball" as it flies by her at 30 miles an hour. The message suggests that he is trying to turn her into the next Maria Yuryevna Sharapova. The motive of other parents is a full-ride athletic scholarship for their children to a university.

- ***Entertainment.*** Spectator sport is a major source of entertainment throughout the world. The telecast of the 2012 (XLVI) Super Bowl was the most-watched program in television history. The New York Giants win over the New England Patriots (21–17) attracted 111.3 million viewers. Of the ten most watched television programs in US history, eight are Super Bowls (including the last six, from 2007-2012). The only non-sport programs in the top 10 were the 1983 finale of the Korean War sitcom *M*A*S*H* (4th all time) and the 1993 finale of the sitcom *Cheers* (9th all time; see Table 1.1).

TABLE 1.1

Top Ten Most Watched Television Programs in US History			
Rank	**Program**	**Year**	**Viewers**
1	Super Bowl XLVI	2012	111.3 million
2	Super Bowl XLV	2011	111 million
3	Super Bowl XLIV	2010	106.5 million
4	*M*A*S*H** series finale	1983	106 million
5	Super Bowl XLII	2008	97.5 million
6	Super Bowl XLIII	2009	95.4 million
7	Super Bowl XXX	1996	94.1 million
8	Super Bowl XLI	2007	93.2 million
9	*Cheers* series finale	1993	93.1 million
10	Super Bowl XX	1986	92.5 million

Note. Adapted from "10 Most Watched Shows of All Time in TV History," http://filmpopper. com/10-most-watched-tv-shows-of-all-time/ and "Super Bowl Ratings Record: Giants-Patriots Game Is Highest-Rated TV Show In US History," http://www.huffingtonpost. com/2012/02/06/super-bowl-ratings-record-tv-giants-patriots_n_1258107.html.

- Internationally, sports also dominate television ratings. In Canada, the most watched event in history was the 2010 Winter Olympics hockey final. Roughly one-half of the country (16.6 million people) tuned in to see Canada defeat the United States in overtime ("Olympic final most watched hockey game in 30 years", 2010). The previous most watched program was the opening ceremony from those Winter Olympic Games (Grohmann, 2010). The two most watched shows in Australian television history were sporting events—the Australian Open men's tennis finals in 2005 and the 2003 Rugby World Cup between Australia and England. Eight of the nine most watched programs in Germany are soccer matches involving their home country team (The Most Watched Programs in TV History, 2010). Finally, in the United Kingdom, the most watched television program is still the 1966 FIFA World Cup soccer final, in which England defeated West Germany 4-2 at Wembley Stadium in London (this match narrowly beat out the funeral of Princess Diana in 1997; Tapper, 2005).

- **Politics.** Because so much of the world is watching, the Olympic Games are used as a political platform. One such platform is for defectors. Tennis star Martina Navratilova defected from her native Czechoslovakia and took refuge in the United States during the 1975 US Open. Recipient of the first perfect 10's in Olympic gymnastics, gold medalist and world champion Nadia Comaneci defected to the United States from her native Romania in 1989, a few weeks before the Revolution.

Another such platform is for dissidents. At the 1968 Summer Olympics in Mexico City, on the medal stand stood two Black Americans (Tommie Smith and John Carlos), recipients of the gold and bronze medals, respectively. As the "Star Spangled Banner" played, they lowered their heads and each defiantly raised a black-gloved, clenched fist; the message each conveyed was black power in America. During the 1972 Munich Olympics, 11 Israeli athletes were kidnapped from the Olympic Village and killed in a gun battle at a nearby airport by Palestinian terrorists. In early 1980, President Jimmy Carter thought he could change the Soviet Union's foreign policy by refusing to participate in the Summer Olympics that year; hence, an American-led boycott of the 1980 games in Moscow took place. Four years later, the Soviet Union initiated a payback by leading 15 nations in a boycott of the 1984 Olympic Games in Los Angeles.

Political baseball is currently taking place in Arizona where a strict immigration law could force players to prove their immigration status at any time. More than one-quarter of professional baseball players were born outside of the United States. The bill, which has potential for stereotyping and racial profiling, created a loud megaphone when activists protested outside Chicago's Wrigley Field and National's Park in Washington, D.C. when they hosted the Arizona Diamondbacks.

Presidential candidates need to at least show interest in sport; it's even better if they have some athletic ability. For example, John F. Kennedy played touch football on the lawn in Hyannisport, Gerald Ford was a star football player at the University of Michigan and helped his team win two national championships, George W. H. Bush captained the Yale baseball team to two College World Series appearances, Dwight Eisenhower golfed, Bill Clinton and George W. Bush jogged, and Barack Obama plays "pickup" basketball. It has become a tradition for the president to call individual athletes or invite the entire team to the White House after winning a championship.

- *Religion.* Super Bowl Sunday is a secular celebration of the masses. It is to sports fans what Christmas and Easter are to the Christian faith. Sport, according to sport philosopher Michael Novak, has quasi-religious properties. Specifically, he referred to asceticism, ceremonies, sacred grounds, and symbols. This well-documented observation is being reexamined here in the interest of clarifying this unique relationship. Further, seriously lacking is a major quasi-religious aspect—rituals/superstitions.

  - *Asceticism.* Athletes have to be disciplined physically or they suffer the consequences of not performing effectively. A discussion of spiritual discipline is not appropriate here; however, athletes do demonstrate their religious beliefs by writing books about their faith, crossing themselves and pointing toward the sky, for example.

◆ ***Ceremonies.*** Sporting events have a prescribed procedure or order which is ceremonial in nature. For example, a baseball game's congregation is its fans, its invocation is the ceremonial first pitch, usually thrown by a celebrity; there is the organist playing "Take Me Out to the Ballgame" during the "seventh inning stretch," and the game is usually nine innings long. Some sporting events are truly ceremonial because they also include elaborate pomp; e.g., the opening and closing ceremonies of the Olympic Games, with the lighting and extinguishing of the Olympic torch.

◆ ***Sacred Grounds.*** In *Field of Dreams*, Ahujai (2001) describes all of the major league ballparks and suggests that there's something about a ballgame that's good for the soul. The original Yankee Stadium, built in 1923, was known as "the House that Ruth Built." Ahujai called it one of the game's true cathedrals. Wrigley Field, home of the Chicago Cubs since 1914, is revered for its neighborhood charm, ivy-covered brick walls, classical hand-operated scoreboard, and "Holy Cow!" There are seats *on* the house, rather than in it. Fans watch the game from roof-top seating on buildings across the street from the stadium.

There are the links at the Old Course in St. Andrews, Scotland where gorse bushes and pot bunkers dot the landscape. It is revered as the home of golf and periodic site of the British Open (Open Championship). The hushed reverence of Augusta National Golf Club in Augusta, Georgia, includes the beauty of pink azaleas, white dogwoods, emerald green grass and, of course, the hallowed grounds of Amen Corner and the Butler Cabin.

Courtesy of Brian Turner.

Wimbledon is the oldest (1877) and the most prestigious tennis tournament in the world. One of four grand slam tournaments, it's the only one still played on the game's original surface—grass (which gave the game of lawn tennis its name). Watching competitors wearing white (strict dress code) play on Centre Court, while sipping champagne, eating strawberries, and looking for the Queen or a Prince in the royal box are part of the majestic experience.

- ◆ *Symbols.* From a religious perspective, a symbol may suggest a visible sign of something invisible (e.g., the lion is a symbol of courage). In sport, symbols are more identified with mottos (short, catchy phrases or statements, such as Nike's "Just Do It!") and logos (specific designs that can be identified with the product, such as Nike's swoosh).

- ◆ *Rituals/Superstitions.* In Carole Potter's (1983) book entitled, *Knock on Wood*, she states that "Little rituals become obsessions. Obsessions become superstitions." (p. 94). Superstitions and rituals are widespread in competitive sport. Rituals create a calming effect from repetition. Athletes believe that such behaviors have a power to enhance their performance and give them confidence. Their appearance, the clothes they wear, the foods they eat, their warm-up routines, and lucky charms, among others, are factors. Tiger Woods wears a red shirt on Sundays when he's competing. Michael Jordon wore his North Carolina Tarheels shorts under his game shorts when he played for the Chicago Bulls. Former Cub and Mets reliever Turk Wendell chewed black licorice and brushed his teeth between innings. Former Red Sox and Yankee's player Wade Boggs was the "chicken man." He habitually ate chicken before every game and started wind sprints exactly 16 minutes before game time.

Maria Sharapova, the tennis star, turns away from the service line and fidgets with her racket strings before turning around to serve again. Rafael Nadal, the Spanish tennis champion, lines up his water bottles carefully. Before each rally, he pulls the back of his tennis shorts and touches his nose. Former University of Nevada at Las Vegas (UNLV) basketball coach Jerry Tarkanian chewed a towel throughout his team's games. Even the late John Wooden, winner of ten national championships in college basketball, had a ritual of holding a folded-up game program in his hand while coaching his team from the bench.

Rituals have been performed to remove curses in sport. One of the classics is the Curse of the Billy Goat. In 1945, die-hard Cubs fan William "Billy Goat" Sianis tried to get his goat into Wrigley Field to watch the World Series. He purchased two box seats. They were turned away and told that Mr. Wrigley, owner of the Chicago Cubs, objected because the goat smelled. That day the Cubs lost. William Sianis sent a telegram to Mr. Wrigley the next day saying, "Who smells now?" He also took the liberty to tell sports reporters that the Chicago Cubs would be hexed until his goat was permitted to attend a game. It's been over 65 years and they have not returned to the World Series. And there's also the matter of fan Steve Bartman. As the Cubs were about to clinch the National League pennant in 2003, Bartman interfered with Cubs' leftfielder Moises Alou at Wrigley Field. The Cubs lost the pennant and the Bartman ball was auctioned, and then exploded to remove its power over the Cubs. Its remains are in a tomb which is a glass case in the entryway of Harry Carey's restaurant in Chicago (and the Cubs have still not won a World Series since 1908).

- *Language.* Our language is littered with metaphorical phrases and sport terms or figures of speech are often used to describe everyday events, occurrences, or circumstances.

  Examples include:

  - Feeling under par (not feeling well)
  - Got a hole-in-one (an amazing achievement)
  - Hit a home run (a successful accomplishment)
  - Keep your eye on the ball (stay focused)
  - Off the hook (no longer in trouble)
  - Touch base (stay in touch)
  - Step up to the plate (get involved)
  - Time out (take a break)

  Logos have a language of their own. The "Golden Arches," which has become a very common phrase in reference to the famous logo for the McDonald's fast-food hamburger chain and the global symbol for the Coca-Cola soft drink company need no explanation. These logos, as is the Nike swoosh, are recognized around the world. Although McDonald's and Coca-Cola are not products directly associated with sport, they have been sponsors of major sporting events around the world (see the sponsorship chapter).

- *Gender.* In 2008, a woman ran for president of the United States, as of 2010, one-third of the Supreme Court justices were women, a select few anchor network news and some serve on the board of directors for Fortune 500 companies; the operative words here are: "a woman ran," "one-third," "a select few," and "some." There also still is gender disparity in sports. Four words in black lettering inform women and our four legged friends that they're not welcome: "No Dogs, No Women." Women are not allowed in the clubhouse at the Old Course at St. Andrews, Scotland (the home of golf) except for social events. Augusta National Golf Club, home of the Masters, is also currently a male citadel.

  However, the empowerment of girls and women through sport has become a major cultural change in America. Although gender stereotypes still exist in sport, women who play them are now embraced as athletes. Sports writer Christine Brennan (2010) shared one of her favorite stories about the then 10-year-old daughter of quarterback Doug Flutie. While watching two sports stars in a 1999 Gatorade commercial, Alexa Flutie asked her dad, "Who's the guy with Mia?" The guy with Mia Hamm, a female trail blazer in US soccer and a product of Title IX, was Michael Jordan.

"You've come a long way, baby" was the tagline for the first women-only professional tennis tournament sponsored by Virginia Slims in 1971. But, in that same year, athletic programs for females generally consisted of cheerleading. And, with the exception of historically black universities, athletic scholarships for women were nonexistent. In the same year, just seven percent of high school varsity athletes were girls. And, female collegiate athletes received only two percent of overall athletic budgets (National Coalition for Women and Girls in Education, 2002). Since Congress enacted Title IX in 1972, female athletes have been afforded tremendous opportunities. As a result, by the 1984 Olympic Games, female competitors had surpassed records set by their male counterparts during the 1960's (Parkhouse, 1990).

Girls and women watch sports, too! If they play, they watch, as well. It is well-documented that Title IX has generated interest among women in so-called men's sports, especially basketball, football, baseball, hockey, and NASCAR. These shifting spectator demographics have significant implications for the sport marketer. According to the *SportsBusiness Journal* (2010), women account for 36%–41% of the fan base for the "Big 4" sports leagues in the United States (MLB, NBA, NFL, and NHL). Women also account for at least 37% of the fan base for NASCAR, MLS, and college football and men's college basketball (see Table 1.2). Additionally, women make up a majority of the fan base for the Women's Tennis Association (WTA; 62% of fan base are women) and the Women's National Basketball Association (WNBA; 60%).

TABLE 1.2

Gender Breakdown of Fans		
League/Organization	% of fans who are male	% of fans who are female
MLB	59%	41%
NBA	60%	40%
NFL	59%	41%
NHL	64%	36%
MLS	60%	40%
NASCAR	63%	37%
College Football	62%	38%
College Basketball	63%	37%

Note. Adapted from "Who the fans are: Breaking down the demos of key sports," *SportsBusiness Journal*, April 19, 2010, 19.

Sports Fans Consider Themselves Experts

Sport consumers are "Monday morning quarterbacks" or "armchair coaches." It's easy to make the decision to either run for a first down or punt when you've had 12 hours to analyze reruns of the actual play. "No other business is viewed so simplistically and with such personal identification by its consumers" (Mullin, Hardy, and Sutton, 2009, 20). The proliferation of sports radio stations has given these "experts" a platform to display their knowledge.

Fans are more informed about sports than traditional products they use on a regular basis. The literature clearly documents the fact that consumers are affected by sport on a daily basis: watching in person or on television, listening to, reading, or talking about it. As more informed consumers, sports fans are also more critical and often feel a sense of ownership or entitlement. The die-hard, loyal sports fan wants to be treated with respect and acknowledged for knowing the game. Arrogant coaches who are confrontational with the press are taken personally.

Sport Leads to Strong Emotional Attachment

"There's no crying in baseball" was a scene in *A League of Their Own*. Boozy Coach Jimmy Dugan (Tom Hanks) reluctantly leads a female team in an All-American Girls Professional Baseball League. It was formed in the 40's when the men were off at war.

Can a consumer develop a passion toward a product? Certainly, a sports car or expensive jewelry can create an emotional response. But, generally, traditional products do not create the emotional attachment or passion that is generated through sport experiences. Grown men do cry! Serious sports fans take losses personally and often reach a depressed state over those which result in such severe consequences as the loss of a championship. Fans also bask in the glory of a win, especially if it's an important one for the home team or an underdog you've been rooting for. Strong emotional attachment is also measured in fond memories, including the sights, smells, sounds, and tastes of the experience. (See the exercise at the end of this chapter.)

The Sport Product Is Intangible

Products are tangible; they can be seen and touched. An automobile (non-sport product) and basketball (sport product) are examples. *Services* are intangible; that is, they have no visible substance. Ushers at a concert and golf lessons are examples. Sport products and services, as fore mentioned, can be categorized as spectator (to watch, as a football game), participant (to work out or play as jogging or participating in a recreational volleyball game) and equipment, including sports apparel and shoes.

The Sport Product Is Inconsistent and Unpredictable

Yogi Berra's well-known phrase, "It ain't over till it's over" suggests that one should not assume the outcome of a sporting event until it's over. Even if the event is predicted as a "shoe in," if one team is superior to another, the outcome is not guaranteed given such as injuries to players, weather conditions, and the home team advantage. The unpredictability of sport is a significant factor that makes it unique and special! This inconsistency creates the backdrop and the suspense. A classic example of such unpredictability is an event called "Miracle on Ice." During the 1980 Winter Olympics in Lake Placid, New York, the men's ice hockey team from the United States won the gold medal, which included a shocking win over the Soviet Union who had just beaten the US team 10–3 less than two weeks earlier.

The NCAA women's and men's basketball tournaments are referred to as "March Madness" because a No. 1 seed can be upset by one ranked ninth or higher in a first or second round. There should be no surprises in traditional marketing. A Big Mac should taste the same every time. "Traveling should be an adventure. Where you stay shouldn't be." was a motto of Holiday Inn's worldwide in the 1990's.

Sport Is Publicly Consumed in a Social Environment

Have you ever attended a sporting event alone? Such an observation is rare. Social interaction with family and friends is a major part of the experience. And, enjoying the event can depend on everyone in your group also having a good time. It's important to develop promotions which maximize this experience for everyone.

The Sport Product Is Simultaneously Produced and Consumed

You can always buy a quart of milk this morning if you forgot to purchase it on your way home last night. But, you cannot sell a seat for yesterday's game today (although later in this chapter you will learn what the Florida Marlins (now the Miami Marlins) did to commemorate a special game). There is no shelf life. The shelf life (the time something lasts) of such traditional products as food can be extended (e.g., storing it in a freezer). Once the spectator sporting event has ended, it ceases to exist. It can be superficially extended via instant replay or taping the event to be viewed at a later time, but the element of unpredictability and the excitement of observing a record breaking, historical moment is gone.

The Sport Product Is Subjective

In a scenario of a family of four attending a baseball game, the husband was involved in the play-by-play action and miscalls by the umpire, his wife looked forward to the post-game fireworks, and their son was engrossed in the antics on the electronic scoreboard, keeping score in the program and how many hot dogs he could devour. Their daughter was more interested in what other fans were wearing and how she could become a bat girl. Did they attend the same game? With so many expectations, it's difficult for a sport marketer to ensure consumer satisfaction.

There Is Little Lead Time to Promote the Sport Product

"Pick Six" is a promotional gimmick used in horseracing to increase track attendance. Individuals who pick six winning horses in one day receive "x" amount of money which is usually substantial. It's similar to the lottery because the prize money is cumulative. That is, this money increases each day until six winners are picked. Little lead-time is also afforded marketers of sports teams in contention for playoffs and championships. Lead-time is rarely a factor in traditional marketing since promotional efforts are not contingent on the outcome of sequential events.

Sporting Events Cannot Be Replicated

Fond memories are measured in time, including moments and seconds. Sport is no exception. And, they cannot be replicated, although replay can extend the length of this experience. To follow are two classic examples:

In 1973 amidst much media hype, Billie Jean King beat Bobby Riggs in three straight sets after he challenged her to a tennis match. Although much older, he boasted about the male's superior athletic attributes. It was dubbed "The Battle of the Sexes."

Brandi Chastain of the United States made a game-winning penalty shootout kick against China in the 1999 FIFA Women's World Cup final. This left-footed kick into the back of the net and her bra-baring celebration afterwards created a cultural phenomenon. Such a phenomenon rarely occurs in traditional marketing. The consumer can always take advantage of that dog food sale next month if it was missed last week.

Emphasis on Product Extensions

While the core product in sports is the game itself, sport is unique because of the emphasis on product extensions. Fans display their loyalty by wearing team jerseys and hats at games. Yankee fans can even buy the same grass seed that is used in Yankee Stadium. In Columbus, Ohio, there are approximately ten stores devoted to product extensions for The Ohio State University Buckeyes. Teams and leagues generate substantial revenue for licensing these product extensions (see Chapter 12 for more information on licensing).

Demand Fluctuates Widely

Some outdoor sporting activities, such as golf and skiing, are obviously restricted by weather. In some northern states, golf courses are only open for business six to eight months out of the year (the same could be said for ski resorts). While you might have a hard time finding an open outdoor tennis court during the spring and summer months, it is doubtful you can play outdoors during the winter months in most parts of the United States.

Demand also often fluctuates for organized team sports. Fans of teams are time and again excited and optimistic at the beginning of the season, but injuries or a losing streak can quickly diminish demand for tickets for most teams. Even a winning record does not guarantee demand. The Atlanta Braves won 14 consecutive divisional titles from 1991 to 2005 (there was no divisional winner in 1994 because of the players' strike) and went to 5 World Series (winning the championship in 1995). However, even with this success, the Braves only sold around 60% of their tickets during the last three years of this impressive streak.

Widespread Media Coverage

While most businesses must pay to promote and sell their product or service, sport organizations get free publicity every day in their local newspapers. Each of these newspapers gives a detailed account of the team's prior game and lets the readers know the exact day and time of the team's next game. Similarly, television stations do stories on area teams each night on their local news shows. Additionally, most major cities in the United States have a sports radio channel that devotes a significant amount of time to sports and teams in that area. On a national level, the ESPN family of networks (ESPN, ESPN2, ESPNU, ESPNEWS, ESPN Classic, ESPN Deportes, and ESPN3.com) give tremendous exposure to the most popular sports (and some not so popular) and leagues, both intercollegiate and professional, in the United States. Sport entities must develop strategies to capitalize on media coverage and utilize this coverage to maximize the reach and impact of their marketing plans. Effective use of media is outlined in Chapter 9.

Sport Organizations Simultaneously Cooperate and Compete

In order to exist, teams must have competitions against other teams. The success of any team, at least to some extent, depends on the success of the other teams in that league. The more teams that compete for championships, the more interest there is for that league (leading to greater revenue for all teams involved). In the Big Ten Conference, the 12 schools share television revenue and post-season revenue for football and men's basketball. The more teams that make post-season appearances, the more revenue each school gets (even those who do not make the post-season). College football teams from the Southeastern Conference (SEC) have won six consecutive Bowl Championship Series (BCS) titles from 2006-2011. These championships have made the conference the pre-eminent league in college football and all member schools have benefited.

Importance of Sport Marketing

With this talk of sport marketing, a central question needs to be asked—"Why is sport marketing important?" Marketing can be seen at all levels of sport. In order to survive (and prosper), all sport organizations must generate revenue. The current economic times has made this a serious challenge for all sport administrators. Sport marketing has never been as important as it is for organizations as it is today. Here is a look at some of the challenges facing sport organizations at various levels.

Professional Sports

Between 2001 and 2011, the National Basketball Association (NBA; +3.2%), National Football League (NFL; +2.4%), and the National Hockey League (NHL; +3.4%) all showed slight increases in average attendance. However, these increases over the 10 year period average less than 1% per year. Average attendance in Major League Baseball (MLB) during the 2011 season was almost identical to what it was in 2001, increasing by only 294 attendees per game, or less 1% over this period (see Figure 1.1). Maybe a more realistic view of attendance is the percentage of capacity (see Figure 1.2). For example, the Boston Red Sox were 8th in MLB attendance in 2011. However, they sold more than 100% of their available tickets. Percentage of capacity takes into account the size of the stadium or arena and lets you know how full (or how empty) they really are.

Even though average attendance in the NFL increased less than 1% per year over the past 11 years, the reality is there were few additional tickets to sell. Average capacity in the NFL was 95.5% from 2001-2011, with a high of 98.2% during two consecutive seasons (2006 and 2007). Overall NFL attendance had declined each year between 2007 and 2010, with a slight increase in 2011. However, this is actually skewed by a few teams. Only six teams in the NFL did not sell 90% of their tickets in 2011, with Cincinnati the lowest at 75.2%. Furthermore, at least one-half of all NFL teams have season ticket wait lists. Most famous is probably the wait list for Green Bay Packers season tickets. The list currently stands at over 96,000. With a season ticket renewal rate of 99.6%, only 126 individuals received tickets for the 2010 season. The Packers estimate that if you put your name on the wait list this year, you will be contacted in 2050! Overall, less than a million tickets went unsold in the NFL during the 2011

FIGURE 1.1

Total Attendance in Professional Sports, 2001–2011

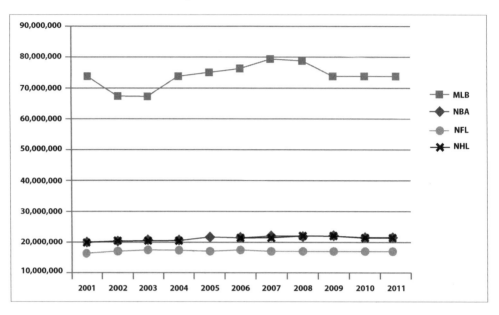

Note: For the NBA and NHL, the year denotes the end of the season (e.g., 2001 shows the capacity for the 2000–2001 season). Also, there was no NHL season in 2004–05. Compiled from attendance figures from ESPN.com.

FIGURE 1.2

Percentage of Capacity in Professional Sports, 2001–2011

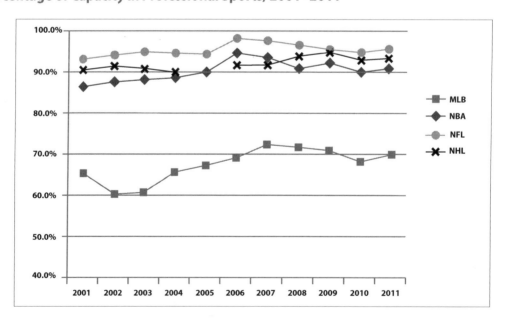

Note: For the NBA and NHL, the year denotes the end of the season (e.g., 2001 shows the capacity for the 2000–2011 season). Also, there was no NHL season in 2004–05. Compiled from attendance figures from ESPN.com.

season. Nevertheless, it should be noted that season tickets sales were down for the third consecutive year in 2010, including a 5% drop between 2009 and 2010 (Vigna, 2010).

The NBA and NHL have comparable attendance figures (not overly surprising since they play the same number of games and in similarly sized arenas). Both were around 90% capacity for the past decade, with the NHL having its best season in 2008–09 (at 95%). During the 2010–2011 NHL season, 18 out of the 30 teams had at least 95% capacity (12 of these teams were at 100% capacity), with the lowest team (New York Islanders) at 67.9% capacity, and the league average at 92.9%. During the same season, exactly one-half of the 30 NBA teams were at 95% capacity, with the overall league average at 90.6%. The Philadelphia 76ers had the lowest percentage of capacity at 74.5%. The NBA and NHL had approximately 2.3 million and 1.7 million unsold tickets, respectively, over that season.

MLB has the most room for improvement with regards to attendance. Overall, about one in three tickets has gone unsold in MLB over the last 11 years. While MLB touted setting attendance records in four consecutive years (2003–2007), attendance has dropped by over 6 million people in the past four years, a decrease of almost 8%. In 2011 MLB teams sold 70% of their tickets, less than all other teams in the other three major US professional sports, with the exception of the NHL New York Islanders (although this number is much better than the 60% capacity MLB had in 2002 and 2003). Only four teams in MLB (Philadelphia Phillies, Boston Red Sox, San Francisco Giants, and Minnesota Twins) had attendance of at least 95% capacity in 2011. The Milwaukee Brewers and Chicago Cubs were the only other teams over 90% capacity. Exactly one-third of all MLB teams averaged less than 60% capacity, with Toronto the lowest at 45.6%. Through the end of July of the 2010 season, a phenomenal 5 no-hitters were thrown in MLB, including a perfect game (one of only 20 in the history of the league). Only 12,288 spectators were in attendance on May 9 to see Oakland's Dallas Braden throw a perfect game (34.9% capacity). Similar attendance figures were seen at no-hit games thrown by Matt Garza of Tampa Bay (17,009; 47.2% capacity), Ubaldo Jimenez of Colorado (32,602; 65.5%), Edwin Jackson of Arizona (18,918; 52.5%), and Roy Halladay of Philadelphia (25,086; 65.1%). The entrepreneurial Florida (now Miami) Marlins' seized the opportunity to capitalize on Halladay's no-hit game in Miami by selling unsold tickets (at face value) as souvenirs after the game (more than 3,000 tickets were sold in the first four hours they were available!; Marlins selling, 2010). Over 31.6 million tickets went unsold in 2011. Using the average ticket price from Team Marketing Report's (2011) *Fan Cost Index* and the number of unsold tickets each team had, MLB had the opportunity to sell an additional $752 million of tickets in 2011, revenue they will never be able to recoup.

Intercollegiate Sports

There is a common misperception that intercollegiate athletic departments in the United States generate a lot of profit. While NCAA Football Bowl Subdivision (FBS) athletic departments do generate a substantial amount of revenue, including nine that have revenues exceeding $100 million per year (see Table 1.3), the reality is only 22 of the 120 programs (18.3%) had generated revenues exceeding expenses in 2010 (Fulks, 2011). The median net generated revenue for these 22 programs was $7,367,000; however, the median net deficit

TABLE 1.3

Rank	Institution Name	Total Revenue
	FBS Schools with Highest Total Revenues, 2010	
1	The University of Texas	$143,555,354
2	University of Alabama	$130,542,153
3	The Ohio State University	$122,739,754
4	University of Oregon	$122,394,483
5	University of Florida	$117,104,407
6	University of Tennessee	$115,729,599
7	Louisiana State University	$111,030,795
8	University of Michigan	$106,874,031
9	Oklahoma State University	$106,362,128
10	University of Oklahoma	$98,512,287
11	University of Wisconsin at Madison	$96,038,912
12	Auburn University	$92,611,558
13	University of Georgia	$89,735,934
14	University of Iowa	$88,735,093
15	Michigan State University	$83,545,892
16	Texas A&M University	$82,774,133
17	University of Virginia	$81,841,633
18	University of South Carolina	$79,879,193
19	University of Kentucky	$79,700,856
20	University of Minnesota	$78,706,900

Note. Compiled from data on the "College athletics finance database", *USA Today,* http://www.usatoday.com/sports/college/ncaa-finances.htm.

for the remaining 98 programs was $11,597,000. Overall, the median deficit for FBS athletic departments was $9,446,000 (i.e., half of the 120 FBS athletic departments lost at least $9.4 million per year).

To counterbalance these losses, universities subsidize their athletic programs. In 2010, there was a gap of $12,962,000 between median revenues and median generated revenues (Fulks, 2011). According to a report by *USA Today*, during the 2009–2010 school year, only seven of the 99 public FBS athletic departments (Louisiana State University, The Ohio State University, Purdue University, Texas A&M University, the University of Nebraska, the University of Oklahoma, and the University of Texas) did not receive funds from their university through student fees, direct state or government support, direct institutional support (general fund money), or indirect institutional support (facilities, energy costs, etc.). On the other end of the spectrum, 31 institutions subsidized at least one-half of their athletic budgets, with 11 of these schools subsidizing at least two-thirds of their budget (see Table 1.4). The average school was subsidized $9.4 million in 2010 (18.2% of budget), an increase of almost 50% since 2005.

TABLE 1.4

FBS Schools with the Highest Subsidies as a Percentage of Operating Budget

School	Total Subsidy, 2010	Increase/ Decrease in Subsidy from 2005 to 2010	Total Operating Revenue 2010	Subsidy as % of Operating Budget
Eastern Michigan University	22,034,322	28.6%	26,270,721	83.87%
Florida International University	17,857,204	47.2%	22,004,418	81.15%
Kent State University	15,626,467	26.3%	19,446,680	80.36%
Ohio University	18,713,965	74.7%	23,905,953	78.28%
State University of New York at Buffalo	19,786,316	37.4%	25,385,009	77.94%
Western Michigan University	18,409,553	29.6%	23,761,393	77.48%
Middle Tennessee State University	15,406,839	35.3%	20,800,017	74.07%
Ball State	14,793,239	40.7%	20,132,632	73.48%
Northern Illinois University	16,129,991	51.7%	22,210,800	72.62%
University of Akron	17,263,774	68.1%	24,012,416	71.90%
Florida Atlantic University	11,080,401	-3.3%	16,284,618	68.04%
Western Kentucky University	15,487,500	54.1%	23,243,348	66.63%
Central Michigan University	16,457,883	39.0%	24,703,101	66.62%
New Mexico State University	16,940,487	109.8%	25,433,613	66.61%
Miami University (Ohio)	17,099,823	18.2%	25,996,018	65.78%
U.S. Air Force Academy	22,500,564	167.3%	34,915,251	64.44%
Utah State University	12,274,044	100.0%	19,201,898	63.92%
Bowling Green State University	11,588,172	4.8%	18,850,778	61.47%
University of Nevada at Las Vegas	34,073,391	255.1%	56,496,233	60.31%
University of Alabama at Birmingham	14,248,839	56.5%	24,273,967	58.70%
Troy University	9,199,857	39.5%	15,783,593	58.29%
San Jose State University	11,181,906	21.8%	20,333,059	54.99%
University of Louisiana Lafayette	6,524,027	101.8%	12,280,070	53.13%
University of Houston	17,420,416	40.1%	33,034,483	52.73%
University of Idaho	8,223,954	23.9%	15,683,183	52.44%
Louisiana Tech University	8,648,134	79.6%	16,587,540	52.14%
San Diego State University	16,966,734	52.0%	32,582,576	52.07%
University of Wyoming	13,949,891	31.1%	26,979,594	51.71%
University of Texas at El Paso	13,697,536	27.3%	26,694,008	51.31%
University of Central Florida	20,305,129	47.6%	40,063,558	50.68%
Colorado State University	13,345,067	110.9%	26,552,383	50.26%

Note. Compiled from data on the "College athletics finance database", *USA Today,* http://www.usatoday.com/sports/college/ncaa-finances.htm.

Using 2009 data, *USA Today* took a closer look at subsidizations, focusing specifically on student fees. Only 11 out of 115 Division I schools examined did not charge student fees to support their athletic programs. These fees ranged from $30 at Louisiana Tech University to $2,022 at Longwood University. Eliminating the 11 colleges that do not charge student fees for athletics and eight others that did not give a specific amount, the average student fee for the other 86 colleges was just over $400 per year. At 17 of these colleges, the student athletic fees account for at least 10% of what undergraduates are paying in base tuition and mandatory fees (see Table 1.5), including Norfolk State University, where almost one-fourth of students' mandatory tuition and fees go to their athletic department. Further analyses showed that students paid $795 million to support intercollegiate athletic programs at 222 Division I institutions. One parent of a Radford student claimed they would be paying $5000 to support the university's athletic department, even though she wasn't an avid fan of the teams. This amount equaled one of the student's loans and could have paid for a year of off-campus housing (Berkowitz, Upton, McCarthy, and Gillum, 2010).

TABLE 1.5

Highest Intercollegiate Athletic Fees as a Percentage of Mandatory Tuition and Fees			
School	**Amount**	**In-State Mandatory Total**	**Athletic Fee%**
Norfolk State	$1,440.60	$6,227.00	23.1%
Longwood	2,022.00	9,855.00	20.5%
Old Dominion	1,133.01	7,708.00	14.7%
James Madison	1,114.00	7,860.00	14.2%
Radford	1,077.00	7,694.00	14.0%
North Carolina-Asheville	620	4,772.10	13.0%
Cal State Bakersfield	672	5,314.00	12.6%
Coppin State	679	5,382.00	12.6%
William and Mary	1,422.00	12,188.00	11.7%
North Carolina A&T	532	4,593.00	11.6%
VMI	1,362.00	12,328.00	11.0%
East Carolina	526	4,797.00	11.0%
Appalachian State	569	5,284.74	10.8%
Western Carolina	617	5,998.80	10.3%
Florida Atlantic	493.5	4,924.10	10.0%
Towson	767	7,656.00	10.0%
North Carolina-Wilmington	541.25	5,415.90	10.0%

Note. Compiled from data from "Analyzing the percentage of tuition that goes to athletics". *USA Today,* September 21, 2010, http://www.usatoday.com/sports/college/2010-09-21-athletic-fees-chart_N.htm.

With colleges and universities struggling financially, the funding of intercollegiate athletic departments has come under fire. The University of California's Academic Senate approved a resolution that urged their chancellor to end financial support for intercollegiate athletics (Williams, 2009). From 2003–2010, the University of California athletic department had approximately $80 million more in expenditures than they did in generated revenues ("UC Berkeley budget crisis," 2009). The athletic department decided to cut five sports to help balance the budget. Additionally, the University of New Orleans decided to start the process of moving down to Division III from Division I after students voted against increasing athletic fees and the department had incurred a deficit of $1.3 million the previous year (Whittaker, 2010).

Interscholastic Sports

While most of the literature and research in sport marketing has focused on the professional and intercollegiate levels, interscholastic athletic departments in the United States also face many similar challenges. After a failed operating levy, South-Western City Schools, the 6th largest school district in Ohio, eliminated all extra-curricular activities, including sports. The district received national attention, including an article on *Sports Illustrated's* website (Staples, 2009) and a feature segment entitled "Game Over" on HBO's *Real Sports*. After a fall with no high school football, voters approved a new operating levy and all extra-curricular activities were reinstated in South-Western City Schools. However, the school district did implement for the first time a "pay-for-play" fee of $150 per student for each sport they play (with a maximum of $500 per family), a practice that is used in 33 states (Halley, 2010). However, this amount is miniscule in comparison with Hamilton-Wenham Regional High School in Massachusetts, where students pay almost $1,000 to play football (King, 2010).

In 2008–2009, at least $2 billion in funding for high school athletics was cut (King, 2010). The Los Angeles United School District cut $1.4 million in their athletic budget alone. With the economic downturn, state high school athletic associations have implemented policies to help their member schools. The Delaware Interscholastic Athletic Association, Idaho High School Activities Association, Mississippi High School Activities Association, New York State Public High School Athletics Association, and Oklahoma Secondary School Athletic Association each decided to reduce the number of contests in their respective states by 10–20% (Julka, 2009; King, 2010). Besides cutting expenses, high schools have also started looking at new ways to increase revenues. Over one-half of the state high school athletic associations have contracts to broadcast their championship events (Seifried, Turner, Christy, Mahony, and Pastore, 2008), and some have investigated the possibility of streaming live championship events (McHugh, 2009). Additionally, state associations have started entering into sponsorship agreements with private companies and started their own licensing programs (like their counterparts at the intercollegiate level). In 2010, the North Carolina High School Athletic Association signed an agreement with Under Armour to become the official outfitter and supplier of athletic apparel, accessories, and footwear for the association. Also, the National Federation of State High School Associations established a licensing program that provides royalties to schools from merchandise sold in retail stores (Dyer, 2009).

Youth Sports

Even less research has been done on youth sports despite the fact that youth sports leagues have grown into a $5 billion a year industry. Little League Baseball has generated a $30 million national television contract with ABC and ESPN alone. In Ohio, there are more than 1,200 non-profit youth sport organizations accounting for $60 million in revenues each year (Jones, Wagner, and Riepenhoff, 2010).

Some of the same issues mentioned at the interscholastic level are also pertinent in youth sports, especially the cost to participate. While pay-to-play is becoming more prevalent in high schools, it has always been a staple in youth sports. However, these participation costs have risen at an astounding rate. According to a survey in the *Columbus Dispatch*, 53% of the respondents reported spending between $500 and $1,500 annually on youth (non-school) sports, with some paying more than $10,000 ("Little leagues, big costs," 2010). A *SportsBusiness Journal* poll of 1,100 senior level sports industry executives found the cost of participation was the biggest threat to youth sports in America (King, 2010).

Summary

In this chapter, you have learned how sport marketing is defined and how it has evolved both as an academic discipline and as an industry. After reading this chapter, you also should understand how sport marketing is both unique and challenging based on consumers' emotional attachments at all levels of sport. You also have learned of the financial and sometimes political obstacles faced by sport entities including those at the professional level. The unique attributes and characteristics of sport combined with ever increasing financial pressures underscore the need for professionals well-versed in the principles of sport marketing. The coming chapters will focus on the key foundational concepts of sport marketing and outline strategies and techniques that may be implemented and utilized when marketing both sport and non-sport products to maximize revenue generation.

Discussion Questions

1. Define sport marketing. How does it differ from "traditional" marketing?

2. How do marketers of traditional products use sport?

3. Explain why sport is unique (as compared to other products and services). Why must marketers approach it differently than they do traditional products?

4. Why is sport marketing important? Give examples for all levels of sport.

Critical Thinking Exercises

1. Although sport marketing has its roots in traditional marketing, explain why marketing traditional products through sport has become such an effective tool over the past 20 years. Include five examples NOT cited in Chapter 1.

2. Spectator sport is consumed for a variety of reasons, some of which may have no relevance to the intended use of the product. A.) Why is it important for the sport marketer to be aware of all of these reasons? B.) Select a spectator sporting event. List and document how each of these consumer expectations will be met.

3. Select an article from the sports section of a major newspaper. Illustrate how this article contributes to the uniqueness of sport marketing.

References

"10 most watched shows of all time," FilmPopper.com, accessed February 7, 2011, http://filmpopper.com/10-most-watched-tv-showsof-all-time/.

Adler, R., *A year in the dark*. New York, NY: Medallion Books, 1969.

Ahuja, J., *Field of dreams: A guide to visiting and enjoying all 30 major league ball parks*. Secaucus, NJ: Citadel, 2001.

"Analyzing the percentage of tuition that goes to athletics," *USA Today*, accessed September 21, 2010, http://www.usatoday.com/sports/college/2010-09-21-athletic-fees-chart_N.htm.

Berkowitz, S., J. Upton, M. McCarthy, and J. Gillum, "How student fees boost college sports amid rising budgets," *USA Today*, accessed September 21, 2010, http://www.usatoday.com/sports/college/2010-09-21-student-feesboost-college-sports_N.htm.

Boswell, T., *Game day*. New York, NY: Doubleday, 1982.

Brennan, C., "Blog to discuss women's sporting chances," *USA Today*, (blog), February 10, 2010, http://www.usatoday.com/sports/genderequity.htm.

"College athletics finance database," *USA Today*, http://www.usatoday.com/sports/college/ncaafinances.Htm.

"Comparing fan demos in sports." *SportsBusiness Journal*, March 2, 2009: 11, 16.

Crosset, T. W., S. Bromage, and M. A. Hums, "History of sport management," In *Principles and practices of sport management*, edited by L. P. Masteralexis, C. A. Barr, and M. A. Hums. Gaithersburg: Aspen Publishers, 1998, 1–19.

Dyer, M., "Nation's high schools cope with recession." *High School Today*, 3(1) (2009): 8–9.

Fulks, D. L., *Revenues and expenses 2004-2010: NCAA Division I intercollegiate athletics programs report*. Indianapolis: NCAA, 2011.

Fullerton, S., *Sports marketing*. 2nd ed. New York: McGraw-Hill, 2010.

Gray, D., and C. McEvoy, "Sport Marketing: Strategies and tactics," *In The management of sport: Its foundation and application*, 4th ed., 228–255, edited by B. L. Parkhouse. St. Louis: Mosby, 2005.

Grohmann, K., "Games opening ceremony is most watched TV event in Canada," Reuters, accessed February 13, 2010, http://www.reuters.com/article/ idUSTRE61C2GL20100213.

Halley, J., "With budgets tight, pay-to-play fees gain currency as way to avoid cuts," *USA Today*, accessed June 11, 2010, http://www.usatoday.com/sports/preps/2010-06-10-pay-to-play_N.htm.

Jones, T., M. Wagner, and J. Riepenhoff, "Children may be vulnerable in $5 billion youth sports industry." *Columbus Dispatch*, August 29, 2010: 140(60), A1, A8–A9.

Julka, B., "How state associations are stretching their dollars." *High School Today*, 3(1) (2009): 24–25.

King, B., "High school sports running on empty." *SportsBusiness Journal*, August 2, 2010: 13(14), 1.

Kotler, P., *Marketing management*. 9th ed., Upper Saddle River: Prentice Hall, 2003.

Lefton, T., "How McDonald's has used sports to package the perfect pitch during most of its 50 year history." *SportsBusiness Journal*, May 30, 2005: 8(6), 15.

Levanthal, J., *Take me out to the ballpark*. New York, NY: Black Dog & Leventhal Publishers, Inc., 2006.

"Little leagues, big costs," *Columbus Dispatch*, http://www.dispatch.com/ live/content/special_reports/stories/2010/youth_sports/index.html.

Mahony, D., and B. G. Pitts, "Research outlets in sport marketing: The need for increased specialization." *Journal of Sport Management*, 12(4) (1998): 259–272.

"Marlins selling Halladay tickets at 'face,'" accessed June 2, 2010, http://sports.espn.go.com/mlb/news/story?id=5236340.

McHugh, P., "Athletic directors face economic challenges." *High School Today*, 3(1) (2009): 16–17.

"Most-watched U.S. telecasts,"CNN.com, accessed February 9, 2010, http://www.cnn.com/2010/ SHOWBIZ/ TV/02/09/nielson.ratings.superbowl/index.html.

Mullin, B., S. Hardy, and W. Sutton., *Sport marketing*. 3rd ed., Champaign, IL: Human Kinetics, 2009.

National Coalition for Women and Girls in Education. "Title IX at 30: Report card on gender equity." Washington, D. C.: National Coalition for Women and Girls in Education, June, 2002.

"Olympic final most-watched hockey game in 30 years," NHL.com, accessed March 1, 2010, http://www.nhl.com/ice/news.htm?id=519476.

Parkhouse, B. L., "A time to speak—You've come a long way, baby...dancing backwards and in heels." *Journal of Physical Education, Recreation, and Dance*, 6(3) (1990): 72–75.

Parkhouse, B. L., and B. G. Pitts, "History of sport management." *In The management of sport: Its foundation and application*, 4th ed., edited by B. L. Parkhouse. St. Louis, MO: Mosby, 2005.

Potter, C., *Knock on wood*. New York, NY: Alice James Books, 1983.

Seifried, C., B. A. Turner, K. Christy, D. F., Mahony, and D. L. Pastore. "An examination of television coverage in U.S. high school athletics." *ICHPER-SD Journal of Research*, 3(2) (2008): 71–77.

Skinner, J., "Welcome to the McDonald's Olympic Champion Crew Program," accessed 2007, https://www.mcdocc.com/c/home.htm.

Staples, A., "The impact of an Ohio school district's decision to cut sports," *Sports Illustrated*, accessed September 17, 2009, http://sportsillustrated.cnn.com/2009/writers/ andy_staples/09/16/nosports/index. html.

"Super Bowl tv ratings," tvbythenumbers.zap2it.com, accessed January 18, 2009, http://tvbythenumbers.zap2it. com/2009/01/18/historical-superbowl-tv-ratings/11044/.

Tapper, J., "The biggest TV audience ever... it is now," Mail Online, accessed May 1, 2005, http://www.dailymail. co.uk/tvshowbiz/article-346942/The-biggest-TV-audience--now.html.

Team Marketing Report, "Fan cost index," fancostexperience.com, accessed 2011, http://www.fancostexperience.com/.

"The Most Watched Programs in TV History," listzblog.com, accessed 2010, http://www.listzblog.com/ top_ten_ most_watched_programs_in_tv_history.html.

"UC Berkeley budget crisis," accessed July 3, 2009, http://budgetcrisis.berkeley.edu/ ?page_id=16.

United States Department of Education, "The equity in athletics data analysis cutting tool," http://ope.ed.gov/ athletics/.

Vigna, P., "NFL season-ticket sales down 5 percent from last year, newspaper reports," pennlive.com, accessed September 8, 2010, http://blog.pennlive.com/ fanbox/2010/09/nfl_season-ticket_sales_down_5.html.

Whittaker, R., "University of New Orleans begins transition to Division III athletics," nola.com, May 23, 2010, http://www.nola.com/uno/index.ssf/2010/05/ university_of_new_orleans_begi.html.

"Who the fans are: Breaking down the demos of key sports." *SportsBusiness Journal*, 12, April 9, 2010: 19.

Williams, Z. E. J., "Resolution urges end to campus athletic funding," *The Daily Californian*, accessed November 6, 2009, http://www.dailycal.org/article/107387/resolution_ urges_end_to_ campus_athletic_funding.

Zmuda, N., "Coke unleashes Olympic blitz." *Advertising Age*, 79(27) (2008): 6.

Courtesy of Sal DeAngelis

CHAPTER 2

Developing a Strategic Sport Marketing Plan

Chris Greenwell University of Louisville
Dustin Thorn Coastal Carolina University

At first, we couldn't be establishment, because we didn't have any money. We were guerrilla marketers, and we still are, a little bit. But, as we become No. 1 in our industry, we've had to modify our culture and become a bit more planned.
Phil Knight, Co-founder and chairman of Nike Inc.

CHAPTER OBJECTIVES

After completing the chapter, the reader should be able to:

- Understand and appreciate the concept of strategic sport marketing.
- Adopt a systematic approach to examining the external and internal environment.
- Understand the process involved in conceptualizing and developing a marketing plan.
- Identify appropriate marketing goals and objectives.
- Demonstrate the relationship between marketing tactics and marketing strategy.
- Appreciate the process of implementing and controlling a marketing plan.

Strategic Sport Marketing

Effective sport marketing does not happen by accident. Whether marketing a mega-event like the Super Bowl or a small, local event such as a youth field hockey camp, marketers cannot rely on guesswork to develop their marketing plan and hope everything will turn out as they like. Instead, organizations need to invest significant time and effort into creating a marketing plan that will help them accomplish what they want to accomplish. In today's business environment, it is vitally important that marketers make the right decisions as most sport organizations do not have the time or budget to engage in trial and error marketing. Mistakes can be costly, as sport marketers operate in a "real time" environment and cannot go back in time to sell unsold tickets for an event that has already passed or sign up participants for last summer's recreation program. Further, competition is especially strong for consumers' sport and leisure spending. If your marketing is not effective, a competitor's might be.

To ensure they are making good decisions, prudent organizations will take a strategic approach to sport marketing. Strategic sport marketing is an approach to sport marketing where organizations engage in careful planning prior to implementing marketing activities designed to meet organizational goals (Shank, 2009). This systematic approach helps management make better marketing decisions by providing direction and identifying activities necessary to move in that direction (Gray, 2001). Organizations do this by focusing on where they are, where they want to be, and what it will take to get there. Organizations also have to understand the environment is constantly changing, necessitating the ability to understand the world around them. Therefore, key questions have to be addressed with an understanding of the marketing environment, their customers' needs, and competing organizations (Bradley, 2003).

The strategic market planning process involves a series of stages including careful assessment of the marketing environment, development of specific objectives, target market identification, development of marketing strategies and tactics, implementation and evaluation. Each stage builds on the prior stage. For example, **target markets** are based on objectives while strategies and tactics are based on target markets, etc. This chapter focuses on the steps necessary to develop a marketing plan and describes the important activities and considerations at each stage.

Preparing the Marketing Plan

A **marketing plan** is a written document outlining an organization's strategy and the course of action necessary to implement that strategy. Regardless of whether your organization is large or small, professional or amateur, a marketing plan can be an invaluable document. Sport organizations typically develop marketing plans on a yearly basis to support their ongoing sport programs. In addition, organizations may develop marketing plans for new programs or products. For example, a parks and recreation department may need to develop a new marketing plan when they introduce a new competitive tennis league or a professional baseball team may develop a marketing plan for a new party deck at their ballpark.

Although there are multiple ways to arrange a marketing plan, the following elements are common to most marketing plans (Stotlar, 2009). The remainder of the chapter describes each of these elements in more detail.

- Introduction
- Data and analysis
- Goals and objectives
- Target markets
- Marketing strategy
- Implementation
- Evaluation
- Summary

While the written plan provides the road map, the process of developing the plan is also vitally important. Organizations need to carefully evaluate their situation and environment, consider potential strategies, and estimate the logistics of implementing the plan in order to make sure they are making sound decisions.

Most organizations will include individuals throughout the organization to generate ideas from different perspectives. Planning groups are typically comprised of personnel involved in developing marketing strategy as well as those involved in day-to-day marketing activities. For example, a marketing director interested in improving customer service may involve ushers, security providers, and concessionaires in the process since those people would have the most direct contact with consumers and have the most direct knowledge about problems and potential solutions.

To facilitate the planning process, many organizations will engage in brainstorming activities when developing the marketing plan. Brainstorming sessions involve members of a group generating ideas related to a problem or issue. This type of activity can encourage new and creative ideas as members work to inspire others' thinking. When brainstorming, it is important for groups to welcome unusual ideas and withhold criticism (Osborn, 1963). Criticisms such as "that is not how we do things around here" or "we've never done things that way" are the best way to stifle creativity and prevent improvement. By being open to all ideas (good or bad), groups open the door to new strategies.

Marketing Plan Introduction

Most marketing plans begin with an introduction providing the reader a basis for understanding the marketing plan. This section may start with a review of the organization's mission and background information on the organization's products and customers. By including this information, the reader (and author) is reminded of the organization's purpose. In addition, this section may include an overview of the marketing plan and a review of prior marketing efforts. This information puts the plan in perspective related to where the organization's marketing efforts have been and where they are going.

Data and Analysis

Within the process of making strategic decisions, sport marketers must take into account the environment in which they operate. Environmental factors can be either internal or external to the organization. Sport marketers must be aware of how both interact with the organization, as they will influence how the organization markets the product to the consumer. The following section will look at some internal and external factors that influence marketing decisions.

Examination of Internal Environment

The internal environment consists of potential influences on the strategic sport marketing process that occur from within the organization. These influences can include the organization's mission, goals, and objectives, organizational culture, and resources within the organization. The following section highlights how each may affect the marketing plan.

Organizational Mission/Vision

Organizations use mission and/or vision statements to communicate the organization's present situation and the direction of the organization. A **mission statement** differentiates the organization from other organizations by declaring what business the organization performs to and whom the organization serves. Mission statements are often accompanied by a **vision statement** that incorporates the primary vision of how the organization activates the mission statement. In the planning process, the development of the mission and/or vision statement is often the link between strategic and operational planning (Hums and MacLean, 2009). Considering this, mission statements play a critical role in influencing marketing decisions.

Marketing decisions need to be consistent with the mission of the organization. One organization that has made marketing decisions based on its mission is Little League Baseball, Inc. The mission of Little League Baseball identifies the purpose of the organization. This purpose will provide the basis for many of their marketing decisions.

Courtesy of Braden Sweeten.

Little League Baseball, Incorporated is a non-profit organization whose mission is to "to promote, develop, supervise, and voluntarily assist in all lawful ways, the interest of those who will participate in Little League Baseball and Softball." Through proper guidance and exemplary leadership, the Little League program assists youth in developing the qualities of citizenship, discipline, teamwork, and physical well-being. By espousing the virtues of character, courage, and loyalty, the Little League Baseball and Softball program is designed to develop superior citizens rather than superior athletes.

(Courtesy of Little League Incorporated.
Reprinted by permission.)

Consistent with this mission, marketing decisions are focused on the ability to attract youth to the sport and expose them to positive values, rather than increasing revenues by extracting as much money as possible from participants, parents, and spectators. The following is a list of marketing decisions enacted to further the organization's mission:

- Establishment of a League program costs a reasonable $16.

- The registration fee for play is not a prerequisite for playing and the league does not permit eligible candidates to be turned away.

- Little League Baseball offers financial assistance to all teams at each level of the Little League International Tournament.

- Admission to Little League World Series games is free.

(Little League Incorporated, 2011a)

Organizational Culture

Organizational culture is the shared values, beliefs, and assumptions of organizational members that guide and establish preferred behaviors within an organization (Shein, 1991). Within the sport industry, there are several examples of how organizational culture affects sport marketing:

- The New York Yankees' organizational culture emphasizes tradition, which lends itself to a more conservative marketing approach. As such, the team has worn the same uniforms for nearly 100 years while many other teams change to keep up with fashion trends (New York Yankees, 2011). Players wanting to grow facial hair are limited to only mustaches and are expected to be well groomed, which is in contrast to many other organizations who expect their players to be "colorful" or "full of character." You do not typically see outlandish promotions at Yankees games that you may see with other, less-conservative teams (Yes Network, 2010).

- Callaway, a leading manufacturer of golf equipment, attributes much of its business success to a culture of innovation. The organization emphasizes research and design by hiring engineers to design golf clubs. As a result, Callaway has developed some of the best golf products on the market and has become the number one seller of irons in golf. This has become a major staple in how Callaway markets and sells irons, as they are the only golf organization that can claim they manufacture "the number one irons in golf" (Callaway Golf, 2011).

- Nike's organizational culture emphasizes the need for employees to explore potential through diversity and imagination. This is done on a 177-acre smoke-free campus that includes two gyms, an Olympic sized pool, indoor and outdoor tracks, hiking trails, soccer fields, and walking paths. The integration of these components in the culture of Nike has led to two of the most recognized marketing slogans: "Just do it" and "If you have a body, you are an athlete" (Nike, 2011).

Organizational Resources

Organizations conduct business using a limited number of resources. These resources range from employees, technology, workspace, money, etc. Therefore, resources within an organization can be considered an internal factor that may affect decisions within the organization. Sport marketers must be aware of how to use available resources in a manner that is effective in achieving organizational goals and objectives. For example, The Ohio State University Athletic Department wanted to increase the number of children in their "Buckeye Kid's Club." They decided to use one of their most valuable resources—historic Ohio Stadium. Potential members were invited to play on the field and meet the cheerleaders and the mascot.

Using the makeup of an organization's employees as an example, each organization is comprised of a unique cohort of individuals. Each individual has a different set of skills, attributes, and experiences the organization can use to achieve desired goals and objectives. However, it is not a guarantee that the employees within an organization at a given time will have the necessary skill sets to maximize potential opportunities that arise.

In addition, financial resources often dictate marketing decisions. Management may have incredibly creative ideas, but if the organization cannot afford to implement those ideas, they are of very little use. In the case of advertising, limited budgets prevent an organization from using television advertising to promote its product. As such, the organization would need to rely on other, less expensive forms of promotion such as outdoor, radio, or Internet advertising.

Examination of External Environment

The external environment consists of influences outside the organization that may affect the strategic sport marketing process. External contingencies may include the economy, environment, technology, social and cultural norms, legal issues, political agendas, educational institutions, and competition. Each of these factors is important for sport marketers to understand as they affect marketing decisions in different ways. The following sections will explain how these factors affect sport marketing decisions.

Economy

Sport consumers use discretionary income to consume sport. Therefore, the sport industry is sensitive to changes in both local and national economies. On a national level, the economy has been tumultuous over the past decade. When the economy is good, consumers and businesses are likely to be willing to spend more on entertainment. During the 1990's and early 2000's, professional sport organizations started emphasizing club seats, suites, and party rooms as a way to extract more money from consumers—and many consumers were willing to pay more for the added luxury, exclusivity, or convenience. When the economy suffered, many of those same organizations were forced to switch focus given that their target consumers had fewer discretionary dollars and were more concerned about paying their mortgages and supporting their children than spending major money for box seats (Sunnucks and Casacchia, 2010). While this was challenging for many organizations, the economy provided a key opportunity to shift marketing strategy to better meet consumer

© Ken Durden, 2012. Under license from Shutterstock, Inc.

demand and need. Specifically, many organizations began to market value packages, afford-able parking, and all-you-can-eat sections, as a way to either drop the price or add value to their offerings (Cyrec, 2009).

The economy's effect on sponsorships can also alter marketing plans. The Ladies Professional Golf Association (LPGA) cancelled three tournaments from the 2009 season and scheduled only 23 tournaments for the 2010 season, down 11 tournaments from the 2008 season. The LPGA has stated their inability to secure tournament sponsors due to the downturn in the economy has led to these organizational decisions. Sponsors like the SemGroup Corporation, Safeway International, and ADT either completely ceased their association with the LPGA or consolidated their sponsorship into lower tiered investments (DiMeglio, 2009).

Physical Environment

The environment is a critical component to sport as it has the ability to affect sport in many ways. The climate of a region can dictate both what and when certain sports are played. Golf courses in Colorado close between the months of October and March due to the cold winters, while courses in Florida are able to be open year round.

© Tim Roberts Photography, 2012. Under license from Shutterstock, Inc.

In recent years, sport organizations have designed venues that can control the environment. Retractable-roof stadiums have become increasingly appealing to sport franchises as they allow the sport organization to control the environment. This is beneficial to the marketing of sport, as now marketers do not need contingency plans for inclement weather. Marketers have the ability to market sport all the time in an environment that is comfortable for both participant and spectator.

Technology

The sport industry is constantly changing with adaptations of new technologies that allow consumers to consume the sport product in a more timely and convenient manner. Sport marketers too must adapt to these new technologies as they relate directly to the marketing process. New innovations, such as smartphone applications, have increased consumers' ability to consume the sport product. No longer must the consumer be at the event or watch it live on television. ESPN offers an application to smartphone users that allows access to score updates, articles, and even live coverage of events on the ESPN3 network. The use of mobile technologies allows sport marketers to increase their distribution agents and incorporate a much larger market of consumers.

Another example of technology influencing the marketing of sport is social networking websites. Websites like Twitter and Facebook have revolutionized the distribution of information regarding sport. Athletes have engaged in sharing both professional and personal information through Twitter accounts. Professional golfer Stewart Cink boasts over 1.2 million followers, and he communicates everything from upcoming events to personal happenings in his life in an effort to help promote and establish a personal rapport with his fan base. Basketball star Shaquille O'Neal has over 3 million followers and has used Twitter to give away tickets to his fans.

Sport organizations have also begun to use Facebook as a distribution agent for communicating information on upcoming events. The 2010 FEI World Equestrian Games established a Facebook page to help promote the event in Lexington, Kentucky. The Facebook page provides updated posts about event happenings as well as a link to the official website where fans can purchase tickets to the event. The use of technologies like Facebook provides sport marketers an alternative to more expensive distribution agents like advertising.

Social/Cultural Trends

In many aspects, sport shares the same characteristics and issues that make up societies. Therefore, it is understandable that social or cultural trends may influence what sports are played, how they are played, and how they are marketed.

Societal norms will often determine how sports are marketed. For example, the Ultimate Fighting Championship (UFC) has sought to expand internationally with mixed results. The sport of mixed martial arts was easily accepted in countries such as Japan, South Korea, Brazil, and the United Arab Emirates where martial arts are understood and respected. However, the organization has experienced roadblocks in much of Europe where many of the locals see the sport as violent and barbaric. Even in North America, the UFC has struggled to gain approval to host events in the major markets, as key legislators do not see the sport as socially acceptable.

Social trends will also influence marketing decisions. A shift in culture away from rigid conservative team sports to a focus on creativity and individualism has helped drive the growth in extreme sports such as skateboarding, snowboarding, inline skating, and BMX. Various extreme sports were built around a culture of individuality and living life to the extreme. This culture is evidenced by the sponsors associated with these types of events, the outlandishness of many of the athletes, and the athletes' approach to competition. For example, Burton, a snowboarding apparel company, designed a two-layer Gore-Tex pant that looked like blue jeans for the 2010 Olympic Winter games. The distressed look of the pants went well with the carefree and loose culture of extreme sport.

A focus on the natural environment is another social trend that has gained more attention in recent years. Over the past several years, sport organizations have been emphasizing preservation of the environment while still maintaining high levels of entertainment. Sport organizations that have incorporated "green marketing" include the NFL's Philadelphia Eagles who have established the Eagles Forest, a 6.5 acre site to grow more than 1,500 trees and shrubs to replace their carbon footprint. The Eagles have also incorporated recycling and use of compostable concession products. The effects of these organizational decisions allowed the Eagles to power Lincoln Financial Field using 100% renewable wind energy for the 2008 season. These organizational decisions have influenced the marketing of the team with the initiation of the "Go Green or Go Home" campaign, playing off the organization's colors and the fact that spectators found littering are now kicked out of games (Philadelphia Eagles, 2011).

© AISPIX, 2012. Under license from Shutterstock, Inc.

Legal/Political Environment

At times sport organizations will need to consider the legal and/or political environment when planning. Legal issues that typically influence sport marketers are trademark infringements, promotional liabilities, and ambush marketing. Sport organizations have an interest in protecting their brand through trademarks. Chapter 13 provides an in-depth discussion of legal issues associated with sport marketing. Outside organizations, attempting to exploit established brands, can engage in trademark infringement. Sport marketers must have established processes for monitoring the sport industry for potential infringements. Sport marketers must also be concerned with legal ramifications from promotional liabilities. On-court/field promotions have become an integral part of the fan experience and serve as creative marketing tools for increasing the sponsor's benefits. However, sport marketers may take an added risk when inviting spectators onto the court/field for a promotional activity. Sport marketers must be legally protected in the event injuries or other concerning issues occur during a promotion. Finally, the legality of ambush marketing is an issue sport marketers must be aware. While most forms of ambush marketing are legal, sponsors are contractually bound to the event/organization and therefore have a right in protecting the exploitation of the sport organizations. When this exploitation is jeopardized by ambush marketing tactics, sport marketers must be informed of any legal protection they can offer to their sponsors.

The need for sport organizations to gain political support is often centered on capital campaigns to build arenas and/or stadiums. Because the cost of arenas and stadiums has grown exponentially in the past 20 years, many sport organizations cannot afford to build these state of the art facilities without assistance. When the University of Louisville decided to build a new riverfront arena for the men's basketball program, the institution needed political support to secure bonds through Goldman Sachs & Co. In order for the university to get the necessary bonds to build the arena, they needed political figures like Mayor Jerry Abramson to support and promote the project. Without the help and support of political figures, they may have never obtained the necessary funds to finance the arena.

Competition

Marketers within the sport industry must have an awareness of how competition can impact the sport organization. An understanding of how competition affects the sport organization allows marketers the ability to make decisions on the marketing mix with less risk. Potential competitors can be in the form of both direct and indirect competition and will vary from market to market. For example, the University of Alabama and UCLA will market their football programs differently due to differences in competition. The University of Alabama has little competition from professional sports in their market area and few intercollegiate teams compete for fans, boosters, or sponsors. UCLA, on the other hand, competes in the same market as the University of Southern California (USC) and eight major league professional sports teams. In addition, their consumers have the option of going to one of many amusement parks, attractions, or beaches rather than attending a game.

Direct competitors consist of organizations that produce goods or services that are identical or very similar in both the product and benefit delivered to the consumer. An example of a direct competitor within the sport industry would be the relationship between the New York Mets and the New York Yankees. Both organizations produce professional baseball entertainment. In addition, both are vying for disposable income of residents within the New York City area. Because of the competition between these organizations, the promotional schedule of the 2010 season revealed no shared dates of promotional events.

Indirect competitors consist of organizations that produce products or services that are not similar but may offer comparable benefits to the consumer. Within the sport industry, entertainment is a core benefit sought by many consumers of sport products. Therefore, sport organizations that produce sport events must understand how other entertainment organizations affect their organization. Examples of indirect competitors to sport organizations consist of many other entertainment organizations such as restaurants, movies, and performing arts shows. For example, The Anaheim Ducks not only have to compete against the other professional teams in the Los Angeles area, but also have to compete with the various amusement parks, tourist attractions, concerts, and various outdoor recreation opportunities.

SWOT Analysis

After identifying relevant influences, organizations often conduct a situational analysis or **SWOT analysis**. In conducting this analysis, organizations identify factors to capitalize on (strengths and opportunities) and factors needing to be controlled or eliminated (weaknesses and threats). Strengths and weaknesses are internal and may include factors such as resources (human or financial), competencies, structural advantages, or product advantages.

Potential Organizational Strengths	Potential Organizational Weaknesses
• Product attributes • Financial capacity • Management experience • Community support • Brand image • Existing technology • Location • Facilities • Processes and procedures • History and tradition • Fan or participant loyalty	• Product limitations • Financial restrictions • Lack of fan support • Brand image or reputation • Levels of product awareness • Technological competence • Lack of facilities or poor location • Lack of history or tradition

While strengths and weaknesses are internal factors, opportunities and threats are external factors (or out of the organization's control). These factors are typically related to the economic, social, technical, legal, or competitive environments.

Potential Environmental Opportunities	Potential Environmental Weaknesses
• Developing markets • Social movements or trends • New markets • Potential sponsors or partners • Economic growth • Advances in technology • Political and/or legal changes • Industry trends	• Competitors • Environmental issues • Changes in community values • Labor, supplier, or transportation disputes • Economic conditions • Political or legal uncertainty

Goals and Objectives

Marketing goals provide direction for the marketing programs. They assist in defining the purpose of your plan, guide the planning process, and define what is to be accomplished. By setting goals, efforts are focused on the most important activities. Without goals, marketing programs are directionless and unfocused.

For example, the mission of the Louisville Sports Commission is to attract, create, and operate sporting events. Without direction, the organization would not know what types of events to bid on or host. The Commission must determine what type of events to target. It must be determined if large events, high-profile events, or the most competitive events should be targeted. Each type of event would take considerable time and effort to attract, and without direction, they may be wasting time on pursuing the wrong events for the city. In 2010, the organization set goals to attract sporting events that would fill hotel rooms, create opportunities for locals to participate in and watch, and promote a healthy lifestyle. As such, the organization has been able to attract events such as the NCAA Division II National Championships Festival and the World Cyclocross Championships. In addition, it has been able to identify which other events to pursue (Karman, 2010).

Although the terms "goals" and "objectives" are often used interchangeably, in this chapter goals are defined as broad, qualitative statements that provide direction. The following are some generic examples of sport marketing goals.

- Increase attendance
- Increase market share
- Increase sales
- Increase membership
- Raise participation numbers
- Increase profitability
- Create value for sponsors
- Enhance organization, cause, or community image
- Raise money for a cause or charity
- Promote a sport, location, or organization
- Create an advantage over competitors
- Enhance customer service

Marketing goals should be consistent with the organization's overall mission and goals. If goals are not consistent, then the marketing plan may not yield favorable results. Different types of sport programs should have different types of goals, since each target different consumer segments. For example, organizations may have goals related to profit, image, or participation.

- Profit related goals (e.g., professional sports, major sporting events)—marketing goals should relate to generating revenue.

- Image related goals (e.g., charitable events, promotional events)—marketing goals should relate to generating awareness levels or generating a positive image.

- Participation related goals (e.g., recreation programs, intramural programs)—marketing goals should relate to generating numbers of participants or increasing repeat participants.

For each goal, **marketing objectives** are established. Objectives represent specific performance targets necessary to achieve each designated goal. Good objectives are specific, measurable, achievable, relevant, and timely (SMART) statements that support each marketing goal.

- Specific—Objectives should specify what needs to be accomplished. In many cases, the unit responsible is identified. Avoid statements like "work harder" or "be smarter." Although they sound good, these types of statements are not measurable and provide little direction as to how to accomplish the stated objective.

- Measurable—Objectives should be quantifiable so that the organization can measure its progress in achieving its goals. It is important to be specific about how the organization should improve. For example, a minor league hockey franchise may desire to increase season ticket sales. The objective should be written to specifically identify what percentage of ticket sales stem from season tickets compared to individual game tickets.

- Achievable—Objectives should be reachable. Performance outcomes that are attainable should be developed relative to the organization's available resources.

- Relevant—Objectives should connect to the goal in that if they are met, the goal will be met. Focus on performance outcomes that will have the most impact on the goal. Avoid objectives unrelated or only tangentially related to the marketing goal or organization's mission.

- Timely—Many objectives will include deadlines for completing objectives.

The following is an example of some goals and objectives that a parks and recreation department offering swimming lessons may use. As you will note, each objective directly relates to the goal.

Goal—Increase participation in summer swimming lesson program.

Objective 1—Retain 80% of last year's swimmers.

Objective 2—Register ten new swimmers for each section by the end of the early registration period.

Objective 3—Recruit eight youth groups to participate in lessons by July 1.

Objective 4—Increase participation in adult swimming lessons by 20%.

The following is an example of some goals and objectives that a professional bowling event may use. In this case, the organization has two goals, and the objectives are particular to each goal.

Goal 1—Increase overall revenue.

Objective 1—Sell 12% more all-tournament packages than last year's event by one month prior to the event.

Objective 2—Sell 200 walk-up tickets per session.

Objective 3—Sell 50 group tickets for each session by one week prior to the event.

Objective 4—Average $6 per spectator in merchandise sales for the tournament.

Goal 2—Raise awareness of bowling in the community.

Objective 1—Double the number of mentions in local news coverage during the 60 days leading up to the event.

Objective 2—Operate ten youth bowling clinics in the 2-week period prior to the event.

Target Markets

One of the most important decisions marketers in any industry determine is which markets they will serve. Therefore, this section of the marketing plan provides an analysis of the consumer base. Customer analysis starts with addressing questions related to the ways in which the organization is meeting customers' needs. Typical questions to consider in this process include:

- What customer need is the organization meeting?
- How are customers currently meeting these needs?
- What can the organization offer to meet customers' needs?

From this analysis, marketers can address strategic opportunities.

- Is there interest in what the organization has to offer?
- Are there underserved markets the organization can reach?
- Can the organization offer new benefits to existing customers?

This section of the marketing plan should also provide a detailed description of the market. This portion of the marketing plan must also include information on market size, market trends, customer profiles, and purchase patterns. The following is a sample of some information a roller skating center may include in its plan in order to better understand its consumer market:

- According to data from a 2009 Synovate online panel, traditional roller skating (2x2) participation went from 8.9 million in 2007 to 7.8 million in 2008, a drop of 11.9%. Inline skating went from 10.8 million in 2007 to 9.6 million in 2008, a drop of 11.2%.

- In 2009, SGMA reported that roller hockey participation dropped from 1.8 million in 2007 to 1.6 million in 2008. Roller hockey participation had dropped 60% over the last eight years. Over 60% of roller hockey players played either at home or at a public facility.

- According to Roller Skating Association International (RSA), traditional roller skating has diminished among adults, but is still popular among 7–14 year old children. They report skating centers receive 23 million visits from "tweens" each year and 18 million visits from younger children.

- According to a Matrix Group survey, more than 20 percent of indoor skaters skate between 31 and 99 times per year, while 12 percent go at least 100 times per year. In that same survey, participants ranked the reasons why they skate: It is fun (94%); my friends go (82%); I like the music (82%); I want to get out of the house (79%); I meet new people (70%); and it is a healthy activity (67%).

This information should be key in segmenting the market and identifying target markets. Organizations rarely try to market to every consumer. Instead, organizations identify smaller, homogenous groups with similar characteristics or similar needs. Marketers often identify segments using the following criteria:

- Demographic segmentation—dividing the market based on attributes such as age, gender, socio-economic status, geographic region, and education.

- Psychographic segmentation—dividing the market based on psychological characteristics such as lifestyle, attitudes, personality, opinions, and values.

- Product usage—dividing the market based on how often or how much consumers use the product.

- Product benefits—dividing the market based on the benefits consumers seek from an event.

After segmenting the market, marketers must identify and select **target markets**. Target markets are the segments for which marketers feel they will have the most success pursuing. Marketers should select targets based on a thorough analysis of consumer data, and choices should be consistent with marketing objectives. By identifying distinct targets, marketers can design strategies and tactics to meet the precise needs of each target. For example, Major League Baseball's Tampa Rays have a program to cater to the needs of their "senior" fans, a significant population in the Tampa Bay area. The Golden Rays are the official seniors fan club of the Tampa Bay Rays. Fans 55 and older can join and receive special ticket offers, invitations to exclusive Golden Rays events, and an official Golden Rays tote bag (Raysbaseball.com, 2011).

Organizations must also consider how they will position themselves relative to competition and in the mindset of consumers. **Positioning** refers to the process in which marketers try to create an image for their organization, goods, or services in the mind of their target markets (Reis and Trout, 1981). Organizations have multiple benefits to offer consumers, but marketers often focus on a few key benefits that are most important to their respective target markets. Many descriptions can be used to describe minor league baseball: traditional sport, family fun, developmental league, low price, interesting ballparks, star players, etc. Trying to communicate all of these benefits to consumers may leave them confused. Instead, marketers will often identify and promote the benefits most important to their target market. For example, minor league baseball's Round Rock Express, realizing its target market consisted mostly of families, positions itself as family entertainment. By doing this, the franchise hopes its target market will perceive its games as an ideal place for family fun. Further, organizations often position themselves against competitors. Curves, a health club, positions itself as a club exclusively for women wanting to include exercise as part of their busy routine. When customers in their target market (women with careers and children) are considering a health club to join, this position makes Curves stand out against the bevy of competitors such as Gold's Gym, Urban Active, and other similar clubs.

Marketing Strategy

In this section, marketers describe their marketing strategies and tactics, or in other words, their game plan (Miller, 1997). Marketing strategies typically refer to what is to be accomplished based on established goals and objectives, and marketing tactics are the strategies developed to accomplish the goals (Stotlar, 2009).

Marketers develop strategies in relationship to the marketing environment. Considering each organization faces different environmental factors and challenges, strategies are likely to vary greatly between organizations. Despite this, marketers can use some basic models to guide the development of strategies. The following section presents two common models marketers often used in identifying marketing strategies: The Ansoff Product-Market Growth Matrix (1965) and Porter's Generic Strategies (1980).

The Ansoff Product-Market Growth Matrix outlines four common strategies determined by the organization's desire to reach existing or new markets or its desire to offer existing or new products. The following is a definition of each strategy with examples of how a horse racing operation might utilize each strategy:

- **Market penetration**—Offer an existing product to an existing market. Organizations achieve this strategy by getting existing consumers to consume more or gain competitors' customers. One example of a horse racing operation utilizing this strategy would be the use of a rewards program offering perks for their customers based on how often they used the facility's services. In this case they are offering the same product (live racing) to the same customers (racing enthusiasts), but they are able to increase their business by getting these consumers to consume more.

- **Market development**—Offer an existing product to a new market. Organizations achieve this strategy by presenting existing products in a way that will attract new consumer groups. An example of market development would be one of the many programs horseracing operations offer to attract new consumers to their products, such as college nights or family promotions. The racetrack is still offering an existing product (live racing), but adjusting or adapting the product to attract consumers beyond the typical racing enthusiast.

- **Product development**—Offer a new product to an existing market. Organizations achieve this strategy by creating or offering something new to current customers. Many horse racetracks have accomplished this by offering simulcasts of races at other tracks during times their racetrack is not hosting live races. Existing customers (racing enthusiasts) now have another product (races at other sites) upon which they can wager.

- **Diversification**—Offer a new product to a new market. Organizations achieve this strategy when they use existing capabilities to create a new venture. Many racetracks, realizing they have existing capabilities to host large events and crowds, have started offering concerts. The organization is offering a new product (concerts) to new customers (music fans) and is able to do so efficiently due to their expertise in event promotion, ticketing, concessions, parking, crowd control, etc.

Porter's (1980) generic strategies are three basic strategies related to gaining a competitive advantage. The following is a definition of each strategy with examples of how a soccer camp could take advantage of each strategy:

- Differentiation strategy—Offer a product with unique attributes or benefits competitors do not offer. A soccer camp may promote itself as the only camp in the region where campers get to participate on a professional field (or receive instruction from professional coaches, or compete against top teams, etc.). The key here is to illustrate the desired attributes or benefits your product offers that your competitors do not offer.

- Focus strategy—Offer a product to a narrow market. This allows you to focus better on the needs of a small group. A soccer camp may choose to become a "goalkeeper camp." While limiting the operation to goalkeepers only, the market is much smaller; however, this may make the camp more attractive to kids playing goalkeeper because it focuses on their specific needs.

- Cost leadership strategy—Offer a product with a price lower than that of your competitors. A football camp may decide to drop its prices to make the camp seem more economical than competitors' camps.

Once planners identify strategies, they move to identifying tactics necessary to implement the marketing plan. Tactical planning addresses shorter-term actions necessary to implement longer-term marketing strategies (Boone and Kurtz, 2010). Marketing tactics are the specific solutions developed to meet marketing strategies, and tactical planning guides the implementation of specific marketing strategies. Marketing tactics often revolve around how to manage the marketing mix. The marketing mix is a set of marketing decisions related to the 4 P's—product, price, promotion, or place (also known as distribution).

Product Decisions

Product decisions are related to the goods and services the organization offers. In sport, the product is usually an intangible service (sporting event, recreational program, club membership, sponsorship, etc.) rather than a good (sporting goods). As such, sport marketers tend to make product decisions based on the experiential nature of the product rather than the physical characteristics. For example, the NBA's Golden State Warriors marketing team has no control over how the team plays, but it can influence how consumers may feel about the product. The organization desired to give its brand image a boost by reminding fans of its glory years. To enhance this strategy, the franchise created a new logo and unveiled new uniforms for the 2010-2011 season which featured a classic design and incorporated the same royal blue and yellow color scheme used from 1964-1997 (Thompson, 2010).

Some examples of product decisions are:

- Product development—what goods and services will you offer?

- Brand image—what will you call your program or event?

- Attributes—what attributes need to part of your goods and services to influence customers?

- Benefits—what are the important benefits your consumers seek from your product?

- Extensions—what are the amenities and related products that add to the consumer's experience?

Price Decisions

Price decisions are related to how much will be charged to spectators, participants, or sponsors for the products offered. Similar to product decisions, pricing decisions can be difficult due to the experiential nature of sport. In addition, the value of sport is often quite subjective, further complicating pricing decisions. For example, the value of a round of golf is only as much as what people are willing to pay or what the market will allow. When the number of rounds played dropped dramatically in 2009, Myrtle Beach's golf courses knew they had to adjust their pricing strategies. Demand had dropped, so area courses dropped their rates and provided other bargains, increasing the perceived value

Courtesy of Sal DeAngelis

to the customer and stimulating golfers to play more rounds. The result was increased revenue due to increased volume (Blondin, 2010). This is a prime example of how an economic threat to an organization can also serve as an opportunity for an organization to reconnect with its consumer base and generate additional revenues.

Some examples of pricing decisions are:

- Purchase price—what price will you set for your various goods and services?

- Pricing strategies—should you set a high price to maximize revenue or a low price to encourage participation?

- Discount policies—when and how would you lower your prices?

- Price lining—should you set different prices for different levels of the product (premium seats, full-service memberships, etc.)?

- Payment policies—when and how will you collect payment?

- Bundling—what added benefits will come with each purchase?

Promotion Decisions

Promotion decisions relate to communication with target consumer segments. In sport, promotion decisions can relate to a variety of goals such as creating awareness, stimulating demand, encouraging product trial, and retaining loyal consumers. In 2009, for example, the San Francisco Giants, with the goal of attracting a new target market, created Filipino-American Heritage night. The team brought in popular boxing champion Manny Pacquiao to throw out the first pitch, offered cultural entertainment from local Filipino performance groups, and gave away a special edition Filipino-themed Giants tee shirt. The team credited the promotion with bringing in an additional 10,000 fans for the night, many of whom were attending their first game (Rovell, 2009).

Some examples of promotional decisions are:

- Promotional objectives—what do you want to accomplish through your promotional program?

- Promotional budget—what will you spend and where will you spend it?

- Message content—what will you say to consumers and how will you say it?

- Promotional strategies—will you use sales promotion, advertising, direct sales, public relations, etc.?

- Media selection—what method will you use to transmit your message to your target audience?

Place Decisions

Place or distribution decisions relate to how you get the product to the consumer or how you get the consumer to your product. It would not make sense to have a great product if your consumers could not access it (Smith, 2008). These decisions typically relate to getting the product to the consumer when they want it and where they want it. For example, the Portland Timbers soccer club plays at a stadium located in a downtown area with little parking. To make it easier for its customers to attend games, the team reached a deal with the local transportation authority to include ride fares on the city's light rail system with ticket plans.

Some examples of place decisions in sport marketing are:

- Location—where will you hold your events or activities?

- Facilities—what facilities will you use?

- Access—where will your products be available?

- Time—when will your products be available? When will you hold your events/activities/programs?

- Duration—how long will your events/activities/programs be?

- Distribution agents—will you use wholesalers, retailers, media, etc., to deliver your product to your consumer?

- Inventory—how will you manage your inventory (tickets, memberships, registrations)?

Implementation

In addition to identifying *what* strategies and tactics are necessary, the marketing plan should identify *how* to implement these tactics. Poor implementation and coordination has ruined many great ideas (Mullin, Hardy, and Sutton, 2007). In these cases, the organization may not have had sufficient resources, appropriate procedures, organizational support, trained staff, or the level of coordination necessary to execute the marketing plan. For example, the Louisville Fire indoor football team planned a team jersey giveaway for one of its home games knowing this would attract many young football fans to the game. The franchise was correct as the team generated increased ticket sales for this event. However, the team had neglected to order jerseys far enough in advance to disperse the jerseys at the designated game. Instead of having happy new fans eager to attend additional games, the franchise faced many angry parents swearing to never attend another game.

Implementation of the plan should address three factors related to each tactic: 1. each task necessary to implement the tactic; 2. people responsible for executing each task; and 3. the timeframe for each task (Luther, 2001). It is important to consider *all* the necessary tasks. Imagine marketing a baseball game with a "wet and wild" promotion predicted to be a major revenue generator. A frozen t-shirt contest, water balloon contests, and a slip and slide for on-field fun after the game has been planned for the event. Marketers must consider what is necessary to ensure the success of the event. Some considerations might include

- Obtaining approval from management to run the promotion

- Securing permission from the grounds crew (they are likely to be protective of their field)

- Generate a budget for the promotion and obtain funding

- Work out the details with the facility

- Train the staff on how to run the event

- Order materials

- Have materials set up and ready to go

- Try out the contests and activities in advance to ensure everything will work

- Consider how to minimize risks to make sure no one gets hurt

- Promote the promotion (the event cannot be successful if no one shows up)

- Schedule activities

- Write the public address script

- Mobilize security and ushers to make sure things don't get out of hand

- Develop contingency plans (i.e., what if it rains? what if someone gets hurt?)

After identifying everything needed to implement the plan, the plan must be implemented. At this stage, the marketer transitions from being a planner to an organizer and a leader (Shank, 2009). Timing and coordination are crucial as many activities occur simultaneously and at multiple times. Consider a management team developing a plan for a college football game. When developing its marketing plan, the need to improve customer service may have been identified and thus, strategies for improvement were developed. The marketers cannot execute this plan single-handedly. Instead, they must coordinate activities with parking attendants, ticket takers, concessionaires, ushers, and a host of other people who encounter the customer.

Evaluation

This section of the sport marketing plan is concerned with evaluating the level of success of the marketing plan. Evaluation is the process of comparing results against objectives to determine whether specific strategies or tactics were appropriate in meeting objectives. If the results of the plan met or exceeded objectives, marketers know strategies are appropriate and should likely continue with established tactics. In cases in which results do not match objectives, marketers must adjust, modify, or completely change future marketing plans.

Evaluation is an ongoing process that takes place throughout the entire planning process as well as the end of the process. This allows decision makers to adjust their marketing plans as issues arise throughout the implementation of the plan. Considering many sport marketing plans cover long periods of time, it is important to build in specific points of evaluation throughout the plan's implementation so that problems can be identified and corrected in a timely manner. For example, a professional football team may review customer service data after each game to rectify problems prior to the next game.

Marketing Plan Summary

The final section of the marketing plan is a summary of the key elements of the plan. In this section, remind the reader of the goals and objectives and summarize the activities necessary to reach those goals and objectives (Stotlar, 2009). Sometimes this section will be in the form of an executive summary, which appears at the beginning of the plan.

Key Questions to Address in a Marketing Plan

Introduction

► What is the organization's mission?

► What are our current products and who are our customers?

► What were the results of prior marketing efforts?

Data and analysis

► What are our internal considerations?

► What are our external considerations?

► How can we assess our strengths, weaknesses, opportunities, and threats (SWOT)?

Goals and objectives

► What are the overall marketing goals?

► What specific objectives need to be set related to those goals?

Target Markets

► How can we describe the market?

► Who are our target markets and how can we describe them?

► How will we position our product in the minds of our target markets?

Marketing Strategy

► What is the long-term marketing strategy?

► What tactics are necessary to accomplish the marketing strategy?

- Product
- Price
- Promotion
- Place

Implementation

▶ What tasks are necessary to implement the tactic?

▶ Who is responsible for executing each task?

▶ What is the timeframe for each task?

Evaluation

▶ How will we evaluate the effectiveness of the plan?

Summary

Effective marketing requires a significant amount of consideration and planning. Without this effort, the overall plan is directionless and much less likely to succeed. A significant part of the planning process involves collecting and analyzing the appropriate data in order to make educated decisions. Then, planners can identify goals and objectives, select appropriate target markets, identify tactics incorporating the four P's, and develop plans for implementation and evaluation.

Discussion Questions

1. What do organizations hope to accomplish through a strategic sport marketing approach?

2. Why is it essential to understand the internal environment and external environment before setting goals and developing tactics?

3. What are the criteria for setting good objectives?

4. In what situations would a differentiation strategy be most appropriate? When would a focus strategy be most appropriate? When would a cost leadership strategy be most appropriate?

5. Why is it important to include a plan for implementation in your overall marketing plan?

Critical Thinking Exercises

Assume you have been chosen to market a Women's Flat Track Derby Association (WFTDA) Roller Derby Regional Tournament. The event will be three days long featuring some of the best roller derby teams in the region. The top three teams will advance to the WFTDA National Tournament. Flat track roller derby is a contact, team-sport featuring two teams of five players on the track at once. Since the sport first gained prominence in 2001, it has grown to include teams in more than 400 leagues. Leagues are mostly made up of young (20–30 year old), amateur, all-girl teams who compete at local roller rinks. Through the sport, organizers hope to promote a positive, athletic, strong, female image.

1. Why would it be important for you to develop a marketing plan for this event?

2. What types of information would you need to market this event?

3. Identify and evaluate the organization's internal strengths and weaknesses.

4. Identify and evaluate environmental opportunities and threats.

5. What would be some appropriate goals and objectives?

6. How would you evaluate the success (or failure) of your marketing plan?

References

Ansoff, I., *Corporate strategy: An analytical approach to business policy for growth and expansion.* New York, NY: McGraw-Hill, 1965.

Blondin, A., "Grand Strand golf courses sees bump in play," Myrtle Beach Online, accessed June 10, 2010, http://www.thesunnews.com/2010/06/09/1522193/strand-sees-bump-in-play.html.

Boone, L. E., and D. L. Kurtz, *Contemporary marketing.* 14th ed. Mason, OH: South-Western College Publishers, 2010.

Bradley, F., *Strategic marketing in the customer driven organization.* West Sussex, England: Wiley, 2003.

Callaway Golf, "Innovation: Overview," accessed September 1, 2011, http://www.callawaygolf.com/Global/en-US/Innovation.html.

Cyrec, C., "Pro sports 2010 game plan centers on value," *Dallas Business Journal,* accessed December 11, 2009, http://www.bizjournals.com/dallas/stories/2009/12/14/focus7.html.

DiMeglio, S., "LPGA schedule shrinks from 2010: 23 events secured," *USA Today,* accessed November 18, 2009, http://www.usatoday.com/sports/golf/lpga/2009-11-17-2010-lpga-schedule_N.htm.

Gray, D. P., "Sport marketing: Strategies and tactics." In *The management of sports: Its foundation and application,* 3rd ed., 300–336, edited by B.L. Parkhouse. New York, NY: McGraw-Hill, 2001.

Hums, M. A., and J. C. MacLean, *Governance and policy in sport organizations.* Scottsdale, Arizona: Holcomb Hathaway, 2009.

Johnson, K., "Monarchs to tout players' athletic skills in effort to lure male fans," Bizjournals.com, accessed May 5, 2008, http://www.bizjournals.com/sacramento/stories/2008/05/05/story11.html?page=1.

Karman, J. R., "Louisville Sports Commission adjusts its focus, pushes to land more events," Bizjournals.com, accessed June 11, 2010, http://www.bizjournals.com/louisville/stories/2010/06/14/story3.html?page=3.

Little League Incorporated, 2011a, www.littleleague.org.

Little League Incorporated, "The mission of Little League," 2011b, www.littleleague.org/learn/about/historyandmission/mission.htm.

Luther, W. M., *The marketing plan: How to prepare and implement it.* 3rd ed. New York, NY: AMACOM, 2001.

Miller, L. K., *Sport business management.* Gaithersburg, MD: Aspen, 1997.

Mullin, B. J., S. Hardy, and W. Sutton, *Sport marketing.* 3rd ed., Champaign, IL: Human Kinetics, 2007.

New York Yankees, "Uniforms & Logos," 2011, http://mlb.mlb.com/nyy/history/uniforms_logos.jsp.

Nike, "Benefits: WHQ Campus," accessed September 1, 2011, http://www.nikebiz.com/careers/benefits/other/whq_campus.html.

Osborn, A. F., *Applied imagination: Principles and procedures of creative problem solving.* 3rd ed., New York: Charles Scribner's Sons, 1963.

Philadelphia Eagles, "Eagles Forest," accessed September 15, 2011, http://www.philadelphiaeagles.com/gogreen/Forest.asp.

Porter, M. E., *The competitive advantage of nations.* New York: Free Press, 1980.

Raysbaseball.com, "Join the official seniors fan club of the Tampa Bay Rays for only $25!" accessed April 5 ,2011, http://mlb.mlb.com/tb/fan_forum/golden_rays.jsp.

Ries, A. and J. Trout, *Positioning: The battle for your mind.* New York: McGraw-Hill, 1981.

Rovell, D., "Giants hit home run with ethnic marketing," CNBC.com, 2009, http://www.cnbc.com/id/30323407

Schein, E. H., "The role of the founder in the creation of organizational culture." In *Reframing organizational culture,* 14–25, edited by P. J. Frost, L. F. Moore, M. R. Louis, C. C. Lundberg, and J. Martin. Beverly Hills, CA: Sage, 1991.

Shank, M. D., *Sports marketing: A strategic perspective*. 4th ed. Upper Saddle River, NJ: Pearson, 2009.

Smith, A. C. T., *Introduction to sport marketing*. Oxford: Butterworth Heinemann, 2008.

Stotlar, D. K., *Developing successful sport marketing plans*. Morgantown, WV: Fitness Info Tech, 2009.

Sunnucks, M., and C. Casacchia, "Arizona's pro sports teams battle for ticket sales," *Phoenix Business Journal*, accessed March 26, 2010, http://www.bizjournals.com/phoenix/stories/2010/03/22/daily76.html.

Thompson, M., "Golden State Warriors' new uniforms, logos bridge eras in franchise's Bay Area history," *Mercury News*, accessed June 17, 2010, http://www.mercurynews.com/ci_15322115?nclick_check=1.

Yes Network, "Some former Yankees enjoying facial hair freedom," accessed April 26, 2010, http://www.myyesnetwork.com/14633/blog/2010/04/26/some_former_yankees_enjoying_facial_hair_freedom.

Courtesy of Kimberly Miloch.

CHAPTER 3

Understanding Sport Consumer Behavior

B. Christine Green The University of Texas at Austin
Matthew T. Bowers The University of Texas at Austin

> *Look at the world around you. It may seem like an immovable, implacable place.*
> *It is not. With the slightest push—in just the right place—it can be tipped.*
> > *Malcolm Gladwell,* The Tipping Point

CHAPTER OBJECTIVES

After completing the chapter, the reader should be able to:

- Identify key motives for consuming sport.
- Describe the factors that influence consumers' perceptions of sport products and services.
- Explain how attitudes and emotions affect sport purchasing.
- Differentiate between consumer involvement and identification.
- Explain ways in which groups can influence individual sport purchases.
- Discuss the process of consumer decision making in sport.
- Determine effective marketing tactics for each stage of the decision process.
- Understand the ways in which new technologies impact sport consumers.

The concept of marketing originally began as little more than a sales exercise. Sport organizations would develop products, services, programs, or facilities and then try to convince people to purchase them. More recently, successful businesses began to shift the way they thought about—and conducted—their marketing efforts. In essence, the focus of marketers changed. No longer did they begin their marketing campaigns with a product or service that they needed to introduce to a group of consumers. Instead, they began by trying to understand the consumers themselves. What needs do consumers have? What are their interests? What type of lifestyles do they lead? Once we, as marketers, know what consumers find useful and meaningful within their lives, we can then set about creating products or services to fulfill their needs. This type of marketing is consumer-centric, and is based almost entirely on understanding consumers. As a consequence of this shift in thinking about how to reach consumers, the area of consumer behavior emerged to form a critical component of any organization's marketing efforts.

Studying consumer behavior tells you why consumers act the way they do—why they watch, attend, or play the sports they do—and why they make the purchases they do. Knowledge of your consumers' behaviors can help you to make more informed business decisions, reach new consumer groups, and retain existing customers. The key to success in any area of business is to understand the way your target markets think, act, and behave in response to internal factors, external factors and situations, and your organization's own marketing efforts. This chapter first examines the internal and external factors that affect customers' consumption behaviors. Internal factors are psychological in nature and vary from individual to individual. Some also vary according to the situation. **Motivation, attitudes, perceptions, emotions, identification, attachment**, and **psychological involvement** with a player, team, sport, brand, or sport organization have all been shown to influence sport consumption behaviors. Individuals are also influenced by external factors such as **culture, subcultures**, friends, and family members. These **reference groups** play a part in shaping sport consumption behaviors, as do situational factors such as geography and climate, place, season, social setting, and even time of day. In addition, the marketing efforts of both you and your competitors also influence the behaviors of sport consumers. Each of these factors can, in turn, influence consumers' purchase decisions.

The next section of the chapter describes the consumer decision process. The decision process begins with need recognition, and is followed by a search for information and an evaluation phase prior to purchase. One might think that the decision process ends with the decision to purchase or not purchase; however, consumers continue to evaluate their purchase decision even after the purchase has been made. We call this **post-purchase evaluation**. Each of the steps in the decision process is affected by the internal and external factors discussed in the first part of the chapter. We further explore some of these factors in relationship to the phases of the decision process. This section concludes with a discussion of effective marketing strategies to influence consumers at each stage of the decision process. The final section of the chapter focuses on specific applications of sport consumer behavior to a variety of sport marketing contexts.

Internal Factors

This section examines the internal psychology of individuals and the ways in which this affects their sport consumption. In short, we want to know what makes consumers think and act the way they do. The first part of this section examines the motives that drive consumers' needs and desires. Next, we explore the impact of consumers' perceptions. Sport consumers take in information in a variety of ways. Even when the message seems to be the same, customers interpret the meaning of the message based on their personal knowledge and experiences. It is important to understand how consumers form perceptions to better understand how to influence their perceptions of your products and services. Attitudes, like perceptions, also influence how consumers feel about your sport organization, event, product, or service. Most advertising is designed to create or change consumers' attitudes. Designing effective marketing messages relies heavily on your understanding of consumers' attitudes and identifying the processes in attitude development that may be impacted by your marketing efforts. Sport teams and brands often elicit strong emotional attachments from fans. As a result, sport purchases can be highly symbolic, thus fanship can become a part of the way sport consumers define themselves. Consequently, the final internal factors considered in this section are the role of identity and involvement in sport consumer behavior.

Motivation

Motivation is the driving force behind our actions. In sport marketing, it can be characterized as the needs and desires of potential fans, participants, and other sport consumers. Sport marketers are successful when they can identify the core needs of their target markets, and design and promote products that meet those needs. An abundance of individual motives have been identified to explain consumers' drives to purchase sport products and services. Although there is some overlap, it is dangerous to assume that motives to watch sport are the same as those to participate in sport or to play fantasy sport or sport video games. Consider what drives you to attend a sporting event? Are these the same reasons that drive you to participate in sport? Probably not. Let's look at some of the key differences.

Spectator sport motives typically fall into one of eight common categories: (1) group affiliation, (2) family time, (3) aesthetic appreciation, (4) self-esteem, (5) economic, (6) eustress, (7) escape, (8) entertainment (Wann, 1995). The need to be part of a group and to spend time with others is a common reason for sports spectating. Most fans attend sports events with friends. However, it is not necessary to watch sport with existing friends for sport spectating to fulfill this need. Consider the popularity of sports bars, as an example. It is quite possible to feel a sense of belonging with other sports fans, merely through the common cause of cheering for your team. Fans of the same team often bond in these situations, sometimes without ever knowing the other fan's name. Bonding plays an important role in family motivation to watch sport too. This motive is more specific than the group affiliation motive in that the group consists of family members, but is essentially the same. Sports spectating can be a time for the family to get together. This is particularly important to married couples and families with children in the home. However, one look around a ballpark suggests that sports spectatorship is intergenerational, and can be driven by a desire to spend time with children, parents, grandparents, siblings, and a wide array of extended family. In fact, sports spectating can create family traditions such as family tailgates, Super Bowl parties, or other gatherings to watch sport events.

Some sport fans are driven to watch sports for the aesthetic beauty inherent in the sport or the athletes' movements. This is perhaps most obvious in the case of artistic sports such as gymnastics or figure skating. However, it is important to consider the old adage, "Beauty is in the eye of the beholder." Soccer fans may appreciate the beauty of a perfectly timed cross; motor sport enthusiasts may appreciate the beauty of a bold passing move; mixed martial arts fans may appreciate the beauty of a particular combination of kicks and punches. Aesthetic motivation is not limited to stereotypically graceful forms of sport. It can also be found in more violent sports. In either case, it behooves sport marketers to determine what constitutes beauty for their target markets and to find ways to use these ideals in their marketing communications.

Self-esteem is a more general need or motivation that can also drive sports spectating. Being a fan of a sports team can enhance one's self-esteem and maintain one's self-concept. Cialdini and his colleagues (1976) call this **BIRGing;** basking in reflected glory. When a fan's team wins, fans extend the win (and achievement) to themselves. Listen the next time your favorite team wins and you are likely to hear the fans exclaim that, "We won!". This phenomena is associated with the *bandwagon effect*, whereby the more a team wins, the more people claim to be fans. Interestingly, fans tend to distance themselves from a loss in order to protect their self-esteem. Rarely do you hear that, "We lost." Instead, it is "They (the team) lost." This is called **CORFing;** cutting off reflected failure.

Courtesy of Gary Southshore RailCats Baseball.

© Aija Lehtonen, 2012. Under license from Shutterstock, Inc.

Economic gain motivates some to watch sports. The most obvious example is sports gambling, where the outcome of the sport event has a direct financial impact on the spectator. Sports betting is a multi-billion dollar industry, with a high proportion of gamblers found on college campuses (Nelson et al., 2007); therefore, sport marketers should be aware of this motive but consider the ethical implications of focusing marketing efforts on meeting this need. Recently, a more indirect economic motive has emerged. Fantasy sport participation has skyrocketed over the past five years (Mahan and McDaniel, 2006). While the potential financial gain from fantasy sports play is not dependent on a single game outcome, fantasy sport enthusiasts' motives for economic gain can change the way they watch sport. Clever sports marketers will recognize this need and shape their products accordingly. For example, broadcasters now sell packages such as the Red Zone offered by Time Warner Cable. This package shows all the scoring opportunities across the NFL in real time. In this way, fantasy sport players can track their "own" players and the points that they generate.

Sports contests can fulfill fans' need for stimulation and excitement. **Eustress,** the positive stress associated with high levels of arousal and excitement, drives many to watch sport competitions. The uncertainty of game outcomes is the primary stimulus for eustress. Sport marketers can, and often do, help to build eustress through the stories they tell through their marketing communications. Rivalries, real or imagined, are a way to increase excitement surrounding a game. In short, the drama surrounding an event can be highlighted by sport marketers to appeal to fans motivated by eustress.

Escape is another motive that stimulates sports attendance and viewing. Sometimes escape works with eustress to help spectators to escape from the boredom of their everyday lives. Sometimes it works in opposition. That is, watching sports can provide an opportunity to escape from the stress and stimulation of everyday life. In either case, sport acts as a diversion. Although sport is intrinsically meaningless, this meaninglessness actually enables sport to serve as a canvas upon which people can ascribe meanings that can be both intensely personal and universally shared. For example, when your local NFL franchise wins the Super Bowl, the experience can become something that the community draws upon to bring its members closer together while also providing individuals with a range of psychic benefits from vicarious achievement to a weekly escape from the winter doldrums—if only for a few hours.

Lastly, many are attracted to watch sport purely for the entertainment it provides. The main sources of entertainment are the game and the competition itself; however, the ancillary entertainment can also attract consumers. The cheerleaders, bands and other music, halftime shows, and even promotional games can be attractive means for attendance at live sporting events. In fact, a festival-like atmosphere may be the most important driver of non-fans' attendance. The challenge for sport marketers is to attract these non-fans motivated by the overall entertainment experience, and then convert them to fans with multiple motives for attendance.

It is highly unlikely that any person is motivated by any single motive. Rather, multiple motives work to attract fans to sport. The same is true for sport participation, as well as hybrid participative/spectator settings such as fantasy sport and sport video-gaming. Common motives for participating in sport fall into three categories: (1) achievement, (2) mastery, and (3) social.

- **Achievement motivation** is driven by the need to win, to compete, and to be the best. Sport participants motivated by these needs require social comparison. It is not enough to improve; they must be better than their competitors. Extrinsic rewards such as trophies, all-star games, and MVP awards are attractive to these participants. Notice that the need to achieve is difficult to obtain via sport spectating. At best, achievement for sport fans is vicarious. Yet it is possible for fans to meet their need for achievement via fantasy sport participation or video gaming.

- **Mastery motivation** does not require social comparison. As such, it is a more intrinsic motivation often represented as competition with one's self. Challenge and learning play a big role in motivating mastery-oriented sports participants. Like achievement motivation, mastery motivation seems quite distinct from the spectator motives discussed earlier. However, sports video games that provide increasing levels of challenge seem ideally suited to mastery needs.

- **Social motivation** is the participation motive most linked to spectator motives. Sport participants with a need for social interaction can clearly find that in team sports and also through the social life surrounding sport competitions. Sports spectatorship also would seem to meet this need. In fact, the spectator motives of group affiliation and family time can be considered social motives. Fantasy sports and video gaming can also meet social needs, albeit in different ways.

While participation motives are not completely unrelated to motives for watching sports, they overlap less than we think. This is why nearly every young athlete participates in youth soccer at some point in their life, yet soccer is still considered a minor spectator sport in the

United States. Similarly, attendance at NFL games dwarfs attendance at most other professional sports events. Women are a prominent market segment for the NFL, yet few women have experience playing football. Clearly, the motives that drive sport participation are different from those that drive spectation and attendance. Whatever sport products or services you are marketing, it helps to understand your consumers' needs, to create or modify your products to meet those needs, and to communicate to your target markets in a way that highlights the ways in which your products and services meet their needs. Consequently, the more motives you can appeal to, the more likely you are to attract a broad base of consumers.

Perceptions

Have you ever attended a sports event with a friend and ended up wondering if you had gone to two different events? You thought the game was boring, but your friend couldn't stop raving about it. It's all about perception. Perceptions are what create different "realities" for different people. Perceptions occur in response to stimuli, and are built through a process of filtering, receiving, and interpreting information. Although the process itself is internal, it is affected by both internal and external influences. Internal influences include motivation, emotions, attitudes, self-concept, prior memories, and experiences, as well as expectations. External factors can include culture or subculture, social groups, and the situation. Perceptions are formed when you attend to particular stimuli, process the information, and interpret that information to give it meaning.

Consider an example of two friends attending a college basketball game. The game is a non-conference game played early in the season between a highly rated Division I team and a local Division II team. Pat played basketball through high school, while Chris has only played recreationally. Pat regularly attends college basketball games. Chris has only been to one other basketball game. Both Chris and Pat have active social lives and go out often with friends. The game is sloppily played; the Division I team wins by a score of 88-61. Do you think Chris and Pat perceived the game in the same way? Probably not. Consider the differences in their previous experiences that could affect the way that they experienced the game. Chris had little basketball knowledge or experience. It is likely that Chris focused on the excitement of the total event rather than the basketball game itself. Pat, on the other hand, has significant knowledge of the game and may have had low expectations for the quality of play. Instead of attending to the band, the cheerleaders, and the other fans, Pat may have focused more on the players and the game. Given the sloppy play and lopsided score, it would not be surprising that Pat perceived the game to be boring. Chris, on the other hand, perceived the experience to be exciting. Notice that Chris would be responding to different stimuli than Pat. Chris noticed all of the entertainment. Chris' lack of basketball knowledge and experience affects the interpretation of the experience, resulting in positive perceptions of the game. The challenge for sport marketers is to understand that no two people view the world (or their product) in the same way, and to determine how to create positive perceptions within a target market.

Attitudes

An attitude is a general evaluation of something. Your customers have attitudes about your brand, your products, your services, your advertising, the quality of your team, the coach, individual players, even the seat they occupy when watching the game. Attitudes can be thought of as liking or disliking and include the strength of feelings toward an object. A large part of sport marketing efforts are designed to change people's attitudes in order to create positive thoughts, feelings, and intentions toward our products and services. Attitudes consist of three components: (1) beliefs, the cognitive aspect of attitudes; (2) feelings, the affective aspect of attitudes; and (3) experiences, the behavioral aspect of attitudes.

Beliefs are the way that people think about your product. For example, consumers in the South might think that hockey is a game for cold climates. This can help to create dislike for the sport (and more importantly, your team). If you are marketing ice hockey in Florida, you might try to change consumers' attitudes toward ice hockey by providing them with information that shows that hockey is a popular sport in the South, or that top hockey players grew up in the South. In other words, change your customers' thinking. Alternatively, you could try to change how your customers feel about your product. To do this, you need to make an emotional connection with your customers. Sports teams readily offer marketers with opportunities to connect emotionally with customers. This can occur through the stories you tell about your athletes and the team. It can occur through the team's association with the host city. It can even occur through the use of rituals and symbols that bring back nostalgic memories of earlier experiences. Sport events have also been successful in changing the way that customers feel about them by partnering with charities that customers already have positive feelings toward. The third component, experiences, references past behaviors. Consider our customer with the negative attitude towards ice hockey. She may have attended a hockey game as a child. If her experience of the game was not positive, that experience is likely to result in a negative attitude toward the sport more generally. However, other experiences can negate that one. Positive experiences of other professional sport contests, a fun evening watching hockey on television with friends may be enough to create a positive attitude. This is yet another point of leverage for sport marketers to change attitudes—create positive experiences.

In summary, although attitudes can be enduring and stubbornly upheld, they are always learned. Consequently, sport marketers have the capacity to modify customers' attitudes, by teaching them to think, feel, and/or act differently. Clearly it is easier to create a new attitude or to confirm an existing positive attitude than it is to change a negative attitude, but it is possible to change even long held attitudes. It is a matter of understanding the issues that affect a customer's negative attitude, and then adjusting your marketing efforts to reshape that attitude to a more positive one.

Identity and involvement

Sport involvement is a function of one's interest in sport and its importance in one's life. Like product involvement more generally, high levels of sport involvement are related to more purchases and higher customer loyalty (Bee and Havitz, 2010; Pawlowski et al., 2009). Fans with higher levels of sport involvement tend to feel more deeply about their team, and be more emotionally attached to the team. These are the hardcore fans. Less involved customers are more correctly labeled as spectators than as fans. These customers are less inclined to think, read, or talk about the team. Fan and spectator involvement should be encouraged whenever possible. Find ways to create "touch points" (Gambetti, 2010) between fans and the team, its players, and other personnel (e.g., coaches, owners, mascots, cheerleaders). The more connected fans feel, the more likely they are to watch games, buy tickets, wear licensed products, and promote the team to others. The more highly involved one is with a team or sport, the more central the team is to one's identity.

Team identification is an important consumer behavior variable. The more a fan sees himself as a fan of the team, the more she supports the team. Importantly, highly identified fans place less importance on the team's performance, know more about the team, find their fan experiences to be more enjoyable, and consume more team-related media and products (Murrell and Dietz, 1992; Sutton et al., 1997). Clearly, these are highly desirable outcomes. Sport marketing professionals can help increase fans' identification by providing opportunities for fans to display their team identification through product purchases, website fan zones, and fan events. Similarly, fan identification can be enhanced by providing spaces and opportunities for fans to interact with other fans, team members, and other parts of the organization. In short, it helps fans to feel and show that they are part of the organization.

External Factors

Sport consumers vary tremendously in their sport choices and consumption patterns. Many of those differences can be attributed to the internal factors discussed in the previous section. Yet these internal differences are not the only influences on our sport purchase behaviors. We are also affected by external influences. In fact, we are socialized into distinctive patterns and types of sport consumption by a host of external factors, including the people closest to us, the groups that we belong to or admire, and the larger culture of which we are a part. Even then, our purchase decisions vary as a function of the situation in which we find ourselves. These external influences are discussed in the following sections.

Reference Groups

Although we rarely acknowledge the impact of others, preferring to think that our decisions are solely our own, we are profoundly influenced by those around us. We may be influenced by different people, and value the thoughts and opinions of different groups. These groups serve as reference groups. Reference groups influence our values, attitudes, perceptions,

Courtesy of Brian Turner.

and even our sense of who we are. They serve as a point of comparison or a sounding board for the choices we make. Reference groups can be either direct or indirect in their influence. Family and friends serve as **direct reference groups** as they are likely to interact with you directly. If you think about the sports you play, chances are you first became interested in the sport or team because your friends played, or perhaps your had family members that also participated in that sport. Similarly, consider your earliest fanship. Chances are that you became a fan of your favorite team because your parents were already fans. They may not have forced you to become a fan of their team, or even directly encouraged you to share their fanship. However, you may have grown up sitting in the living room with your parents as they cheered on their team. In fact, you may have learned how to watch a game by mimicking your family members. If they shouted at the television, you may have been socialized into seeing that as a "normal" behavior for watching a televised sport event. Peer groups are particularly important socializing agents for adolescents. Think about all the ways that your peers signal which sports are acceptable to play and which are not. Chances are that you never noticed unless you tried a sport that was considered socially unacceptable in your town or for your gender or for people of your social class. While direct reference groups have the capacity to create the most powerful support (or sanctions) for sport consumption choices, indirect reference groups also play an important role in consumer socialization.

Indirect reference groups include groups to which you aspire, subcultures, social institutions such as media, religion, and political and educational systems, and even ethnic and national cultures. We tend to be so embedded in the larger social institutions and culture that we have difficulty seeing their influence, yet they exert a powerful influence on our norms, values, attitudes, beliefs, and consequently, on the decisions we make. Sport marketers create powerful brand images for their teams, events, and organizations. Sport teams also can take on the characteristics of their community. For example, the Pittsburgh Steelers are seen as a blue collar team that embodies the city's industrious work ethic, while the Lakers are seen as a team whose players and style reflect the glitz and glamour of Hollywood. The image represented by these teams (or by individual athletes on a team) can be aspirational. That is, sport consumers may aspire to be like those players. Sport fans can also aspire to be like other fans they see on television or read about on the Internet. Fans can be impacted by these images without ever coming into direct contact with any individual represented by those images. Marketers use sport teams and athletes as spokespersons or in advertisements to take advantage of their position as an **aspirational reference group**.

Subcultures operate in ways similar to aspirational groups. Sports often have very strong subcultures. Outsiders may view the values and norms of a subculture in stereotypical terms. Consider a scenario in which you wanted to become a snowboarder. Chances are that your knowledge of the snowboarding subculture would influence what kind of clothing you would wear to snowboard, what kind of music snowboarders listen to, and what equipment and brands are valued. You might even be familiar with some of the snowboarding lingo before ever setting foot on the mountain. Marketers reach aspiring snowboarders by offering them products and services that will identify them as part of the subculture. While actual subcultural membership is more complex than this, marketers can at least help novices to look like part of the group.

Culture profoundly influences our views of what is acceptable, thus accepted within the culture. Attitudes and behaviors are shaped by the values instilled through our ethnic and national culture. The sports we play are largely determined by our culture. Netball is a very popular sport for girls and women in Commonwealth countries such as Australia and Great Britain, but most Americans have never heard of it. Table tennis is a highly competitive and popular sport in many Asian countries. While we have competitive table tennis in the United States it would be considered a minor sport at best. Even the way we watch sport is affected by culture. For example, African-Americans are socialized to interact with their environment. Consequently, they often verbally engage with televised sport broadcasts by talking to the players and referees on screen, and with fellow viewers on site (cf. Hale-Benson, 1986).

Reference groups can shape consumers' attitudes and perceptions as they socialize consumers into the norms and values of the group. In the main, socialization occurs through the processes of modeling, prompting, and reinforcing desired behaviors. Modeling can occur indirectly by watching other fans' behaviors or directly by copying the behaviors of those close to you. For example, watching other fans to determine when you should sit or stand at a college basketball game. Behaviors can be prompted or cued by reference groups. Reference groups also serve to reinforce desired behaviors directly and indirectly. A father taking his daughter to her first baseball game may smile and laugh when she boos the umpire, thus reinforcing the behavior. An advertisement featuring a favorite player chewing a particular brand of gum can reinforce a fan's decision to purchase that brand of gum. Alternatively, undesired behaviors can be sanctioned. According to de Mooij (2011), four things must happen for the reference group to exert influence over consumers' behaviors. First, the reference group must make the consumer aware of your product or service. Second, there must be an opportunity for the consumer to compare himself or herself with the reference group. Third, the reference group must influence the person to adopt values and behaviors consistent with the group. Lastly, group membership must support the consumer's decision to use the same product or service that is used by the group. The resulting behavior is still subject to situational factors.

Situational Factors

The attitudes, perceptions, and behaviors of sport consumers are also impacted by the situation within which they occur. Situational factors can take a number of different forms. Perhaps the most easily identifiable situational factors are the time and place within which the decision occurs. At the most basic level, time and place can refer to the time of day or time of year, and the geographical and climate-related surroundings. Are you more likely to buy snow skis during the winter months because you associate the winter season with cold-weather outdoor sports? What about if you live in a state like Florida with no snow? Clearly the time and place can play a significant role in influencing consumption. On an even more personal level, the temporal and physical surroundings can offer smells, sights, sounds, and many other stimuli which might impact your decision-making process. For example, some sporting goods stores have hardwood basketball courts and putting greens in the store to help transport the consumer closer to the physical environment that they would use a particular product in. Social surroundings also impact decision-making. If you wanted to go bowling but your friends wanted to take advantage of nice weather and go golfing instead, there is a good chance the pressure to conform to the desires of the group would lead you to lace up your golf cleats instead of slipping on a pair of bowling shoes. Finally, the technological resources you have access to may also impact what and how you consume sports. The opportunities to watch sports or buy sport/fitness equipment could vary tremendously, depending on the technology to which you have access. A person living in an isolated, rural environment who only has basic cable and dial-up Internet service would have much less to choose from than a person with satellite television (and subscription sports packages) and broadband Internet when choosing between different sports viewing options. In summary, situational factors can have a significant impact on influencing the decision-making process.

The Decision-Making Process

Consumers engage in a decision-making process every time they consider buying a ticket to watch a game, putting their kids in a local youth sport program, or purchasing a licensed jersey for a loved one. The time it takes to make a decision varies from person to person and from situation to situation, but generally follows a five-stage process. The first stage in the decision process is need recognition. If there is no perceived need in the mind of the consumer, there is unlikely to be consumption. Once the consumer recognizes a need or desire, he then begins to search for information about potential products and services to meet the identified need. This stage is followed by a period in which the purchaser evaluates the information collected and makes a choice. The fourth stage is the purchase stage. At this stage in the process, a consumer will choose to either purchase or not purchase the product or service. Case closed? Not quite. The final stage of the decision process is postpurchase evaluation. At this stage the buyer evaluates her purchase and decides whether she is pleased with it. This stage does not always end happily. The purchaser may experience "buyer's remorse" at this stage. Buyer's remorse occurs when the purchaser regrets making the purchase. Clearly, we are more likely to entice customers to purchase our products and services again if they are happy with their initial purchase.

Each stage of the process seems fairly straightforward. Yet the decision process is actually quite complex. Each stage in the decision is affected by three things: the internal state of the decision maker, the external forces acting on the decision maker at the time and place of purchase, and the actions that you take as a marketer to win the person's business. A good understanding of your customers and their needs and desires dramatically improves your chances of winning their business and creating loyal fans. While decision-making can be affected by one's mood (affective state), it is predominantly a cognitive process. Consequently, much of the process occurs internally and is difficult to see. By understanding the decision process and the needs of your consumers, you will be better able to recognize the stages through careful observation of your customer. Let's look at each stage more closely.

Stage 1: Need Recognition

At this stage, the customer recognizes a need. This may be a long-standing need that has just crystallized, or it could be a fleeting desire. In either case, the need emerges from a perceived gap between the customer's actual state (i.e., feelings, thoughts, and perceptions of the current situation) and a desired state (i.e., the way the customer wants to be/feel at that time). Let's examine three cases. In the first, Pat has recently moved to another state and doesn't know anybody in her new home town. She feels lonely and recognizes a need to socialize and to make new friends. Pat's need emerges from an internal analysis of her current situation. Alternatively, consider the case of Chris. Chris has just returned home from his first year of university study. Although he is glad to be home, his friends and family comment on how much weight he has gained in his time away. Chris translates these comments into a need to lose weight. Chris' need is influenced by external social forces: his family. Now, consider a third situation. Devin is enjoying the broadcast of the Australian Open tennis championships. An ad appears for lessons at the local tennis center. Devin recognizes a desire to learn to play tennis. Devin's need is also stimulated externally. However, he is made aware of a need through the marketing efforts of his local tennis center.

Each of these scenarios illustrates the multiple forces acting on potential purchasers during the need recognition stage. The way that each person defines their specific need is influenced by their own motives, perceptions, attitudes, and self-concept. Each is also influenced by significant others, reference groups, culture, subculture, and the specifics of their current situation. Each can be (and in the case of Devin, already was) influenced by your marketing efforts. Let's look at Pat's case again.

Pat feels lonely. She has happy memories of spending time with her friends cheering on their favorite basketball team. She is motivated by a desire to socialize with others. While she is lonely, she also thinks of herself as shy. Notice that each of these reflects her internal state and might be difficult for an outsider to recognize. Pat's need is also influenced by external forces. For example, she may have grown up in a family that valued large group outings where happiness was equated with having many friends and family members around and being alone was labeled odd. If Pat internalized these values, which is likely, it is not hard to see how she would recognize a need for friends in her current situation. So far, marketing has not played an explicit role in Pat's need recognition, but could it? Of course!

What if you were the Marketing Director for Pat's local NBA-Development League team? The needs to socialize and to meet new people are fairly common. Moving to a new city is also a common occurrence. Thus, Pat's case may not be unique. Could this group be a valuable target market for your organization? Perhaps, but it would have to be reachable. Most cities have organizations that welcome new people to the area. Realtors, apartment locators, and moving companies can be useful partners in locating customers new to the area. Welcome Wagon, Newcomers Club, and similar organizations offer welcome packs to families new to the area and solicit offers from local businesses to include in those packages. Social media sites can also help you to reach new members of the community. Clearly, not everyone who moves is lonely and seeks new friends. The point is that this group may be more receptive to messages which suggest that they need to make friends in their newly chosen town. Your task is to help them to become aware of this need. Your marketing communications should highlight both the need and the way that attending your team's games can help to meet that need. Finally, you should consider creating activities and opportunities at the game for people to meet and connect with one another to build friendships. That is, make sure that you deliver on your message.

Stage 2: Information Search

This stage of the decision process is characterized by the consumer's search for potential solutions to the need recognized in the first stage. Information search may be passive or active. The more urgent the need, the more active the consumer searches for information. In fact, some purchasers skip the information search entirely. Three purchase situations are associated with consumers' failure to search for information: (1) impulse purchases like that giant foam finger you bought the last time you went to a football game; (2) routine purchases like athletic tape; and (3) purchases of products to which the consumer is intensely loyal. Loyal fans of the WNBA's Washington Mystics, for example, are unlikely to search for other area teams' ticket packages before deciding to purchase Mystics tickets.

Most sport purchase decisions do not fall into these three special categories. They do, however, vary in the urgency and meaningfulness of the purchase. For less urgent purchases, consumers first gather information passively. Once a need has been identified, the consumer is open to receiving information about potential ways to satisfy the need. The beginnings of information search are often internal. Consumers will first fall back on their own attitudes and experiences to determine which types of solutions will satisfy their needs. They begin to notice or attend to information that may not have seemed relevant prior to need identification. Consider Chris' recent observation that he needs to lose weight. Weight loss is a function of diet and physical activity. Thus, potential solutions could include changes in diet, increases in activity, or a combination of the two. Chris falls back on his attitudes and experiences. He may think back to a time in his life when he was lean and fit. That experience could be associated with sport participation. His roommates may be a key reference group for Chris. If they eat pizza, drink beer, and generally scoff at the thought of dieting, Chris may rule out dieting as a viable option. In this way, Chris has framed his weight problem as a lack of physical activity rather than diet. Consequently, his information search will center on ways to increase his physical activity. Prior to realizing that he needed to become more active, he may have passed notices around campus advertising the fitness center run by the campus recreation department without ever processing (or even noticing) them. Once he identifies his need for physical activity, he is more likely to tune in when his friends are discussing recruiting players for an intramural sports team. He may begin to notice fitness advertisements in the newspaper, magazines, television, or the Internet. In short, he opens himself up to messages that are relevant to fitness.

As the need becomes more intense, consumers become more active in their information search. Instead of noticing advertisements for sport and fitness programs, Chris may begin to collect more information about the advertised services. This process could take a variety of forms—collecting marketing collateral, phoning for information, searching the Internet, and asking friends and family for opinions and recommendations.

The marketing task at this stage of the decision process is two-fold. First, identify the information sources that are most influential to your target market. Then, make sure that information about your product or service is available there. Your website is a critical medium through which you can provide information to prospective purchasers. Advertisements, displays at expos, and trade shows are other ways to provide detailed information to prospective purchasers. Consumer experiences are a pivotal source of information for many sport services and products. For example, to help Chris gather relevant information about your fitness bootcamp program, you may offer a free trial class. Similarly, customer service programs designed to maximize customer satisfaction creates walking, talking advertisement for your program. Word-of-mouth advertising, when delivered by a trusted member of a reference group, is an incredibly effective method for delivering information while also differentiating you from your competitors. While there are clearly budget constraints on the number and types of channels you use to provide information, it pays to deliver your message in multiple ways.

Stage 3: Evaluation of Alternatives

While the information search phase is a divergent one, evaluation of alternatives begins the convergent phase of the decision process. The information collected in the previous stage is now evaluated and assessed. In a truly rational evaluation process, the consumer will determine specific criteria to use in an evaluation of alternatives, evaluate each option on those criteria, and weight the relative importance of each criteria to determine which alternative (if any) will be purchased.

Let's examine a hypothetical list of options generated by Devin in the information search phase. Devin's search, based on the interest generated by watching the Australian Open, produced the following three alternatives:

- **Play Like a Pro.** This option includes six private, one-hour lessons with a US Professional Tennis Association (USPTA) professional, three sessions with a personal trainer, a one-hour consultation with a dietician, and three sports massage sessions. Lessons take place on weekday evenings at a private tennis-only facility near Devin's workplace. Ancillary services are also offered at the facility, but must be scheduled separately. Marketing materials highlight the competitive accomplishments of players who have trained with Play Like a Pro, the educational qualifications of staff, and the quality of the facilities. The price for this package is $1800.

- **City Recreation Department Classes**. This option includes eight weeks of group instruction at the public tennis complex. Lessons last 1½ hours each and the instructor is a former Division I college tennis player. Classes are offered for Beginners, Advanced Beginners, Intermediate, and Advanced players. Marketing materials focus on schedule information and show images of players of all ages, ethnicities, and genders. The price for this package is $75.

- **Stunning Views Country Club.** This option requires membership in the local country club, which offers golf, tennis, swimming, a fitness center, pro-shop, and clubhouse. Tennis services include participation in US Tennis Association leagues, private and group lessons with US Professional Tennis Association certified tennis professionals, weekly adult clinics, tournaments and regular social mixers. Marketing materials emphasize the wide range of services offered to patrons, and show images of the views from the tennis courts as well as players socializing in the clubhouse. Full club membership is $3000 per year. Tennis only memberships are $2000 per year. Lessons are not included in the membership.

Devin can evaluate these three options in two ways. He can make an attitude-based choice or an attribute-based choice. First, Devin could list the needs the tennis lessons must fulfill. Let's assume that these needs are: (1) to develop skills to be competitively successful; (2) to improve his body appearance; (3) to fit into his current lifestyle; and (4) to meet other competitive tennis players. These needs could be weighted based on their importance to Devin. Then, each option would be scored based on the degree to which the service meets each of his needs. The option meeting the most (and most important) needs would be selected. Alternatively, Devin could evaluate each feature for each program. Features might include price, individual attention, instructor qualifications, competitive opportunities, and support services. The option that provides the most valued features would be selected.

The marketing challenge at this phase is to differentiate your product or service from your competitor, and to show that your product is superior to your competitor on the attributes that matter to customers in your target markets. Alternatively, or additionally, your marketing materials should communicate the benefits of your product over your competitors, particularly the benefits that meet the core needs of your target markets. If your target market is focused on skill development and competition, for example, you may not need to emphasize the social events available. However, if social events differentiate your tennis program from your competitors and other features do not, include this feature in your marketing communications and explain how this feature meets the needs of your target market. For example, social events provide opportunities to interact with other players to arrange matches or to recruit a doubles partner.

These examples have emphasized a rational evaluation of alternatives. Alas, many sport products are highly emotional, symbolic purchases linked to one's identity and self-esteem. Decision rules tend to disappear in the face of emotional purchases. Instead of a rational evaluation of options, sport fans sometimes purchase based on what feels right. Highly identified fans evaluate purchases based on the degree to which the purchase will support their fan identity, even if that purchase seems unwise based on other criteria. Consider the decision to attend a sports fantasy camp. Fantasy camps are part vacation, part training camp with competition and instruction from professional athletes, and an opportunity for grown men (and women) to interact with their sports idols (cf. Haydari, 2007). These camps cost upwards of $4000 per day. For most, attending a fantasy camp is hardly a rational decision. Yet, it may just be the ultimate vacation for a highly identified fan. The chance to play and compete with their sports idol provides a highly symbolic experience that can easily override the rational evaluation of vacation alternatives. Fantasy camps are just one example of fans' willingness to purchase sport products and services for their symbolic value. Licensed product purchases are also a testament to the value of sports symbols. A polo shirt from the same manufacturer demands a significantly higher price when it carries the logo of a favored team: fans are willing to pay more to demonstrate their affiliation. Why would anyone spend $100 on a three-inch plug of grass? Well, it's not *just* grass, it's freeze-dried sod from the original Yankee Stadium. For Yankee's fans, this is a piece of history. It symbolizes all that the Yankees represent. At the same time, ownership of this sod/history provides them with a way to display their identity as a Yankee fan. In short, it proclaims that, "I am a part of this team/organization. The team's success is my success." The emotional investment in one's attachment to the team and the resulting boost to one's self-esteem overrides the rational choice model of decision making.

The emotional attachment that exemplifies fanship is not guaranteed, but is something that can be nurtured by your sport marketing efforts. Although winning and success can lead some to become fans, winning is neither under the control of the marketing department nor an assurance of long-term fanship in and of itself. Consider the bandwagon effect, whereby casual fans increase their involvement with a team as it wins its way through the play-offs. Hard-core fans scoff at these fans, labeling them "fair weather fans." Yet, the positive emotion of a play-off run can create an opening for sport marketers to reach these fair weather fans and convert them to more loyal fans by deepening their level of involvement and identification with the team. First, however, you must understand how these consumers differ from your core fans. In other words, examine the internal and external factors influencing their current fanship, and design your marketing efforts to either expand of make use of additional factors to retain their fanship.

Consider the case of Carla and Bob. Carla moved to the San Francisco Bay Area three years ago. She enjoys sports, but does not consider herself a sports fan. She has watched Major League Baseball (MLB) games at social gatherings, but feels no particular interest in the sport and no attachment to any particular team. Bob, on the other hand, has lived in the Bay Area all his life. His entire family considers themselves sport fans, and in particular, fans of MLB's San Francisco Giants. He has strong memories of attending games with his father throughout his childhood, and currently gathers with friends and family to watch Giants games at someone's home or a local sports bar. He owns numerous shirts and hats with the Giants logo, and prides himself on supporting the Giants through good times and bad. Currently, the Giants are making a strong move toward advancing to post-season play in the hopes of winning the National League pennant. Their late-season run has generated intense interest throughout the Bay Area. Both Carla and Bob find themselves caught up in the excitement. Should you market to each of them in the same way? Let's look at the forces at work.

Carla's new fanship is motivated largely on the basis of a need for belonging and socializing. Her friends and colleagues talk about the Giants play-off run incessantly. Many of their social events now occur at local bars where the games are shown. Her office even organized a group to attend a game at AT&T Park. Carla enjoys the feeling of being a part of something larger than herself, takes pleasure in the elation of winning, and even purchased a Giants jersey to wear to the game. She now finds herself reading the sports page of the newspaper and has visited the team's website for more information about the team. Carla is now a fan, but will her fanship last beyond this season?

Bob's fanship is longstanding and he considers himself a loyal Giants' fan. He enjoys the social aspects of fanship, but would also be happy watching the game by himself. The Giants' current success is exciting, but Bob has more attachments to the team than that. He is very knowledgeable about the players, coaches, and the general manager. Consequently, he is able to share in the individual successes of players and coaches, as well as the team's success. Bob has at least a 20-year investment in his fanship. Being a Giants fan is part of Bob's identity.

On the surface, Carla and Bob are both excited fans of the San Francisco Giants. Yet, Carla's fanship is more tenuous than Bob's. Your job as a marketer is to understand how these fans differ and to design strategies and tactics to appeal to each. The big challenge in this situation is to find ways to build on Carla's fragile new fanship in order to deepen her involvement with the team and the loyalty she feels toward the team. In short, your task is to mold a "fair weather fan" into a highly identified, loyal fan of the team. This doesn't happen automatically. Unlike Bob, Carla does not have strong attachments to the team itself or to the players. In fact, her attachments are to the other fans—her friends and colleagues. Consequently, it is not difficult to imagine Carla abandoning her fanship to pursue other social opportunities after the season. So, how do you get her back once the season starts again? Well, you know that she enjoys the social component of her fanship, so perhaps you create fan parties in the off-season. She also knows that she has few attachments to the players, perhaps because she lacks knowledge or she hasn't had a chance to connect with the players. To build multiple attachments, marketers should provide fans with opportunities to interact with players and coaches, to make a personal connection. You also know that Carla likes being part of something larger than herself. Partner with a cause for in-season and out-of-season events in the community, and facilitate opportunities for fan involvement. In short, help Carla to maintain, strengthen, and deepen her ties to the team, its personnel, and its links to the community. At the same time, you, as a marketer, can become an integral part of her social experience.

Stage 4: Purchase

After a consumer has generated alternatives, evaluated each alternative, and selected the best option, she is ready to purchase. However, customers do not always choose to purchase at this stage. A purchase is made only when the customer feels that the selected alternative has value. It could be that in evaluating each alternative, the consumer does not feel that any of them (even the best alternative) provides the value that she is seeking. Value isn't just about price; it also encompasses elements of quality and perhaps, symbolic value. The emotional attachment that fans have for their sport teams can be the deciding factor in the final decision to purchase or not. The impact of fans' emotions can most clearly be seen in impulse purchases made in the euphoric moments following a big win. How often do we hear about fans lining up outside stores the day after an important victory to be the first to purchase an item commemorating the accomplishment?

The marketing challenge at this phase of the decision process is to ensure that it is easy for consumers to make a purchase and that the consumer understands the value of the purchase. Emotional enthusiasm is short-lived. Products should be available before this emotion disappears. Sports leagues and teams understand the importance of this lesson. For example, merchandise touting both teams participating in the Super Bowl as the Super Bowl Champions will be produced prior to the game. The actual winner's merchandise will be sold immediately; the loser's will be destroyed or donated to third-world countries. On a much smaller scale, you can make it easy for fans to purchase your merchandise by embracing multiple payment options, selling through multiple outlets, and bringing products to places that fans go (e.g., games, tailgates, airports, college bookstores, the Internet). Fans are no longer limited to the geographic region in which they play. Consequently, web-based purchasing is an increasingly important purchase venue. In summary, find ways to make it easy for your customers to purchase your products and services.

Stage 5: Post-purchase Evaluation

You made the sale—isn't this the end of the purchase decision? If you never intend to sell to that customer again, you can stop paying attention. However, repeat purchasers are the lifeblood of a successful sports organization. Marketers estimate that it costs five times more to recruit a new customer than it does to sell to an existing customer (Bhattacharya, Rao, and Glynn, 1995). So, pay attention to how your customer feels *after* making a purchase. Did the experience meet or exceed expectations? Does the customer feel good about her purchase? Good enough to come back? Will she encourage others to purchase?

Most consumers experience some degree of reflection after making a purchase. In this phase, consumers may wonder whether they made a good decision or whether they should have waited or perhaps purchased some other product or service. These concerns occur as a result of cognitive dissonance, an uncomfortable tension that results from holding two conflicting or incompatible thoughts at the same time. For example, after purchasing Final Four tickets, a consumer may think, "My family will really enjoy attending the Final Four." At the same time, he may think, "These tickets were overpriced. I can't afford these." This cognitive dissonance is an internal battle that will be resolved in one of two ways. Either the customer will find information that supports his decision to purchase the tickets, or he will feel guilty about the purchase and experience "buyer's remorse." If your fans feel remorse after purchasing your products, they are unlikely to become repeat customers. Further, satisfied customers are more likely to encourage others to purchase your products and services. Word-of-mouth is often one of the best forms of advertisement, as people tend to trust the attitudes and opinions of people they know. Consequently, your role as a sport marketer is to ensure that customers feel good enough about their purchases to provide word-of-mouth advertising for your products.

So, how do you go about making your customers happy with their purchases? Well, one way is to make sure that you deliver on your promises. What types of messages are you sending to your customers? Sports events are unpredictable. One sure way to make your fans unhappy is to promise them a victory and deliver a loss. Sport marketers are often tempted to make promises about things that are not under their control, like winning and losing. Other messages can go astray in their implementation. Consider a minor league hockey team that markets itself as a family friendly entertainment experience. The experience (i.e., your product) must then meet consumers' expectations that it is interesting and appropriate for people of all ages, including children. Scantily clad dancers may not meet this expectation. Replays of violent checking and on-ice fights might be exciting, but many parents would not feel these to be appropriate for their children. Half-price beers may attract the young adult market, but may also create an environment not suitable for families with young children. Be diligent in creating and monitoring the fit between the design of your product experiences and the promotions and messages that you use to market those experiences. Otherwise you may create buyers' remorse in some or all of your target markets.

Another way to help your customers feel good about their purchase is to provide them with access to information and messages that support the value of their purchase. Testimonials are one way to use reference group influences to support a purchase decision. Consider a testimonial from a fan that met her husband at your Singles Night Promotion. Announce the number of single women in attendance. Provide a cost comparison of your ticket packages with other entertainment options to help customers see the value of their purchase compared to alternatives. Highlight external awards your organization has won such as "Best Family Night Out." Your customers are looking for information that confirms their decision to purchase. Provide it.

Sometimes, no matter how careful you are, a customer will have a negative experience. A negative experience does not necessarily lead to buyer's remorse. It depends on (1) whether you know about the negative experience, and (2) what you do about it. Even if you never know that a customer had a negative experience, chances are that the customer will tell others about it. If you don't know about it, you can't fix the problem. Consequently, it is important to implement a customer service program which reaches out to customers and encourages them to tell you when they've had a bad experience or want to complain about their experience. Then, empower your employees to make the situation right for the customer. Research shows that customers who have had a problem with their purchase and have had that problem resolved in some way by the organization are even more loyal to the organization than customers that have never had a problem. Now that doesn't mean that you should create problems in order to solve them, but it does suggest that it is possible to turn around a negative situation and create loyal fans.

Shortcuts in the Decision Process

The majority of sport purchases are considered high involvement purchases. That is, they are not routine purchases, and they are purchases that have psychological meaning to the customer. These purchase decisions tend to move through all five phases of the decision process. However, there are a few notable exceptions to this. Impulse purchases, low involvement purchases, and purchases by deeply loyal fans do not always conform to the five phase model. Instead, these purchasers often skip the information search and evaluation of options phases, moving directly from need to purchase. Impulse purchases are often emotional purchases. Fans get caught up in the moment and feel and emotional need to connect with their team, most often by purchasing licensed products. This can occur prior to a game when fans may feel the need to showcase their fanship to other fans. It can also occur in the emotion laden end of a hard fought victory.

In both cases, sport marketers can take advantage of the emotion of the moment with emotional appeals and plenty of opportunities for purchase. Theme parks have become the gold standard for organizations wanting to encourage impulse buying by organizing their facilities to capture the fleeting moment of excitement from each ride. Amusement park riders are routed through a store selling themed merchandise designed to evoke the emotion of the ride. Riders must make their way through the store to exit the ride. It is not much of a stretch to funnel sports fans through or at least past stores and tents selling licensed merchandise as they exit the stadium.

Low involvement purchases, like impulse purchases, tend to be made with little thought. These purchases have none of the emotion of impulse purchases. Instead, they are usually routine purchases of products that are difficult to differentiate, like concessions, athletic socks, or perhaps tennis balls. If the product is not easily differentiated from its competitors, and the customer is unlikely to take a significant risk by purchasing a different brand or product, it is probably a low involvement purchase which has no need for information search or evaluation phases to make a confident purchase decision.

The last type of purchase that can shortcut the decision process is not really a type at all. Rather, it describes any number of purchases by deeply loyal customers—that is, the deeply committed fans. These consumers don't bother to search, not because the purchase doesn't matter, but because it matters greatly to them. For these loyal fans, there are no options: it's your product or service or nothing. Consequently, there is no reason for them to search for, or evaluate, alternatives. The brand loyalty of these customers represents a highly attractive target market. Because loyal fans are unlikely to switch to another team, event, or program, marketers may choose to spend their time and energy to attract new markets or to increase the involvement of other fans. Clearly that is important, but your loyal fans also need to be continuing focus of your marketing efforts. Loyal fans are not as price-sensitive as casual fans. Consequently, they will often pay for bigger, more expensive ticket packages and will consume more of your other products. However, this loyalty comes with a price. Loyal fans and long-time supporters expect more from the organization. They are highly identified with the team; so much so, that they may come to believe that they are actually a part of the organization. Marketers can cater to this market with special invitation-only events that enhance fans' sense of being an insider. Interactions with players, coaches, and other team personnel are particularly treasured. In short, find ways to make your most loyal fans feel special.

Applications

During the early eras of sport in this country, opportunities for consuming sport were restricted to simply attending games and contests within immediate geographical proximity, or, for those who could read, the newspaper reports. Prior to the construction of transcontinental railroads in the latter half of the nineteenth century and the advent of communication technologies such as radio and television, consumers of sport had few entertainment options and limited access to mostly regional forms of participatory sport. As these new communication technologies proliferated, and socio-historical conditions afforded workers more time for leisure pursuits, sport became more of a presence in the lives of the general public. Whether it was Albert Spalding touring the country with his baseball all-stars, or radio broadcasts of a Jack Dempsey boxing match, technological advances around the turn of the twentieth century ushered in new opportunities for the average person to consume sport. While the historical developments related to technology, particularly with respect to mass communication media, have essentially enabled sport consumption to exist on a broad enough scale to merit study, our focus in this chapter is concerned more with the

© iofoto, 2012. Under license from Shutterstock, Inc.

present and future of sport consumer behavior. It is important as sport managers, however, that we always understand how history has shaped sport as we know it today.

The relationship between sport and the media has anchored the exponential growth in sport consumption over time. Without the media, sport fans would be restricted to consuming only the live sports contests that took within close enough geographical proximity to allow you to physically attend. Thanks to radio, television (cable, satellite, and pay-per-view), and the Internet, sport consumers today can watch virtually any sporting event that takes place around the globe. For example, a former Tampa, FL resident who now resides in Austin, TX can watch the Tampa Bay Buccaneers play every week through DirecTV's NFL Sunday Ticket package even though he no longer lives within the geographical range of the local broadcast. Or, a young Chinese boy can cultivate his NBA basketball fanship by watching Internet broadcasts of his countryman Yao Ming's Houston Rockets' games. In short, the opportunities for sport consumers to connect with any sport, team, or player around the world are virtually limitless. In the following examples, we will take a closer look at new ways that sport consumers at every level are using new technologies to strengthen their ability to connect with their desired sport product. While the examples hardly represent an exhaustive list of the seemingly endless ways in which people now consume sport, they are intended to provide a glimpse at some of the important developments that sport managers and marketers should know. It should be no surprise that many of these developments take advantage of the instant connectivity and interactive nature of the Internet.

Video Games

In November 2010, the video game developer Electronic Arts announced that its EA Sports FIFA Soccer franchise surpassed 100 million units sold over the lifetime of the franchise; this coming after its FIFA Soccer 11 game became the fastest-selling sports video game of all time following its 2.6 million copies sold in the first five days after its release (Steve_OS, 2010). Although these individual figures are remarkable, they are also indicative of the fact that sport video games represent one of the largest and fastest-growing areas of sport consumption in the world. What makes sports video games such a compelling means of connecting fans with the sports they consume is that video games give players an opportunity to put themselves into the world of the athletes and teams they follow. Not only can players take over the virtual representations of their favorite sports figures (often reproduced in life-like detail down to personalized batting stances and free throw routines), but players can also create their own avatars and insert themselves into the game alongside their heroes. With online play increasing as well, players now have the opportunity to team up with other virtual players and play, for example, a game of pickup basketball without ever leaving the comfort of their home. Although some researchers lament the amount of time that video game players spend in physically sedentary activity, the influence of sports video games on the consumer behavior of sports fans in undeniable.

© Yuri Arcurs, 2012. Under license from Shutterstock, Inc.

Fantasy Sports

Perhaps nowhere is the need of fans to connect with sport organizations more evident than in the exponential growth in fantasy sports over the past decade. With the advancements in digital media that have emerged as a result of Web 2.0 (the shift toward web applications that enable consumers to take a more participatory role in creating and sharing information) fantasy sports have become a pervasive outlet for sports consumers to cultivate their fanship in a more interactive forum. Now, not only do sports fans passively watch the games of their favorite teams, but they also actively work to connect with and watch other players and teams whom they have an interest in solely as a result of fantasy sports. The major sports leagues and broadcast media now work to facilitate fantasy sports through fantasy-related programming and live scoring updates. For example, NFL Sunday Ticket, the subscription package that allows consumers to see every NFL game across the country regardless of media market, has added a premium feature to its package that allows fans to receive customized alerts on their screen each time one of their fantasy players scores a point. This is good news for fantasy sports players, but it is also good news for the league. Fantasy sports encourage fans to watch a broader array of games than they ever would have if they were simply following their favorite, local team. Viewing more games in turn leads to fans being exposed to more advertisements, which encourages companies to partner with the NFL and/or purchase advertising space. At the same time, this can also increase television ratings such that the NFL can demand higher rights fees to broadcast its games. In short, fantasy sports have become a means for sport consumers to take a more active, immersive role in the cultivation of their fanship, and have also proven to be an effective diversification strategy for sport leagues and broadcast media looking to find more meaningful ways of connecting with consumers.

Premium Website Subscriptions

Subscriptions to premium websites that provide insider access to favorite professional sports teams and college programs have emerged as a primary means of consumption for fans who are deeply committed to following a particular organization. Perhaps nowhere has the emergence of these subscription-based websites been more dramatic than within the realm of college sports. For example, Rivals.com began in 2001 as a subscription service that offered insights about news and rumors related to college football recruiting for "serious sports fans" (Rivals.com, 2011). Ten years later, the website now provides overarching coverage of college sports while simultaneously housing subsidiary websites related to each major conference's college athletic programs, with a yearly subscription rate for each college team's website that can surpass $100. Billing itself as providing the "Ultimate Fan Experience," Rivals has since merged with Yahoo! Sports, and in January of 2009, had over 11.5 million unique visitors to its websites. The success of Rivals stems from "integrating its exclusive expert content into a network of team-based sites with message boards and various community tools that encourage and result in ever-increasing fan knowledge and involvement." In other words, Rivals provides consumers of college sport the opportunity to pay a premium for access to content in which only the most dedicated fans would be interested. In so doing, the website has offered hoards of college sport consumers the opportunity to immerse themselves even further into their favorite programs, which in turn allows them to connect in a deeper, more exclusive manner.

Athlete Use of Social Media

Another emerging technological advance related to sport consumer behavior via the Internet relates to the use of social media by athletes. Thanks to Facebook, YouTube, and Twitter, athletes of all levels can now interact with others in a way that was impossible a mere five years ago. Whether you are a high school football player who posts his highlight films to YouTube in the hopes of being discovered by college scouts, or a professional athlete connecting with fans on a more personal level, social media allows for unprecedented access between sport consumers and the teams and the athletes they follow. Lance Armstrong, for example, has nearly 3 million followers on Twitter, where fans can not only receive the tweets that Armstrong puts out, but are given the opportunity to respond to these tweets as well, offering a level of intimacy (albeit virtual) for sport consumers that has not historically existed until recently.

Summary

Studying consumer behavior provides sport marketers with key insights allowing them to make informed business decisions, reach new consumer groups, build fan retention, and consumer loyalty. Understanding the demographics and psychographics of consumer segments is the foundation for marketing strategy. This chapter has examined internal and external factors influencing spot consumer behavior and factors impacting consumer purchase decisions. Strategies and application of these concepts to various consumer segments were also highlighted.

Discussion Questions

1. How do sport marketers benefit from understanding consumer behavior?

2. What categories of internal factors play a role in sport consumption? How?

3. How do reference groups influence the decision-making process?

4. How is consumer behavior both a "divergent" and "convergent" process?

5. Explain ways in which groups can influence the consumption behaviors of individuals.

6. What are the five stages of the decision process? How could you influence consumers at each of the stages? Are there decisions that do not go through all the stages? Explain.

7. How has the development of new media impacted sport consumer behavior? Can you think of other examples not mentioned in the chapter?

8. How could you use social media to increase fan identification?

Critical Thinking Exercises

You have just been hired as the marketing intern for the Round Rock Express, the AAA minor league affiliate of the Houston Astros baseball team. Upon being hired, members of the organization shared with you their concerns regarding declining attendance figures over the last few seasons. As your first assignment, the Director of Marketing has asked you to assist in developing a new marketing strategy for attracting families, the target demographic, to the ballpark. Unfortunately, that is the only information that the Director of Marketing provided to help you with your new project. With little information to draw from, you decide that your best bet is to start simple and put yourself in the place of the consumer. Using the Purchase Decision Process model as your guide, explore a family's decision to attend a Round Rock Express game. After examining all of the factors and simulating through the stages of the purchase decision process, provide the Director of Marketing with your comprehensive assessment of the factors and stages where the Express can improve their marketing efforts. Then, develop a strategy and supporting tactics to reach families at each stage of the decision process.

You are currently working for USA Football, an independent non-profit organization leading the development of youth, high school, and international amateur football. You have been assigned to the International Federation of American Football (IFAF) to oversee the ticket sales for the World Championships, which will be held next year in Cologne, Germany. Your first task is to gather information about potential ticket buyers in Germany. Consider how you will go about this process. Be sure to consider how your knowledge of Americans' consumption of football can help you and how it will not. Draft a detailed agenda for your first meeting with your sales team leaders. What aspects of consumers' behavior are most likely to be similar for Americans and Germans? Which would you expect to be most different? Why?

References

Bee, C. C., and M. E. Havitz, "Exploring the relationship between involvement, fan attraction, psychological commitment and behavioural loyalty in a sports spectator context." *International Journal of Sports Marketing and Sponsorship* 11 (2010): 140–157.

Bhattacharya, C. B., H. Rao, and M. A. Glynn. "Understanding the bond of identification: An investigation of its correlates among art museum members." *Journal of Marketing,* 59(4) (1995): 46–57.

Cialdini, R. B., R. J. Borden, A. Thorne, M. R. Walker, S. Freeman, and L. R. Sloan, "Basking in reflected glory: Three (football) field studies." *Journal of Personality and Social Psychology,* 34 (1976): 366–375.

de Mooij, M., *Consumer behavior and culture: Consequences for global marketing and advertising.* Thousand Oaks, CA: Sage, 2011.

Gambetti, R. C., "Ambient communication: How to engage consumers in urban touch-points." *California Management Review,* 52(3) (2010): 34–51.

Hale-Benson, J. E., *Black children: Their roots, culture, and learning styles.* Baltimore, MD: John Hopkins University Press, 2010.

Haydari, F., "Fantasy sports camps," *Travel + Leisure,* November, 2011, accessed January 30, 2011, http://www.travelandleisure.com/articles/fantasy-sports-camps.

Mahan, J. E., and S. R. McDaniel, "The new online arena: Sport, marketing and the media converge in cyberspace." In *Handbook of sports media,* edited by A. A. Raney and J. Bryant. Hillsdale, NJ: Lawrence Erlbaum, 2006: 443–459.

Murrell, A. J., and B. Dietz., "Fan support of sport teams: The effect of a common group identity." *Journal of Sport and Exercise Psychology,* 14 (1992): 28–39.

Nelson, T. F., R. A. LaBrie, D. A. LaPlante, M. Stanton, H. J. Shaffer, and H. Wechsler., "Sports betting and other gambling in athletes, fans, and other college students." *Research Quarterly for Exercise & Sport,* 78 (2007): 271–283.

Pawlowski, T., C. Breuer, P. Wicker, and S. Poupaux, "Travel time spending behavior in recreational sports: An econometric approach with management implications." *European Sport Management Quarterly* (2009): 215–242.

Rivals.com, "About us," accessed April 3, 2011, http://www.rivals.com/content.asp?CID=36178.

Steve_OS, "FIFA soccer franchise sales top 100 million lifetime, FIFA 11 Ultimate Team free now," November 4, 2010, accessed April 3, 2011, http://www.operationsports.com/news/454740/fifa-soccer-franchise-sales-top-100-million-lifetime-fifa-11-ultimate-team-free-now/.

Sutton, W. A., M. A. McDonald, G. R. Milne, and J. Cimperman, "Creating and fostering fan identification in professional sports." *Sport Marketing Quarterly* (1997): 15–22.

Wann, D. L., "Preliminary validation of the sport fan motivation scale." *Journal of Sport and Social Issues,* 19 (1995): 377–396.

Courtesy of Kimberly Miloch.

CHAPTER 4

Marketing Information

Chad Seifried Louisiana State University
Todd Hall Georgia Southern University

> *Facts are available to everyone; it is interpretation and implementation that is key.*
>
> Rick Simcock, British advertising executive
> *"The Best Marketing Research Quotes"*

CHAPTER OBJECTIVES

After completing the chapter, the reader should be able to:

- Discuss the importance of marketing research to sport marketers.
- Describe the basic steps of the marketing research process.
- Compare and contrast various types of research designs.
- Summarize various methods of data collection.
- Discuss the importance of gathering and maintaining a database of quality information.

The people promoting sport entertainment products and services may not conduct their own research, but it is important for the sport industry to understand **marketing research** processes and database management efforts and activities that are necessary to effectively and efficiently run their respective organizations. The material and evidence gathered through marketing research strategies maintained in databases provide important information for decision makers to identify available marketing strengths, weaknesses, opportunities, and threats for their sport organizations. The application of this research with all types of consumers, audiences, and clients is conducted for planning and future decision making.

The data collected allows sport organizations to segment markets and identify critical characteristics of target markets to evaluate their current market position and to develop the material basis for marketing mix decisions. Marketing research endeavors may also supply answers to questions regarding a variety of topics. For instance, sport organizations may ask questions on topics such as consumer attitudes toward new products and services, how advertising strategies affected purchase decisions of those consumers, and the recruiting potential of perspective clients. Marketing research can also prompt solutions to customer satisfaction problems and pricing issues related to price threshold and the zone of tolerance (i.e., range of customer service/product expectations related to the desired and minimum acceptable benchmarks). Brand image, loyalty, and commitment can also be measured and stored through marketing research to help sport organizations identify necessary changes to their sport, event, or venue. Multiple other questions can also be evaluated, measured, and answered with appreciation of the various steps in the marketing research process and database management. This chapter reveals relevant information related to marketing research and database management and communicates their value for use in the sport industry.

Marketing Research

The purpose of marketing research centers on the discovery or collection of information through exploration, description, explanation, and evaluation to enhance the decisions made throughout the marketing process (Aaker, Kumar, and Day, 2006). **Descriptive research** endeavors help sport marketers stay abreast in the constantly changing landscape of sport and consumer behaviors/preferences. **Explanatory research** efforts aim to answer the critical questions of how and why, associated with sport consumption, to help predict future trends, behaviors, and preferences. Focusing on causation, explanatory research goes beyond simple description. **Exploratory research** is a flexible and dynamic type of research aimed at gaining a deeper understanding about a particular problem, idea, and/ or issue that has not been clearly identified. With little previous information to provide a base, exploratory research can be useful to help conduct future research and with subject selection to provide guidance about the study of a specific or general topic of interest. Evaluation requires research investigations to focus on judgments, results, and the effectiveness of established tactics, programs, and organizational activities to determine if those achieved success or failed in relation to investments (i.e., time and financial). In the end, discovery makes use of observation and other data collection efforts to explain results and find solutions for future inquiries and problems.

Several important groups and individuals conduct research for sport organizations. For example, government agencies, private commercial organizations, consultants, and venue managers all exist as possible sources of external information. Consultants, in particular, appear useful because they provide information related to an area of expertise established within their organization or institution (e.g., academic institution). With the ability to pay special attention to specific projects, consultants are used frequently within the sport industry with facility construction/renovation efforts, advertising agencies, and other industry clients to offer advice and findings related to consumer preferences, staff behaviors, industry competition activities and performances, and product and service quality outcomes to managers who make strategic decisions.

Marketing research involves a systematic process approach involving the collection, organization, examination, and presentation of information on a defined area of study to enhance decisions throughout the strategic marketing process. Marketing research must be systematic to show it is both well organized and unbiased during the execution and operation of the strategic marketing plan. Establishing a foundation for the operating of a marketing research process involves several basic steps. The steps in this process are interdependent and thus the choice to change one part of the plan will affect or influence the decision to use another. As an example, changing the target market to investigate can change the sample selection technique and possibly the data collection tool to record consumer thoughts, opinions, and/or activities. Below is a review of the basic steps in the marketing research process (Mullin, Hardy, and Sutton, 2007; Sayre, 2007; Shank, 2009).

Basic Steps of Marketing Research Process

1. Identify and Define Area of Need or Opportunity
   a. Refine area through establishing research objectives
2. Develop and Design Proper Approach/Research Design
   a. Identify and select information sources/resources
   b. Determine method/tactic to assess data
   c. Design data collection forms
   d. Establish sampling method and size
   e. Decide on budget and set timeframe
3. Collect and Organize the Data
4. Perform Data Analysis
5. Prepare and Present Final Research Findings/Report

Step 1: Identify and Define Area of Need or Opportunity

Problem/opportunity identification and definition is the first and most important step of the marketing research process. Notably, this phase directs researchers to establish a clear and precise understanding of the phenomenon through developing a research problem statement. Critically, the researcher must identify and define the problem to prevent irrelevant activities affecting the outcome. This goal is accomplished through refining research objectives and utilizing existing records/information. It is recommended that researchers use previous internal and external sources such as data reports, sales records, purchasing patterns, theoretical research, and customer feedback to develop an accurate and specific definition regarding the area of study.

Step 2: Develop and Design Proper Approach/Research Design

Designing a flawless research approach involves many important activities. First, the researchers must utilize the goals and objectives developed in Step 1 to help them identify and select the necessary information and resources to complete the project. The next step within designing a proper research approach should center on determining and selecting the appropriate methods to assess data. This may require the design, modification, or reuse of collection forms. The researcher should follow this by attempting to search out the best sample method (i.e., purposive, random, convenience, stratified, etc.) and size to complete the research inquiry. Finally, the researcher should decide on a budget and establish a timeframe for completion of the study if necessary. Naturally, this step is critical to the success of the research endeavor and will be the most time-consuming part of the process due to the careful thinking and precise execution required from the various activities employed.

Courtesy of Kimberly Miloch.

Choosing the appropriate research design framework is important because each and every study is likely to be unique and require different attention to reach the planned goals and objectives of the research endeavor. It should be noted that exploratory, descriptive, historical, and causal designs are most common in marketing research.

Exploratory designs emerge as useful devices when research problems are difficult to explain and little previous information exists on a particular topic of study. Possessing vague characteristics, numerous data collection efforts are possible within the exploratory design format. For example, the executive management group for the Lethbridge Hurricanes, a WHL hockey team, was concerned about the in-game experience and entertainment provided for spectators. The researcher may recommend interviewing managers responsible for the entertainment, and/or having similar discussions with fans, or attending similar sporting events to assess fan experiences amongst competitors (Hall and Ma, 2001). A discussion of data collection techniques is included below.

Descriptive designs are appropriate for targeted group study and the examination of a correlation or relationship between two or more variables connected to the target group. Knowing the direction or shape of a correlation helps marketers answer the who, what, where, when, why, and how often questions critical for establishing/creating the appropriate marketing mix. The English Premier League recently invested significant resources to gain a thorough understanding of not only their fan base, but also of non-fans. The results of their 2009-2010 Fan Survey can be found on their website. It contains a demographic breakdown, and match attendance information, as well as media consumption and the impact of the global economic woes on consumption behaviors.

An additional example involves the Houston Dynamo of Major League Soccer (MLS). The Dynamo also recently conducted a study to get a better understanding of their fan base along with their consumer preferences and behaviors. From responses to an online questionnaire, Dynamo management were able to get a better understanding of their fan demographics, game attendance behaviors and preferences in terms of days and times of competitions, as well as media consumption. Some of the questions asked in this study, which are common in descriptive research endeavors can be seen in Table 4.1 (Hall, 2008).

Historical methods trace the various aspects of culture and change in society within narrative and analytical forms to promote the sequential understanding of events/activities through the cultural products people create such as architecture, art, and literature (Seifried, 2010). Also described as a process of critical evaluation (i.e., verifying, interpreting, presenting), these records which survive the past also present opportunities to uncover how the subtle and unknown contextualize decisions and activities for the future. Sport marketers benefit through the historical research of archival data to help establish marketing trends and changes related to consumer behavior. Marketing research through the historical method can also lead to a quality review of strategic issues and the corresponding decisions of a sport organization along with that impact on consumer activities. Understanding how to relay messages better to potential and current target markets is an outcome of historical research (Seifried, 2010).

Finally, **causal designs** are useful to examine if changes in one variable develop changes in the outcome or behavior of another variable being measured. Also known as cause-and-effect, a dependent variable (i.e., variable predicted or measured) is manipulated in some manner by the independent variable (i.e., causal event or activity). To use a causal design it is critical that the problem or topic of inquiry is clearly defined. Several other points must also be satisfied and respected to establish a causal design. For instance, researchers should accept the possibility that although cause-and-effect may vary based on the magnitude of one variable (i.e., Mill's Method of Concomitant Variation) other variables may exist which could produce changes on the outcome. Those outlying variables should be eliminated from consideration when determining the cause-and-effect relationship between the dependent and independent variables. Furthermore, researchers should recognize that although the production of an event (i.e., effect) can occur simultaneously with the cause, a causal event must also precede the effect. Marketing researchers generally try to ascertain cause-and-effect through descriptions and explanations provided by the data (Rudd and Johnson, 2010). Causal descriptions suggest a specific causal relationship or covariance between independent and dependent variables while causal explanations attempt to connect or recognize the specific mechanism(s) that created the relationship(s). Below, in the experimental design description, a causal design can be seen.

TABLE 4.1

Descriptive Questions Asked of Houston Dynamo Fans (Hall, 2008)

1 Gender
Male _____   Female _____

2 What year were you born?
_____

3 The highest level of education achieved:
_____ Some high school
_____ High school graduate
_____ Trade or technical diploma
_____ Some college
_____ College graduate
_____ Graduate degree
_____ Professional degree
_____ Don't know/decline to respond

4 Your racial/ethnic group ancestry:
_____ African American/Black
_____ Asian/Pacific Islander
_____ Hispanic/Latino 1st generation
_____ Hispanic/Latino 2nd generation
_____ Hispanic/Latino 3rd generation
_____ Native American
_____ White/Caucasian
_____ Other
_____ Decline to respond

5 Your household income:
_____ < $20,000
_____ $20,000 to $34,999
_____ $35,000 to $49,999
_____ $50,000 to $74,999
_____ $75,000 to $99,999
_____ $100,000 and up

6 Are you a season ticket holder?
Yes _____   No _____

7 About how many Dynamo games do you attend each season?
_____ None
_____ 1 to 3
_____ 4 to 6
_____ 7 to 10
_____ 11 or more

8 How likely are you to watch a Dynamo match on the following station?

	Very Likely	Likely	Neutral	Unlikely	Very Likely
ESPN2	_____	_____	_____	_____	_____
TeleFutura	_____	_____	_____	_____	_____
Fox Soccer	_____	_____	_____	_____	_____
Channel 43	_____	_____	_____	_____	_____
Channel 55	_____	_____	_____	_____	_____
HDNet	_____	_____	_____	_____	_____

9 Which day of the week typically provides you the best opportunity to attend a game?
_____ Sunday
_____ Monday
_____ Tuesday
_____ Wednesday
_____ Thursday
_____ Friday
_____ Saturday

Source: Hall, T. 2008. "Houston Dynamo spectator/fan snapshot". Unpublished raw data.

Step 3: Collect and Organize the Data

This step in the research process involves field-related activities embraced and approved by the organization to track patterns of consumption and behavior needed for the creation of marketing profiles and needs assessments. Activities such as primary and secondary source searches, interviews, focus groups, surveys/survey campaigns, and experiments are completed by specifically assigned and trained individuals or representatives. Data collection can occur through telephone, Internet surveying, mail surveying, and a host of other activities. Becoming knowledgeable on a variety of data collection techniques/sources is promoted by this work. For instance, **quantitative research** measures may offer a tightness of control (e.g., how many people attend sporting events and venues as live or remote spectators) but they cannot reveal a true measure of what to charge advertisers because the threat of contextual influence always remains to affect their claims or results. To answer the why questions associated with live and remote spectator attendance, for example, **qualitative research** methods may be employed because they can provide rich descriptions of reality. Yet, qualitative methods can experience difficulty with generalizations due to its special attention in a specific environment. Appropriately, combining several methodologies serves as a viable option to help sport organizations carry out research endeavors and create synergy associated with past and/or future research undertakings related to present and future strategic marketing decisions.

Data can typically be classified into the two general categories of **primary** and **secondary data**.

Primary sources emerge directly from those involved with events or activities associated with the specific research question related to the study. Within reasonable limits, a wide range of primary sources is recommended for data collection. Primary source documents may include a variety of organizational items such as company minutes, reports, income statements, balance sheets, and memorandums, along with personal items like diaries, letters, memoirs, autobiographies, speeches, interviews, focus groups, and oral evidence/testimony. These primary sources aid research efforts because they provide official reasoning for decisions by individuals and/or organizations along with possible personal accounts and influences. Other preexisting forms of primary sources may include existing relics and buildings/venues, manuscripts such as laws, files, official publications, and maps, and visual evidence from films, newspapers, paintings, and pictures.

Secondary sources differ from primary sources because the information is generally collected at a previous point in time, but can still be relevant to the current research question. Similar to primary sources, secondary sources can exist in a variety of forms but all can serve as an excellent base or foundation for multiple types of inquiries. For example, in 2008, the organizing committee for an Olympic-style regional sporting event for senior citizens in central Texas was interested in discovering what event attributes or characteristics influenced athlete participation (Ferreira and Hall, 2011). The sport marketing researchers relied on several academic and industry research projects published between 1991 and 2005 to identify ten such attributes. The secondary sources of data proved instrumental in helping determine which of the attributes were important and which were not. Additional examples of secondary sources include: governmental research reports and investigations (particularly those compiled by the US Census Bureau), standardized industry information, trade and professional society publications and collections, books, and journals offered daily, weekly, monthly, and annually.

In-depth interviews are regularly used as a data collection technique for a variety of research purposes. Structured or unstructured, in-depth interviews allow the researcher to explore a variety of issues related to the area of study. With a goal of collecting information, in-depth interviews allow the researcher to collect the subtle and possible unknown reasons for consumer or client behavior that cannot be extrapolated from other methods/tactics. For example, complex decisions may be difficult to see from simple survey devices. The amount of detail or depth of information that can be gathered from employing this technique is the main advantage. A primary disadvantage of depth interviews is related to the time and costs associated with gathering information from one individual at a time.

Focus groups similarly act to gather valuable information related to some area of study; furthermore, they are typically used for exploratory research. Led by a structured series of questions, six to ten people offer opinions on a specific area of study in focus group interviews. As an exploratory technique, focus groups can be particularly effective in brainstorming sessions, product concept testing, and developing team logos and/or names. For instance, the San Jose Sharks conducted focus groups with fans and players before introducing new logos and uniform designs prior to the 2007-2008 National Hockey League (NHL) season (M. Bordelon, personal communication to author, May 11, 2010). The Columbus Blue Jackets (NHL) similarly used a series of focus groups during the design process of a new third or alternative jersey for 2010-2011. Working with both the Blue Jackets' in-house designers and Reebok, the NHL jersey provider, the focus group helped create a jersey which used a vintage style to highlight the Civil War heritage of the team and honor their late owner and founder John H. McConnell ("Columbus Blue Jackets Unveil New Third Jersey", 2010).

© Terry Gilliam/AP/Corbis.

Survey instruments are useful to capture information on an area of study during a single moment in time. As snapshots, surveys typically help researchers examine and analyze topics related to satisfaction, awareness, loyalty, lifestyle choices, and general behavioral tendencies, but they also help in collecting information related to other areas of interest and important demographics. Survey instruments are generally employed for descriptive types of research investigations and may come from a variety of sources (i.e., mail, telephone, computer/Internet, and on-site).

On-site surveys are generally distributed to customers, attendees, or consumers prior to the beginning of an event. Because they capture the thoughts and views of individuals during a brief moment in time, they may be unreliable unless follow-up surveys are conducted to reduce or guard against bias. For the best results, on-site surveys should be simple and quick for the participants. Also, it is important to note that on-site surveys only capture information from those who are already there; you do not get information from people who do not attend your event. *Telephone surveys* are useful to target and recruit a specific audience related to question of an organization. Like the on-site survey, telephone surveys can be performed at one location but recent legislation related to the National Do Not Call List registry

Courtesy of Kimberly Miloch.

may prevent some targeted calls from reaching the desired audience. *Mail surveys* are also commonly used to gather information from targeted consumer groups. While advantages of this method of data collection include relatively little expense and standardization of questions to a large sample, a primary disadvantage is that mail surveys often realize a low rate of response (Trochim and Donnelly, 2007). To improve response rates, surveyors should organize the instrument to be as simple as possible and centered on specific statements to avoid confusing prospective respondents. Remember, the respondents are not "in the moment" like they would be on-site when reviewing mailed survey instruments. Finally, *computer/ Internet surveys* are gaining popularity in marketing research circles because the researcher can design an interesting and visually stimulating instrument to attract the attention of prospective participants and their commitment to finish the survey tool. A major advantage of computer surveys allows the surveyor to design the instrument to provide for the redirection of respondents to questions applicable to their previous answers. Also known as skipping or branching, participants can finish surveys quicker and surveyors can ask more under the computer/Internet survey method. Another advantage of computer-based instrumentation is highlighted by the usefulness of the computer to immediately or more readily calculate statistical information for both practical and academic research.

Experimental research endeavors may exist as the most appropriate research device to employ for causal-comparative research because they utilize the manipulation of variables against constants. The researcher within the experimental design enjoys the opportunity to control the conditions and variables of the study. Test marketing of new products and/ or services exists as an example of experimental research. Generally limited by geographic area, sport marketers can collect important information related to sales potential, market preferences/attitudes, and competitor thoughts/reactions. Experimental research should be acknowledged as capable of imposing high financial cost and time commitments. For example, new productions techniques, promotional plans, and distribution channels could inflict tremendous anxiety through financial commitments and the likelihood that competitors could react with quick imitations and/or discounted products and services of their own.

An example of experimental research was recently conducted with sport management students at a mid-size university in the Southeast United States. The goal of the study was to understand how potential sport event spectators use sponsor relationships as signal of event quality. More specifically, the researchers wanted to determine if a sponsor related to the sport and if the size of the sponsor had an impact on perceptions of the quality of a fictional sporting event. As such, the two manipulated (or controlled factors) were sponsor size (national vs. local) and sponsor relatedness (functional similarity vs. no similarity). In this experiment, the sporting event was a golf long drive competition. Student received one of four sponsor-event scenarios. One scenario matched an unrelated national sponsor (Chili's restaurant), while the second matched an unrelated local sponsor (a local ethnic restaurant). The other two scenarios contained sport-related sponsors at the national level (Callaway) and at the local level (Hacker's—a local driving range). The results of this experiment suggest that potential spectator perceptions of event quality were influenced by relatedness to the event (i.e., golf-oriented companies), but not by the size of the sponsor. An important takeaway for event managers would be to focus selling sponsorships to sport-related organizations (Walker, Hall, Todd, and Kent, in press).

Step 4: Perform Data Analysis

Following the collection of data to the appropriate threshold, relevant data should be systematically organized and analyzed by the researcher and organizational decision makers. Activities such as clustering, data mining, and the use of various statistical analysis programs (i.e., SPSS, SAS, AMOS, NVivo, etc.) emerge as viable options. Coding of the data will likely be necessary to represent specific responses, but looking at the "big picture" is also important to keep track of the "picture or puzzle" established with your information. Central tendency (i.e., mean, median, and mode) and dispersion (i.e., range, variance, and standard deviation) are the most capable of helping to create a basic picture of your results.

Step 5: Prepare and Present Final Research Findings/Report

It is of critical importance that researchers report the findings in an interesting and clear manner to their intended audience without overwhelming them with technical jargon and unnecessary information. Properly documenting and accounting the findings of the analysis serve to enable higher management of the data for more efficient and effective decisions regarding the area of study. To present the findings, descriptive statistics, conceptual models, ideal-types, causal-comparative analysis, and general reviews of data appear best to accurately and clearly communicate important messages revealed by the data analysis. Descriptive statistics and conceptual models are useful devices that can be employed to present findings related to the "big picture." Causal chains and ideal-types also serve as methodological tools to express understandings and may be most useful for issues related to social phenomenon and public behaviors/preferences. Causal chains utilize patterns which were established in a sequential order to explain a cause-and-effect relationship concerning observations. Ideal-types exist as a heuristic device designed to draw meaning from social phenomenon and activities to reduce error in the interpretative gap.

Theoretical research may use these various techniques and methods to create conclusions about a topic of investigation through deductive reasoning and the use of data explored. Many research investigations conducted by sport enterprises utilize academic based theoretical research studies to guide their own marketing research campaigns. Overall, marketing research plays an important role for all sport industry members that desire to engage in quality policy making, planning, and resource management toward the goals they established as an organization.

Database Management

Database management is the use of customer and client-oriented databases/information to enhance the marketing productivity of the sport organization to obtain new consumers, as well as to retain satisfied consumer groups. In this section of the chapter, we elaborate on this definition and provide additional information related to the importance of database management. In the end, readers should understand the importance of making a financial and organizational commitment to gather and maintain useful information that will ultimately assist in the attainment of strategic marketing objectives.

In today's competitive sport information and business environment, database management has developed into a critical area for sport organizations to address in order to achieve and assure success of organizational goals and objectives. Database management can be defined as the controlling and overseeing of critical information, established in real time, using comprehensive, updated, and relevant information, about the relationship an organization shares with its customers and clients to answer important inquiries and problems for the purpose of identifying and creating a long-term responsive customer and client group capable of generating and offering repeat business (Hoffer, Prescott, and Topi, 2009). Database management includes the development of predictive models which focus on responsiveness to consumer and client preferences and attitudes to help increase the organization's rate of success associated with profit achievement.

Readers should note this definition utilizes carefully chosen passages which focus on the purpose of marketing (i.e., activities the firm uses to enhance customer/client value). For instance, database management is centered on current or potential customer and client information and needs. Exponentially growing in size and complexity, database applications provide opportunities for sport organizations to record and comment on consumer and client demographics, purchase intentions, psychographic information, and their attitudes/preferences regarding sports products and services. Next, database management prompts evaluation of marketing productivity and the effectiveness (i.e., success and failure) of marketing programs and services. Database management also is useful for targeting specific, current, and potential consumers and clients because it helps manage how consumers and clients can be acquired (i.e., increase number of consumers and clients), retained, and developed (i.e., increase duration, volume, and frequency of business-customer activity).

The San Diego Padres provided an interesting example of how database management can help achieve many of the information gathering objectives mentioned above. The Padres operated the "Frequent Friar Rewards Club," which fans can opt to join after they purchase tickets online or at Petco Park. Fans earned points based on the purchase of single-game tickets. The more tickets a fan purchased, the more points they earned. An important caveat to this reward program is that club members were required to provide a valid email address. This provided the Padres with an important point of contact for future marketing and sales activities. During the process of purchasing tickets and joining the Frequent Friar Club, the Padres gathered demographic, actual purchase, and purchase intention (multi-game flex packs) information. They also obtained product preference information when fans purchased tickets based on opponent, day of the week, and number of tickets. Location of the tickets in the stadium can also provide insights into product preferences, as well as socio-economic status. More detailed psychographic information can be gathered as fans begin to cash in their points for a variety of rewards, which include discounted tickets, an assortment of promotional items, and a behind-the-scenes tour of Petco Park. In total, this rewards program allowed the Padres to gather significant data about their fans, all of which is managed in a database (Frequent Friar Rewards Club, 2011).

Interestingly, the software and computer access networks utilized in database management for data entry, saving, and retrieving are marketed as Customer Relationship Management (CRM) software or CRM-based technology. CRM similarly emphasizes consumer relationships. For example, the sporting goods store salesperson may learn much about a current and/or potential client through repeated visits. Based on regular interaction, the salesperson begins to understand the preferences and attitudes of the current and/or potential client to enhance or establish a connection between the client and the store. However, CRM may need assistance from database management because large businesses may offer conditions which prevent a more personal connection to clients. Thus, database management allows salespeople and organizational members to get to know a person better if they do not genuinely engage in regular interaction with which to enhance customer relationships.

Database management emphasizes the analysis of rich data sources through a process that originates from the sport organization's marketing strategy, mission, and legal obligations (e.g., privacy issues). Combined, these factors create research initiatives and lead strategy to how their problems or questions will be solved or answered to help provide valuable insight about potential consumer/client behavior. Most of the work incorporating database management items involves information technology experts, marketing analysts, and campaign leaders over a period of time. The work of those individuals and groups may be translated from one program or design to another before the implementation of future marketing tactics/strategies. In the end, adequate database management may become a competitive advantage for sport organizations.

Live and remote spectators exist as audience members with available contact information capable of fluid interactions with events and venues. Spectator-based information collections may serve as a long-term marketing tool to service organizational missions, goals, and objectives because they possess the critical information to deliver important messages on behalf of the organization and/or its clients to provide for a more satisfying consumption of the event/venue.

More than just a simple list of audience or patron names and addresses, a highly respected database contains information related to consumer and client lifestyle and behavior patterns, detailed demographic information, financial records related to purchases and purchase intentions, and responses to promotional strategies and the selected media used. Interestingly, external lists specifically created for database management do exist for sport organizations to consume outside of in-house creations, which also center on matching current or potential consumers and clients to behavioral tendencies/patterns. For example, the Atlanta Hawks, at different points of their business cycle, subscribe to a service called BusinessWise, which allows them to gain access to a specific target market in the local area (J. Green, personal communication to author, February 24, 2011). Additionally, external lists can result from commercial or professional list organizations, mail-order databases, competitor entertainment venues, magazine subscribers, association memberships, mail-order forums, and a variety of other list-serve opportunities. Furthermore, these opportunities can create revenue for the host organization which can be sold or rented to other organizations to help them advertise their products and services.

Building your own database should be valued over external lists because internally-created databases resulted from people actually interested and/or involved in your product or services. Internally-created databases can also be "developed ... to store and maintain this information, as well as accept new data" (Zeigler, 2007, 312). The construction of this resource would allow sport marketers or marketing researchers to track research already completed (i.e., avoid the waste of time) and create new research questions to answer to help improve the effectiveness and efficiency of marketing product and services. The Atlanta Hawks (NBA) practice such a philosophy. As an example, during the 2001-2002 season, the Hawks began to utilize an internally-developed lead management program called ONYX to track individual game buyers—specifically gathering information from those who purchased tickets online (J. Green, personal communication to author, February 24, 2011).

Similar to the steps in the management research process, database management also requires careful attention during the collection, inputting, organization, and examination of consumer and client information. Again, taking a systematic approach appears best to create an adequate and mistake-free representation of consumers and client data. Below is a review of the basic steps in the database management process to locate, collect, and record information on the thoughts, opinions, and/or activities of current and/or potential consumers and clients (Mullin, Hardy, and Sutton, 2007; Hoffer, Prescott, and Topi, 2009).

Basic Steps in Database Management Process

Step 1: Locate Quality Information

    a. Coordinate and possibly collaborate with potential data collection partners

    b. Standardize data collection procedures and responsibilities with participating researchers (i.e., review coding responsibilities, create operational definitions, etc.)

    c. Identify errors and possible corrections related to: where, when, what, why, and how

    d. Pay attention to redundancy and consistency of data sets

Step 2: Collect Information

    a. Complete basic data statistics and frequency analysis items (e.g., means, median, mode, standard deviation, range, etc.)

    b. Eliminate redundant information and sources through cross-comparison

    c. Separate and segment data for profiling and theme analysis

Step 3: Record Information

    a. Follow established protocol to note any significant changes

    b. Routinely back-up data collection (i.e., digitally and hard copy/original)

    c. Re-check data quality and quantity

    d. Prepare and publish data for documentation

Step 4: Monitor and Manage

    a. Update software

    b. Update information

    c. Back-up data

Summary

Sport organizations can and often do invest significant resources, in both time and money, gathering information related to consumer and competitor intelligence. In fact, savvy sport managers realize that being aware of and sensitive to consumer needs, as well as being knowledgeable about competitor product offerings and strategic moves, are the first two steps of achieving a market orientation. The third and final characteristic of being market oriented is being responsive to those needs and market conditions in providing timely solutions. This is the primary purpose for conducting market research or gathering information—to assist the sport manager in the decision-making process.

The systematic gathering of information through the described marketing research process allows the sport manager to obtain accurate, unbiased information. While such information can be stored in databases, it is ultimately useless unless the manager applies the newfound knowledge to the strategic marketing process. Using information gathered through the marketing research process does not guarantee success, but can certainly increase the likelihood of success when applied appropriately to decisions regarding segmenting, targeting, pricing, and marketing mix decisions among many others.

Discussion Questions

1. Why is marketing research important for sport marketers?

2. What steps are involved in the marketing research process?

3. What steps are involved in the database management process?

4. What is the most important step of the marketing research process? Why?

5. What are advantages/disadvantages of collecting qualitative and quantitative data?

6. Explain how secondary data sources are typically employed in marketing research endeavors.

Critical Thinking Exercises

1. You have recently been hired as the Marketing Manager for the Savannah Sand Gnats, a local minor league affiliate of the New York Mets. Your first course of action is to identify who is attending the games. Much of your strategic marketing plan will be derived by identifying potential target markets. Design a 15-item questionnaire with the goal of gathering as much pertinent information as you can about the fan base.

2. As a database management specialist, you are currently serving as a consultant to the Louisiana State University's (LSU) athletic department. The athletic department is planning a capital campaign to raise money for extensive renovations of Tiger Stadium (i.e., south end zone expansion and north end zone renovation). Make a detailed list of information that you will want to gather from donors.

3. Search the web to identify three secondary sources of information related to basketball shoe sales in the United States.

4. Conduct an abbreviated focus group with your classmates regarding their satisfaction with attending local university or professional football games.

References

Aaker, D. A., V. Kumar, and G. Day. *Marketing research,* 9th ed., New York: John Wiley and Sons, Inc., 2006.

"Columbus Blue Jackets Unveil New Third Jersey." *Columbus Blue Jackets Website,* November 24, 2010, accessed March 4, 2011, http://bluejackets.nhl.com/club/news.htm?id=544478

Ferreira, M. and T. Hall. "Understanding senior sport participants' choice of regional senior Olympic Games using a preference map." Manuscript in preparation, 2011.

Frequent Friar Rewards Club. *San Diego Padres Website,* March 4, 2011, http://mlb.mlb.com/sd/fan_forum/frequent_friar.jsp

Hall, T. [Houston Dynamo spectator/fan snapshot]. Unpublished raw data, 2008.

Hall, T., and D. Ma. Fan perceptions of in-game entertainment. Unpublished manuscript, University of Lethbridge: Alberta, Canada, 2001.

Hoffer, J. A., M. B. Prescott, and H. Topi. *Modern database management.* 9th ed., New York: Pearson-Prentice Hall, 2009.

Mullin, B. J., S. Hardy, and W. Sutton. *Sport marketing.* 3rd ed., Champaign, IL: Human Kinetics, 2007.

Rudd, A. and R. B. Johnson. "A call for more mixed methods in sport management research." *Sport Management Review,* 13 (2010): 14–24.

Sayre, S. *Entertainment marketing & communication: Selling branded performance, people, and places.* Upper Saddle River, NJ: Pearson-Prentice Hall, 2007.

Seifried, C. S. "Introducing and analyzing historical methodology for sport management studies." *International Journal of Sport Management,* 11(4) (2010): 1–21.

Shank, M. D. *Sports marketing: A strategic perspective.* Upper Saddle River, NJ: Pearson-Prentice Hall, 2009.

"The Best Marketing Research Quotes", Marketing with Dave, December 13, 2011, http://www.marketingwithdave.com/2008/03/best-marketing-research-quotes.html.

Trochim, W. M. K, and J. P. Donnelly. *The research methods knowledge base.* 3rd ed., Mason, OH: Thomson, 2007.

Walker, M., T. Hall, S. Y. Todd, and A. Kent. (in press). "Does your sponsor affect my perception of the event? The role of event sponsors as signals." *Sport Marketing Quarterly.*

Zeigler, E. F. "Sport management must show social concern as it develops tenable theory." *Journal of Sport Management,* 21(3) (2007): 297–318.

CHAPTER 5
Sport Market Segmentation

Coyte Cooper University of North Carolina, Chapel Hill

> *We had something going almost every day, for in our three and a half years in Cleveland every day was Mardi Gras and every fan was king…We gave a lot of gifts to other fans, too. Among other things, we had 20,000 Princess Aloha orchids—all beautifully packaged—flown in from Hawaii in a special temperature-controlled plane. They were presented to the first 20,000 women to come through the turnstiles (Veeck and Lynn, 2001).*
>
> *Bill Veeck*
> *(on early gender-based promotions)*

CHAPTER OBJECTIVES

After completing the chapter, the reader should be able to:

- Gain an understanding of the unique challenges facing sport marketers in today's competitive entertainment industry.
- Comprehend the concept of segmentation and how it can help sport marketers become more efficient in their interactions with consumers.
- Develop the ability to use the bases of segmentation to creative innovative products in the sport industry.

In today's competitive entertainment industry, segmentation has become a necessary strategy for sport organizations looking to enhance their marketing efforts. In response to the challenges discussed in this chapter, sport organizations have turned to strategic marketing initiatives in hopes of improving their relationships with current and potential fan bases. In particular, sport marketers have become reliant on streamlined products and delivery strategies when attempting to reach "segmented" groups of consumers. In simple terms, these marketers have chosen to focus on specific target markets so that they are better able to deliver a quality product that builds the brand image of sport organizations. As competition continues to increase in the future, sport marketers will need to continue to develop their innovative approach to segmentation.

The chapter will focus on providing a sound understanding of segmentation and its implications on the sport industry. Following the discussion of the challenges facing sport organizations, the chapter will outline the specific implementations of segmentation as they relate to various elements of sport marketing. Further, the disciplinary nature of segmentation will be discussed to develop a framework for future innovation in the sport industry. The following structure has been included in the chapter to provide a sound understanding of marketing segmentation and how it can improve interactions with consumers.

Introduction to Market Segmentation

In the sport industry, **market segmentation** has been defined as the process of dividing a large, heterogeneous market into smaller groups of more homogeneous groups with similar wants, needs, and/or demands. In essence, this process is characterized by the ability to identify specific consumer segments (e.g., college-aged students) with unique characteristics (e.g., limited disposable income) that sport organizations can strategically target in their marketing efforts. While there are a variety of benefits realized through market segmentation, the basic driving force behind the process is to develop, communicate, and deliver a quality product that is designed for specific groups of consumers. Through this streamlined process, sport marketers foster the ability to create loyal consumers who are willing to support the organization in a variety of different capacities. Regardless of the end process, the unique nature of the entertainment industry has made it critical for sport organizations to consider segmentation strategies when developing marketing plans.

Need for Market Segmentation

With the evolution of the entertainment industry, the reality is that most sport leagues and organizations are facing unique challenges that threaten their sustainability at all levels. As a measure to enhance the marketability of the sport product, marketers must understand these challenges so that they are able to develop competitive strategies that allow sport organizations to be successful in their interactions with consumers.

While there are a variety of obstacles present in the sport industry, this chapter will focus on the identification of universal challenges facing sport organizations at the local, regional, national, and global levels. In order to fully grasp the concept of market segmentation, the chapter will emphasize the basic understanding of the following two challenges: (1) creation of a competitive marketplace and (2) constant evolution of consumers. These specific challenges will be discussed in-depth in the following sections before moving on to the potential responses available to sport marketers.

Creation of a Competitive Marketplace

One of the greatest challenges facing sport organizations at all levels is the extensive number of entertainment options that are available to consumers. In the United States alone, there are thousands of sport-related consumption opportunities that are available to individuals on a daily basis (Howard and Crompton, 2004). However, when focusing solely on the sport entertainment industry, these marketplace challenges become somewhat more focused for sport organizations. In terms of television viewership, there are more channels available for sport broadcasts than ever before (Nielsen, 2010). Similarly, the growing popularity of the Internet has provided sport organizations and teams with an avenue to broadcast their events live or on a "delayed" basis across the United States and the world (Nielsen, 2010). While these technological platforms certainly create new broadcast opportunities for niche sporting events, they also create more competition for established sport entertainment entities. Thus, when considering the evolution of the sport industry, it is safe to say that sport organizations must move away from a mass marketing approach if they want to be successful with segmented populations.

Constant Evolution of Consumers

In direct relation to the competitive marketplace, another challenge facing sport marketers is the fact that consumer preferences are constantly evolving as individuals interact with innovative product lines and delivery strategies being offered in the entertainment industry. In essence, when consumers are constantly provided with products that exceed their expectations, they then have a new **quality reference point** to gauge their consumption decisions. For example, the inclusion of state-of-the-art amenities (e.g., cigar bar, themed club) in the Vito Anthony "Bunker" Suites at the Palace of Auburn Hills creates elevated expectations for the high-end clientele that invest in these types of premium seating options (Howell, 2010). More importantly, these extravagant entertainment options create a competitive benchmark for sport and entertainment entities looking to reach high-end clientele. Similarly, the improved offerings within ticket packages create a situation where consumers have higher expectations across the board at sporting events.

Building on the previous expectation challenges, sport marketers also face a major challenge when interacting with younger generations of consumers. With the inclusion of a technological "arms race," younger generations are constantly provided with new opportunities to consume entertainment information via the Internet and mobile applications. While this seems like a minor consideration, it is something that sport organizations must consider because of the growing popularity of the Internet among this consumer segment. As these technological mediums continue to evolve, this creates a unique challenge for sport marketers because they must continually find new ways to deliver innovative content in a quick, concise manner that is expected from younger generations of consumers. In order to be successful from a marketing standpoint, the expectations of key consumer segments must be taken into consideration prior to developing products and delivery strategies.

Implementation of Market Segmentation

In response to the culminating effects of the previously defined challenges, sport organizations have turned to segmentation to improve their relations with current and potential consumers. As an initial step, marketers must attempt to define key target markets that have a potential interest in the product being offered by the sport organization. However, this process can be made significantly more efficient if marketers first consider the **bases for segmentation** that are available in the surrounding designated market area (DMA). In addition, once these bases have been considered, sport marketers should also use the criteria for segmentation to determine whether they should invest their resources in defined target markets. When a target market is determined as a potential solid investment, then the sport organization can move on to the development of a product that meets the wants, needs, and/or demands of the group being targeted. Each of these individual areas of emphasis in the segmentation process will be discussed in depth in the following sections.

Bases for Segmentation

In the sport industry, there are several bases that sport marketers consider when making segmentation decisions. In essence, these bases for segmentation are the consumer characteristics that sport organizations consider when developing specific marketing plans. While there are a variety (and combination) of bases for segmentation, the decisions on which target markets emphasize are often influenced by the following characteristics:

- *Demographics:* The process of segmentation in which marketers make their decisions based on the fundamental characteristics of the consumers being targeted. Coined as "state-of-being" segmentation (Mullin, Hardy, and Sutton, 2007), this method of can be described by the creation, communication, and delivery of product based on the individual's background information.

- *Psychographics:* The process of segmentation where marketers make their decisions based on the psychological preferences of the consumers being targeted. Described as an innovative marketing strategy, this method is characterized by the use of an individual's "mindset" to make business decisions.

- *Behavioral:* The process of segmentation where marketers make their decisions based on the unique needs of the consumers being targeted. In essence, this encompasses the creation, communication, and delivery of a product based on the specific needs of the identified segment.

- *Hybrid:* The process of segmentation that uses a combination of demographics, psychographics, and behavioral influences to make marketing decisions.

Each of the four bases of segmentation will be discussed in depth prior to touching on the specific criteria that need to be taken in to consideration when making segmentation decisions.

Demographics

In the sport industry, the most common form of segmentation occurs when marketers use demographic information to make business decisions. While there are a variety of demographic dimensions that marketers consider, segmentation decisions are generally made with the following consumer characteristics in mind: age, gender, income, ethnicity, sexual orientation, geographic location, and family life cycle. In essence, sport marketers use these characteristics to determine whether there are certain groups of individuals (e.g., men age 18–24) that have an interest in their sport product. It is the effective use of these demographics that allows sport organizations to identify target markets with unique wants and needs that marketers can leverage in the delivery of their ticket packages and promotions.

An early innovator in the area of segmentation based on demographics was Bill Veeck. While setting attendance records as the owner of several Major League Baseball (MLB) teams, Veeck implemented creative promotional strategies designed to enhance interest in a variety of different consumer segments. For example, as owner of the Cleveland Indians, he created a themed "Thank U Night" promotion (e.g., colored tents, palm trees, and a vaudeville show) to show appreciation to the fans across the state of Ohio. Similarly, Veeck also attempted to access the female demographic when featuring a "Princess Aloha Orchid" giveaway to the first 20,000 women as they came through the turnstiles for a home game (Veeck and Lynn, 2001). It was this innovative approach that set the precedent for the themed promotions that are present at today's sporting events. Some individual examples of demographic segmentation in the sport industry are provided in Table 5.1.

TABLE 5.1

Examples of Demographic Segmentation in the Sport Industry		
Consumer Segment	**Variables**	**Promotional Strategy**
Men 21–30	Age, Gender	*"Bud Light Six Pack" Promotion*[1] Package: Choice of six games and beer giveaway
Corporations	Income	*"Bunker Suites" Promotion*[2] Package: High-end amenities and entertainment
Minority Groups	Ethnicity	*"Ethnic Heritage Night" Promotion*[3] Package: Themed cultural entertainment/giveaway
Lesbians	Sexual Orientation	*"Human Rights" Promotion*[4] Package: Recognition of gay and lesbian groups.

Note. Promotional strategies presented by the following sport organizations: [1]Phoenix Suns (NBA), [2]Detroit Pistons (NBA), [3]San Francisco Giants (MLB), [4]Seattle Storm (WNBA).

As illustrated in Table 5.1, there are a variety of innovative demographic segmentation strategies that are present in the sport industry. In an effort to extend their reach with consumers, the San Francisco Giants have segmented their market based on the ethnicity of the individuals in their DMA. With a diverse culture in the surrounding area, the Giant's marketing staff has used the following themed promotional nights to appeal to specific ethnic groups: Filipino Heritage Night, Indian Independence Day, Irish Heritage Night, Italian Heritage Night, Japanese Heritage Night, Jewish Heritage Night, and Polynesian Heritage Night ("San Francisco Special Events Calender," 2010). For example, the Japanese Heritage Night promotion included a Masanori Murakami jersey (first Japanese player in MLB) and a seat in the heritage section. In addition, the ticket sales from the promotion all went to local Japanese charities in the San Francisco area ("San Francisco Special Events Calender," 2010).

Psychographics

Another form of segmentation that has become increasingly more common in the sport industry is the delivery of product based on **psychographics**. The term psychographic, or the emphasis on the consumer's "mindset," takes place when organizations make decisions based on the lifestyles of the individuals being targeted ("Market Segmentation," 2010). While there are a variety of lifestyle dimensions, the most common methods of psychographic segmentation take place when marketers consider the attitudes, behaviors, and preferences of consumers (Barry and Weinstein, 2009). However, to enhance the practical application of this concept, this chapter will focus on the implementation of specific consumer preferences in sport industry environments.

In the sport industry, the use of consumer preferences has become more common among marketers making segmentation decisions. At the intercollegiate level, marketers have emphasized the reasons why consumers attend sporting events when creating specific ticket packages. For example, the National Wrestling Coaches Association (NWCA) has used market research to guide their decisions when marketing their All Star Classic and National Duals event. Following the identification of the most popular consumer preferences (see Table 5.2), the NWCA has tailored their promotional strategies to increase consumer interest at their events. For example, the strong preference for achievement and individual match-ups has encouraged the NWCA to highlight the accomplishments of wrestlers at their All Star Classic (Cooper, 2011).

Behavioral

The third base of segmentation that is common in the sport industry is the formation of target markets based on the needs of consumers. In addition to focusing on individual expectations (e.g., readiness to purchase, usage rate, and user status), sport marketers at all levels

TABLE 5.2

Wrestling Consumers' Responses to Sport Motivational Preferences		
Sport Fan Motives (*N* = 975)	*M*	*SD*
Individual Match-Ups *I consume to follow marquee match-ups between top ranked wrestlers.*	5.36*	1.03
Achievement *I consume because I enjoy following wrestler's great achievements.*	5.36*	0.97
Wrestling Loyalist *I consume because I enjoy supporting college wrestling.*	5.33*	1.01
Team Affiliation *I consume to follow a team competing in college wrestling.*	4.90*	1.48
Individual Wrestler Affiliation *I consume to follow an individual wrestler competing in college wrestling.*	4.63*	1.49
Entertainment *I consume for the entertainment options offered in college wrestling.*	4.41*	1.56
Social *I consume for the opportunity to socialize with other wrestling fans.*	4.18	1.43
Learning Opportunity *I consume to learn strategies/techniques from top collegiate wrestlers.*	3.96	1.58

Note. The scale ranged from Strongly Disagree (1) to Strongly Agree (6). Information was obtained from article in *Sport Marketing Quarterly* (Cooper, 2011). *$p < .001$ ($\mu \geq 5$).

have made segmentation decisions based on the benefits sought by consumers. In short, this method is often successful because it develops products, communication methods, and delivery strategies based on the unique characteristics of the segment being targeted.

As a marketer, the behavior segmentation method is extremely effective because it focuses on the unique needs and wants of different groups of consumers. The truth is that many segmentation decisions do not fall within the demographic and psychographic realms. In fact, many segmentation decisions can be based on the fact that groups of individuals have unique characteristics that are not being met in traditional ticket packages. For example, many working professionals (at all income levels) have time constraints that limit them from committing to a full- or half-season ticket plan. It is a marketer's job to use behavioral segmentation strategies to respond to these needs. Similarly, many of these young professionals also have an interest in networking opportunities to advance their careers. As illustrated by marketing expert Bill Sutton (see Table 5.3), sport organizations can enhance their relations with these young professionals when creating themed networking packages.

TABLE 5.3

Networking at the Game

The program content or the event could include a meal and a speaker or might be just a gathering with hors d'ourves and a cash bar. The program should be different each month to create a fresh experience. A sample program might look like this:

Game 1: Networking mixer and outline of the program; speaker on how to network and develop an effective business network.

Game 2: Presentation by head coach or GM about coaching/managing and how to improve performance.

Game 3: Sport marketing as a business development tool.

Game 4: Team owner talks about his/her primary business.

Game 5: Barnes & Noble or Borders' sponsored night; author of a contemporary new business book speaks.

Game 6: One of the team sponsors speaks about how they have used sponsorship as a business development tool.

Game 7: Program is designed based upon a survey of the networking membership.

Note. The information was gathered from article in *SportsBusiness Journal* (Sutton, 2009).

Hybrid

With an emphasis on maximizing interest in the sport product, it is important to realize that sport marketers often combine the bases of segmentation to enhance their efficiency with consumers. It is not uncommon for sport organizations to first use demographic segmentation to identify potential consumer groups that are present in the surrounding DMA (e.g., college-age students). However, marketers have also improved their efficiency when considering the psychographic influences within particular demographic segments. For example, when focusing on the college-aged students, sport organizations can use psychographic considerations such as consumer preferences to further segment their markets. The three bases of segmentation can be used in coordination with one another to improve marketing initiatives.

Criteria Considerations for Segmentation

For the marketing process to be effective, sport marketers must consider five key criteria prior to investing in segmentation initiatives: (1) **identifiability,** (2) **accessibility,** (3) **substantiality,** (4) **responsiveness,** and (5) **retention potential** (Kotler and Keller, 2005; "Market Segmentation," 2010). As illustrated in the previous section, the identification criterion starts when sport organizations scan their surrounding DMA and determine potential target markets in the area. However, it is critical that a sport marketer ask himself or herself whether or not the target market makes sense from an efficiency standpoint before moving ahead with a segmentation decision. In other words, there must be an opportunity to achieve the desired goals for the target market (e.g., financial return, increase in publicity) if segmentation is going to take place. For example, if a sport organization is looking to sell

$500,000 in suite inventory (ten suites at $50,000), then the potential segment must have the income capacity to embrace the high-end premium seating options that are being offered. Further, marketers should consider whether or not the segment is in a geographic range that makes sense for consumers being targeted. If the sport organization determines that the target market is clearly identifiable, then they are ready to assess whether or not the segment is accessible.

Once a target market has been identified, it is important to move on to the second criteria for determining whether a sport organization should segment a market. As explained by Mullin, Hardy, and Sutton (2007), it is always important for a sport marketer to ask himself or herself whether a target market is accessible before moving forward with marketing endeavors. From a practical standpoint, this means that sport organizations should consider whether or not the consumer segment could be reached through traditional communication mediums (e.g., advertisements, cold calls). If the organization has the ability to reach the target market in an efficient manner, then the marketer can then move on to the third criterion focusing on the responsiveness of the potential consumer segment.

In addition to determining whether the potential target market is identifiable and accessible, an effective sport marketer must also consider substantiality in the segmentation decision-making process. In essence, the term substantiality is primarily concerned with determining if a potential segment is large enough (and/or with enough resources) to justify the investment in a segmentation process. If the sport organization feels that the target market is a substantial consumer segment, then the marketer can move on to the identification stage of segmentation.

The fourth criterion when considering segmentation relates to the responsiveness of the consumer segment being targeted. In many ways, this is the most important segmentation criterion because it determines whether a potential target market will be interested in your product. More importantly, it offers the sport organization the opportunity to enhance their operational efficiency by focusing on consumer segments that will respond favorably to the product being offered. Sport marketers can improve their effectiveness in this criterion by asking themselves the following question: Will the target market respond to the communication, product line, and delivery strategy that you have implemented? If the sport marketer can say yes to each of these areas, then the organization is ready to move on to the fifth criterion for segmentation.

The final criterion for consideration when making a segmentation decision relates to whether or not the consumer segment can become repeat purchasers. While retention is not necessarily a mandatory segmentation criterion, it is at least important to consider because it provides sport organizations with an understanding of the working environment they are facing as they move forward with their marketing initiatives. For example, if individuals within a specific target market are not likely to become loyal customers, the sport marketer can make plans to re-package their inventory for identified consumer segments in the future.

Developing a Segmented Product

The advancement through the five criteria for segmentation is only one step for a successful sport marketer. Once marketers have advanced through these criteria, they have the information that is necessary to start to finalize their understanding of their target markets. In addition to identifying their primary target markets (e.g., college students age 18–24), it is extremely important that sport organizations take the time to understand all of the needs, wants, and characteristics of the individuals who they are targeting. In essence, it is this process that allows sport marketers to understand the type of product and communication strategy that they must develop to be successful in their marketing endeavors. In other words, when you have a product that is unique to your specific consumer segments, then you give yourself a great chance to develop initial interest and loyalty among your consumers. However, it is important that sport marketers recognize the different product areas that are relevant to the segmentation process. These product areas will be discussed below before moving on to a discussion of the innovative segmentation strategies in the sport industry.

- *Ticket Packages:* The foundation for creating an innovative product for target markets is largely dependent on the ticket packages that are presented by sport organizations. When ticket packages are successfully crafted to meet the demands of consumer segments (e.g., mini-packages for individuals with limited time and disposable income), then sport organizations have a significantly greater chance of maximizing interest in their core product. Marketers must strategically create packages that are diverse in nature if they hope to meet the needs and wants of different target markets.

- *Entertainment:* In coordination with the ticket packages, sport marketers must also be concerned with the entertainment that they are offering to their target markets when they attend sporting events. More importantly, the entertainment options (e.g., music, giveaways [see promotions below]) should cater to the majority of the consumer segments attending the event. While this is a challenge, effective marketers find a way to incorporate entertainment for everyone.

- *Promotions:* In many ways, promotions can been seen as a form of entertainment for sport marketers. However, promotions are important enough that they deserve their own category in this section. When focusing on the different ways to create interest in sporting events (e.g., giveaways, Facebook videos), it is imperative that sport organizations highlight promotions that are specifically designed for their target markets if they want to be successful in their marketing endeavors. With themed promotions included in designed ticket packages, sport organizations have a greater chance of pleasing their consumers.

- *Concessions:* Along with the previous product areas, sport organizations should also consider the food options that they are offering to their consumers. When concession options are provided that satisfy the preferences of key target markets (e.g., ethnic options for Heritage Nights), then sport organizations increase their chances of developing loyal, repeat purchase consumers.

- *Merchandise:* Similar to the concession options, marketers must also be aware of the merchandise options that are available at their events if they are going to maximize their effectiveness. For example, with a new emphasis on attracting the female demographic, sport organizations must be sure to provide women's apparel options (see pink NFL jerseys) if they are going to extend their reach to new consumer segments.

Courtesy of Kimberly Miloch.

- *Sponsorship:* When making segmentation decisions, it is important to envision the corporations that can be approached for potential sponsorship agreements. In particular, marketers should try and engage in relationships with "matching target markets" so that the consumers, sponsoring corporation, and sport organization all benefit. This is a major consideration because a successful sponsorship agreement provides the sport organization with an opportunity to provide added value to key target markets.

- *Internet:* With the growing popularity of the Internet, it is important that sport marketers use technology in a way that is beneficial and desirable to key target markets. Similar to the previous product areas, the ability to create a streamlined product allows sport organizations to enhance their relationships with consumers. This area will be discussed more in-depth in Chapter 9.

When sport marketers develop a well-rounded product that is specifically designed for their key target markets, they provide themselves with an opportunity to attract and retain large groups of consumers. From start to finish, a sport marketer's job is to create a themed experience with amenities and entertainment opportunities that encourage consumers to want to come back to future events. This means that a marketer must constantly focus on the consumer segment's needs and wants if he or she wants to succeed from a marketing standpoint. Some examples of successful uses of segmentation at all levels will be discussed in the following section.

Applied Segmentation in the Sport Industry

As a marketer, it is important to consider your environment when making segmentation decisions. The reality is that each sport organization has an individualized product that has its own strengths and weaknesses. More importantly, each sport organization has a surrounding DMA with consumers featuring unique needs, wants, and characteristics that must be met for marketers to be successful. Thus, it is extremely important that sport organizations take their environment into consideration when making decisions on how to market their product to consumers. To help illustrate this concept, segmentation examples will be presented at the youth, high school, college, professional, and global levels.

Courtesy Brian Turner.

Youth Sport

At the youth level, there are a myriad of sporting events that are offered across the United States and the world. While there are a wide range of different types of benefits offered at each of these sport events, there are some clear consumer segments that marketers should consider when working at the youth level. First, from a participation standpoint, it is imperative that marketers focus on the development of promotional strategies to encourage young athletes (ages 4–18) to turn out for sport activities. In addition, when focusing on fan consumption, marketers should create materials to encourage families in the surrounding area to attend local sport events. These strategies should be designed with the cultural preferences in mind. An example of applied segmentation at the youth level is provided below.

Sport Event: Houston Little League Baseball

Key Target Market: Families in surrounding Houston area

Segmented Marketing Strategy: Through a partnership with the Houston Astros and Minute Maid, the City of Houston created a "Grand Slam for Youth Baseball" program that provides kids (4–18) with an opportunity to participate in baseball and softball. In addition to free t-shirts, caps, and equipment, the program also provides scholarship opportunities to selected individuals who participate in the program ("Grand Slam for Baseball," 2010).

High School Sport

Similar to the youth level, high school sports have a variety of different sport events to consider when engaging in marketing initiatives. However, at the high school level, the marketing has become slightly more refined because athletic departments have a vested interest in increasing consumer interest in their product(s). Regardless of the institution and/or sport event, it is safe to say that high school students and alumni are a primary target markets for athletic departments. In addition, parents and community members in the surrounding areas are consumer segments that offer the potential to increase attendance at high school sport events.

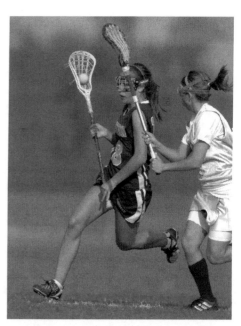

© Shawn Pecor, 2012. Under license from Shutterstock, Inc.

Sport Event: High school athletic events (13 state associations)

Key Target Market: High school students (age 14–18)

Segmented Marketing Strategy: In an effort to improve their marketing efforts, over 4,000 high school athletic departments have partnered with Home Team Marketing to improve their relations with consumers. Through the partnership, athletic departments have developed relationships with Fathead that allows them to offer consumers logos and football helmets in a decal format. In addition to offering a quality product to consumers for $49.99, athletic departments also get a share of the proceeds to fund their operations (Smith, 2010).

© Jeff Schultes, 2012. Under license from Shutterstock, Inc.

College Sport

At the college level, marketing has become important enough that many athletic departments have chosen to invest in personnel to improve their relations with consumers. However, the level of promotional commitment by the athletic department depends a great deal on the sport team on which they are focusing. With the "arms race" at the intercollegiate level, many Division I athletic departments invest a great deal of their time and energy on marketing activities that will grow men's basketball and men's football. As a result, there is more segmentation that takes place when promoting these types of sporting events. In contrast, there is generally significantly less emphasis on nonrevenue, Olympic sport teams (e.g., men's wrestling and women's volleyball) when it comes to marketing endeavors. However, regardless of the sport type, it is safe to say that all sport teams are reliant on younger athletes (age 5–18) in their respective sport when attempting to maximize interest in their events. In addition, college students (and segments within college [e.g., fraternities and sororities]) are primary target markets for all sport teams.

Sport Event: Stanford Football games
Key Target Market: Non-loyal consumers
Segmented Marketing Strategy: To increase attendance at their 55,000 plus capacity football stadium, the Stanford athletic department offered "Grid Iron Guarantees" to consumers who purchased their new season ticket and "Family Plan" buyers. In essence, the athletic department guaranteed a full refund for any fan that was not satisfied with the "entertainment value" of the product at the end of the season (Smith, 2008).

Professional Sport

The pinnacle of segmentation in marketing exists at the professional level of sports. With more competition in the entertainment industry and less disposable income among consumers, it is becoming more and more imperative for sport organizations to engage in segmentation activities to maximize their attendance at events. In particular, while it is necessary for all sport leagues and organizations, it is critical for MLB teams to segment their markets sharply because of their extended 162 game seasons. With this being the case, there is a wide range of segmentation strategies that professional sport organizations implement to enhance their marketing endeavors. However, a few examples of segments being targeted by these sport organizations are the following: college age students, ethnic groups, Millennials (younger generation of consumers who have grown up with technology), women (all ages), and youth athletes (age 6–13).

© Jerry Sharp, 2012. Under license from Sutterstock, Inc.

> *Sport Event:* National Football League (NFL) games
> *Key Target Market:* Youth athletes (age 6–13)
> *Segmented Marketing Strategy:* To continue to establish a loyal fan base in the future, the NFL has created youth flag football leagues throughout the United States in hope of engaging youth in their sport. In 2009, the NFL hosted eight regional tournaments held in NFL cities that offered the opportunity to advance to play in a championship held prior to the Pro Bowl at the Dolphin's stadium (Show, 2009).

Global Sport

Moving beyond professional sports at the national level, another level of segmentation exists for marketers responsible for promoting global sport events. On one hand, the level of segmentation is similar to professional sports because events such as the Olympics and the World Cup must segment sharply to reach their consumers effectively. However, the segmentation at global events is far more complex because marketers must consider the unique characteristics of consumer segments within each of the individual countries that are being targeted by the host event. Thus, there are a myriad of segmentation strategies that exist within each country because of the cultural differences present in each territory. The World Cup is an event where innovative segmentation strategies exist to attract younger generations of consumers across the world.

© sportgraphic, 2012. Under license from Sutterstock, Inc.

Sport Event: World Cup Soccer 2010
Key Target Market: American youth soccer players
Segmented Marketing Strategy: In an effort to grow soccer in the United States, the South African Tourism Bureau partnered with US Youth Soccer and Coca-Cola to create a fun, web video contest. The grand prize was a trip to South Africa for an entire team for eight days and seven nights, with a match against a South African youth soccer team occurring during the World Cup ("South Africa Tourism launches World Cup Promotions," 2010).

Summary

As the sport industry continues to evolve at all levels, it will be increasingly important for sport organizations and marketers to invest in segmentation initiatives if they are going to remain as a viable option in the entertainment industry. With more entertainment options being presented to consumers, there is a growing need to design products, communication strategies, and delivery mechanisms specifically for target markets at each level. When consumers are provided with interactions that are specifically tailored for their needs and wants, then they are much more likely to become loyal fans who engage in repeat purchase activities. These are the types of fans that will allow sport organizations to be successful at all levels in future years.

Discussion Questions

1. What is market segmentation and how can it help sport organizations to enhance their relationships with current and potential consumers?

2. What criteria would you suggest that sport organizations consider prior to making final decisions on how to segment markets?

3. Based on your experience, what is one example of innovative demographic, psychographic, and behavioral segmentation in the sport industry?

4. What are the most common (and effective) target markets at the global, professional, college, high school, and youth levels of sport?

Critical Thinking Exercises

1. You have recently been hired as the Director of Marketing for the Ultimate Fighting Championship (UFC). After talking to President Dana White, he is interested in extending the reach of the UFC to consumers across the United States. In an initial meeting, he asks you to outline a plan to create new UFC fans in the future. In particular, he is interested in knowing what consumer segments you plan to target and how you plan on reaching them. What would be your response as the new Director of Marketing?

2. Mike Moyer, Executive Director of the National Wrestling Coaches Association (NWCA), is interested in hiring you to be a marketing consultant for college wrestling programs. After an initial meeting, you learn that he is interested in developing promotions to increase interest in the following target markets: college students, high school and youth wrestlers, and fraternities and sororities. What marketing strategies would you suggest to encourage these target markets to attend wrestling events at the local, grassroots level? How would you make sure that these target markets become repeat customers in future years?

References

Barry, J., and A. Weinstein. "Business psychographics revisited: from segmentation theory to successful marketing practice." *Journal of Marketing Management,* 25(3/4) (2009): 315–340.

Cooper, C. G. "The Motivational Preferences of Consumers Attending Multiple NCAA Wrestling Events." *Sport Marketing Quarterly,* 20(1) (2011): 35–42.

Grand Slam for Baseball. *The Houston Astros Official Website,* 2010, http://mlb.mlb.com/hou/community/youth_baseball.jsp

Howard, D. R., and J. L. Crompton. *Financing sport.* 2nd ed., Fitness Information Technology: Morgantown, WV, 2004.

Howell, D. "The Palace introduces Presidents Club and Vito Anthony Suites," 2010, http://www.nba.com/pistons/tickets/sterlingbankclub_vitoanthonysuites.html.

Kotler, P., and K. Keller. *Marketing management.* 12th ed., Prentice Hall: Upper Saddle River, NJ, 2005

Market Segmentation. *NetMBA Business Knowledge Center.* http://www.netmba.com/marketing/market/segmentation/

Mullin, B. J., S. Hardy, and W. Sutton. *Sport marketing.* 3rd ed., Human Kinetics: Champaign, IL, 2007.

Nielsen year in sports. Nielsen, 2010, http://en-us.nielsen.com/content/dam/nielsen/en_us/documents/pdf/White%20Papers%20and%20Reports/Nielsen%20Year%20in%20Sports.pdf

San Francisco Special Events Calendar. *San Francisco Giant's Official Website,* 2010, http://mlb.mlb.com/sf/ticketing/group_special_events.jsp

Show, J. "Leagues aim to build next generation of fans." *Street & Smith's SportsBusiness Journal,* August 17, 2009:18.

Smith, M. "Home Team widens collection of high school associations." *Street & Smith's SportsBusiness Journal,* January 4, 2010: 5.

Smith, M. "Football program at Stanford provides a money back guarantee." *San Francisco Chronicle,* 2008, http://www.seattlepi.com/cfootball/376648_stanford27.html

Sutton, B. "Networking package could be a huge hit with young professionals." *Street & Smith's SportsBusiness Journal,* September 7, 2009: 17.

"South Africa Tourism launches World Cup Promotions." *Official Travel Pulse Website,* October 30, 2009, http://www.travelpulse.com/Resources/Editorial.aspx?n=62917

Veeck, B., and E. Linn. *Veeck—As in wreck: The autobiography of Bill Veeck.* The University of Chicago Press: Chicago, IL, 2001.

Courtesy of Kimberly Miloch.

CHAPTER 6

Creating the Marketing Mix

Andrea N. Eagleman Indiana University-Purdue University Indianapolis

> *In business, one of the challenges is making sure that your product is the easiest to experience and complete a sale.*
>
> Mark Cuban, owner of the Dallas Mavericks

CHAPTER OBJECTIVES

After completing the chapter, the reader should be able to:

- Develop a strong understanding of the five elements of the marketing mix.
- Understand what makes the sport product unique from other products and services.
- Learn how the marketing mix is applied in three sectors of the sport industry—youth, collegiate, and professional.

Introduction

In order to survive and compete, organizations in the sport industry must focus a great deal of their efforts on marketing. Sport marketing is unique in that sport is essentially a service industry due to the intangible nature of the sport product. Therefore, it is difficult to control aspects such as the outcome of the game, the weather on the day of a game, or how exciting a game or performance will be for the audience. For example, if a fan purchases tickets to the National Hot Rod Association (NHRA) US Nationals in Indianapolis, he or she cannot be

© Walter G. Arce, 2012. Under license from Shutterstock, Inc.

entirely sure what the weather will be like on the day of the race. If it rains, the drag races will be delayed until officials are able to ensure that the track is completely dry. The fan cannot be sure if the races will be close at the finish line, and therefore more exciting for the fans to watch.

Sport marketers are not able to control these aspects of the event, but what they can control are the various elements involved in marketing the sport product. This chapter provides a detailed look at those elements: product, price, promotion, place, and public relations. The first four in this list are often referred to as the "Four P's" (Mullin, Hardy and Sutton, 2000, 38) of marketing, and in recent years, public relations has been added as a fifth P to form the "Five P's" (p. 38). Together, these elements combine to make up what is referred to as the **marketing mix**. It is important to remember that all sport organizations utilize the elements of the marketing mix, including those sport organizations whose products are primarily tangible, such as an apparel and equipment manufacturer like Nike.

This chapter is designed to introduce each of the marketing mix elements to readers in a way that explains each element in detail, and also provides real world examples from a variety of different sport organizations. The chapter includes the following sections:

Elements of the Marketing Mix

Product

At the core of the marketing mix is the sport **product**. The product is that which is being marketed. It can take many forms, but typically "product" refers to the sport contest or game itself. For example, if North Senior High School is hosting a girls' basketball game in its home gymnasium on Friday night against South Senior High School, the sport product is the actual basketball game that will take place between the two teams. Because North Senior is the host of the game, it is likely that the athletic administrators from this school will take on the responsibility of marketing the game to the community. Conversely, from a tangible sport perspective, the product might be the pair of running shorts that Under Armour sells at Dick's Sporting Goods stores.

Product Extensions

Along with the core product, it is quite common for sport organizations to offer **product extensions**, which help make the intangible product more tangible for those consuming it. Examples of frequent product extensions at a high school basketball game such as the one mentioned above include paper tickets, game programs, souvenirs such as t-shirts, mini megaphones, pom-pons, and other merchandise with the team's logo or school name. All of these product extensions can be taken home after the product (or game) has been consumed, and therefore serve as a tangible reminder of the game for the fan who attended. Product extensions are not required for the sporting event to take place, but they enhance the fan's experience at the game, and serve as a reminder of the game for the consumer at a later date. If the consumer had a positive experience, seeing one of these product extensions might remind them of the good times they had at the game, and could encourage future purchases.

From a collegiate and professional sport perspective, many teams and franchises have begun hiring photographers to walk through the stands during the game to take pictures of fans. After the game, fans can log-on to the team's website to order prints of their picture with the team's logo or stadium as the background image. This is yet another product extension offered to the fans.

Aside from product extensions that can be taken home as souvenirs or mementos, other product extensions exist in sport settings as well. Examples of other product extensions include concession stands, cheerleaders or dance teams, halftime performances, and games or trivia contests that take place on the scoreboard. All of these extensions seek to ensure that the customer is entertained throughout the duration of the game, and can contribute to a consumer having a positive experience at the game even if their favorite team loses or performs poorly.

Because the core sport product is difficult for sport marketers to control, they often have to focus their efforts on product extensions and attempt to please consumers in this way.

© fstockfoto, 2012. Under license from Shutterstock, Inc.

Price

In its simplest form, **price** is the amount that a customer pays for a product. It is extremely important in sport marketing because it is a highly visible element associated with the product. If a consumer sees a price that they deem to be too high, they might not pay attention to any of the other P's associated with that product such as promotion, place, or public relations, because in their mind the decision about whether or not to purchase has already been made.

Along with being highly visible, price is also arguably the easiest element of the marketing mix to change. If demand for a product is greater than the supply, sport marketers might make the decision to increase the price slightly, because they suspect there is enough demand to account for a price change, which in effect will bring in greater profits to the sport organization.

When determining the price of a product, sport marketers must keep in mind that price is often associated with quality in the consumer's mind. Therefore, if the price is set too low, consumers may equate the product as having a lower quality and could be hesitant to purchase it. Similarly, a product's price is also associated with its value. If a price is set too high, consumers might not feel that the value of the product is worth the price associated with it, and will choose not to buy it. In these especially hard economic times, it is important for sport marketers to make consumers feel as though they are getting a highly valuable product for a reasonable price.

Place and Distribution

Place refers to the location from which the product can be purchased. It is also often referred to as **distribution**. It is quite common that a sport product will have several different places where it can be purchased. For example, to purchase tickets to a Chicago Cubs baseball game, consumers have many different options. One option would be to go to the stadium and purchase tickets directly from the box office. Another option, which is likely more convenient for most, is to purchase tickets online from the Cubs' website. Still, others may choose to call the box office or a ticketing company like Ticketmaster to purchase tickets. Finally, for games that are sold-out, consumers have the option of purchasing from other consumers on online auction sites such as eBay, or from scalpers on the streets surrounding the stadium. Even when tickets are sold online from the team site or from websites like eBay or StubHub, there are still distribution-related concerns. Will the tickets be mailed to the consumer's home? Held at the will-call window? Emailed to the consumer to print at home? Sent via text message so that the consumer has to show his or her phone at the turnstile?

Similarly, an Oakland Raiders football fan who wishes to purchase merchandise featuring the team's logo has many options for the place to purchase the product. They could buy it from a gift shop in the Oakland Coliseum, where the Raiders play, from the Raiders' website or any other sporting goods website, or from a sporting goods store in or near Oakland.

Although there are many different places to purchase sport products, it is important to remember that the core product, the game itself, can only be consumed *in person* at the stadium or facility in which the game is taking place. It is possible, however, for a fan in one state to consume a game taking place three states away via live broadcasting on the television, radio, or Internet.

Place is an extremely important element in the marketing mix because unlike the elements of price, promotion, and public relations, it is a difficult element to change or revise easily. Sport facilities are costly to build, and therefore, teams need to be mindful of the location they choose for a stadium prior to building it. Several considerations must be taken into account when making such a decision: parking, transportation to and from the stadium, proximity to hotels, restaurants, and shops, crime rates in the surrounding neighborhood, and the aesthetics of the facility and its surroundings. One example of the importance of facility location can be seen when comparing the Chicago White Sox and Chicago Cubs MLB teams. Although it is difficult to compare the teams based solely on the location of their facilities, it is interesting to note that in 2011, the teams had comparable seasons in terms of their records. In terms of attendance, however, the Cubs filled Wrigley Field to an average of 90.5% capacity in their home games, while the White Sox filled U.S. Cellular Field to an average of only 60.8% capacity ("MLB Attendance Report," 2011). Anyone who has visited both ballparks knows that Wrigley Field is located in the middle of a young, vibrant neighborhood filled with restaurants, shops, and sports bars surrounding the stadium. Public transportation is plentiful, and most hotels are just a few miles away in the downtown area. The neighborhood also enjoys a very low crime rate. Visiting the neighborhood surrounding Wrigley Field is just as exciting as visiting the ballpark itself for some fans. Conversely, U.S. Cellular Field is located in an area of the city that experiences much more crime, and there are very few restaurants or other attractive locations for fans to enjoy before or after a game. Public transportation is available, but many sports fans are hesitant to use public transport to and from U.S. Cellular Field because of the crime associated with the ballpark's neighborhood.

Up to this point, this section has focused heavily on service-related businesses. In terms of retail businesses in the sport industry, place is also a very important consideration. For example, an organization such as Brooks, a specialty running shoe brand, has many considerations to make regarding the distribution of its shoes. The following is a list of some of the distribution-related choices Brooks must make:

- Should they open their own Brooks retail stores, in which they must staff and manage every store from the company's headquarters in Bothell, Washington?

- From which sporting goods stores, if any, will they sell their shoes? Will they supply their shoes to major national and/or international sporting goods chains such as Dick's Sporting Goods, or will they supply their shoes only to specialty running shops?

- Where will their shoes be available for purchase on the Internet? Will they sell shoes directly from their own website, or will they sell only through running retailers such as Road Runner Sports?

- Will they distribute their shoes only in the United States, or internationally? If they choose to distribute internationally, in which countries will Brooks shoes be available?

This list provides only a brief snapshot of the distribution-related issues that Brooks faces in selling their shoes. As one can see, the decisions Brooks makes can have a major impact on several areas of their business and the marketing mix. For example, if Brooks chooses to distribute their shoes to a retailer that is viewed by customers as being a "low-cost" retailer, it could dampen their brand image in the minds of consumers, which could have consequences on the price Brooks assigns to their shoes.

As you can now begin to see, all of the P's of marketing are interrelated and depend on each other to ensure a successful product.

Promotion

The **promotion** aspect of the marketing mix is the method used by the sport marketer to create awareness of the sport product in the minds of consumers. It is the primary mechanism for creating an image of the product in the consumer's mind, and the goal of promotion is to create a positive image that elicits a response in the form of a purchase. Promotion can take on many forms, including advertising, personal selling, publicity, and sales promotion.

When many people think of promotion, they immediately think of **advertising**. This is a powerful promotional tool, but it should not be viewed as the only promotional tool. Advertising is a paid form of non-personal communication in which the sport organization controls the message. Therefore, the sport organization must position the sport product in the best possible light via its advertising efforts, while also creating an advertisement that is unique enough to catch the consumer's eye. Americans are exposed to up to 5,000 advertising messages every day, so one key to advertising is the ability to break through the clutter of all the other messages being thrown in a consumer's direction (Story, 2007). Sport organizations may choose to advertise through traditional forms such as the newspaper, magazines, radio, billboards, or television, or they might also explore new media such as the Internet, cell phones, or digital signage such as billboards, signage at a stadium, or even signage in the bathroom stalls of public restrooms. Above all, advertising should at the very least make the consumer aware of the product or service being offered.

Aside from advertising, **personal selling** is another form of promotion. Personal selling involves any face-to-face communication between the seller and a potential consumer. It has the ability to be effective because of its personal, interactive nature. While personal selling could include a ticket sales representative from a sport organization visiting a local business in an attempt to sell the organization season tickets, it also includes any interaction that an employee of a sport organization has with a potential customer. This includes not only front office employees, but athletes and coaches as well. For example, when the North Junior High School soccer team sells tickets for their pancake breakfast fundraiser, they will most likely set up a booth in their school or at other school sporting events, and the players will attempt to sell the tickets to their peers, families, and teachers.

A third category of promotion includes **publicity**. This is media exposure for the sport organization that the organization does not actually pay for. Examples of publicity include newspaper, magazine, or website articles and/or pictures of the sport organization, or any

Courtesy of Brian Turner.

other coverage in a news publication that the organization did not pay for. The concept of publicity will be covered in greater length in the next section about public relations.

Finally, the concept of promotion also includes **sales promotions**. These are paid forms of communication, and as the name suggests, this communication typically centers on information regarding the purchase of a product or service. Examples of sales promotions include coupons, rebate offers, product sampling, promotional giveaway items, and displays. Sales promotions provide an ideal activation method for many sport organizations' sponsorships. For example, the Colorado Rockies MLB team has a coupon for Sports Authority sporting goods stores printed on the back of every Rockies ticket, showcasing one of the team's sponsors, while also driving traffic to Sports Authority stores.

Promotion strategies are strongly linked with the price element of the marketing mix. Promotions in the form of coupons or other discounts must be carefully considered to ensure that the organization can still generate enough revenue to make a profit. Additionally, promotions must take into consideration the place or distribution of the product. Promotions should ideally be present in the locations where the product is sold or consumed, and should be appealing to the fan demographics in the area in which the promotion will take place. For example, it would not be logical for the University of Colorado to use beach towels as a promotional giveaway item at their late season home football games, as the weather is generally cold and potentially snowy in Colorado during this time of year. The University of Miami in Florida, however, might have great success with this type of giveaway even in November because of the warm climate in Miami.

Public Relations

Public relations, or the fifth P of the marketing mix, is in its simplest form the sport organization's relationship with all of its publics, and those publics' relationship with the organization. Sport organizations attempt to maintain as positive a relationship with their publics as possible, and public relations, or PR, efforts seek to enhance this relationship.

Some examples of sport organization publics, or stakeholders, include its fans, community, sponsors and potential sponsors, shareholders (for public companies), media, its employees, and any other person or organization who might somehow come into contact with the organization.

Within the larger realm of public relations are two sub-functions which often merit their own departments within a sport organization: media relations and community relations. **Media relations** is primarily concerned with maintaining strong relationships with the media at a local, regional, and sometimes national or international level. Media relations professionals often work closely with media members to pitch stories about the sport organization, provide more detailed information when a media member is working on a story regarding the sport organization, or to facilitate interviews with athletes, coaches, or other key members of the sport organization. Media relations also involves setting up and managing the press functions at events to ensure that the members of the media have wireless Internet connections, power outlets for their laptops, and anything else that is pertinent to the media member performing his or her job.

The second sub-function of public relations is community relations. This involves maintaining favorable and strong relationships within the community surrounding the sport organization. For example, at Indiana University, located in Bloomington, IN, the Athletic Department recognizes that towns surrounding Bloomington also view the IU Hoosiers as their hometown teams, and therefore the Athletic Department seeks to form relationships with leaders in the surrounding communities such as Bedford, Ellettsville, Martinsville, and Nashville, and also holds community relations events in these locations, such as meet-and-greet opportunities with IU coaches and administrators. Community relations is often equated with charity or advocacy, and indeed, this type of work can be included in this category. The NBA and WNBA have a league-wide "Read to Achieve" program, which is an educational initiative designed to help children develop reading as a lifetime hobby. Players from the various NBA and WNBA teams will take time out of their schedules to read to groups of children throughout their communities as part of the program in order to encourage reading among their communities' youth.

Finally, public relations is certainly related to the concept of publicity, as stated in the previous section. Public relations professionals work with the media constantly in an attempt to place positive stories about their sport organizations in the media. Publicity is a nonpaid form of communication, so sport managers view it as an inexpensive way to distribute their messages to the various publics. In order to reach all of the possible publics, as well as to compete with other organizations in an increasingly cluttered media landscape, PR practitioners must develop story ideas that are unique and catchy. Instead of placing the same type of story in a media outlet over and over again, PR practitioners must think of creative ways to include information about their organization in the media. One example to illustrate this concept could be an NHRA Full Throttle Drag Racing team. Because there are at least 64 professional class drivers competing in most NHRA national events, the ability for teams to place stories in local media where the race is taking place is often limited to the teams who are performing the best at the time of the event. A team whose driver is not racing particularly well must develop creative story pitches to attract local media. An example of one such method might be contacting local television weather reporters rather than focusing solely on local sports reporters. Drag racing is highly dependent on the weather conditions of the day, which can have major impacts on the car and the way the crew chief tunes the engine. Explaining this to local weather reporters provides a new twist on the weather report, and is a topic that most teams would not think to pitch. In doing so, the team who is struggling might actually get greater media attention than those teams who are in the media because their driver is doing well in the race.

Marketing Mix Orchestration

Now that a basic understanding of the marketing mix and the five P's has been established, it is important to illustrate the ways in which various sport organizations carry out the marketing mix. This section will provide examples from three areas of sport: youth, collegiate, and professional.

USA Gymnastics

USA Gymnastics, the governing body of the sport of gymnastics in the United States, is continually faced with the challenge of maintaining and increasing participation in gymnastics among the country's youth. In 2006, the organization launched an initiative in partnership with Tyson Foods called the "Tyson Fitness Challenge" in an effort to promote healthy, active lifestyles for children, and to increase participation in gymnastics in USA Gymnastics' wide network of member clubs across the country. According to the Tyson Fitness Challenge website, the program is "an eight-session fitness initiative geared to help today's youth achieve healthy, active lifestyles. The program is not about teaching gymnastics skills; it is about gymnastics clubs helping kids increase their flexibility, strength, and endurance, as well as learn about the importance of a well-balanced diet."

The program was designed for kids between the ages of 6 and16, and is available to USA Gymnastics member clubs free of cost. Registration can be completed on the Tyson Fitness Challenge website, after which the club receives an administrator's handbook, promotional posters, and a DVD containing program ideas and demonstrations. Non-USA Gymnastics members may also join, but must pay $29.95.

In addition to providing member clubs with promotional materials about the Tyson Fitness Challenge, USA Gymnastics implemented several of its own initiatives to create awareness for the

© Laura Stone, 2012. Under license of Shutterstock, Inc.

program. Advertisements in its two member publications, *Technique* magazine (sent to professional members such as coaches and judges) and *USA Gymnastics* magazine (sent to professional members and competitors) have increased awareness among all of the organization's members. Additionally, an interactive Tyson Fitness Challenge Zone is set up at USA Gymnastics events such as the US National Championships to allow youth the opportunity to learn about the four fundamentals of fitness and to practice some of the exercises found in many Tyson Fitness Challenge programs across the country. Finally, USA Gymnastics secured media placement in news outlets such as the *Cleveland Business Journal* and *Parents* magazine.

While no official figures are currently available to assess the success of the program in increasing participation at gymnastics clubs across the country, the 2010 Sporting Goods Manufacturers of America's "Sports Participation in America" report showed that among children ages 6–17, gymnastics ranked second behind cheerleading in terms of participation (Sporting Goods Manufacturers of America, 2010).

Saint Mary's College of California Athletic Department

Saint Mary's College of California is a small, private, Lasallian college located in Moraga, California that competes in NCAA Division I athletics. One of the athletic department's challenges in the early 2000s was finding ways to attract students to attend the school's various athletic events. In response to this concern, the athletic department designed a student marketing initiative to attract more students to all of the athletic events on campus, and it has been highly successful in creating awareness about athletic events on campus, bringing in student fans, and therefore, making the atmosphere at athletic contests a difficult one for opponents. The club is called "Gael Force," a play on the school's mascot, the Gaels, and upon the completion of the 2009-2010 academic year, it was the largest student club on campus with over 1,200 members (or nearly half of the school's undergraduate enrollment). Student members of Gael Force receive free admission to any SMC home athletic event, priority seating at men's home basketball games, road trips to away sporting events, and an official t-shirt each year, among other benefits. The price paid by students to join is dependent upon their year in school, as freshmen they pay the most at $50 per year, followed by sophomores at $40, juniors at $30, and seniors at $15 (Gael Force, n.d.).

The Gael Force initiative would not have experienced the same level of success without the proper marketing mix. In order to maximize the number of Gael Force members, the athletic department understood that it had to keep prices set at a level that was deemed affordable by college students, and the membership should provide benefits believed to be of value by the students. Secondly, the students would not sign up for the club if they were not aware of it. Efforts were made to promote the club throughout campus, such as information given to freshmen during their SMC orientation, announcements made in classes by current members, information readily available on the athletic department's website, and finally, public relations efforts in the form of media coverage for the club. For example, following a 2009 NIT Tournament loss at Saint Mary's home basketball stadium, McKeon Pavilion, Davidson University coach Bob McKillup said in the post-game press conference, "Is this the atmosphere that they have for every game? It just blows my mind that they have this kind of crowd. This is very similar to [Duke's] Cameron [Indoor Stadium] in terms of the noise level, the heat, the intensity, the passion. Saint Mary's deserves credit for having a crowd that's that supportive." The quote was published in news outlets throughout the country, such as ESPN.com (Associated Press, 2009), and the publicity Saint Mary's and the Gael Force received as a result only assisted in the efforts to attract more students, as evidenced by the increase in membership the following academic year.

San Jose Sharks

When one thinks of ice hockey, the Bay Area of California likely does not come to mind as a mecca for hockey fans. With a sunny and warm climate year-round, cities such as San Jose and San Francisco are not often associated with the sport of ice hockey. The San Jose Sharks, however, have become one of the National Hockey League's (NHL) most successful franchises since their inaugural 1991–1992 season, largely because of the team's marketing mix.

The Sharks have averaged yearly attendance figures of at least 99.5% of stadium capacity at the HP Pavilion since 2006 (NHL Attendance Report, 2011). During the 2009–2010 and 2010-2011 seasons, attendance figures reached 100.4% of arena capacity. The Sharks routinely average more fans per game than teams in traditional hockey locations such as Colorado, Detroit, New York, and Boston ("NHL Attendance Report," 2011).

The Sharks' success in selling tickets did not come easily, and rather it is the result of strategic marketing efforts by the organization and its owner, Silicon Valley Sports & Entertainment (SVSE), involving strong community relations and public relations programs. Among the many initiatives started by SVSE and the Sharks, one was to raise awareness of the Sharks' organization among the community's youth, resulting in school visits by the Sharks' mascot, Sharkie, a "Reading is Cool" program for all Kindergarten through Grade 6 schools in Santa Clara County, and the creation of youth hockey leagues. In addition to getting children involved in the sport of hockey at a young age, SVSE also opened and began managing three hockey rinks in three different Bay Area locations: the Oakland Ice Center, Sharks Ice at Fremont, and Sharks Ice at San Jose, thus bringing the sport of hockey to the entire community.

With regard to public relations, the Sharks compete in a media landscape that is heavily saturated with sport organizations, such as the San Francisco and Oakland professional teams, several minor league teams, and college and university athletic programs such as Stanford and the University of California-Berkeley. Instead of battling with other sport organizations for space in the local media outlets during a time in which most media outlets were downsizing in terms of the number of journalists they employed, the Sharks took it upon themselves to constantly create unique content for their website, and to serve as the number one news source for Sharks-related information. The result has been daily news stories on the site, in-depth interviews with players and personnel, and exclusive video content, as well as an online "Fanzone" that includes a chat room, message board, blogs, and a presence on social networking sites such as Twitter and Facebook.

Along with the Sharks' strong community and public relations efforts, the team has been able to keep average ticket prices fairly low compared to the rest of the NHL. In the 2009 season, the Sharks' average single game ticket cost $43.07, which was the 8th lowest average cost out of the 30 NHL teams, an impressive feat for a team located in an area with one of the most expensive cost of living averages in the United States (Team Marketing Report, 2009).

Summary

As you have learned throughout this chapter, the five P's that comprise the marketing mix are important for every sport organization, and must work together in order to successfully carry out an organization's marketing mix. The following exercises allow students to discuss and think critically about the information presented in this chapter.

Discussion Questions

1. How are the five P's of marketing related? Give an example of a sport organization that you know of, and describe how it utilizes the five P's.

2. The chapter described several product extensions offered at sporting events. What other product extensions have you seen at sporting events? What ideas do you have for additional product extensions that might enhance the game experience for fans?

3. Look at the list of distribution-related issues facing Brooks on page 119. Based on what you know about Brooks, discuss these questions and determine the distribution strategy or strategies that you believe would work best for Brooks.

4. After learning about the five P's of marketing, discuss and explain how each P is related to the other four P's.

5. Discuss each of the examples given under the "Marketing Mix Orchestration" section. Determine the product, price, place, promotion, and public relations elements in each example, and discuss how each piece of the marketing mix worked in conjunction with the others to ensure successful marketing for each of the organizations.

Critical Thinking Exercise

Imagine that you are a marketing manager for a local parks and recreation department in an affluent and historically conservative community in Northern Michigan, whose population is around 15,000 people. Following the success of snowboarding at the past few Winter Olympic Games, the department decides to introduce a new winter competitive youth sports league in the sport of halfpipe snowboarding for children ages 6–17. The department already has successful, established winter youth sports leagues in ice hockey, figure skating, and downhill skiing, and recent figures show that 75% of the community's youth are enrolled in at least one of these programs. Prices for participation are traditionally higher than the national average for such programs in order for the parks and recreation department to maintain its facilities and employ instructors and coaches. The department built a new state-of-the-art ice rink three years ago to accommodate the ice hockey and figure skating programs. A large department-owned park is used for the skiing program in the winter, and is used for other outdoor activities in the summer. No halfpipe facilities currently exist, though there is room to build one in the department-owned park if two tennis courts are removed. Based on this limited knowledge of the parks and recreation department, explore the five P's of the marketing mix in order to develop a marketing plan for the new snowboarding program. Outline the details of each of the P's and explain how each one works in conjunction with the others.

References

Associated Press. "Mills' double-double carries Saint Mary's to NIT quarterfinals," March 23, 2009, http://scores.espn.go.com/ncb/recap/_/id/290832166/davidson-wildcats-vs-saint-marys-gaels

Gael Force. (n.d.) http://www.smcgaels.com/ViewArticle.dbml?DB_OEM_ID=21400&ATCLID=1483263

MLB Attendance Report. http://espn.go.com/mlb/attendance/_/year/2011

Mullin, B. J., S. Hardy, and W. Sutton. *Sport marketing.* 2nd ed., Champaign, IL: Human Kinetics, 2000.

NHL Attendance Report. 2011, http://espn.go.com/nhl/attendance

Sporting Goods Manufacturers of America. "SGMA study identifies active segments of U.S. population." July 20, 2010, http://www.sgma.com/press/237_SGMA-Study-Identifies-Active-Segments-of-U.S.-Population

Story, L. "Anywhere the eye can see, it's likely to see an ad." *The New York Times,* January 15, 2007, http://www.nytimes.com/2007/01/15/business/media/15everywhere.html?pagewanted=1&_r=1

Team Marketing Report. "Team marketing research," 2009, http://teammarketing.com.ismmedia.com/ISM3/std-content/repos/Top/News/nhl%20fci%2009-10.pdf

Tyson Fitness Challenge. (n.d.) http://www.tysonfitnesschallenge.com

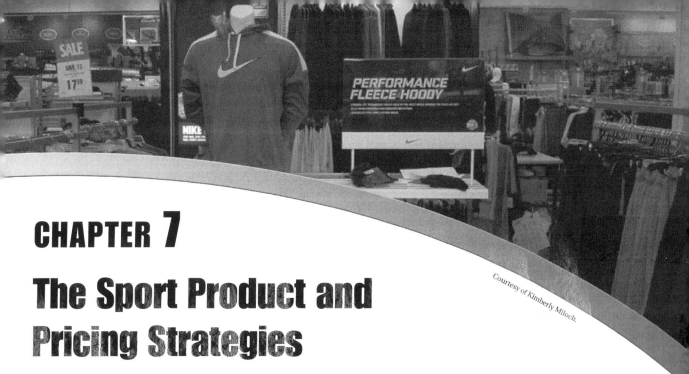

Courtesy of Kimberly Miloch.

CHAPTER 7

The Sport Product and Pricing Strategies

Dr. David Rylander Texas Woman's University
Amy Rundio University of Texas at Austin
Jacquelyn Wilson Texas Woman's University

> *I have discovered, in twenty years of moving around a ball park, that the knowledge of the game is usually in inverse proportion to the price of the seats.*
>
> *Bill Veeck*

CHAPTER OBJECTIVES

After completing the chapter, the reader should be able to:

- Understand the nature of sport products.
- Recognize the importance of branding and positioning.
- Identify how quality can be defined in multiple ways.
- Understand the factors that influence sport pricing.
- Recognize the psychological aspects of price.
- Understand alternative pricing strategies.

Sport Products

As noted in the previous chapter, the sport product can take many forms, but the term often refers to the sport contest or game itself. Sport consumers buy tickets, pay for parking, and navigate the venue to find their seats. In today's sport marketplace, sport consumers expect and demand more than just a ticket for their time, effort, and expense. Expenditures of both time and effort are part of the price paid by consumers in exchange for a product. When the product is a new smart phone or microwave oven, it is relatively easy to define what consum-

Courtesy of Ricky Edison.

ers receive in exchange for their expenditures. However, sport products are more complex and less tangible than traditional products, and they include much more than the competition between two teams.

In many ways, a ticket to a sport event features competition on the field of play and an entertainment or fan experience featuring all elements of the *sportscape* (i.e., all components surrounding the product of sport and the design through which fans experience the product). These sportscape components could include the parking at the sport venue, the in-game promotions and entertainment, and even the interactions with event staff and replays on the jumbotron. The sport product has evolved into a complex and multifaceted product centered on a competition that builds and reinforces emotional attachments and socialization among consumers. This chapter explores the nature of sport products, highlights the unique characteristics of sport products, and outlines the dynamics of pricing sport products.

A product (or offering) can be a tangible good, service, or a combination of the two that provides benefits to a customer as part of an exchange of value. In a broad sense, sport products are offerings directed to spectators, participants, or sponsors (see Table 7.1). Sport products can be categorized as spectator sports (amateur or professional; live or media-based), participation sports (amateur or professional), or sporting goods (including apparel, athletic shoes, equipment and other sports-related products; Fullerton and Merz, 2008). Sponsors, who can include sport marketers or non-sport marketers, can seek access to potential customers through any of these types of sport products.

TABLE 7.1

Spectators	Participants	Sponsors
Amateur (NCAA, NAIA, MiLB, NBA D-League)	Amateur (Little League, High School Sports, Road Races)	Access to potential customers
Professional (MLB, NFL, NHL, NBA, MLS)	Professional (MLB, NFL, NHL, NBA, MLS)	Location to display product/advertising
Can be consumed live or through medium (TV, Internet, radio)	Sporting Goods (apparel, athletic shoes, equipment)	Association with sport team

The sport product can be described in terms of features (e.g., athletic contest, players, sporting arena), but perhaps a more meaningful approach is to define the product as a "bundle of benefits." Benefits for a sport spectator (or fan) could include emotional excitement and camaraderie. Benefits for a sport participant could include improved health and social bonding. Sport sponsors seek benefits such as brand exposure and engagement with potential customers. These benefits of sport products are powerful economic drivers, leading to a gross domestic sport product in the United States estimated to be approximately $168 billion dollars per year (Milano and Chelladurai, 2011).

Goods Vs. Services

Goods are defined as tangible products with physical features that offer benefits to customers. **Services**, as opposed to goods, are intangible, less standardized, perishable from a time perspective, heterogeneous, and often inseparable from the provider. (See Chapter 1 for more service aspects of sport products.) The *intangibility* of the service aspects of sport means that many features and benefits are not easily seen or touched. The entertainment of watching a sporting event is mostly intangible. With intangible products, more emphasis is placed on adding tangible qualities and building a strong brand image. Sports teams add tangibility by emphasizing arena features (e.g., seat comfort), promoting the team brand and/or mascot in a more tangible way (e.g., the University of Texas Longhorns with mascot Bevo), or giving tangible evidence of the experience (e.g., ticket stubs, programs, player autographs).

Tangible sporting goods, such as balls and equipment, are easier to *standardize*. Consistent quality can be manufactured with little variability. However, the quality of a game itself is highly variable. One of the key attractions to sport is the uncertain outcome associated with

Courtesy of Brian Turner.

competition. While consumers enjoy rooting for the Cinderella team and the underdog, they also like knowing their team has a fair chance of winning. While this uncertain outcome can attract fans to the venue, it can also result in levels of dissatisfaction among consumers if their team does not perform well.

Tangibilty/Intangibility

Intangibility refers to the aspects of sport that are not easily seen or touched. Examples include the game itself, the entertainment surrounding the event (during timeouts and at halftime), the atmosphere (loudness at a football game, quiet calm at a golf tournament) and the service provided by staff (polite, friendly, etc.). Without the intangible aspects, the sport product would either not exist or be pretty uninteresting.

© Joyce Michaud, 2012. Under license from Shutterstock, Inc.   © photofriday, 2012. Under license from Shutterstock, Inc.

Adding tangible qualities to sport can enhance the experience of the event and provide evidence of the experience. Stadium design (aisle width, seat comfort, etc.), giveaways and souvenirs (posters, foam fingers, baseball caps), and ticket stubs give evidence of the experience. Adding value to the event through tangible qualities can reduce the risk of attending an event that is primarily intangible.

© Nicemonkey, 2012. Under license from Shutterstock, Inc.

Examples of tangible qualities can include:
- Giveaway items: posters, t-shirts
- Facility features: aisle width, seat comfort, sight lines
- Ticket stubs and programs: game programs and commemorative editions of ticket stubs and programs for special events
- Souvenirs and merchandise: baseball caps, t-shirts, foam fingers
- Concessions: souvenir cups, unique foods

© Eric Broder Van Dyke, 2012. Under license from Shutterstock, Inc.

Given the unpredictability of on-field performance, sport marketers strive to consistently create a high quality entertainment experience to enhance value and satisfaction among consumers. The sportscape has become a core product extension in sport. Particularly, the sportscape is encompassing the factors that the average consumer will appreciate—elements like the comfort of venue seating, leg room, visibility from venue seating, and steepness of walkways. These items are considered to be aesthetic factors; however, they can become important in fan experience and satisfaction.

Elements of Sport Products

The term "sport product" can apply to a variety of offerings. Figure 7.1 illustrates some of the major types of sport products, including sporting events, participatory sports, sport sponsorship, and sports accessories. Each type of sport product has different characteristics and must be marketed in different ways. This section focuses primarily on the sporting event (e.g., professional or collegiate sports). This type of sport product can be experienced in various ways, including in-person attendance at an arena or stadium, viewing on television, listening to the radio broadcast, and viewing or tracking on the Internet. Each of these modes of consumption has a unique mix of product and service elements, as described in Figure 7.2.

FIGURE 7.1
Elements of Sport

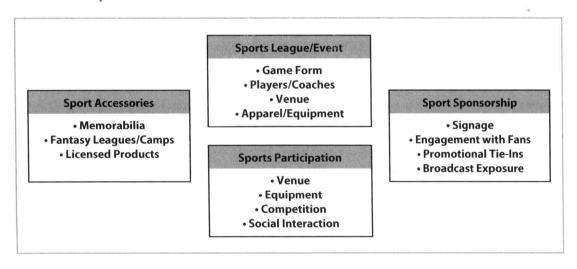

FIGURE 7.2
Ways to Consume Sport

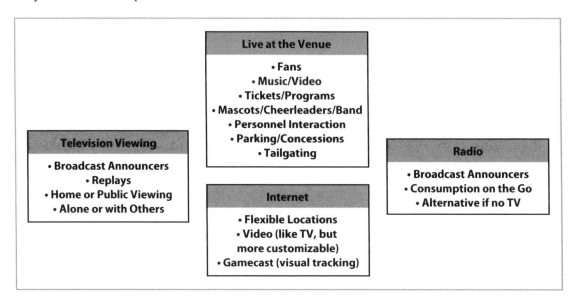

The Sport Product Mix

A group of related products is typically organized into a *product line.* These products may be similar in terms of use, distribution, type of need satisfied, and/or type of customers reached. The total assortment of product lines then becomes the *product mix.* The number of product lines in the mix is described as the *width,* or *breadth,* of the mix. The number of variations within a product line is referred to as the *depth* of the line. Width and depth will vary depending on the type of sport product. For example, the National Football League (NFL) has a primary "product line" of football franchises that field teams which compete against each other. This product line is currently 32 teams deep. Of course, the teams and players are the products that attract the fans (i.e., customers), but the NFL also offers lines of merchandise (e.g., jerseys, pennants, concessions, etc.) to sell to those fans. Some sport leagues may have less depth (i.e., fewer teams) or less width (i.e., fewer lines of merchandise).

There are two specific ways to analyze sport as a product. The core product is the actual competition, including the players, coaches, and sport activity. Additional parts of the sport product are product extensions, which can include ancillary items, such as the mascot, music, halftime or in-game entertainment, plus other factors that bring life and excitement to the game.

For example, the National Basketball Association (NBA) has a primary product line consisting of professional basketball teams. In early years, they had as few as eight teams, but they have now extended their product line depth to 30 teams. In addition, the NBA added a second product line under the Women's National Basketball Association (WNBA) brand. The WNBA began with eight teams, and now operates with 12 teams. The NBA also extended their product mix to the NBA Development League, which serves to develop players on behalf of NBA affiliate teams. Sports league expansion into other products, such as apparel or sporting goods, will often entail licensing, where separate marketers pay to sell merchandise under the league name. Media products such as NBA TV, the NBA's television channel that shows past games, current news, and live games and the NBA's website are other examples of product extension. The NBA has also begun to expand their product globally, through sponsorships, promotions, events, and arena management in China with the ultimate goal of creating an NBA-affiliated league.

Courtesy of Kimberly Miloch.

A sporting goods company would have a more conventional type of product mix. Modell's Sporting Goods has an extensive product mix of tangible sport products, including apparel, sports equipment, exercise equipment, and sport accessories. The product lines can be divided by gender, age, type of sport, type of equipment, or other relevant characteristics. There is no exact science to organizing a product mix and product lines, but it should be done in a way that makes sense from a manufacturing, distribution, usage, and/or customer viewpoint. The drop-down menus on Modell's Sporting Goods website offer an illustration of how the company organized its product mix.

Branding and Positioning

To most sports fans, the names "New York Yankees," "Dallas Cowboys," "Notre Dame Football," "NCAA Final Four," or "Manchester United" conjure up images of the team or event. Images such as the team's logo, script writing, and name all represent a brand that the organization has developed. A **brand** is a verbal or visual way of identifying the sport product as distinguished from other sport product, such as a name, design, symbol, or some combination of the three. Branding is a vital element of the sport product, as it sets it apart from similar products, and will be discussed in more detail in Chapter 12.

The image that comes to mind when you see a brand is called the "position" of the brand. **Brand positioning** refers to "a relatively stable set of consumer perceptions (or meanings) of a brand in relation to competitive alternatives" (Kates and Goh, 2003, 59). Sport marketers will try to position their brands in a special way that has meaning to their fans and helps build brand loyalty. The Yankees may position themselves as "champions," while the Dallas Cowboys have held a position of "America's Team" for over 30 years. Positions may change over time, and sometimes a brand's position is not what was intended, such as the Tampa Bay Devil Rays. In these cases, the sport marketer will try to **reposition** the brand, often using various types of promotion to communicate the intended position.

Tampa Bay Devil Rays

In March 1995, Tampa Bay was awarded a new MLB franchise after a long pursuit. They were positioned as the team that the area had been waiting for. However, they were plagued by poor records, off the field player troubles, and an outdated stadium that caused consumers to lose interest in the product. Their brand position had changed from an exciting new team to one of a perennial last-place team that had lost respect from the baseball and local community.

Then, in 2008, as an effort to reposition the team, the team's new owners unveiled new uniforms, new colors, and a new name. "We were tied to the past, and the past wasn't necessarily something we wanted to be known for. Nobody's running from it or hiding from it, and we're proud of certain aspects of it … I hope and expect the fans who come out will see it as a new beginning," said new principal owner Stuart Sternberg. Since the changes were put into place, the team's record has drastically improved and they have made the playoffs twice. Attendance has also increased by about 30% since the repositioning.

http://www.baseball-reference.com/teams/TBD/attend.shtml

http://sports.espn.go.com/mlb/news/story?id=3101213

Positioning a sport brand can be based on characteristics of the team, the host city, and/or the fans. The Chicago Cubs are positioned as lovable losers, a team that has a devoted following of fans who have endured over 100 years without winning a championship. The team would actually lose some of its brand identity if they were to win the World Series! In the 2011 NBA Championship, the media helped position the Dallas Mavericks as the underdog group of veteran players, led by Dirk Nowitzki, who worked hard and played as a team. They were pitted against the "big three" of LeBron James, Dwyane Wade, and Chris Bosh of the Miami Heat. The Miami Heat were positioned as the super talented (but perceived as arrogant and entitled) team that most fans loved to cheer against. The effective positioning helped attract a large television audience to a championship series that was lacking some of the NBA's more glamorous teams.

Sport brands can be positioned in relation to team attributes, benefits of being a fan, history of the sport franchise, types of fans, how the team compares to other competitors, or possibly even how the team relates to its location. For example, the New Orleans Hornets, as a relatively new NBA team, had to deal with the New Orleans Saints football team winning the Super Bowl. Although they are in different sports, the Hornets still have to compete for emotional and financial support among sport fans in New Orleans. The immense popularity and success of the Saints made it difficult for the Hornets to get media attention and create an identity. They had to find ways to stand out and communicate a consistent positioning message to their fans. Their new position was based on the slogan, "Passion. Purpose. Pride." (Apostolopoulou and Biggers, 2010).

Quality of Sport Products

Consumers expect high quality, but what does that mean for sport products? For tangible sports equipment and apparel, quality can be defined by factors such as performance, durability, and aesthetics. **Service quality** is a more challenging concept, especially in relation to sports. What defines a quality football game? For some, it is the emotion and excitement of the experience. For others it is the quality of play or competition. Some fans might view quality simply as their team winning. Other spectators might be more interested in seeing a close, competitive contest with an exciting finish, regardless of who wins. Quality of the game experience can also be judged based on factors such as comfort, parking convenience, responsiveness of personnel, social interactions, and supplemental entertainment.

The key to defining quality is to view it from the customer's (fan's) perspective. Different customers will seek different dimensions of quality, including product performance, features, reliability, conformity, durability, serviceability, aesthetics, and perceived quality. A sport marketer must identify segments of customers by their varying perceptions of quality, using the different dimensions, in order to attract and retain consumers. This can be a challenge for those in sport management. People working in a sport likely have a strong interest and commitment to the sport, but they might not understand that many fans do not have the same passion. Some fans are more interested in the quality of the ancillary activities. The full game experience must then be designed to appeal to the most important quality dimensions for the targeted segments.

Innovation and the Product Life Cycle

As with any industry, the sport industry is constantly evolving. While tradition is important in sports, innovation can be critical to staying relevant. Even the traditionalist sport product of Major League Baseball (MLB) has added lights, indoor stadiums, the designated hitter, additional playoff teams, and even instant replay in select instances. The NFL and the National Hockey League (NHL) consistently change rules to protect the safety of fans and players, and to enhance the game. In more traditional sports, small innovations can help improve the experience for fans, without interfering with the fundamental nature of the sport.

A greater degree of innovation is necessary when new or niche sports are invented or popularized. There are always new sports being invented, such as Bossaball, a combination of volleyball, soccer, gymnastics, and capoeira. Other sports have been around longer but are newly developed for larger markets. For example, the X Games have elevated BMX and skateboarding to larger scale televised sports. The X Games began as the Extreme Games in 1995, with 198,000 spectators and seven sponsors ("Overview: A brief history of the X Games," n.d.). The event has grown into Summer and Winter X Games, with multiple extreme sports, including Moto X, Rally Car, snowboarding, new ski events, and snowmobile. Younger people in particular are attracted to new sports and games, so innovation can attract a young market. The X Games have scored well with the young male market, but they will have to continue to innovate as the novelty erodes.

When new products (e.g., new sports) are introduced, they enter what is called a **product life cycle (PLC)**. The *introduction stage* is when a new sport or product is introduced and customers begin trying it. Some products are not accepted at this stage and immediately decline, while other products find a market and begin to grow in acceptance. New sports, such as Bossaball, must find ways to educate and engage people in the introduction stage. This can be difficult when specialized equipment or playing arenas are required, or if the sport is too complicated. People are more apt to adopt the new sport if it is easy to learn and try.

A new sport product that has a successful introduction will advance to the *growth stage* of the PLC. This is where product adoption begins to rapidly expand to new markets. This stage can last a long time if the product continues to expand internationally. In growth, the marketer must: (1) establish a strong market position to defend against potential competition, (2) make necessary adjustments and build a long-term strategy, and (3) repay initial investments and generate enough profit to justify continuation of the product.

When growth slows, the sport product enters the *maturity stage* of the PLC. This is a point where most potential markets have been reached and the product should be generating strong cash flow. With traditional products, maturity usually means a large number of competitors and downward pressure on pricing. Sport products, however, might experience more of a monopolistic effect. For example, as Mixed Martial Arts (MMA) approached maturity, the Ultimate Fighting Championship (UFC) brand acquired the top fighters and began to rise as the dominant league for that sport—just as the NBA and NFL became the "monopolistic" leagues in basketball and football. The NCAA holds a similar position of strength in college sports. Successful sport leagues can enjoy extended time in the maturity phase, and even periods of new growth.

There is no prescribed length for PLC stages, and the maturity phase can last a long time (e.g., the main professional sports leagues in the United States) or a short time (e.g., fads that come and go quickly). A sport or other product can also be in different PLC stages in different parts of the world. Soccer has been a strong, mature sport for a long time in most of the world, but it is still in the growth stage in the United States. There are several ways a sport product can stay in maturity longer; some examples are: (1) develop strong brand loyalty; (2) develop leagues for children and amateurs that generate interest and feed into professional leagues; (3) have consistent quality, but make changes that enhance the experience for players and fans; (4) develop partnerships with other brands, media outlets, and cities; and (5) continue to expand to new markets.

Eventually, all types of products will likely reach the *decline stage* of the PLC. This could be due to loss of interest, more attractive competition from other products or any number of political or social changes. Most sports are enjoying strong attendance, but boxing is a sport that is seeing some decline. The twentieth century experienced a run of popularity for boxing, as multiple stars dominated the scene. The twenty-first century, however, has lacked the big names, especially in the heavyweight division. More champions have also come from places outside the United States. These factors have contributed to a decline in United States popularity. Another major factor is the rise of MMA. This sport has drawn away from boxing the attention of fight spectators and the media. Now many fans are more likely to splurge for a pay-per-view MMA night than for a boxing night. Boxing is not dead, but the sport must

Product Life Cycle Graph

It can take years, decades, or longer for a product to progress through all of the stages in the product life cycle. With technology, however, the product life cycle is much shorter, as new technology quickly replaces older technology today. For example, the DVD was introduced in the late 1990s and began replacing the older VHS movies, and the DVD is being replaced today by Blu-Ray and Live Streaming of movies. Another example from technology includes mobile phones. The original cell phone came out in 1984, and was the size of a brick. Phones quickly became smaller and easier to carry. Today's phones have even advanced beyond merely making phone calls and can take pictures, surf the Internet, play music, and more. The graph below shows what the product life cycle looks like in terms of sales and time, and shows products in each stage of the life cycle.

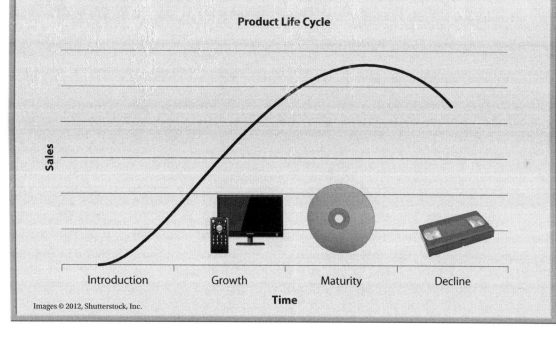

Product Life Cycle

Sales

Introduction   Growth   Maturity   Decline

Time

Images © 2012, Shutterstock, Inc.

re-position itself and develop some star fighters that people will want to see. Products in decline can still find some success and maybe even begin to grow again, but the decline stage is a time to re-evaluate the future and consider what changes are necessary for long-term success.

Pricing of Sport Products

As mentioned in the previous chapter, price is the amount a customer pays for a product. A well-designed sport product has value to customers, and that value is captured by the price. The price in sport marketing is highly visible and can greatly influence sales. The price is easy to change, but the response to the change may be difficult to predict. There are many elements to consider when determining a price, and numerous strategies for presenting the price.

Factors Influencing Sport Pricing

Setting the appropriate price for a sport marketing product depends on multiple factors. These influences can be examined in a "5 C's" framework: company, costs, customers, competition, and conditions.

Company factors include the mission, objectives, and business philosophies of the organization. This includes the organization's goals and all costs associated with producing the event or product. Sport organizations can be driven by profit objectives (i.e., targeting a specific rate of return; trying to maximize profit), volume objectives (i.e., maximizing total revenue or attendance), or image objectives (i.e., maintaining a prestige image; winning even if it means losing money). The objectives of the sport company will drive the basic approach to setting prices. Some organizations want to maximize attendance, so they would keep prices lower. Other organizations seek to maximize profit or revenue, which could lead to higher pricing. Some seats might be priced extremely high to establish the prestige of sitting there.

Costs must factor into any pricing decision. If revenue (generated by price × quantity sold) does not meet or exceed total costs, then the organization loses money. Therefore, price and cost decisions must be made together. How do you know how much you can pay an athlete (a cost to the organization) without having an estimate of expected revenue? How can you set a price without knowing that the price will be enough to exceed the cost? This is further complicated by fixed versus variable costs. Many of the costs of a sport organization are *fixed,* meaning they must be paid regardless of how many people come to the events. Fixed costs include guaranteed player contracts and fixed facility expenses (e.g., basic labor needed to run the facility, ownership, or lease costs). The *variable* costs are only incurred for each fan who attends the sport event. These can include ticket handling costs and variable facility costs (e.g., restroom use, cleanup). Most sport products are high in fixed costs but low in variable costs. That is, the cost of one additional fan attending a sport event is very low, but the total revenue must be enough to cover the high fixed costs of the event. Therefore, the base price should be high enough to target total cost coverage, but selective price discounting can be a valuable strategy for adding sales volume. Even a half-price ticket will provide more than enough revenue to cover the variable costs associated with the additional customer.

Customers are critical to the pricing equation. Consumers determine what the market will bear in terms of price, and they determine the value associated with ticket price. Sport marketers need to understand influences on customer demand and how consumers will respond to price changes, which is explained by the *price elasticity of demand,* which is the degree to which demand for a good or service varies with its price (Mankiw, 2009, 90–98). If the percentage change in customers is greater than the change in price, then you have *elastic* demand. If the percentage change in customers is less than the change in price, then you have *inelastic* demand. If the change in demand equals the change in price, you have *unitary* demand.

As an example, if a ticket price was increased from $20 to $25 (25% increase) and corresponding attendance dropped from 30,000 to 24,000 (20% decrease), then you have inelastic demand. If attendance dropped by more than 25% in this example, you would have elastic demand. Under normal circumstances, this indicates that a company can increase revenue by increasing prices if demand is inelastic. However, in a sport marketing context, the reduction in fans might not be worth the increase in revenue. If demand is elastic, the sport marketer can increase revenue *and* attendance by lowering prices. In the case of many popular sports teams, demand tends to be more inelastic. Top college football teams, many NFL and NBA teams, and select other teams (e.g., Boston Red Sox) are able to sell out all of their tickets to just about every game. In most cases, a price increase would not deter a sellout, meaning the demand is inelastic.

Competition is the fourth "C" that must be considered when establishing prices. Competition can be same-sport, same-level (e.g., two major league baseball teams in Chicago), same-sport, different-level (e.g., college football team in same city as a professional football team), different sports (e.g., hockey and basketball running concurrent seasons, sometimes sharing an arena) or non-sport competition (e.g., other types of entertainment). Sports in major cities will likely face heavy competition at all of these levels. Sports in smaller markets may have more limited competitive alternatives. Sport customers might make price judgments based on any of these types of competitors. For example, a $40 ticket to a professional basketball game might seem high compared to a $15 ticket to a college game, but the same ticket seems low compared to a price of $75 for a concert.

The final "C" is *conditions*. This includes any aspects of the external marketing environment that could have an effect on costs or pricing perceptions. The major types of conditions include the economy (e.g., may have to reduce prices in a recession since sport products are not necessities), technology (e.g., new technology allows lower cost and more convenience in delivering tickets over the Internet or through mobile devices), cultural (e.g., growing Hispanic population opens new market opportunities for some sports), legal (e.g., laws restricting ticket resale) and physical (e.g., weather effects). Sport marketers must track trends in these areas and understand possible impacts on their customer demand and pricing approaches.

Given the complexity and intangibility of many sport products, pricing is often one of the most challenging elements of the marketing mix. If a price is too low, profits can suffer and the image of the sport product can be weakened. If a price is too high, attendance can drop and fans may be lost for a longer term. The price to attend a football game, for example, can include the ticket (which varies according to seat location, services, etc.), parking (which may be bundled with the game ticket), concessions, souvenirs, and the time and monetary costs of getting to the game. The sport marketer's job is to ensure that the experience of the game is perceived to be worth the summation of perceived costs to the fan.

Value

Price is a key variable influencing customers' perceived value of the sport experience. *Value* is defined as the perceived benefits of the sport product divided by the perceived price. It is important to note that "perceived price" might not be equal to the actual price paid for a ticket. Customers may perceive price in different ways, especially if the ticket was purchased as part of a bundle of tickets or other products. The perceived price can also include the other additional costs involved with attending the event (e.g., parking, distance driven, concessions, time).

One way to view the total perceived cost of an event is the Fan Cost Index (FCI), where the cost to attend a sporting event is analyzed on the pricing for a family of four. It includes the following items to determine the cost to attend an event:

- Four "average" tickets
- Two small draft beers
- Four small soft drinks
- Four hot dogs
- Two game programs
- Two adult-size caps
- Parking for one vehicle

The Fan Cost Index allows pricing to be compared to other events and illustrates the expenditures necessary for a family to attend a sport event. As seen in Table 7.2 from the Team Marketing Report, the FCI can vary greatly within a professional sport league as well as between sports. The variations are most closely related to demand differences and other market factors.

TABLE 7.2

Fan Cost Index—2011	
League—Team- High, Average, Low	**Price**
Major League Baseball—Boston Red Sox (H)	$339.01
Major League Baseball—Average	$197.35
Major League Baseball—Arizona Diamondbacks (L)	$120.96
National Football League—New York Jets (H)	$628.90
National Football League—Average	$427.42
National Football League—Jacksonville Jaguars (L)	$319.06
National Basketball Association—New York Knicks (H)	$505.64
National Basketball Association—Average	$287.85
National Basketball Association—Memphis Grizzlies (L)	$173.72
National Hockey League—Toronto Maple Leafs (H)	$626.45
National Hockey League—Average	$326.45
National Hockey league—Dallas Stars (L)	$223.78

Source: https://www.teammarketing.com/btSubscriptions/fancostindex/index

Psychology of Pricing

As mentioned previously, customer perception is a critical factor when it comes to concepts like quality, value, and price. Why would one person think it is an acceptable value to spend thousands of dollars for seat licenses and season tickets for a professional football team, while someone else thinks that $50 is way too much for a ticket to see the same team? Why do customers respond violently to price changes in one situation, but not respond at all to price changes in another situation? Much research has been directed at the psychology of pricing. Some of the key psychological concepts related to sport marketing are briefly explained here.

Courtesy of Kimberly Miloch.

Consumers often judge a price based on some **reference price**. This can be a competitor's price, a stated "regular" price, or a price someone expects based on previous experience or value judgment. A price of $40 for a basketball game can seem high if the reference price is based on similar games that charge only $25. The same price can appear low to someone who is accustomed to paying $75 for concerts or other events. Giving customers the right frame of reference (i.e., a high reference price) can help them perceive price as lower or as a better value.

Price can also be used to communicate a distinct image through **prestige pricing**. The Boston Red Sox charge unusually high prices for certain seats to help maintain an exclusive image. NBA courtside seats enjoy a similar aura of prestige, with a corresponding high price. Those seats can have even higher perceived worth when you could be sitting close to Jack Nicholson or Spike Lee. High profile boxing matches will likewise set prestige prices for ringside seats, which are frequently occupied by celebrities.

Many other psychological pricing concepts can play a role in consumer perceptions. **Odd-even pricing** involves prices that are just below whole number (e.g., $49.95 instead of $50). Consumers perceive the lower price as a greater value despite the small difference. The concept of just noticeable difference (JND) also plays a role in perceptions. There is a range of change that most consumers will not notice. When a price is changed beyond this JND range, consumers will react more dramatically to the change in price. Thus, price increases should be below this level, while price decreases must be big enough to be noticeable. The "magic" amount of price change varies for different products and situations, so it requires some research and judgment.

On the other hand, sometimes it is difficult to change prices at all. This is the case with **customary pricing**, where customers expect a certain traditional price, such as $5 "cheap seats." Customary pricing is especially strong where consumers are used to consuming their sports for free. Major sports have long been able to be seen for free on broadcast or packaged cable television. They are able to continue offering the broadcast for free as long as advertisers are willing to pay to sponsor the programming. A move to pay-per-view would be difficult for most fans to accept. Some core fans would pay the price, but the sport would risk losing many other fans who refuse to pay (and therefore stop watching the sport).

Sport Pricing Strategies

Taking into consideration the many influencing factors and psychological factors of pricing, sport marketers have several approaches to consider in determining a pricing strategy. Products and services can be priced individually or **bundled**. Season tickets or partial season ticket packages will often be bundled with ancillary items such as parking or other specialty products or services. An opposite approach is to charge a single price for a ticket, but then charge separate (and typically high) price for other items. This *captive pricing* strategy might keep the ticket price reasonable, while charging unusually high prices for food, drinks, and souvenirs. Customers are not as price sensitive in this case since they do not have alternative choices and are likely to expect higher prices in those situations.

Price discounting is another important decision area. Discounting (i.e., lowering) a price is a promotional tool that can stimulate demand or reward desired behaviors. Discounts can encourage customers to buy more tickets (e.g., quantity discount for groups or multi-game ticket packages), to buy seats that are not expected to sell for a particular game, or to encourage early purchasing or off-season purchasing (e.g., reducing ski resort prices during slow times). Many sporting events have a low marginal cost for each additional fan. That is, the cost of selling one more ticket is low (printing of the ticket, marginal utility, and cleanup cost). Therefore, it can make sense to discount the ticket. The sport marketer still makes a marginal profit and can earn more profit from the higher margin concession sales.

Promotional discounting is a tempting tool for boosting sales or attendance, but there are potential dangers. When you discount the price of a product, you are saying that it might not be worth the full price. This can discount the value (and reference price) of the product/brand in the minds of consumers. In addition, too much discounting leads to consumers expecting to pay less. It will then become increasingly difficult to sell at regular prices. Discounts cut into profit margins, so this approach should be used with strategic discretion. Discounts can also start price wars with competitors, in which companies continually lower prices in order to stay competitive and sell their product. The prices can be driven so low that profit margins become negligible.

Sport pricing strategies also include structured tools like the break-even analysis, cost-plus pricing and variable ticket pricing. The **break-even analysis** for sport product pricing is the point at which total costs (i.e., fixed costs + variable costs) equals total revenue. This is figured by dividing the fixed costs by the contribution margin, which is price minus the variable cost per unit (i.e., fan). The equation below is used to calculate how many unit sales would be needed in order to break even (i.e., make exactly zero profit). Once the break-even point (BE) has been reached, any sales above that point go toward profit.

$$BEunits = \frac{F}{PV}$$

Assume fixed costs (F), including stadium rental, taxes, and equipment, are $500,000. Variable costs (V), including wages, materials, and cost of food and drink at concessions, are $10 per fan attending an event. If the price (P) paid per fan is $30, the break-even point is determined as

$$500{,}000 \ / \ (30\text{-}10) = 500{,}000 \ / \ 20 = 25{,}000 \text{ units (fans)}$$

Another tool for pricing is **cost-plus pricing**, where a fixed percentage mark-up is added to the cost of a product. This is more common with tangible sport products, such as equipment or souvenirs. The cost for an item could include material and labor costs, licensing costs and other supplemental costs in the production or distribution of the item. The seller adds a mark-up to the cost in order to arrive at the final price to the customer. For example, if the total unit cost for an autographed football is $40, a mark-up of 50% would add $20, resulting in a selling price of $60.

Break-even analysis and cost-plus pricing are basic formula approaches for determining prices and expected profit. Today, sport organizations are beginning to practice more complex pricing models. **Variable ticket pricing** involves multiple price points. This idea of "smoothing" or variable pricing is where two different prices are changed based on prime and non-prime schedules. This has been most noticed within the sport product category with seat location within a stadium or venue. There are several factors that enhance the variable ticket price, such as proximity to the field or court, line of site and extras (e.g., parking, food service, or even a swimming pool beyond the outfield wall). At some events, tickets can range from $7 for outfield seats to $170 for seats box seats. Organizations are able to charge this because the ticket demand will allow it.

Another way in which variable ticket pricing is evident is the day or date of the scheduled event, a game on a Tuesday at 2:05 p.m. could be lower priced than Saturday night at 7:05 p.m. Special event games tend to be higher priced, like opening days in baseball and homecoming in football. This expanded variable pricing has led to **dynamic pricing** by many sport teams. In this case, prices can change daily based on a set of variables (Muret and Lombardo, 2010). For example, the San Francisco Giants use approximately twenty variables to determine fluctuating prices for 2,000 of their seats (Lemire et al., 2009). People are willing to pay more when a star pitcher is on the mound or if the Giants are hosting the rival Dodgers in a close race for the division lead. This dynamic pricing approach is similar to the complex algorithms used by airlines to frequently alter the prices of their tickets according to demand patterns.

In the end, sport marketers provide a multi-faceted product, much of it intangible, and try to capture value through appropriate pricing. The more the product is enhanced or differentiated (e.g., winning team, popular players, nicer stadium, attractive promotions), the more power they have to charge higher prices.

Variable Ticket Pricing

Variable ticket pricing has allowed many sport organizations to maximize revenue by adjusting prices based on many factors. Dynamic pricing has allowed sport organizations to go one step further and constantly adjust their prices based on an even wider variety of factors. Sport organizations that have utilized dynamic pricing include teams from the MLB, NHL, NBA, MLS, and even NASCAR tracks.

The St. Louis Cardinals introduced dynamic pricing in 2011 using a computer program that allowed the team to adjust ticket prices daily based on changing factors like team performance, opponent performance, pitching matchups, and weather. Their primary goal was to "get more fans to more [of our] games," according to Joe Strohm, Vice President of Ticket Sales. Dynamic pricing also allows them to widen the ticket-purchasing fan base, to reward those fans who buy earlier in the season, and to protect season ticket holders' value.

Source: St. Louis Cardinals website, http://mlb.mlb.com/stl/ticketing/dynamic.jsp.

Variable ticket pricing has been utilized in college football at the University of Texas and Texas A&M football teams. As you can see below, each team has adjusted their prices based on the quality and popularity of the opponent, allowing each team to sell as many tickets as possible for each game.

Variable Ticket Pricing in College Football

University of Texas 2011 Home Football Schedule			Texas A&M 2011 Home Football Schedule		
Sep. 3	Rice	$70	Sep. 4	SMU	$50
Sep. 10	BYU	$85	Sep. 17	Idaho	$50
Oct. 8	Oklahoma (in Dallas)	$110	Sep. 24	Oklahoma State	$80
Oct. 15	Oklahoma State	$85	Oct. 15	Baylor	$80
Oct. 29	Kansas	$75	Oct. 29	Missouri	$80
Nov. 5	Texas Tech	$95	Nov. 19	Kansas	$70
Nov. 19	Kansas State	$75	Nov. 24	Texas	$100

Source: University of Texas Athletic Website, http://www.texassports.com/tickets/m-footbl-ticket-info.html and Texas A&M University Athletic Website, http://www.12thmanfoundation.com/ticket-center/football/home-game-tickets.aspx.

For consumers, it will be less expensive to attend games against weaker or less popular opponents, but more expensive to attend the games that everybody else wants to be at. Consumers who might not have gone to a game before, might go to a less expensive game because the opportunity cost is less for them. Diehard fans, however, are likely to still attend all games and pay the higher prices.

Discussion Questions

1. Compare a tangible sport product (e.g., a football) with a less tangible one (e.g., watching a football game). How will the marketing be different for each product?

2. Look at the product mix at www.modells.com. How wide is their product mix (i.e., number of product lines)? How deep are their product lines (i.e., number of variations in each line)?

3. Think of two professional sports teams with very different images (e.g., Dallas Cowboys and Oakland Raiders). How are the teams' brands positioned differently? What has contributed to these different positions (i.e., brand images)?

4. Discuss the quality of the experience of attending a baseball game from different perspectives of quality: emotional, social, and practical aspects.

5. Explain reasons why it might be a good strategy to raise prices for a professional sporting event. Consider product, customer, cost, and other potential influences.

6. Why might some people view $20 as too much for a ticket to a sporting event, while others view $50 as a bargain? Think of multiple possible reasons.

7. Name three sport products that are currently in each stage of the Product Life Cycle (PLC).

Critical Thinking Exercises

1. Select three sport products. Conduct an analysis of those products and determine each product's stage in the Product Life Cycle. Develop a marketing strategy or promotion for each product based on its stage in the Product Life Cycle. Share your strategies or promotions with your classmates, and discuss why the strategies or promotions you developed are most appropriate for each product in its respective stage in the Product Life Cycle.

2. Select at least three sport entities providing similar products (i.e., minor league baseball, major league soccer, major league hockey, high school sport events, college athletic events). Conduct a ticket pricing analysis for each sport entity. Your ticket pricing analysis should include the sport pricing strategy utilized as well as the tangible and intangible benefits of purchasing tickets (or in many cases season tickets, mini season ticket plans, group tickets, etc.). Compare the ticket pricing and benefits for each sport entity. Based on the comparison, develop and write recommendations for modifying the pricing strategy or enhancing the tangible and intangible benefits offered to sport consumers. Share your findings and your recommendations with your classmates.

References

Apostolopoulou, A. and M. Biggers. "Positioning the New Orleans Hornets in the 'Who Dat?' City." *Sport Marketing Quarterly,* 19(4) (2010): 229–234.

Fullerton, S., and G. R. Merz. "The four domains of sports marketing." *Sport Marketing Quarterly,* 17(2) (2008): 90–108.

Garvin, David A. "Competing on the Eight Dimensions of Quality." *Harvard Business Review,* November–December 1987.

Kates, S. M. and C. Goh. "Brand morphing: Implications for advertising theory and practice." *Journal of Advertising,* 32(1) (2003): 39–68.

Lemire, J., M. Bechtel, S. Cannella, and K. Kennedy. "Tickets with Flex." *Sports Illustrated,* 110(8) (2009).

Mankiw, N. G. *Principles of economics.* 6th ed., Mason, OH: South-Western Cengage Learning, (2009): 90–98.

Milano, M., and P. Chelladurai. "Gross domestic sport product: The size of the sport industry in the United States." *Journal of Sport Management,* 25(1) (2011): 24–35.

Muret, D. and J. Lombardo. "NBA clubs adopt dynamic pricing." *Street & Smith's Sportsbusiness Journal,* 13(16) (2010): 6.

Overview: A brief history of the X Games. (n.d.) http://www.espneventwrapups.com/xgamesfourteen/About/Overview.aspx

Wakefield, K. L., J. G. Blodgett and H. J. Sloan. "Measurement and management of sportscape." *Journal of Sport Management,* 10 (1996): 15–31.

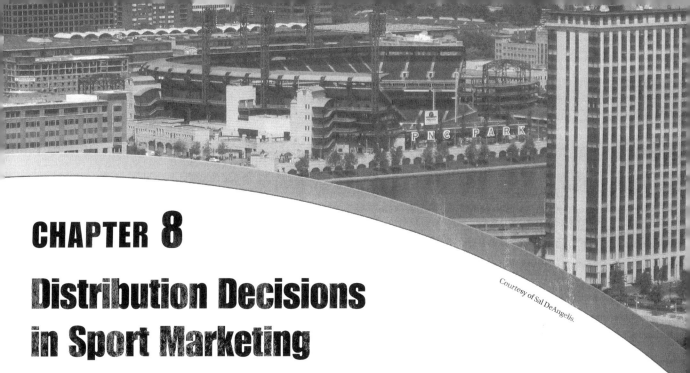

Courtesy of Sal DeAngelis.

CHAPTER 8

Distribution Decisions in Sport Marketing

Salvatore DeAngelis Philadelphia Phillies
Chad Seifried Louisiana State University
Bonnie L. Parkhouse

> *No matter where you live and what team you root for, the baseball park evokes emotions unlike any other kind of athletic facility. Even in a time when the sport is struggling to compete with increasingly popular team sports like football, basketball, and even hockey, the baseball field holds a special place in the hearts and minds of generations of fans. New parks continue to be greeted with great enthusiasm by local communities. Fans travel hundreds or thousands of miles to experience the sights, the sounds, the smells, and the tastes of these baseball homes.*
>
> *(Leventhal, 2006, 6)*

CHAPTER OBJECTIVES

After completing the chapter, the reader should be able to:

- Discuss the importance of operations/facility management to sport marketing.
- Differentiate between mission statements, goals, and objectives.
- Appreciate that marketing mix including facility elements such as accessibility and transportation issues, facility design, venue amenities, and staffing.
- Understand that event and facility aesthetics impact satisfaction and relationships with prospective clients.
- Recognize that security and risk management programs are essential to ensuring all participants (i.e., spectators, media, players, administrators, vendors, etc.) experience a safe environment.
- Realize that high-quality customer service is the life-blood of any sports and entertainment venue.

Introduction

Facilities have numerous components requiring management, and the failure of any single component can have a disastrous impact on other components or the entire event (Fried, 2009). Appropriately, facility operations managers enjoy numerous duties to make sure that every aspect of the event runs smoothly. Their responsibilities generally focus on creating the most consistent, safe, aesthetically appealing, and accessible environment possible for invitees (i.e., live and remote) and participants. Five elements characterize job description of operations managers: Consistency, Location, Aesthetics, Security, and Service (CLASS). Appreciating the meaning of these words allows operations managers to achieve their primary goals: safety for all spectators, athletes, and employees, and the creation of value associated with their product and services.

Consistency

Facility managers are responsible for a myriad of disciplines including construction, security, housekeeping, capital projects/improvements, human resources, and customer service. Excellent managerial, organizational, and time management skills are a necessity for this profession because facility operations managers, like marketers, have no control over the core product (i.e., game or event). Of course, it is easier to market a facility and event when the team wins. Whether the core product is ineffective or not, the operations manager should capitalize on and use product extensions (e.g., concessions, promotions, ticket discounts) and features of the facility (e.g., cleanliness, sightlines) to entice consumption and loyalty among fans. Recognizing several key managerial functions will help facility managers and marketers involved with operations management establish consistency through effectiveness and efficiency in coordinating financial, physical, and human resources.

Managerial Functions

Bridges and Roquemore (1996) famously identified four primary functions of management: planning, organizing, implementing, and controlling. Planning should be considered as an important activity because it appears futuristic and helps minimize potential problems. Appropriately, sport operations managers should seek to work ahead or anticipate possible outcomes and events because it helps create a more effective, efficient, and knowledgeable/skilled end product to deal with invitee and participant problems, requests, or preferences. Organizing emerges as an important function because it helps guarantee everyone involved with operations management works or learns together toward common goals and objectives. During the organizing function, an administrator coordinates these resources (i.e., financial, physical, and human) to accomplish objectives. Overall, the activities of planning and organizing help operations managers maximize the efficiency of all resources and participants (i.e., coaches, students, parents, etc.) and in production of valuable end products and services.

During the implementation phase of management, operations managers need to understand the work habits and skill sets of employees. They must also possess a firm understanding of the culture and climate among personnel in order to most appropriately implement policies and strategies that benefit the achievement of the organization's operational goals and objectives. Finally, controlling acts as an important function of operations management. Controlling serves to make sure everyone learns and performs at the appropriate pace and that the program's events and personnel and services continue to operate on schedule and that the organization is functioning in a manner that will maximize efforts to meet organizational goals and objectives. Summative and formative evaluations of job performance are useful in assessing strengths and weaknesses of employees and assessing their respective roles in assisting the organization in meetings its goals and objectives. Bolino and Turnley (2003) suggested using evaluations in this manner tends to be more accurate because it helps provide important information related to job performance versus the alternative (i.e., rewarding generalized personality traits), which may occur during the formal evaluation process.

In order to achieve success with these functions of management, the operations manager and marketer should focus on the organization's *mission statement.* A mission statement provides operational direction and sets the foundation for the development of organizational goals and objectives (Bartkus and Glassman, 2005). As a written guide to reflect policies and procedures within an organization, the mission statement serves to broadly describe the firm's stakeholder management philosophy.

The mission statement for the Pro Football Hall of Fame in Canton, Ohio can be found on their website.

Goals and Objectives

Mission statements should not be confused with goals or objectives. **Goals** are broad based or general statements designed to provide programmatic direction and typically focus on ends rather than means (Allison and Kaye, 2005; Le Blanc, 2008). Goals are most appropriate when they identify or categorize major responsibilities or pursuits and areas of need programmatically or organizationally. Goals should precede objectives, and be developed based on the mission statement. **Objectives** are then developed from the organization's respective goals and outline details or strategies for meeting each goal. (Allison and Kaye, 2005; Le Blanc, 2008). In order to write these statements of action, objectives must be measurable, realistic, clear and concise, specific, and possess some respect for time (i.e., time-limited/phased through dates and time).

Generally, two types of objectives will be created by operations managers: **outcome objectives** and **process objectives**. Outcome objectives identify the end result or outcome for users of the organization's products and services as a result of their participation. Outcome objectives typically begin with phrases like "to improve, to reduce, to upgrade, to demote, etc." and are aimed at helping to change client or consumer behavior, skill, or awareness (Allision and Kaye, 2005). Process objectives serve to specify a tactic, action, or means to achieve outcome objectives. Also known as action objectives, these objectives generally use terms such as "to implement, to develop, to establish, to conduct" as a way to characterize activities or tactics used by the firm (Allison and Kaye, 2005, 238).

Personnel Organizing

In order for operations managers to adequately achieve their assigned responsibilities, they must be able to delegate tasks. Excellent human resource management and great leadership qualities are vital in operating a successful venue. Finding an employee with the right skill sets for a specific job is not an easy task. To do this, managers may have to rotate personnel into different positions or change job descriptions to best suit both employees' and the organization's needs. This transition may be unpopular and employees may not support their new roles. Thus, continuous evaluation of the transition is necessary.

Proper resources and training should be provided to employees, particularly when transitioning to new positions. Training and orientation programs and guided facility tours serve as excellent examples to improve employee performance. In addition to creating specific job descriptions, defining job qualifications, providing resources, and identifying appropriate responsibilities, a manager must also specify and adhere to organizational relationships (Fried, 2009). Organizational charts are a symbolic representation of an organization's hierarchy, but they do not always guarantee a leadership dedication. The Ohio State University Department of Athletics has created a complex organizational chart/structure to support its position as one of the most comprehensive athletic programs in the country. The graphic on the following page represents an order of responsibility and obligations but not necessarily a following or dedication to leadership.

Location

One could argue that sports are no different than any other real estate venture—the most important factors are location, location, and location. Since the core sport product is typically a competition or a game of some form and since it is simultaneously produced and consumed, it is prudent that the venue should maximize exposure. Location of the stadium or venue, coupled with pleasing aesthetics and surroundings, is critical to the experience of every participant (i.e., live or remote). As a central element of any sports gathering, the sport venue acts as an essential element to the marketing mix and includes a number of components that influence the attractiveness of the event. This consists of accessibility and transportation issues, design, amenities, and staffing.

Accessibility and Parking

Sport facilities should be close to major highways and public transportation systems to maximize accessibility to potential spectators and consumers of their products and services. This concept is particularly important to those facilities within urban settings and to those targeting senior citizens, youth, and lower economic groups. The history of this practice is strong and dates to the nineteenth century when sport entrepreneurs decided to build sport facilities close to local trolley and railroad lines. This allowed potential consumers located outside the city centers easier and often direct access to the venue (Seifried and Pastore,

The Ohio State University Department of Athletics Organizational Chart (2010)

As of 10/10

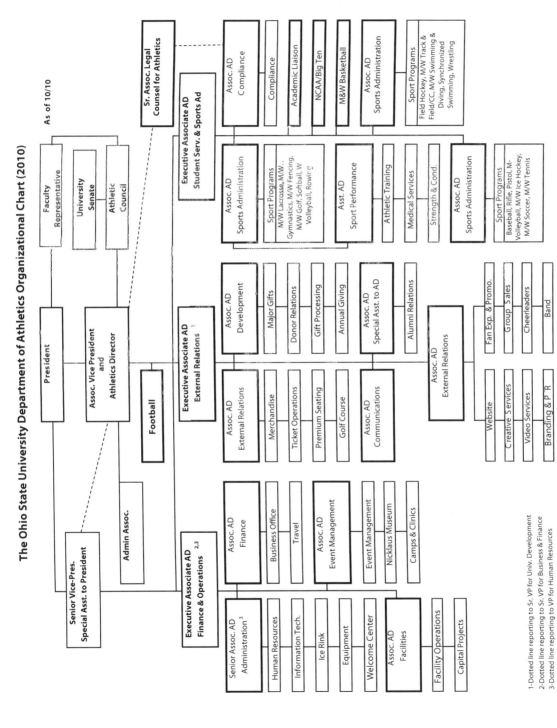

1-Dotted line reporting to Sr. VP for Univ. Development
2-Dotted line reporting to Sr. VP for Business & Finance
3-Dotted line reporting to VP for Human Resources

Courtesy of The Ohio State University Department of Athletics. Reprinted by permission.

Courtesy of Sal DeAngelis.

2009a). As ballparks, stadiums, and arenas continued to move away from city centers during the "cookie cutter era" of publicly funded facilities, highway access became critical to the survival of any potential ballpark or venue because car loving Americans desired to drive their personal automobiles to the event (Seifried and Pastore, 2009b).

Appropriately, firms recognized the need for accessible facilities and designed venues to incorporate and address traffic demands prior to, during, and following events. As an example, the sports complex in South Philadelphia (Citizens Bank Park, Lincoln Financial Field, and Wells Fargo Center) is easily accessible by two major highways (i.e., Interstate 95 and 76). Further, a small percentage of subway riders attend Philadelphia games even though the facility has more than 20,000 on-site parking spots. Most professional venues today utilize a similar parking strategy to invite people to their respective events, but some venues are heavily enclosed and do not have ample parking. For instance, Fenway Park (Boston), Wrigley Field (Chicago), Yankee Stadium (New York) produce a much higher use of public transportation ridership due to the limited parking available in their neighborhood settings.

From these examples, traffic flow appears to be an extremely important part of a patron's visit to a major facility. One of the most common complaints at events that draw very large crowds is the time it takes consumers to get into and leave the facility's parking lots (Parkhouse, 2005). Traffic flow includes both the movement of the public on the streets to the facility and the flow within the actual parking areas provided by the venue (Parkhouse, 2005). Although public streets are typically controlled by the local police, the facility should make every effort to coordinate traffic flow.

The maximization of parking typically accompanies traffic congestion which may disrupt and negatively impact the experience of spectators. Thus, maintaining a satisfied crowd parking at the venue is critical because the direct collection of parking fees on a per-car basis is one of the most common revenue generating methods for sport organizations, and is often a significant generator of revenue. For example, the University of Hawaii Manoa Campus (2010) indicated that Aloha Stadium generated approximately $209,000 in parking revenue during the 2008 season, while athletics overall generated a gross revenue of roughly $400,000 from parking. Additional sources of parking revenue can be secured from selling preferred or personalized parking spaces; per-event/all-event/season/annual passes; valet parking, and oversized parking fees for RVs and motor homes where tailgating is prevalent.

Aesthetics

Many sport managers and scholars have noted the need to enhance the fan experience at sporting events as attendance has always been at the core of sports business (Steeg, 2010). As a result, teams and leagues have sought to enhance the fan experience and generate additional revenue streams while doing so. Fans are able to experience the five senses while at the stadium: sound, sight, touch, taste, and smell. Each guest has unique interests and teams should attempt to tap into each of these senses to create lasting memories. The *sportscape* or entertainment experience allows fans to experience each of the five senses while at the stadium. From music and scoreboard videos to food and merchandise, the entertainment experience is as much a part of the event as the on-field competition. Sport marketers must strive to provide a high quality entertainment experience to enhance fan satisfaction and encourage repeat consumption. Elements of the fan experience are discussed in greater detail in Chapter 7.

Operations managers need to appreciate that the fan experience begins well before anyone passes through the turnstiles. Television and radio programs should provide viewers and listeners alike with exclusive content, promotional updates, and foreshadow what the fan will encounter at the venue. Creating a pre-game ambiance or environment is necessary to position the fans in the appropriate state of mind (i.e., see value from your sport product and/or services). Post-game programming is equally important as it provides news, analysis, and player interviews for fans as they leave the stadium. Each of these forms of communication provides a unique opportunity to shape fans' expectations for the event and in turn assist in managing their satisfaction levels. Additionally, social media provides a unique opportunity for sport organizations to disseminate a direct and unfiltered message to fans, and as such, should be strategically utilized as part of the marketing mix. Chapter 9 provides greater insight specific to the use of public relations and media as a means of shaping fan perceptions. Next, there is only one chance to make a first impression and stadium operators should adopt that mantra when training game-day staff (e.g., security, ushers, ticket takers). This is critical since these personnel are on the "front lines," and are often the first and only personnel fans may encounter. Fans do not often interact with a team's president or general manager, but they do see (and talk to) employees in their seating section. Fans also have an opportunity to enjoy unique experiences related to their senses and the production of the event. Below is a breakdown of elements that should be of primary focus when creating the fan experience.

Sound

The sound system is a key component in enhancing the fan experience. Fans must feel connected to the action even when they are not watching the game. The radio and/or television broadcast of the game should be audible in the concourses and restrooms. Music should be played when there are stoppages and before/after each game. Sound should not be limited to the inside of the stadium. This experience should start when the fans exit their vehicles or step off the subway. Fans always need to be connected to what is happening no matter where they are located. This may be why a new trend in sport facility construction or renovation practices includes the incorporation of a viewing plaza outside of venues. For instance, at Cowboys Stadium, home of the National Football League's (NFL) Dallas Cowboys, eight Daktronics portable modular LED display units sit in the venue's AT&T Plaza to bring HD broadcasts, movies, sounds, and interactive fan opportunities (e.g., crowd prompts, live scores and statistics, updated standings, pre/post-game interviews) to intensify the crowds connection to Cowboy events (Cohen, 2009). These technologies also provide unique elements of sponsorship inventory that enhance the experience for fans and assist in generating additional revenue streams for the sport entity.

Sight

Equally important in enhancing the fans' in-stadium experience are video boards (Steeg, 2010). It has been documented that teams are only using a small percentage of existing boards and there is too much emphasis on advertising or static graphics. The production of video segments that are "sponsored" are far better than having disengaged fans. Dallas Mavericks owner Mark Cuban has blogged about the fan experience. He wants fans to never look down and correctly stated that, at most events, the memory is the experience, not the score (Steeg, 2010). Known for his fan friendly focus, Cuban's philosophy recognizes the importance of entertaining the fans and providing them with ample activities so they always have something to see or do while at the venue. Similarly, the NFL's Houston Texans created a halftime show in response to fan feedback. After learning its fans desired a halftime show similar to what they would see on television, the Texans teamed with a local news station to develop a halftime show with highlights, commentary and analysis, and statistics pertinent for fantasy football (Kaplan, 2004). This allowed the Texans to enhance its halftime show and also add to its sponsorship inventory by partnering with the local news station.

In order to help franchises improve fan interaction with the event environment, many sport firms are utilizing high-definition video boards to produce crystal clear pictures and sounds. The standard for all high-definition boards again exists in Cowboys Stadium. Opening in 2009, Cowboys Stadium provides views of events taking place in that venue on the world's largest 1080p television. Stretching roughly 180 feet and weighing nearly 600 tons, the $40 million video board provides, according to Cowboys Stadium owner Jerry Jones, every seat the equivalent of a 60-inch HDTV experience. The size of this board also provides fans with standing room only tickets in the upper plaza levels of the stadium to similarly enjoy the event up close. Therefore, on game days the roughly 80,000-seat facility services 100,000 spectators.

Touch

Technology advances have made it possible for fans to gather and to receive information via phone services. Offering Wi-Fi coverage throughout the stadium and parking areas is a necessity in today's technological advanced world. League-designed applications, such as MLB.com At Bat, and NBA Game Time, provide other game broadcasts, highlights, and real-time statistics. Teams must augment that information in-stadium. Developing a team- and venue-specific application or texting service that provides game information, but most importantly, traffic/parking, concession/merchandise specials and emergency services information could also be crucial to future success (Steeg, 2010).

Interactive exhibits and playgrounds enhance the fan experience, especially for those with short attention spans or not interested in the action on the field. As an example, AT&T Park (San Francisco-MLB) incorporated a 17,000 square-foot Coke bottle shaped playground into its structure, while Atlanta's Turner Field (MLB) developed an arcade area for its young and old attendees. Comerica Park (Detroit-MLB) also integrated a Ferris wheel, carousel, and giant waterfall for similar audiences looking to escape from the action but stay at the venue. Minor league sports similarly understand these entertainment needs and erected "fan zones" to enhance entertainment inside and outside venues (Steeg, 2010). Seifried (2010) suggested these exhibits and digital opportunities were established to help attendees live the experiences they will enjoy and desired from home. This desire of fans to experience at the ballpark what they would experience at home must be addressed when marketing the sport product, or fans may simply stay at home to watch the game or event.

Taste and Smell

Concession operations are critical to fans' impressions and they have been transformed since the 1980s to eventually become just as beneficial to revenue generation as tickets sales (Seifried, 2010). Operations managers should recognize that different sports require different concession demands. For instance, baseball facilities need expansive concessions within large open concourses so that people can select from a variety of items in the spring and summer seasons without missing any action. Football facilities, by contrast, require a high volume of concession areas in order to accommodate waves of fans quicker and with more efficient service during downtimes in action, such as at halftime or during television timeouts.

A need also exists for recognition of the importance of venue signature items. Opportunities like "Boog's BBQ" at Oriole Park at Camden Yards adds value to each ticket. Fans famously crave Fenway Franks when attending Red Sox baseball games in Boston and seek to purchase one of those hot dogs as part of their ballpark experience. Importantly, these items and others at ballparks, arenas, and stadiums throughout the world aid in the ability to create "tastes" and "smells" in the venue.

Nostalgia

Collectively these elements and special structures, edifices, and displays also possess the ability to evoke nostalgia on which operations managers can capitalize. Sport facilities create nostalgia by offering structures which mythologize the past through promotion. Promoting past heroic achievements and utilizing

Courtesy of Sal DeAngelis.

authentic displays such as monuments, statues, or produced videos/films, and incorporating halls of fame or museums importantly connect fans to real sport experiences (Seifried and Meyer, 2010). Operations managers and marketers should realize these tactics can be quite beneficial in creating and maintaining relationships with prospective clients. Recognizing the fact that early social experiences often influence the level of identification and attachment to brands (Fairley, 2003) is also critical for the sport operations manager to understand. This is because the degree to which people participate and interact with sport is somewhat influenced by those early experiences with the sport product and its associated services (e.g., concessions, parking, technology, etc.).

Appropriately, many NFL and MLB organizations utilize entertainment zones and products which evoke nostalgia (Seifried and Meyer, 2010). Those organizations moving into new buildings in recent years also understand that it is critical to move the "ghosts" and traditions of an old venue into the new structure (Seifried and Meyer, 2010). As an example, literature on MLB and NFL franchises suggests the leagues went to great lengths to move fan groups and their traditions into their new venues as a way to maintain allegiances (Seifried and Meyer, 2010). Further, those renovating took great care not to lose nostalgic aspects of their venues during the incorporation of technology and other revenue generating structures (Seifried and Meyer, 2010). As an example, the Boston Red Sox added seats to the "Green Monster" between 2003 and 2010 but were careful to keep that structure as close to the original as possible (Boston Red Sox Tour, personal communication to author, July 2010).

Courtesy of Sal DeAngelis.

Safety

Security Management

Security is the process of protecting or safeguarding an item, person, or place (Fried, 2009). Security personnel are responsible for creating the necessary plans to ensure safety for all of the aforementioned. Items that need to be secured can include televisions, equipment, and supplies. The individuals inside the venue must be protected at all times as well. This includes staff, participants, officials, media, and fans. Finally, the facility and all ancillary areas must always present a safe environment.

Security Staff

The most appropriate way to ensure proper security management is to have a well-trained staff. It is a common misconception that only "security guards do security." Everyone in a sports facility should be trained in security protocol. Ticket takers should be able to recognize fans that are visibly

Numerous crowd-related problems have arisen in stadiums and arenas when jubilant or impaired fans have caused serious security issues:

- A fan was Tasered at The Player's Championship (PGA) in 2010 for acting disorderly, as was a teenager who ran onto the field at Citizen's Bank Park in Philadelphia.
- Toronto Maple Leaf's player Tie Domi squirted water onto a heckling fan while he was sitting in the penalty box. The spectator lunged over the dividing glass and wrestled with Domi.
- Three individuals were detained at gunpoint at Pittsburgh's Heinz Field in 2010 for trespassing. The stadium was closed to the public at the time.
- Kansas City Royals coach Tom Gamboa was attacked on the field by two fans in 2002. Even though Gamboa was not seriously hurt, it was discovered later that one of the fans possessed a knife.
- Tennis star Monica Seles was stabbed in the back by an obsessed fan at the French Open in 1993. His reason for attacking Seles was to allow Steffi Graf to regain the number one world ranking.

intoxicated. Ushers should conduct pre-game inspections of their sections to ensure they are clear of debris or suspicious packages. Maintenance staff may be a valuable source of information as they are often in a position to observe unusual activity. Specific security personnel should be able to conduct bag inspections prior to entering the facility, handle basic fan ejections, and clear the venue when the event has concluded.

Weapon use should never be a substitute for proper training. The misuses of firearms and physical restraints have caused great concerns at facilities. Carrying weapons may create a greater risk than if the staff had no weapons. Many larger stadiums supplement their security staff with local law enforcement officers who are properly trained to use firearms and also have arresting rights in case of more serious security issues. A significant amount of training in interpersonal communication and dispute resolution is required for those individuals serving as security personnel who are not involved with local law enforcement. These individuals should be well-versed in the facility's policies and procedures. Pre-season classes are often held as a refresher for returning employees, as well as new ones.

Orientation classes should also be held for all other employees to cover administrative issues such as reporting times, work schedules, and policy changes. This time can also be used to tour the employees in order to familiarize them with the facility. Site-specific training focuses on protocols and procedures for handling specific security issues. On-the-job training is often the best way for the "rookie" staff members to learn the idiosyncrasies of each specific position. New employees should be paired up with existing ones so real-life experiences can be taught. These are often more valuable learning tools than a classroom setting. This phase can also include specific training such as how to work specific sections of the facility.

Ongoing training can include refresher courses or focus on new technology (some advances in technology are explained later in this chapter). Some facilities conduct weekly, informal meetings where the employees are updated on policy changes and security concerns.

Supervisors and full-time employees may be required to attend advanced managerial courses such as tabletop exercises. Also known as TTX, these exercises analyze how team leaders would respond in a crisis. Security directors from many professional sports facilities attend these classes on a regular basis. Events are typically hosted by the Department of Homeland Security and present faux-disaster and subsequent evacuation of stadiums. Sports executives and law enforcement officials work together through many different phases of the incident to determine the appropriate actions to be taken should a catastrophe occur.

Crowd Management

Facility and security managers understand that whenever there is a large gathering of people there are potential risks. Crowd management is the process of taking proactive steps before a crowd becomes unruly or other incidents occur. While security issues are sure to arise inside a sports facility, a security manager is not appropriately prepared if little is done to prevent violence outside of the facility. Parking lots, surrounding streets, and the perimeter of the building are just as important as the venue. Listed below are some examples where security was necessary outside of the facility:

- In 2011, a man was critically injured during opening day of the Major League Baseball season after the game between the Dodgers and Giants.
- In 2009, another man was beaten to death in a parking lot by three individuals outside of Citizens Bank Park after a Phillies game. The incident began inside the stadium and reignited when the two parties became confrontational after the game.
- In 2005, a man detonated a bomb and blew himself up outside of Oklahoma Stadium during a college football game.

Security Strategies

Staff Size

No matter what event is taking place in a facility, an appropriate number of security/police personnel must be used to secure the entire building. The force must match the needs of the event. For example, a high school varsity football game would require less security than an NHL playoff game. Some facilities use a formula when implementing a security staff (e.g., one security guard for every one hundred fans).

Law Enforcement

As stated earlier, larger facilities may opt to hire local law enforcement for sold-out, high-profile events. These individuals are often used as a show of force at entrance gates and on the playing field to deter wrongdoers. Police officers can be used in the seating bowl to assist game-day staff by diffusing altercations and escorting unruly fans who may need to be ejected and/or arrested. Sometimes animals can also be utilized inside facilities. Officers mounted on horses can quickly respond to incidents, aid in dispersing large crowds, and allow security personnel to see above the fans. Dogs can be used to inspect illegal items and unauthorized areas. For contests which host heated traditional rivalries, it is best to make sure security and law enforcement are enlarged. As an example, it is not uncommon for San Francisco police to dress in riot gear when the Los Angeles Dodgers come to town (Lacques, 2011).

Technology

Proper training and adequate personnel can be complemented by high-tech security mechanisms. Technological advancements have resulted in many new products that were not considered years ago (Fried, 2009). Video surveillance is probably the most frequently used technology in sports facilities as many venues built today include security rooms to monitor the crowd and unsupervised areas. Closed-circuit televisions systems (CCTV) have also significantly advanced over the years and can pan, tilt, and zoom in on any area or on any fan in the venue. This technology changes quickly and operations managers must be able to adapt.

Many buildings, including non-sports facilities, also issue "proximity key-cards" to all employees. These cards double as identification for staff members and allow access to a certain area only if the staff member has the right to enter that restricted area. Doors are programmed to remain locked if access is denied. Using the same guest paging system

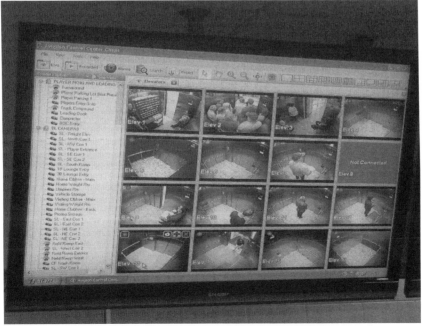

Courtesy of Sal DeAngelis.

implemented at restaurants for waiting patrons like JTECH transmitters, also allow employees direct communication with their colleagues without utilizing two-way radios or the telephone. Staff members can press one of four buttons on the transmitter to summon their supervisor, security personnel, medical and/or cleaning staff. This technology is less expensive than supplying all of the staff members with two-way radios and the communication is instantaneous.

Courtesy of Sal DeAngelis.

Ticket Distribution protection is also a good example of how changing technology can affect the fan experience. Years ago the only way to purchase tickets was at the box office. New electronic technologies, especially the computer, expanded the possibilities of ticket distribution and the protection of seat holders, largely because computerized ticketing eliminated the problems of duplicate tickets, excess stock, and limited choice. Some of the new distribution protection programs or outlets that sports facilities used include:

Team Website

Approximately 70% of all tickets sold in 2010 for the Philadelphia Phillies were sold on Phillies.com. Fans are able to purchase tickets for individual games or group outings and enjoy discounts through the use of promotional codes.

Courtesy of Sal DeAngelis.

Call Centers

Whether automated or speaking to a live person, fans can phone into a call center to purchase tickets for upcoming events. Many ticket buyers still prefer speaking to sales representative, especially when selecting locations for season tickets.

Partnerships with Ticket Firms

Today's sports market is dominated by Ticketmaster. Fans can log onto websites to purchase tickets for their favorite sports and entertainment events. A secondary market was created with StubHub. com which allows fans to legally "scalp" and/or purchase tickets from other fans.

Ticket Kiosks

Many teams have started using kiosks to distribute tickets. Similar in look to bank ATMs, these kiosks allow fans to purchase and print their tickets without standing in long lines during peak traffic times.

Ticketless Systems

Teams also need to be able to distribute tickets to fans in the fastest, most convenient, and most attractive way possible. Along with the travel industry (e.g., airlines) ticketless event attendance is an emerging norm that operations managers should understand. Ticketless event attendance surfaced because it saves time, money, and the environment. A number of professional sport organizations, such as the Phoenix Suns of the National Basketball Association (NBA), have recently begun to utilize a ticketless system which uses simple credit card swipes to secure entry into venues. The Suns started their interest in the ticketless system to capture more demographic and psychographic data about their fans, control costs (i.e., reduce personnel and print costs), and improve event security. Overall, the ticketless systems helps the Suns franchise better see or anticipate changes in consumer behaviors/preferences and reduce the problems associated with scalpers surrounding their venue in addition to reducing costs (Roso, 2009).

Alcohol Management

Alcohol sales generate a significant amount of revenue for facilities, but they also present operations managers with significant risks. Venue managers must establish ways to monitor and manage responsible alcohol sales and consumption. Some techniques supported by the International Association of Venue Managers (Adelman, 2010) include:

- Limit the number of alcoholic drinks a patron can purchase at a time (usually 2 per person) and look at the tab which records the total number for the event on their credit card.

- Alcohol servers are instructed to "card" fans that appear under the age of 30 and ask who the second purchased beverage is for.

- Disallow fans to enter the facility that are visibly intoxicated.

- Provide "dry areas" (often called family sections) in the facility where alcohol is not served.

- Cutting alcohol sales at a certain time (e.g., end of 7th inning or 3rd quarter).

- Developing and promoting designated driver programs.

- Requiring employees (servers and security) to attend TEAM classes: Techniques for Effective Alcohol Management. These courses train staff how to identify appropriate

Courtesy of Sal DeAngelis.

IDs, intoxicated fans, and other indicators as they relate to irresponsible
alcohol management.

- Stop selling alcohol like the Toronto
Blue Jays did in two games during
their 2009 season and the New York
Jets, who completed their 2007 and
2009 home schedules with dry games
at Giants Stadium.

Courtesy of Sal DeAngelis.

Fan Education

The best-trained and best-equipped security staff has very little value if fans do not know how
to respond and care for their own safety (Fried, 2009). Fans should have the basic knowledge
about how to evacuate the facility (knowing the closest exit), ways to communicate with staff,
and other general information as it refers to safety. Many professional sports teams show a
"fan warning" on their video boards during an event. This graphic can outline smoking policies, security measures, risks of attending sporting events (e.g., balls or bats that may leave
the field), and ramifications if a fan acts in a disorderly manner. Fans also enjoy the ability to
communicate with security personnel from the comfort of their own seats in many venues.
Telephone "hotlines" have been instituted at venues where fans can report unruly behavior
via their cell phones.

A newer feature is text messaging, which allows spectators an immediate and dis-
crete way to communicate with security. For example, the San Francisco 49ers maintain
that they are "committed to creating and maintaining a safe and enjoyable experience for all
guests visiting Candlestick Park" (Fan Behavior, 2010). To assist the 49ers, they ask patrons
to immediately report unruly fan behavior that negatively affects the event experience by
texting to "41513" and typing the keyword "BADFAN" and a <space> which is to be followed
by a description of the issue and location of the unruly behavior. The 49ers also provide customers with the opportunity to dial (415) 656-4949 to speak with a 49ers representative to
report poor fan behavior (Fan Behavior, 2010). Similarly, the St. Louis Rams developed their
own text messaging opportunities with their guest services department for fans to report on
unruly behavior. Again, texting "41513," the keyword "RESPECT," and describing the issues
along with the seat location, Rams patrons can quickly eliminate poor behavior in the crowd
("St. Louis Rams Fan Code of Conduct," 2010).

Evacuation

Unfortunately, sports facilities sometimes have to be evacuated. Reasons can include dangerous weather, a fire, or a terroristic threat. When events like these occur, facilities must
implement an Emergency Action Plan (EAP). It is not enough to just construct this document. Managers and employees must be well-versed on what to do in case of an emergency/
evacuation. Response to an emergency situation by the facility staff must be prompt and

professional. The difference between a well-trained response and an erratic, poorly trained response could be the difference between life and death. An emergency response plan should be devised for all perceivable emergency situations. It is vital to thoroughly train all personnel who will most likely be involved in these response procedures. Sometimes this is not doable. So, at a minimum, every employee in the facility should know the primary and secondary evacuation routes as they relate to the sections they are working. Public address warnings should also be used and provided, but if ignored, repeated.

Risk Management

It is essential to develop alternative methods to reduce the risks associated with holding a sporting event. No one is immune from litigation. A good risk management plan should be designed primarily to allow participants, employees, and fans a quality experience in a safe environment. When this is accomplished, facility managers protect themselves from potentially being sued. The plan should protect anyone associated with the event from undue risk. Effective facility managers should be able to identify, assess, and treat potential risks. Once this is done, standard operation procedures can be formalized.

Identification Stage

At the risk identification stage, the facility manager must discover the various risks that may cause losses during any given event. There are several factors that must be addressed in order to reduce the likelihood of losses to the sports facility. The primary factors are related to the base of operations at every sport facility and within almost complete control of the sport facility manager. Therefore, each sport facility manager must consider them when trying to reduce risk.

Identifying risks can begin with categorizing the types of losses and hazards. For example, losses may include property, contracts, tort liability, and financial operations. Hazards include environmental, programmatic, transportation infrastructure, and emergency response. It should be noted that while a well-trained staff is the risk manager's best tool for identifying risks, staff members can also be risks themselves when they do not apply the same rules to themselves as they do their client (Parkhouse, 2005).

Risk Assessment and Treatment

The assessment of risks should occur next and be systematic, using amount and frequency of loss as the two main criteria. A matrix can be created that allows a consistent approach to the assessing process (See Table 8.1). Risk treatment is based on the severity and frequency of occurrence. Generally, avoidance, transfer, elimination, or reduction are the four most frequently used types of risk treatment (Parkhouse, 2005).

Operations managers should avoid or eliminate risks that cause great harm or frequently occur (Parkhouse, 2005). As an example, a facility should never hold an event that has caused great damage to sport facilities elsewhere (e.g., Disco Demolition at Comiskey Field on July 12, 1979). The promotion, Disco Demolition Night, serves as a superior example of this. A crate of disco records exploded on the field between games of a doubleheader between the Chicago White Sox and Detroit Tigers and encouraged fans to run onto the field to increase the destruction. Interestingly, the promotion overflowed the 55,000-seat ballpark. Another 40,000 fans allegedly waited outside but 10,000 were able to sneak into the venue using grappling hooks and other methods to help cause destruction to the playing field and the cancellation of game two of the doubleheader (La Pointe, 2009). Effective risk managers reduce or eliminate all potential losses that may occur.

Transferring risk should occur as a viable option when it is accepted that certain losses will likely occur, but it is difficult to determine the approximate loss involved or the frequency of those episodes. The matrix below identified these risks more or less as middle-of-the-road risks. Looking at the matrix, however, does reveal that some very high losses are included (Parkhouse, 2005). These risks do not need to be avoided because the frequency of their occurrence is moderate or low. Also, the risks that occur very frequently are moderate and therefore should not be avoided.

Retaining and reducing risks is a final option for treating risks. The matrix below shows that risks that are kept and decreased are those that have low or very low potential for loss. Sports facilities can accept these risks because there is very little chance of suffering substantial losses. This assumes that once the facility manager decides to keep the risk, proper precautions are taken to decrease the occurrence of, and the monetary loss associated with, the risk. This is accomplished by developing standard operating procedures, which is the final step in the risk management process (Parkhouse, 2005). The table below shows facility managers several categories and examples of risks which can be classified by their treatment and frequency.

TABLE 8.1

Treatment Recommendation Based on Categorization of Loss and Frequency			
Frequency	**Severity of Injury or Financial Impact**		
	Catastrophic Loss	**Critical Loss**	**Moderate Loss**	**Low Loss**
High Frequency	Elimination	Elimination	Transfer (e.g., Players injured from condensation on court due to melting ice below)	Transfer or Retain and Reduce (e.g., Ticket scalping of counterfeit tickets)
Medium Frequency	Elimination or Transfer	Transfer	Transfer or Retain and Reduce (e.g., Officials injured from fans throwing snow)	Transfer or Retain and Reduce (e.g., Broken condiment dispenser spills on customer clothing
Low Frequency	Elimination or Transfer (e.g., Disco Demolition at Comiskey Field)	Transfer (e.g., Customer becomes sick from perishable item sold at concession stand)	Retain and Reduce (e.g., Hockey puck deflected into the crowd)	Retain and Reduce (e.g., Parking attendant pockets cash from direct-car sales)

Adapted by Chad Seifried from *Sport Facility Management Organizing Events and Mitigating Risks*, Robin Ammon Jr., Richard M. Southall, and David A. Blair (2005). Morgantown, WV: Fitness Information Technology.

SERVICE

Guest Services

Great customer service focuses on interaction throughout the venue. Everyone in a venue interacts with fans at some point, so facility managers must train not only their event staff, but also managers and front office personnel. One-time training is often not enough and employees should be constantly reminded that giving "world-class" customer service is paramount. Companies like *Dale Carnegie* develop the performance of people for business, while building a corporate culture where employees are happy about work. *Dale Carnegie* instructors teach the necessary "tools" to employees so they are able to provide excellent customer service to all that attend events. According to Fried (2009), the operations manager serves three audiences: a) customers; b) internal constituents; and c) external constituents.

Customers

The life-blood of any sports and entertainment venue are customers. Customers provide much of the revenue needed to operate the facility. They can be a very demanding group who knows what they want, when they want it, and how they want it served. Pleasing everyone is impossible, but an operations manager must strive to give the same service to the fans seated in the upper deck as they do to those located in luxury suites. Customers attending events are not the only customers within a facility. Promoters that book events at facilities want the same excellent customer service. If facility managers do not extend such courtesies, then the promoters will be inclined to take their events (and revenue) elsewhere. Many times facility managers have multiple tenants housed in the venue. This is evident in arenas that host both professional basketball and hockey. Primary tenants, like the aforementioned teams, take precedence over smaller tenants (concessionaire, housekeeping, etc.).

Internal Constituents

Anyone working at the facility is considered an internal constituent. Employees, investors, and government officials all have a vested interest in the building. This influences facility managers to constantly improve the venue and to provide superior service.

External Constituents

The facility operators must reach beyond their own buildings to those who can exert influence on the sports venue. While they may never step foot in the building, bankers, politicians, and the media can control the decisions of a facility manager. Many government entities interact with facilities, especially if the venue is municipally owned. Facility managers experience many challenges when dealing with local and state officials. Laws are constantly changing and sports facilities must adapt quickly. If the city passes a smoking ban inside all private-sector buildings, then the sports facilities must adhere to this new law. Buildings must always be up to code, apply for appropriate permits when doing construction, and follow all of the rules set forth by the **Americans with Disabilities Act**.

Summary

In this chapter, we demonstrated that facility and operations managers must be able to adapt quickly to social, legal, and economic changes/challenges during their tenure and that safety should remain a priority. As stated early in this chapter, a facility manager should focus on Consistency, Location, Aesthetics, Security, and Service (CLASS) to achieve and appreciate these points of interest. *Consistency* begins with coordinating the managerial functions of planning, organizing, implementing, and controlling. In order to achieve success with these functions of management, mission statements, goals, and objectives should be established to reflect the policies, procedures, and operational direction of the organization. Organizational charts represent the hierarchy of an organization in order to police such efforts.

Next, *location* of the sport venue exists as a critical component to the shared experience of every participant (i.e., live or remote). As a central element of the marketing mix, internal and external accessibility, parking, and transportation design surface as important items toward maintaining a happy crowd and the development of a consistent revenue stream. To ensure the realization of an *aesthetically* pleasing experience for all attending sporting events, facility managers should challenge themselves to attend games as a fan and identify their level of satisfaction with the above areas (i.e., sound, sight, touch, taste, and smell). Enjoying all that a facility has to offer will help decide what it is fans want and need to make the game-day experience fulfilling for all that pass through the turnstiles and possibly create nostalgia for the venue and events that take place there.

Safety, through the analysis of a variety of components (i.e., security, staff size, law enforcement, alcohol and crowd management, technology, and fan education) is also critical to the development of a useful and effective risk management program. Risk management allows participants, employees, and fans to experience events and activities inside and outside of the venue under safe conditions. When a safe environment is achieved, facility and operations managers service their organization by protecting them against unforeseen risks (e.g., financial, human, and legal). Risk management plans should include the identification and assessment of potential risks and involve an appreciation for the potential outcomes different treatment techniques will create. Finally, *service* which concentrates on customers, internal constituents, and external constituents should be used to maximize event experiences. It is easy to enjoy a job in sports when the team is successful. However, happy employees will many times translate into happy fans more consistently than winning alone.

Discussion Questions

1. List and describe the types of constituents an operations manager serves.

2. Compare and contrast the differences between a mission statement and goals and objectives.

3. List and describe the types of training security managers should afford their staffs.

4. What strategies can be utilized by security managers to help reduce potential risks or hazards?

5. Describe the instances when you would avoid/eliminate, transfer, or retain and reduce risks?

6. Identify the aesthetic elements of the facility/event which lead customers, clients, and participants toward a better fan experience.

7. Search the Web for mission statements of sport organizations. Select 1–3 mission statements. How are they written? How are values and brand of the organization reflected in its mission statement?

Critical Thinking Exercises

1. Although 45,000 fans leave a sporting event without incident, one creates a problem (e.g., enters field of play, starts a fight). What impression does that lone person leave on fellow spectators, event participants, game officials, and event operations managers? Does their behavior affect the play and management of the next event?

2. As a facility manager, what are the steps that should be followed in a risk audit? What are some concerns that should be addressed?

References

Adelman, S. A., Esq. "I'll drink to that: Minimizing the risk of intoxicated patrons." *Facility Manager,* August/ September, 2010, http://www.iavm.org/Facility_manager/pages/2010_Aug_Sep/OperationsEvents.htm

Allison, M., and J. Kaye. *Strategic planning for non-profit organizations: A practical guide and workbook.* 2nd ed., Hoboken, NJ: Wiley & Sons, Inc., 2005.

Bartkus, B. R., and M. Glassman. "Do firms practice what they preach? The relationship between mission statements and stakeholder management." *Journal of Business Ethics,* 83 (2005): 207–216

Bolino, M. C., and W. H. Turnley. "Going the extra mile: Cultivating and managing employee citizenship behavior." *Academy of Management Executive,* 17(3) (2003): 60–73.

Bridges, F. J., and L. L. Roquemore. *Management for athletic/sport administration.* Decatur, GA: ESM Books, 1996.

Churchill Downs, Inc. (n.d.) "Mission statement." http://www.churchilldownsincorporated.com/

Cohen, D. "Daktronics displays decorate Cowboys Stadium outdoor plaza." *Sports Video Group,* September 24, 2009, http://sportsvideo.org/main/blog/2009/09/24/daktronics-displays-decorate-cowboys-stadium-outdoor-plaza/

Fan Behavior. "San Francisco 49ers Fan Behavior and Code of Conduct," 2010, http://www.49ers.com/stadium/stadium-info/policy.html

Fairley, S. "In search of relived social experience: Group-based nostalgia sport tourism." *Journal of Sport Management,* 17(3) (2003): 284–304.

Fried, G. *Managing sport facilities.* 2nd ed., Champagne, IL: Human Kinetics, 2009.

Kaplan, D. "For halftime, Texans go to the highlights." *SportsBusiness Journal,* March 15, 2004.

Le Blanc, R. *Achieving objectives made easy: Practical goal setting tools & proven time management techniques.* Maarheeze, Netherlands: Cranendonck Coaching, 2008.

Lacques, G. "Giants fan remains in coma after attack at Dodger Stadium." *USA Today* April 4, 2011, http://content.usatoday.com/communities/dailypitch/post/2011/04giants-fan-still-in-coma-after-attack-at-dodger-stadium/1

La Pointe, J. "The night disco went up in smoke." *New York Times,* July 4, 2009, http://www.nytimes.com/2009/07/05/sports/baseball/05disco.html

Leventhal, J. *Take me out to the ballpark.* New York: Black Dog and Leventhal Publishers, 2006.

Mullin, B. J., S. Hardy, and W. Sutton. *Sport marketing.* 3rd ed., Champaign, IL: Human Kinetics, 2007.

The Ohio State University. "Department of Athletics organizational chart," April 2, 2010, http://ohiostatebuckeyes.com/fls/17300/pdf/hr/org-dept-of-ath.pdf?DB_OEM_ID=17300.

Parkhouse, B. L. *The management of sport: Its foundation and application.* 4th ed., New York, NY: McGraw-Hill, 2005.

Pro Football Hall of Fame. (n.d.) "Mission statement". http://www.profootballhof.com/hall/missionstatement.aspx.

Roso, R. "Phoenix Suns experiment with new ticketless technology System". *Ticket News,* March 26, 2009, http://www.ticketnews.com/news/Phoenix-Suns-experiment-with-new-ticketless-technology-system309267.

Seifried, C. S. "An ideal-type for the evolution of sport facilities: Analyzing professional baseball and football structures in the United States". *Sport History Review,* 41(1) (2010): 50–80.

Seifried, C. S., and K. Meyer. "Nostalgia-related aspects of professional sport facilities: A facility audit of Major League Baseball and National Football League strategies to evoke the past". *International Journal of Sport Management, Recreation & Tourism,* (2010): 51–76.

Seifried, C. S., and D. Pastore. "Analyzing the first permanent professional baseball and football structures in the United States: How expansion and renovation changed them into jewel boxes". *Sport History Review,* 40(2) (2009a): 167–196.

Seifried, C. S., and D. Pastore. "This stadium looks and tastes just like the others: cookie cutter era facilities from 1953–1991". *Sport History Review,* 40(1) (2009b): 30–56.

St. Louis Rams Fan Code of Conduct. Edward Jones Dome, 2010, http://www.stlouisrams.com/edward-jones-dome/fan-code-of-conduct.html

Steeg, J. "On game day, teams must set the tone, deliver the Experience". *Street & Smith's SportsBusiness Journal,* 15 (2010): 25–31.

University of Hawaii-Manoa. "Funding athletics at UH-Manoa", 2010, http://www.hawaii.edu/uhmfs/documents/faculty%20senate%20presentation%201.19.11.ppt

CHAPTER 9

Promotional Mix, Public Relations, and Emerging Technologies

Stephen W. Dittmore University of Arkansas
Galen Clavio Indiana University
Kimberly S. Miloch Texas Woman's University

We have a lot of success with using unique experiences in leveraging sales, and even more so in building relationships with our current customers. Everybody wants to feel like they are getting something that nobody else is receiving.
Brandon Schneider, Golden State Warriors as quoted by Hogan (2011).

CHAPTER OBJECTIVES

After completing the chapter, the reader should be able to:

- Understand and explain the role of the promotional mix in sport marketing.
- Recognize and outline the elements of the sport promotional mix.
- Articulate the unique nature of the sport promotional mix compared to traditional industries.
- Recognize and identify the role of public relations, emerging technologies, and social media in the sport promotional mix.
- Recognize and understand the best practices in implementing effective sport promotional mix strategies.

Introduction

Previous chapters have discussed the key concepts that provide the foundation for appropriate and effective sport marketing plans and strategies. This chapter details elements of the marketing mix including the promotional mix and public relations with a special focus on emerging technologies.

When establishing the most appropriate promotional mix for a specific sport entity, sport marketers must consider the target markets, the overall marketing objectives of the organization, the desired outcomes of the promotion, and the most impactful combination of communication channels for achieving desired marketing outcomes. Shank (2008) defines the **promotional mix** as "the combination of tools available for sport marketers to communicate with the public" (277). The concept of the **sport promotional mix** may be further defined as the strategic utilization and integration of communication channels designed to achieve sport marketing objectives and reinforce brand image. Traditional elements of the promotional mix include advertising, public and community relations, and sales strategy and promotion. Most recently, emerging technologies and **social media** have provided marketers with a direct and interactive communication channel for reaching consumers and enhancing the promotional mix. Additionally, sport sponsorship and endorsement represents a unique form of advertising that proves beneficial for many companies when seeking enhanced awareness, increased consumer consumption, and reinforcement of brand image for products. Both sport sponsorship and endorsement are discussed in detail in Chapter 11.

FIGURE 9.1
Sport Promotional Mix

Framework developed from Irwin, Sutton, and McCarthy (2002); Mullin, Hardy, and Sutton (2007) Pedersen, Miloch, and Laucella (2007); Shank (2008).

Advertising

Advertising, by its nature, is intended to persuade consumers to engage in purchase behaviors. In designing any type of advertising, sport marketers must know and understand the characteristics of their respective target markets. Advertising campaigns should be designed with the marketing objectives and the target markets as a central focus. For an advertising campaign to be impactful, it must resonate or relate to the sport entity's target markets. Knowing and understanding the demographics, psychographics, and lifestyle characteristics of the target consumer base is vitally important when designing advertising campaigns that will impact consumer purchase behavior. The manner in which the advertising campaign is designed is also relative to the specified marketing objectives. Advertising campaigns designed to create consumer awareness will likely differ from those designed to encourage repeat purchasing or increased consumption of the sport product. Regardless of the specific desired outcome, advertising campaigns should always seek to reinforce the brand image of the sport entity and relate to the overall strategic marketing plan of the organization.

The most appropriate advertising campaigns clearly and concisely communicate to target consumers, tout the benefits and features of a product, differentiate the product and its features from competition in the marketplace, and are repetitive and memorable. Effective advertising campaigns are clear and concise in messaging. The messages are clearly and quickly communicated to the targeted consumer base. When advertising campaigns lack clarity in messaging, it may create confusion or misperceptions among the target consumer base. This, of course, would prove ineffective in achieving marketing goals and yield a poor return on investment of marketing expenditures.

FIGURE 9.2
Characteristics of Effective Advertising

- Focused on Target Market
- Linked to Achievement of Marketing Objectives
- Clear and Concise
- Illustrates Product Benefits & Features
- Differentiates from Competition
- Repetitive & Memorable

Adapted from Pedersen, Miloch, and Laucella (2007) and Shank (2008).

Advertising strategy should also include a focus on the product's features and benefits of use while also differentiating the product from its competition. Many major league franchises benefit from a geographic monopoly and lack direct competition from another sport specific, major league franchise. Regardless, a focus on benefits and features of attendance at the venue is key in persuading sport consumers to purchase tickets. Other sport products, such as apparel, equipment, and minor league sport venues do not possess a strategic geographic advantage. In this competitive marketplace, it is imperative to focus on the benefits and features of the product and to also differentiate the respective product from its competition.

To leave a lasting impression on consumers, advertising campaigns should be repetitive and memorable. Consistency and repetition in messaging is central to increasing consumer awareness and placing the product in the consideration set of consumers. A lack of awareness means consumers may not consider the product at the time of purchase. Thus, advertising messages should focus on creating awareness among consumers and directly connecting the product to the consumer.

In its most recent 2011 marketing campaign, the Women's Tennis Association (WTA) utilized a promotional mix grounded in traditional television and print advertising and also integrated with digital and social media. The efforts focused on the WTA's "Strong is Beautiful" slogan and featured many of the tour's professional players including Denmark's Caroline Wozniacki, Serbia's Ana Ivanovic, and China's Na Li. The athletes share personal stories of triumph, and the ads highlight their strengths both on and off the court. The central focus of the campaign is intended to engage and attract new fans to the sport and to increase loyalty among the WTA's existing fan base (WTA Launches, 2011; WTA Looking, 2011).

The National Hockey League's Florida Panthers have also created its 2011-2012 season marketing campaign with a "We See Red" advertising theme. The "We See Red" theme is the central focus of the franchise's advertising for the season and was selected to exemplify passion and commitment. It has been incorporated into all elements of its promotional mix. The team debuted a new home jersey during the 2011 NHL draft and is utilizing traditional media via radio, television, and print advertisements. It is also utilizing its website to share videos focusing on its "We See Red Manifesto." Additionally, the team also created a special ticket package to incentivize and attract new consumers. The full or half season "We See Red Pack" includes tickets in the lower level of the arena and numerous benefits such as the "We See Red" Panthers home jersey, an autographed stick by the team, an invitation to the team's welcome party, and entry into a road trip contest (NHL Panthers, 2011).

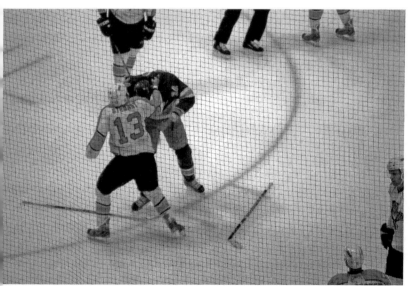

© Daniel M. Silva, 2012. Under license from Shutterstock, Inc.

In addition to the sport promotion mix, companies have consistently utilized sport and athletes to appeal to the masses in advertisements. Effective and appropriate examples of sport in mainstream advertising and the use of athletes as endorsers are examined in detail in Chapter 11. Equally important to the role of advertising in the promotional mix is the utilization of public relations strategies and techniques. While advertising relies on paid forms of communication, public relations represents a form of unpaid communication. As illustrated in the subsequent pages, sport public relations focuses on communications with key publics that serve to reinforce the overall marketing plan and brand image of the sport entity.

Public Relations

The importance of **public relations** to sport organizations has been heightened in the New Media era. This has made the job of a public relations professional both easier and more difficult. More tools, such as social media, are available than in the past, and no longer do organizations need to rely on media to carry organizational messages. However, a greater need exists for the development of long-term, meaningful relationships with key publics.

Two recent definitions of sport public relations speak to this by emphasizing aspects of relationship-building. Hopwood (2007) called public relations the "management of corporate image through the proactive and professional management of relationships with the organization's publics" (293). Similarly, Stoldt, Dittmore, and Branvold (2012) defined sport public relations as a "managerial communication-based function designed to identify a sport organization's key publics, evaluate its relationships with those publics, and foster desirable relationships between the sport organization and those key publics" (2).

Those two definitions have several commonalities. First, both emphasize the role of management and the importance of public relations for overall organization reputation management, not just dealing with media or fluff pieces such as spin doctoring. Second, both stress the need to create and maintain positive relationships with specific organizational publics. Both definitions are grounded in well-established models of public relations.

Public Relations Models

Most public relations literature points to Grunig and Hunt's (1984) conceptualization of one-way and two-way models of public relations as the definitional approach to viewing public relations communications.

One-Way Models

One-way models of public relations focus on the dissemination of information about an organization to its publics, functioning like a monologue. Specifically, the **press agency model** involves seeking attention in almost any form. These are among the most traditional in sport, usually relying on the mass media to aid in the dissemination process. For example, consider the antics of boxing promoters seeking media coverage at a weigh-in prior to a big title fight. The **public information model** focuses on the dissemination of accurate and favorable information about the organization. This approach gained traction in the early part of the twentieth century as a way to combat muckraking newspaper stories (Grunig and

Grunig, 1992). Specific tactics such as Tweets, news releases, and press conferences are still essential tools for today's public relations practitioners, though most public relations theorists now emphasize the relationship-building activities of two-way models.

Two-Way Models

Two-way models, on the other hand, place much more emphasis on interaction and dialogue. Grunig and Grunig (1992) suggested **asymmetrical communication models** were imbalanced in that information leaves the organization and attempts to change the public's behavior. **Symmetrical communication models** are balanced and use both research and dialogue to adjust the relationship between an organization and its publics. Understanding, rather than persuasion, is the principal objective of two-way symmetrical public relations.

The two-way symmetrical model has been described as "the normative model for public relations—that it describes how excellent public relations should be practiced" (Grunig and Grunig, 1992, 291). The authors stressed that dialogue is one of the most important elements of this model. As Stoldt, Dittmore, and Branvold (2012, 27) noted, "the element of dialogue is crucial to modern public relations practice as it places much more importance on practitioners as receivers of information rather than merely information disseminators."

The ultimate objective of two-way symmetrical communication is a relationship in which the actions of either entity, the organization or the public, positively impacts the economic, social, political, or cultural well-being of the other entity (Ledingham and Bruning, 1998). To accomplish this, organizations can utilize a number of tactics to foster relationships with key publics.

Hopwood (2005) examined the use, and non-use, of two-way symmetrical public relations in her case study of English country cricket clubs. She concluded that organizations which overlook the benefits of public relations do so in favor of organizational functions which are perceived as being more lucrative or cost-effective. Sport clubs, she argued, "which depend upon continual replenishment of supporters for their long-term viability, need to be especially mindful of the implications of ignoring the basic principles of public relations" (Hopwood, 2005, 182).

The use of dialogue has emerged as a successful principle in two-way symmetrical communication. Kent and Taylor (1998) defined dialogic communication as a give and take tactic, calling it a "negotiated exchange of ideas and opinions" (325). One commonly used tool to exchange those ideas and opinions is an organizational blog. An organizational blog is a website with dynamic content and posts by organizational representatives displayed in reverse chronological order. A unique feature of the blog is the ability for readers, and subsequently the author, to post responses to a particular entry, creating a virtual dialogue.

Dittmore, Stoldt, and Greenwell (2008) found evidence that a professional baseball team's organizational weblog was an effective tool in establishing both a human voice and a relational commitment with its fans. In this sense, weblogs appear to aid in the generation of long-term commitments with publics.

The benefits of two-way communication are not limited to just fans. Cleland (2009) noted a growing interdependence in the English Premiership on the part of the media and the clubs for news, information, and content. Development of new media streams has eliminated the reliance on old communications models, such as the one-way and two-way models discussed earlier, and created an environment where the overall importance of local media to organizations has been reduced (Cleland, 2009). The result of this has been increased negative media coverage of the clubs (Birmingham City and Northampton Town). This may be corrected through better relationship management.

Given this emphasis on dialogue, it is not surprising that in the preface of their book, *Putting the Public Back in Public Relations,* Solis and Breakenridge (2009) suggested the following definition of social media and its impact on public relations: "Participation is the new marketing. And to participate, we must become the people we want to reach. The New Media landscape is creating a hybrid of PR, online marketers, market analysts, and customer advocates, to effectively and genuinely engage in the conversations that define social media and create relationships with customers" (xx).

Their definition suggests that today's social media combines the concepts discussed throughout this book. Social media is both public relations and marketing. It creates dialogue, meaning that it is two-way, engages conversations, and creates relationships.

Audiences for Public Relations Activities

Many different ways exist to conceptualize the audience for public relations. Most definitions will use the term "stakeholder" or "public" to classify groups of individuals to which the organization may wish or need to communicate. However, Stoldt, Dittmore, and Branvold (2012) view the two terms as distinctly different in the world of sport public relations. They suggest stakeholders are used to describe large groups of people who hold similar standing to the organization, while publics are specific groups of people within stakeholder groups.

Hopwood (2007) relied on the public relations theoretical approach known as "license to operate." She concluded business success for sport organizations "can only be sustained if it exists within a supportive operating environment" (296).

Common publics which may influence a sport organization's ability to operate include, but are not limited to: individual attitudes by customers, suppliers, consumers, employees, investors, and the community; legal and regulatory bodies; industry associations and standards; industry reputation; media; and more (Hopwood, 2007). It is important to note that not all of these publics are applicable to all organizations and that each organization may identify publics which are specific to its organization and operations.

Identification and Influence of Publics

As Stoldt, Dittmore, and Branvold (2012) suggested, multiple public groups make up a larger stakeholder group. For example, a college athletic department might identify several distinct publics all of which are important to the operation of the department. Consider a stakeholder group such as alumni. This broad group might be subdivided into smaller publics such as former letterwinners, alumni who donate to athletics, and alumni who do not donate to athletics. The athletic department will likely treat each public differently based on how they contribute to overall operation of the athletic department.

Smith (2005) compartmentalized publics in four ways, based on the unique relationship each category has with the organization. *Customers* of the organization are individuals who receive the products or services an organization distributes. This category should include not only current and potential customers, but also secondary customers, or the customers of the organization's customers (Smith, 2005). Consider the college athletic department again. Its customers might be ticket holders, donors, and sponsors, each of whom contribute significant resources to the department. Each group will likely react differently to changes in the quality of the athletic department product, and therefore might not be treated as one singular public.

A second way to categorize publics is through *producers* of the organization. These individuals provide inputs needed for the organization to function. Inputs can be human (employee or volunteers), physical (suppliers of raw materials), or financial (stockholders, venture capitalists, donors, sponsors; Smith, 2005).

A third category of publics are *enablers* to the organization. These individuals serve as regulators or agencies which establish norms and standards for the organization as well as groups which can hold influence over potential customers and can assist in making the organization successful, such as the media and stock analysts (Smith, 2005).

The final category of publics proposed by Smith (2005) is *limiters,* or those publics which can somehow adversely affect the operations of the organization. These can include activist groups, competitors, and individuals opposed to the organization.

Messaging for Publics

Given the potential that many different publics will be interested in what an organization communicates, it is important for a public relations professional to be focused on reaching each public in a meaningful way. The current environment of online communication through websites, blogs, and social media such as Twitter and Facebook makes that job both easier and more difficult.

Syme (2010) advocated for the two-way public relations tactic of dialogue to aid in this process. She recommends assessing a cross section of sport organization's fans to determine how they are using the technology, and then prioritizing changes to how the organization uses social media to meet fan usage patterns.

Without a doubt, the current technology makes it easier than at any point in history to communicate an organizational message directly to targeted publics without worrying about it being misrepresented, misinterpreted, or taken out of context. On the other hand, it is more difficult than ever to have a message break through all of the forms of content which exist and have the message resonate with the intended public.

Community Relations

Community relations is frequently overlooked as a significant and influential area of public relations (Pedersen, Miloch, and Laucella, 2007). Activities within community relations are designed to enhance the sport organization's ability to develop those long-term two-way relationships with key publics. The tools utilized to develop those relationships have been described as unmediated communications, and have been found to be effective at establishing and enhancing relationships with various publics (Stoldt, Dittmore, and Branvold, 2012).

Unmediated communication tactics possess three distinct advantages as public relations tools (Stoldt, Dittmore, and Branvold, 2012). First, it is face-to-face, allowing for a personal contact between the organization and a public. This would include specific tactics such as speeches, clinics, and player, coach or mascot appearances. Second, individuals who attend these activities are likely already identified with the organization and have a favorable attitude toward the organization. And third, the organization enjoys a high degree of control over the messages being delivered and how they are presented in these settings.

A growing line of sport-related literature focuses on the importance of **corporate social responsibility** (CSR; Bradish and Cronin, 2009). Sport organizations which engage in CSR are frequently considered to be involved in "cause-related marketing." This engagement manifests itself in a variety of forms such as event programming, environmental sustainability, and corporate citizenry. Specifically, Sheth and Babiak (2010) identified five common practices relating to CSR in their survey of US professional sports teams: donating to charities; supporting social causes; conserving resources and reducing wastes; treating employees fairly; and complying with equal employment opportunity practices. These practices often result in diverse specific programs.

For example, Babiak and Wolfe (2009) noted the types of CSR programming prominent in professional sports leagues varies considerably from the National Basketball Association (NBA)'s "Basketball Without Borders" program where young people attend a basketball-themed camp designed to promote goodwill, education, and friendship through sport, to the National Hockey League (NHL)'s "Hockey Fights Cancer" program where funds are raised to support cancer research.

Investor Relations

Numerous sport organizations are publicly owned and, as such, must consider investor relations to be one of their critical public relations functions. Often nested within an organization's corporate communications department, the goals of the investor relations function are to enhance the value of a company's stock and to reduce the cost of obtaining new capital from investors (Cutlip, Center, and Broom, 2000). Investor relations practitioners must not only be accomplished public relations professionals, they must also possess expertise in finance. Specifically, investor relations professionals need knowledge in government regulations relating to financial publicity, policies of national stock exchanges, an understanding of financial statements, and the operational strategies embraced by their companies (Miller, 1998).

Specifically, investor relations professionals may be asked to produce annual reports, plan shareholder meetings, and coordinate interactive communications with investors and the media. Annual reports function to disclose financial information to shareholders, investment firms, and financial media (Treadwell and Treadwell, 2000). Annual shareholder meetings provide shareholders an opportunity to hear directly from a corporation's management team as well as vote on board members and other proposals submitted for shareholder approval.

Employee Relations

Organizations with an employee relations unit commonly house the unit in the human resource department where other important administrative aspects of the organization are kept, such as employee benefits and policies. As Sheth and Babiak (2010) pointed out, a significant portion of CSR is treating employees fairly. Therefore, it is critical for a communications or public relations professional to not overlook the importance of reaching out to this public. Stoldt, Dittmore, and Branvold (2012) have identified three unique features of managing employee relations which cover nearly every level of sport organizations.

First, because of the popularity of sport, employees often enjoy a feeling of social stature or prestige based on their affiliation. Therefore, it is important for sport organizations to build employee commitment by stressing organizational pride. Following the bid scandal of 1999, the Salt Lake Organizing Committee for the 2002 Olympic Winter Games held regular all-employee meetings in which prizes and gifts were raffled off and senior managers were often roasted by other employees (Romney and Robinson, 2004).

A second unique feature is the heavy reliance by sport organizations on volunteers for the successful staging and organization of events. Finally, the third unique feature relates only to professional sports and involves labor relations and the possibility of work stoppages through either labor lockouts or strikes. Such was the case during the National Hockey League's year-long work stoppage from 2004–2005 when league officials announced that nearly two-thirds of its employees would be laid off due to the labor-management lockout.

The use of both advertising techniques and public relations are vital to developing a successful promotional mix. Those tools may often be used with sales strategy to more fully integrate the promotional mix. Sales strategy and promotion are outlined in the subsequent paragraphs.

Sales Strategy and Promotion

In the past, sport marketers were criticized for a "win and they will come mentality" relative to marketing and sales promotions (Mullin, Hardy, and Sutton, 2007). As sport marketing has evolved, so too have the **sales promotions** utilized by sport marketers. "Sales promotions are short-term incentives, usually designed to stimulate immediate demand for sports products or services" (Shank, 2005, 277). Sales promotions are integral to the success of the sport promotional mix. As with other elements of the sport promotional mix, these promotions should be designed with consideration for both the target markets and marketing objectives. One encounters numerous examples of sales promotions daily including "buy one, get one free" incentives, "clearance sales," time sensitive pricing, coupons, and even "bundled" pricing for media such as cable, Internet, and phone.

Sport marketers have recognized the value of integrating sales promotion as part of the promotional mix. The New Jersey Nets offered "early bird" season ticket renewals for season ticket holders for the 2011–2012 season. "Early bird" renewal purchasers earned special discount pricing (Coast to Coast, 2011a). As Broughton (2010) notes, Major League Baseball (MLB) relies on specific promotional giveaways in order to increase ticket sales. Franchises report that bobbleheads are still one of the most attractive giveaways to consumers, and typically result in an increased attendance at games when they are distributed (Broughton, 2010). Franchises may also take advantage of seasonal promotions such as the Golden State Warriors' "Tickets and a Turkey" incentive. For this ticket promotion, the franchise offered consumers two or four tickets (depending on the location in the arena) and a $15 gift card to a local grocer during the Thanksgiving holiday season. Franchise personnel noted the promotion contributed to sell out games (Hogan, 2011). Similarly, the Seattle Mariners have developed a ticket promotion centered on starting pitcher Felix Hernandez. During the games in which he pitches, the team will offer specially priced $30 tickets in a section of the ballpark it deems "King's Court." Included in the ticket purchase is also a "King's Court" t-shirt (Coast to Coast, 2011b).

Increasingly apparent in today's sport marketplace is the need to focus promotional efforts that most attract and resonate with sport consumers. Hogan (2011) reports that team marketing personnel have noted specific needs and desires among consumers. These include ticket promotions that provide both flexibility and a unique experience for sport consumers, as well as those that also guarantee an "added value" with the expenditure. Promotions with added value may include as part of the promotion merchandise, free or discounted food, special parking, or exclusive offers. Additionally, unique experiences may include invitations to special franchise events, access to players or coaches, or photos in the venue (Hogan, 2011).

Increasingly important as an element in the promotional mix are emerging technologies and social media. These are discussed in detail in the subsequent paragraphs.

Emerging Technologies and Social Media

The ever-changing face of technology has provided both great opportunities and great challenges to sport promotion mix managers. The advent of mobile devices capable of delivering a rich assortment of real-time content, combined with the ability of sport teams and leagues to customize that content in whatever way they see fit, has given companies more control than ever over how their product is portrayed to sport consumers.

Courtesy of Kimberly Miloch.

However, the effective utilization of these technologies requires a mastery of skills for which many sport organizations are unable or unwilling to commit. For some organizations, emerging technologies can appear as a threat to their standard ways of doing business, forcing them to adapt to a seemingly foreign method of communication and marketing. Other organizations suffer from a lack of progressive thinking in top management positions, with decision makers having cut their teeth in an era where face-to-face communication ruled the day, leading them to favor that type of promotion over all others. Still other organizations become concerned with the cost and rapid obsolescence of emerging technologies, unwilling to commit time and financial resources to methods of promotion and marketing which may disappear within five years.

Despite these concerns, emerging technologies provide sport organizations with remarkable methods of reaching their customers, and doing so in a way that adapts the organization's message and image to the social and cultural preferences of the newest consumer generation.

Defining New Media

Most emerging promotion and communication technologies in sport rely on **new media**, which may be defined as a merging of traditional media forms (such as audio, video, and written word) with interactive digital technology, frequently through the moderating factor of the Internet. New media's focus is on interactivity and individual consumer focus, as opposed to the broader audience approach of traditional media. Whereas traditional media content is designed for thousands, new media content can and should be personalized for each of the individuals within those thousands.

The new media term has grown to encompass both the hardware on which content is generated and received and the software for which it is designed. Therefore, a computer laptop or handheld smartphone would be considered new media, but so too are the software applications that those hardware items are designed to run. Furthermore, cross-platform network software, such as Twitter and Facebook, fall definitively into the new media category.

It is important to draw a distinction between actual "new media" and the representation of traditional media within the new media realm. The former promotes an atmosphere of interactivity, personalization, and community, where the media consumer can both choose which content being generated by the media source that they receive and interact with that content dynamically, either through responding to the content in a discussion setting or through creating their own content. The latter creates an environment where the traditional, non-interactive media content is simply reproduced in a digital format, with no possibility of customization or response.

As an example, a sport team's website would seem to be unquestionably a new media content source. However, if there are no interactive elements on the site, such as the ability to comment on team stories or correspond with team personnel, then ultimately the site is portraying a traditional media presence, as opposed to a new media one.

Metapersonal Connection

New media's personalized and interactive elements help to promote the concept of **metapersonal connection** between the sport organization and the team. The concept of metapersonal connection states that sports fans are increasingly interested in electronically mediated personal engagement from their sources of sports entertainment, in addition to (or as opposed to) face-to-face personal engagement. As Generations X and Y continue to age and become progressively larger parts of the sport marketplace, they bring with them both a technological adeptness and a desire to be communicated to on an individual basis.

Whereas sports fans of the previous decades were satisfied with simply following along with their sports heroes and favorite teams through blanket coverage provided by traditional media sources, many of the emerging new media-enabled fans desire a feeling of special access and privilege. These new media fans are interested in interacting with their sports idols, or at the very least gaining a window into their thoughts and emotions.

Furthermore, these fans want to feel special and appreciated by the athletes and teams that they follow, and they look upon new media as a vehicle for such interaction. While such a relationship would have been impractical from both the fan perspective and the sport figure's perspective prior to the arrival of the new media age, the capabilities of digital, interactive technology have made such connections possible.

Promoting an atmosphere of metapersonal connection in the sport promotional mix requires that the organization be willing to engage fans on an individual level. Some methods for doing so include utilizing **social networking** to provide exposure for players, coaches, and team personnel, promoting the usage of blogs by team personnel, encouraging feedback from fans on a variety of issues, and running contests and giveaways specifically geared towards the new media-enabled audience.

Blogging and Podcasting

The emergence of the web log, or **blog**, in the first decade of the twenty-first century was initially met with skepticism by media consumers. For the first several years of its existence, blogging was almost solely the domain of the writing hobbyist, a place where individuals could express their feelings and opinions on topics to an audience that would never have been available prior to the advent of widely-available Internet connections. Very few media sources took blogging (or bloggers) seriously, and even fewer sports organizations expressed any interest in the medium, except as a domain to be ridiculed due to its content producers' penchants for being critics of team personnel and decisions.

However, as traditional media have continued their downward financial spiral, sport organizations have realized the potential of the blog as a method of mastering the promotion and communication mix, through the advancement of unique, consumer-friendly material which promotes the organization's agenda. As consumers have embraced Internet-based media content, they have demonstrated an interest in hearing directly from current and former players, coaches, and front office personnel. The blog provides a perfect avenue for this type of material.

A successful organizational sports blog provides fans with a window into the thoughts or actions of members of the team. In some cases, this may be a key member, such as a general manager, coach, or star player. However, fans have also demonstrated an interest in reading blogs written by individuals who might not be considered of front-line importance. There are popular organizational sports blogs written by radio play-by-play broadcasters, assistant coaches, backup players, and even mascots. Some popular sport blogs include Dallas Maverick's owner Mark Cuban (blogmaverick.com), Yahoo and ESPN blogs, college sport blogs, and individual athlete blogs. Other popular blogs include those written by athletes, coaches, or journalists during a live event such as the FIFA World Cup, the Olympics, or the Super Bowl.

Podcasts are similar to blogs in that they are easy to produce, tend to focus on items not covered by traditional media, and are easily consumed by new media users. A podcast is an audio or video content package which is distributed through digital means. In most cases, the term podcast is synonymous with audio content, and this audio content is normally distributed as an MP3, which is generally a small, compressed audio format that is playable on a variety of hardware, including home computers, smartphones, and personal music players.

Podcasts allow for the sport organization to offer unique content in a generally non-interactive form. Unlike traditional radio programming, podcasts are almost never listened to while they are being recorded. Instead, the podcast is captured live and then disseminated after the fact. This allows the sport organization to include the content that they want, without immediate feedback. Generally, podcasts are posted on a website, and often fans are invited to comment on the podcast after the fact. Some enterprising sport organizations will include particular comments or questions in the next podcast they create, providing fans with a sense of possession and community. The NHL's Washington Capitals regularly include podcasts as features on the team website as do most sport entities. Sports news sites such as ESPN also include a myriad of podcasts providing audio content for fans.

Social Media and Networking

While most media are focused on the spreading of content from an initial source to many receivers, the advent of social networking could provide sport organizations with a fundamental shift in the way news and content is disseminated among fans.

Social networking can best be defined as a collection of individuals who share connections, and through those connections are able to exchange information and opinion. The most popular social networking site is Facebook, which is an information-rich, self-contained social network that originally started as a website aimed specifically at college students. Created at Harvard University in 2004, it has evolved into an all-encompassing social network which allows members of all age groups to join and connect with other users.

The standard setup of a Facebook user's personal profile allows individuals to post a variety of information, photos, videos, and other content about themselves on the site. Users then have the ability to connect their profiles with other users' profiles, allowing for each to view the others' information. Users may post messages and links on their page which are then distributed through a news feed, and connected users are able to see the content of each other's news feeds. Users may also comment on other users' feeds. This often occurs when one user wants to make a statement about an item that another user posts on his or her profile.

Companies and organizations are not left out of the equation on Facebook. The software allows for these entities to create a "page," which is basically a profile specifically set up for a business. Users are then able to "like" that page, which then places any articles or stories that the organization posts on its page into the user's news feed. As of 2010, several teams have started to utilize these Facebook pages to distribute stories and run giveaway contests. As an example, the Indianapolis Colts of the National Football League utilized their Facebook page to post exclusive video content, links to press releases from the team website, and give away tickets to pre-season games.

Another popular social networking site is Twitter. While Facebook's focus is on providing an information-rich, highly personalized environment for users, Twitter relies on almost the exact opposite approach.

Individual users sign up for a Twitter account, and the personalization of that account is limited to a picture, a background page scheme, and a 140-character biographical sketch. The Twitter user then creates connections to other Twitter users' profiles. The focus of Twitter is on the "feed," which consists of the messages created by both the user and the users that they follow. These messages, or "tweets," are very information-poor, in that they are limited to 140 text characters, which in many cases is only enough room for one or two sentences. Users may also post links to stories, links to pictures, and may "re-tweet" the messages of other users.

While the technological constrictiveness of Twitter's messages may make the network seem unappealing compared to Facebook, the reality is that Twitter is very popular, for completely different reasons than Facebook. Twitter's popularity almost certainly lies in its brevity; tweets are easy to consume, easy to create, and promote an informational focus that can get lost in the richness of Facebook's information feed. Additionally, Twitter is arguably more suited for mobile technology than Facebook. While both have numerous smartphone-based applications, reading and creating content on Twitter is less time-consuming and generally easier than doing the same on Facebook, again due primarily to the constriction of information.

While some sport organizations have begun to use Twitter in a collective sense, the medium has found perhaps its most appropriate calling as a venue for individual athletes and coaches to create a direct connection to fans. Due to the asynchroneity of Twitter, it is entirely possibly for a sports figure to have thousands of followers on Twitter without having to follow those users back in return, something that Facebook's technology has only recently begun to allow.

It is also possible for sport figures to selectively reply to an individual user's tweets in a public manner, thereby showing all users who follow that sports figure that they have a chance at being recognized by the figure. This possibility is very appealing to many sport Twitter followers, and allows for the sports figure to appear personally connected to fans without the potential pitfalls of face-to-face interaction.

Although primarily concerned with distribution of video content, the popular Internet site YouTube is in fact a social networking nexus as well. YouTube allows for both individuals and organizations to post their own video content in a standardized format, and each user account comes with a series of features that promote interactivity and community. These features include the ability to comment on others' videos and the ability to "like" or "dislike" the video without registering a comment.   Many sports organizations have embraced YouTube as a method of providing unique content not available on traditional media channels. Major League Soccer, for instance, has created a number of YouTube-specific programs, including "Extra Time," a weekly examination of MLS games and league-related issues, and "Goal of the Week," which allows for fans to vote weekly on which scored goal was most impressive. These efforts help to increase the promotional value of MLS efforts by providing new media-enabled fans with unique items that would most likely not have been available in a traditional media environment.

As illustrated in previous paragraphs, sport entities are embracing the advantages of using forms of new media as part of the promotional mix and to reach sport consumers. The NHL's New York Islanders recently launched a new mobile phone application specific to iOS users that will allow them to view game broadcasts and retrieve news on the team from its website (Coast to Coast, 2011a). Fox Sports South utilized digital technology in its billboards in the greater Atlanta metropolitan area. The billboards display live game statistics for both the Atlanta Hawks and Atlanta Braves (Coast to Coast, 2011a). In an effort to better connect with fans, both the Kansas City Royals and Milwaukee Brewers developed promotions to enhance fan relations. The Royals held a FanFest Digital Digest Contest that selected fans to use social media to report on the event from its location. Collaborating with *The Milwaukee Journal Sentinel,* the Brewers invited fans to submit recipes for consideration in its concession stands via its "Create a Concession" contest (Coast to Coast, 2011c). The winning fan's personal menu will be featured in the Brewers concessions. The United States Tennis Association utilized Wii Tennis stations at Times Square to connect with consumers and promote ticket sales for the US Open. Fans were allowed to snap pictures with the US Open trophy, play tennis on a mini court, and enter to win various prizes (USTA Kicks Off, 2011).

Discussion Questions

1. What are the key concepts related to the promotional mix?

2. How is the promotional mix unique in sport compared to traditional industries?

3. What is the role of advertising and public relations in the promotional mix? How are the two elements distinctly different?

4. Why are sales promotions an important component of the sport promotional mix?

5. Why is it important for sport organizations to become adept at utilizing emerging technologies? What benefits do these technologies provide?

6. How might social media best be used as part of the sport promotional mix?

7. What are the reasons why a sport organization might be unable or unwilling to invest time and effort in emerging technologies?

8. What types of blogs, Twitter feeds, or Facebook pages do you follow or read regularly? What factors influence your desire to follow these athletes or organizations?

Critical Thinking Exercises

1. Consider that you are the media manager for a Major League Baseball team, and your task is to design a comprehensive new media campaign to help your team reach more fans. You have decided to start with a Facebook page and a blog. What elements will you include in each, and how will those elements help your team extend its promotional mix?

2. You have recently been hired as the athletic director of a BCS school's athletic department. Your associate and assistant athletic directors have a great deal of experience in the traditional ways of doing their jobs, but have very little experience (and even less interest) in learning how to modify their approach to include new media and emerging technologies. What steps will you take to create an atmosphere that is pro-technology in your office?

3. You have just been named the marketing director for an expansion franchise in the National Hockey League. Outline your marketing plan, and identify what your promotional mix will be relative to your overall marketing plan. How will your promotional mix assist you in achieving your marketing goals?

4. You have recently been hired as the Associate Athletic Director for one of the largest school districts in your state of residence. Your Athletic Director has indicated that you will need to start a social media campaign and begin writing blogs for the various sports. What type of content will you include on the blogs, and how will you connect with key stakeholders utilizing social media? Either in groups or individually, develop a plan for implantation and share with the class.

References

Babiak, K., and R. Wolfe R. "Determinants of corporate social responsibility in professional sport: Internal and external factors". *Journal of Sport Management,* 23 (2009): 717–742.

Bradish, C., and J. J. Cronin. "Corporate social responsibility in sport". *Journal of Sport Management,* 23 (2009): 691–697.

Broughton, D. "Caps, bobbleheads top list of MLB team giveaways/promotions". *SportsBusiness Daily,* November 3, 2010.

Cleland, J. A. "The changing organizational structure of football clubs and their relationship with the external media". *International Journal of Sport Communication,* 2(4) (2009): 417–431.

Coast to Coast. "Coast to coast: Rangers beat ticket sales mark". *SportsBusiness Journal,* March 14, 2011a.

Coast to Coast. "Coast to coast: Royals, speedway assist with tornado relief". *SportsBusiness Journal,* May 30, 2011b: 24.

Coast to Coast. "Coast to coast: Timbers grow sales". *SportsBusiness Journal,* January 10, 2011c: 34, 35.

Cutlip, S. M., A. H. Center, and G. M. Broom. *Effective public relations.* 8th ed., Englewood Cliffs, NJ: Prentice Hall, 2000.

Dittmore, S. W., G. C. Stoldt, and T. C. Greenwell. "The use of an organizational weblog in relationship building: The case of a Major League Baseball team." *International Journal of Sport Communication.* 1(3) (2008): 384–397.

Grunig, J. E., and L. A. Grunig. "Models of public relations and communications". In J. E. Grunig (Ed.), *Excellence in public relations and communication management.* Hillsdale, NJ: Lawrence Erlbaum and Associates, 1992, 285–325.

Grunig, J. E., and T. Hunt. *Managing public relations.* New York: Holt, Rinehart & Winston, 1984.

Hogan, M. "From the ticketing trenches". *SportsBusiness Journal,* May 23, 2011: 22.

Hopwood, M. K. "Applying the public relations function to the business of sport". *International Journal of Sports Marketing & Sponsorship,* 6(3) (2005): 174–188.

Hopwood, M. Sports public relations. In J. G. Beech & S. Chadwick (Eds.), *The marketing of sport.* London: Prentice Hall/Financial Times, 2007, 292–317.

Kent, M. L., and M. Taylor, "Building dialogic relationships through the World Wide Web. *Public Relations Review,* 24 (1998): 321–334.

Ledingham, J. A., and S. D. Bruning. "Relationship management in public relations: Dimensions of an organization-public relationship". *Public Relations Review,* 24 (1998): 55–65.

NHL Panthers. "NHL Panthers launch new 'we see red' marketing campaign". *SportsBusiness Journal,* June 6, 2011.

Miller, E. "Investor relations". In P. Lesley (Ed.). *Lesley's handbook of public relations and communications.* Lincolnwood, IL: NTC Business Books, 1998, 161–206.

Mullin, B. J., S. Hardy, and W. Sutton. *Sport marketing.* 3rd ed., Champaign, IL: Human Kinetics, 2007.

Panthers Launch. "Panthers launch 'we see red' marketing campaign," 2011, www.panthers.nhl.com.

Pedersen, P. M., K. S. Miloch, and P. C. Laucella. *Strategic sport communication.* Champaign, IL: Human Kinetics, 2007.

Romney, M., and T. Robinson, *Turnaround: Crisis, leadership and the Olympic Games.* Washington, DC: Regnery Publishing, 2004.

Rubel, S. "The attention crash", June 11, 2007, accessed November 1, 2009, http://www.micropersuasion. com/2007/06/the_attention_c.html

Scott, D. M. *The new rules of marketing & PR.* Hoboken, NJ: John Wiley & Sons, 2009.

Seltzer, T., and M. A. Mitrook. "The dialogic potential of weblogs in relationship building". *Public Relations Review*, 33 (2007): 227–229.

Shank, M. *Sports marketing: A strategic perspective.* 4th ed., Upper Saddle River, NJ: Prentice Hall, 2008.

Sheth, H., and K. Babiak. "Beyond the game: Perceptions of practices of corporate social responsibility in the professional sport industry". *Journal of Business Ethics,* 91(3) (2010): 433–450.

Smith, R. D. *Strategic planning for public relations.* 2nd ed., Mahwah, NJ: Lawrence Erlbaum Associates, 2005.

Solis, B., and D. Breakenridge. *Putting the public back in public relations: How social media is reinventing the aging business of PR.* Upper Saddle River, NJ: Pearson Education, 2009.

Spoelstra, J. *Marketing outrageously.* Marietta, GA: Bard Press, 2001.

Stoldt, G. C., S. W. Dittmore, and S. Branvold. *Sport public relations: Managing organizational communication.* Champaign, IL: Human Kinetics, 2006.

Syme, C. "Social media 101: Part One: You need a PIE," November 17, 2010, accessed November 22, 2010, http://cosida.com/news.aspx?id=2975

Treadwell, D., and J. B. Treadwell. *Public relations writing: Principles in practice.* Boston, MA: Allyn and Bacon, 2000.

WTA Launches. "WTA launches strong is beautiful campaign", May 12, 2011, www.wtatennis.com/news

WTA Looking. "WTA looking to attract casual fans with new ad campaign", *SportsBusiness Journal/Daily.* May 12, 2011, http://www.sportsbusinessdaily.com

USTA Kicks. "USTA Kicks off U.S. Open ticket sales with Times Square event", *SportsBusiness Journal/Daily.* June 13, 2011, http://www.sportsbusinessdaily.com

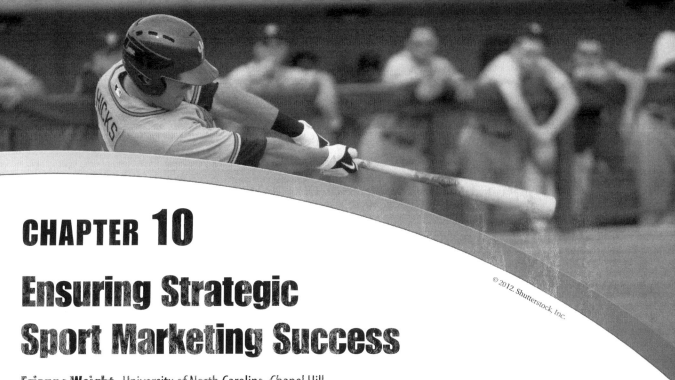

© 2012. Shutterstock, Inc.

CHAPTER 10

Ensuring Strategic Sport Marketing Success

Erianne Weight University of North Carolina, Chapel Hill
Matt Walker University of Southern Mississippi

> *Next to doing the right thing, the most important thing is to let people know you are doing the right thing.*
>
> John D. Rockefeller

CHAPTER OBJECTIVES

After completing the chapter, the reader should be able to:

- Understand the importance of strategy in sport marketing and it's increasing prevalence in the industry.
- Define strategy and purpose and understand how they differ.
- Understand proper change management techniques.
- Discuss strategies to ensure that strategy remains in the forefront of all marketing efforts.
- Discuss rewards programs and one-to-one marketing efforts in the sport industry.
- Understand customer relationship management.
- Define and describe social responsibility in terms of the strategic marketing mix.
- Discuss why social responsibility should matter to sport marketers.
- Discuss why sport organizations have a responsibility to pursue goals above and beyond profit maximization.
- Describe the organizational assets reaped from engaging in socially responsible programs and activities.
- Provide examples of current social responsibility practices in sport.

Introduction

The term strategy is a derivative of *strategos,* a Greek word used to describe a high-ranking military officer. While the concept of strategy (as we study it today) has evolved from these early roots it nonetheless still entails skill acquisition necessary to out-maneuver, fight, and ultimately conquer an enemy. As sport marketers, strategy is probably more familiar than it may be to the general populace as most individuals have a passion for playing and/or watching sport that is generally driven by competitive strategy. Just as your favorite sport star tries to out-maneuver his or her competition, so too do sport marketers strive to out-maneuver their competition in the battle for consumer discretionary income.

It has become popular practice to adorn many traditional business sub-disciplines with the word strategy. If you peruse course offerings, you may see strategic management, strategic marketing, and even strategy as independent courses. This text and chapter each have the word included as integral elements of their titles. This was purposeful to illustrate that strategy echoes the intense competition that exists in the sport industry, for when there is no enemy (or competition), there is no need for strategy. In order to succeed in the battle to attain and retain consumers, it is imperative to frame your marketing and management efforts with the concept that it is foundational in our current competitive marketplace—business is an industrial war for market share.

In Chapter 2, we discussed developing a strategic plan, surveying the internal and external environment, performing appropriate analyses, and developing sport marketing plans. Within Chapters 3–9, elements of the marketing plan were discussed—each forming a critical element of our arsenal. Within this chapter, we will discuss how to best strategically manage and implement the plan in order to ensure success. In addition, the chapter will discuss how aspects of social responsibility have emerged as a new way for sport marketers to add "secondary value" to their brands beyond the traditional "on-field" sport product. In particular, we will elucidate situations where marketers can strategically capitalize on their ability to foster reputational, relational, and partnership assets through social responsibility, social responsiveness, corporate citizenship, and cause-marketing efforts.

Strategic Marketing Management

> ... *All men can see these tactics whereby I conquer, but what none can see is the strategy out of which victory is evolved.*
>
> *(Sun Tzu, 1993)*

Because of the inherent level of uncertainty present in strategy development, it is common for managers to cling to various tangible tactics (Horwath, 2006). One of sport's greatest strategists, John Wooden, once stated "... we are easy to scout but tough to play against" ("Sport: John Wooden's Simple Strategy," 1974). This quote demonstrates the fundamental difference between tactics and strategy. On paper, most of the UCLA Bruin's tactics were simple—and easily defended. But the orchestration of these tactics fit into a well-rehearsed and overall plan which gave the Bruins a competitive advantage week in and week out. This basic example illustrates why it is critical to keep strategy at the forefront of marketing management.

Any competitor can copy, mimic, and counteract elements of your marketing mix, but when these tactics are driven by a strategy, a competitive advantage can ensue.

As discussed in previous chapters, a strong strategic foundation is necessary to support a marketing manager as he/she implements and manages the marketing plan. However, a firm belief in the vision of the organization and the overarching goals of the strategic plan need to be at the forefront of every tactical decision. This sustaining theme begins with a thorough market analysis balancing trends in the industry with specific strengths of the organization

Courtesy of Kimberly Miloch.

and examination of competitors through perhaps utilizing **Porter's 5 Forces model, Value Chain Analyses,** a **SWOT analysis,** and/or other strategic industrial analysis tools (Porter, 1998). Based on relative competitive opportunities, a consumer target market (or segment) is solidified as the organization would strive to attract and satisfy consumers through marketing efforts, and then the marketing mix would be catered to drive that consumer base toward adoption behaviors. The selected strategy would have a purpose to accomplish a variety of specified objectives including increasing revenue, increasing on-the-court performance, facilitation of recruiting, enhancing fan-identity or school spirit, boosting short-term cash flow, enhancing organizational visibility, providing opportunities, protecting and fortifying a community asset, and/or increasing market-share.

Integration of Marketing Concepts

As the integration of tactics and implementation of strategy evolve and progress, a strong belief in the elements and methods delineated in the strategic plan is necessary in order to reinforce the importance of the strategic planning process. At this point, the **marketing management philosophy** specific to the chosen strategy needs to be at the forefront. Generally (in the sport industry), management philosophy is one of a market orientation where the organization strives to focus on customer wants and needs in an effort to satisfy them. However, some organizations integrate their marketing efforts through a production (company-centered), or a sales orientation (sales-centered). Regardless of the specific orientation, target market, promotion techniques, or product decisions, the success of the marketing strategy depends on an integrated process guided with and centered in the strategy.

Because integration is a critical function of marketing efforts, a large portion of a marketing manager's job is to "sell" the strategy to other operational areas of the organization and ensure and facilitate various **process management** techniques. Fundamental to the process, management is making certain the strategy is in line with the staffing and financial resources available. A thorough, internal understanding of the organization's strategy-specific marketing orientation, and each individual or department's unique role is necessary in order to ensure that the external consumer's messages are consistent.

Implementation of Marketing Plan

Implementation of a marketing plan is essentially delivering what you said you would do—putting strategy into action. This involves following up with the specific objectives stated in the marketing plan and creating action assignments for the implementation of the objectives. These assignments then need to be coordinated with other involved parties and facilitated by the marketing manager in order to ensure they are conducted in a way that sustains the vision of the strategy. This process involves extensive communication between and among all parties integral to the planning, budgeting, timelines, job assignments—all the while emphasizing customer relationship management. An organization may have a brilliant strategy, but ineffective implementation is a sure recipe for disaster. If the ball is fumbled on the snap—it doesn't matter how brilliant the play might have been, because the play will be over before it began. Thus, it is critical to have the right people in the right places with a clear understanding of their duties for the plan to be successful.

Communication

In order for a strategy to successfully come to fruition, it must be championed by a leader who strongly believes in the plan. If the strategy represents substantial change within the organization, an implementation of change management protocol is highly suggested. Kotter (2005) developed an eight-step change management model that is recommended reading for any manager implementing change (see Table 10.1).

Generally, individuals are hesitant and/or skeptical when it comes to change. If a new path is to be forged within the organization, following Kotter's eight-step process will greatly facilitate the process and lead to greater levels of success. When communicating the strategy, your message will have strong competition from other messages circulating within the company. In order for the strategy to take root and flourish, it needs to be communicated frequently and powerfully. Depending on the leadership style of the strategy champion and the culture of the organization, this can take shape through formal lines of communication (e.g., meetings, memos, and emails), or through more informal methods (e.g., water-cooler discussions, calendars, paperweights, and screen-savers with strategy key-words). Regardless of the method, regular (even daily) reminders of the strategy will facilitate a strategic directional focus on the task at hand.

Detailed Budgets, Job Assignments, and Timelines

When implementing the marketing plan, integrating all departments involved with the strategy is imperative. Clear, specific, and measurable job assignments and timelines with associated budgets for task-completion are essential. Each department head or individual in charge of the elements should be very clear on their authority and responsibilities. Depending on

TABLE 10.1

Kotter's Eight-Step Change Management Model	
Step One: Create Urgency	In order for stakeholders to buy in to the strategy/change, they need to believe that change is needed.
Step Two: Form a Powerful Coalition	Change will be facilitated if you create a team of influential people who believe in the strategy—their power may come from longevity, status, expertise, and/or political clout.
Step Three: Create a Vision for Change	Simplify the strategy into a form that encapsulates its potential and is easily understood by all stakeholders.
Step Four: Communicate the Vision	Communicate the strategy frequently and powerfully. Demonstrate the type of behavior integral in the plan, and openly address ideas and potential concerns.
Step Five: Remove Obstacles	Alter any structures or processes that can impede the implementation of the plan. Eliminate any barriers to progress.
Step Six: Create Short-term Wins	Success breeds success, and can be a strong motivator. Set short-term targets that can be celebrated along the journey toward complete implementation of the marketing plan.
Step Seven: Build on the Change	Be careful not to declare success too soon. After each victory, analyze what was done right, and what could be better. Strive toward continuous improvement.
Step Eight: Anchor the Changes in Corporate Culture	In order for the strategy to stick and remain grounded in the organization through time, it is important to communicate progress often, and emphasize ideals of the strategy in hiring and training of new staff members.

(Source: Kotter, 2005)

the scope of the project, it can be helpful to utilize critical chain project management in order to best utilize resources throughout the project. Critical chain project management encourages mapping each event with a focus on constraints. Based on these constraints, events and event-chains are sequenced and resources (human or physical) can be optimally allocated in order to fulfill the strategic plan and ultimately satisfy your consumers.

Customer Relationship Management

Imagine yourself as a marketing manager focused on event-chains, budgets, timelines, and job assignments. As you put yourself in this role, it is easy to understand how one might get bogged down in the details of tactics utilized in a strategy rather than remain focused on the vision of the strategy. Just as it is common to lose sight of the big picture, it is easy to stray from the market orientation central to most marketing strategies. Paramount to successful marketing management is an emphasis on **customer relationship management (CRM)**. CRM is a business strategy designed to maximize profitability and customer satisfaction through the coordination of initiatives to build, nurture, and sustain fan identity and/or consumer loyalty. Defined by Morgan and Hunt (1994) as "... all marketing activities directed toward establishing, developing, and maintaining successful relational exchanges" (22), CRM refers to marketing investments geared toward developing long-term relationships with consumers (Algoe and Haidt, 2009). Relationship management continues to be an important topic among marketers. To foster relational exchanges, organizations utilize a number of marketing activities in order to engage new customers and strengthen bonds with existing ones.

At its core, CRM is nothing more than a cultivated relationship between a salesperson and a consumer. A successful salesperson develops a relationship with his or her clients through tracking purchase behavior and preferences. The salesperson may educate, inform, and instruct their customer about new products, services, and technology. Often the salesperson can predict what their customer will need before the customer is even aware of a need. This kind of thoughtful attention is possible through the proper implementation of a CRM informational technology system which can track customer purchasing behavior and preferences and ultimately get to know consumers on an individual basis. This focus on customer relationships is driven by the axiom that customer retention is generally much more profitable than customer acquisition. This can be evidenced by applying lifetime value (LTV) calculations to a simple example (Wakefield, 2007).

Imagine your favorite restaurant in town that you frequent often. Say you go there once a week (except for a few weeks—50 times throughout the year) and spend $6.50 on your meal at each visit. You repeat this practice for the four years you are in college. Your LTV calculation would be:

- LTV = amount spent per visit × visits per year × number of years

- LTV = $6.50 × 50 × 4 = $1300

In this anecdotal example, your LTV simply throughout four years at one restaurant would be $1300. As a manager, utilizing a lifetime value paradigm for customer interactions can be very influential. Just as you would suspect that one might get better service if they spent $1300 rather than $6.50, when lifetime value is emphasized in sales and service training, the most loyal fans, season-ticket holders, and "regular" customers should be treated *better* than the rest. Referring to the **80/20 principle**—80% of a company's revenue is generated from 20% of its customers, it is important to be able to identify these customers. This is made possible through the development of a CRM system and data mining to identify the best customers.

A prerequisite to the creation of unique value propositions for select customers, or individualized promotions and packages for all consumers, is knowledge about the consumer, and a quality CRM database founded on customer data. As discussed in Chapter 4, obtaining high-quality, actionable data is critical to all marketing efforts. Data essential to a successful CRM system involves the collection of information about customers through investigation or first-hand information gathered in customer interactions. Initial data may include responses to questionnaires, information gathered at the point-of-sale, purchase behaviors on the web, activity and preferences tracked through a reward card, etc.

As an example, Veritix is an organization quickly growing as a leading ticketing and marketing organization within professional and collegiate athletics. The company has replaced the traditional (antiquated) ticketing system with FlashSeats—an electronic ticketing system, to provide ticket buyers with the unique opportunity to choose any form of electronic ID (credit card, driver's license, etc.) as their method of entry to a given event. Through this, consumer purchase behaviors can be tracked enabling customized value propositions directly from the ticketing system (Veritix, 2010).

Ideally, all of your customers are getting optimal service, but there are methods to reward repeat customers to make them feel valued. Most consumers are very familiar with customer loyalty programs. These reward programs are growing in popularity among sport organizations. With the often implicit inclination toward identity, reward programs within sport organizations can be very successful as fans often feel that they are supporting their team through purchases. One of the first fan-reward systems implemented in a sport organization was the San Diego Padres' Compadres program. To become part of the program, Padres fans were asked to fill out a short questionnaire (which provided valuable information to the organization), and then the fans were given cards that make it possible for the Padres to track consumption behavior, while fans build up points and earn discounts and special perks.

There are numerous strategies to aid marketing managers in their effort to enhance customer relationships. The emphasis on customized, individualized value propositions is one method. This practice is often referred to as **one-to-one marketing**. In this practice, a sport marketer strives to cater individualized products, promotions, and avenues of communication unique to each buyer. Similar to receiving customized coupons from your grocery store based on what you buy using your value-card, or email offers from Amazon.com based on past purchases, sport organizations can offer similar individualized offers to their customers. If a particular fan purchased three tickets to evening games and hot dogs and sodas at each game, a unique package catered specifically to attract this fan could be sent—*the evening hot dog package* enticing them to purchase five tickets to evening games with deals on hot dog value meals. Because of this fan's prior purchase behaviors, this individualized package might move them up the escalator of commitment to attend five games this year rather than his previous season attendance of three games.

Whatever the system utilized, it is important to remember that customer relationship management is a philosophy. Certainly programs and databases help, but just as networking is much more than the simple act of exchanging business cards, CRM involves a concerted effort to build and sustain *relationships*. Depending on the size of the organization and the number of consumers to sustain, the efforts and possibilities differ. A good practice is to begin a CRM process by building a theoretical picket fence dividing the very loyal customers from all others. Begin with efforts to reward and foster loyalty to this manageable group behind the picket fence, and slowly expand the fence to include more of the customer base. Many database management systems are available to aid sport marketers in consumer relationship management. The key is to make sure the database is user-friendly, adaptable, and integral in the strategic plan.

Accountability and Social Involvement

Sport organizations have the opportunity to capitalize on their relational and community connections by implementing and utilizing various strategies aimed at bolstering their relationship management platform. To build and sustain such relationships, organizations should deploy marketing information in a manner consistent with the philosophy of relationship management. However, in the wake of many recent business transgressions (e.g., British Petroleum, Global Crossing, Enron, Martha Stewart Worldwide, etc.) the emergence of a new business era has increased many marketers' interest in how social involvement[1] and socially responsible information can add substantively to the overall marketing mix. As mentioned throughout this chapter, marketers serve an important role in the development of corporate strategy and as the job entails, are continually looking for new and innovative ways to reach their desired audiences. From a *business-society-relationship* perspective, the description of what was traditionally considered to be a "marketing strategy" has become somewhat blurred. This has partly occurred because traditional marketing theory assumes that the customer is only interested in the company's marketing mix (i.e., product, price, product availability, customer service, etc.). However, increasing societal concerns about the social role of modern business has illustrated that the customer can also be influenced by the ethical standards and social policies of the company behind the products and brands they purchase.

In today's competitive business environment, the need for increased organizational legitimacy through transparent business operations has become paramount, as the phrase "inclusive company" now dominates much of the popular press. An inclusive company is one that understands their stakeholders' needs and incorporates these needs, which are central to achieving sustainable growth, competitiveness, and differentiation into an operational strategy. Therefore, marketers (now more than ever before) understand that the attitudes of their stakeholders (particularly consumers) are critical when analyzing frameworks that guide "inclusive" business choices, part of which are predicated on the company's record for social involvement. Given that social involvement "... can be much more than a cost, a constraint, or a charitable deed—it can be a source of opportunity, innovation, and competitive advantage" (Porter and Kramer, 2006, 1), many sport organizations are now heavily involved in marketing their social initiatives to a broad range of organizational constituents.

Consumers are important stakeholders with regards to ethical and pro-social information and sport organizations are beginning to realize the strategic business implications their awareness of such efforts could have on marketing strategy. Correspondingly, this new era of so called "ethical consumerism" has increased consumer expectations for businesses to participate in addressing (and moreover rectifying) various societal issues such as health and education, fair-trade and worker equality, community development, environmental issues, and to generally (proactively) consider the effects their business operations have on society.

Particularly in recent times, as heightened accountability and increased transparency among big business has expanded, so, too have large-scale marketing initiatives aimed at communicating the "good" things that companies do. Given this surge in socially responsible communication, there is likely no doubt that you have heard or perhaps even discussed the terms: **corporate social responsibility (CSR), corporate citizenship (CC), corporate social responsiveness (CSR$_2$),** and **cause-related marketing (CRM)**. However, disentangling these concepts can be quite tricky because they oftentimes have divergent outcomes that can affect a broad range of organizational stakeholders. One primary question remains though, why should you (i.e., as a business owner, marketing manager, or entrepreneur)

---

[1]The phrase "social initiatives" is used as a collective representation of the business-society relationship.

care about these social involvement areas? The answer is quite simple: strategic community investments (and the subsequent marketing of these activities) can yield **reputational, relational,** and **partnership assets** which in turn can lead positive organizational results (e.g., increased sales, image perceptions, reputation management, etc.).

So of course, why wouldn't a company want to be socially involved and give back to the community? You would think if a company donates money to a few charities they have performed their duty and then might be dubbed a "good corporate citizen." As a result, their business grows and all the executives go home happy—right? Not quite. Before you go and tell your boss to start emptying his pockets to any cause that pulls at your heart strings you need a strategy. Does your investment in the community tie back to your business and marketing objectives? Is there a strategic fit between your organization and the cause you are intending to support? What are the most pressing local, national, or transnational social issues that could yield the most "bang for the buck?" As a marketer, understanding that an organization's contribution to the community is an investment, made with the anticipation that over time, there will be a true impact and bring a positive return.

Given the meteoric rise of social networking (e.g., Facebook, Twitter, etc.) and the relative ease of other types of electronic communication (i.e., e-newsletters), messages about various CSR, CC, and CRM activities are continually being pushed to organizational stakeholders. The problem is that these activities can all mean different things to different people and as such, their true meanings and strategic underpinnings often get blurred. Thus, the marketing manager needs to fully understand the dynamics associated with the various concepts in order to effectively communicate them to the public. The trend of marketing and communicating social and ethical messages has been adopted as a new way for organizations, especially those in the professional sport industry, to attain "secondary value" (Walker and Kent, 2009, 744) beyond the scope of their core product (i.e., the on field competition, for example golf, football, baseball, etc.). This new institutional trend is particularly germane for sport marketers because many businesses now understand the need to act responsibly and moreover, consumers want to live in a community led by socially conscious business leaders. Thus, the strategic focus on community engagement has shifted from a "whether or not" to a "how" approach—in other words—from something organizations could do, into something they ought to, or even should do.

Disentangling the Terms

The confusion surrounding the concepts of responsibility, responsiveness, citizenship, and cause marketing necessitates the need to juxtapose the definitions in order to distinguish these seemingly close-knit concepts.

First, corporate social responsibility (CSR) implies that businesses are responsible for assessing their wider impact on society and regardless of specific labeling, the concept has been applied to how managers should handle public policy and other social issues. Accordingly, Waddock (2004) opined that "... CSR is the subset of corporate responsibilities that deals with a company's discretionary relationships with its societal and community stakeholders" (10), in order to minimize or eliminate any harmful effects on society and maximize any long-run beneficial impacts. To serve their many stakeholders, organizations often proactively implement CSR activities ranging from community enrichment and development programs to environmental initiatives. For example, philanthropic events (e.g., donations to local organizations), volunteer activities (e.g., camps and clinics), community appreciation events (e.g., ethnic heritage days, kid's or senior's days, autograph signings, etc.), educational programs (e.g., school reading and safety programs), and general community involvement (e.g., opening a Boys and Girls Club, rebuilding homes, etc.) are all examples of CSR seen in sport.

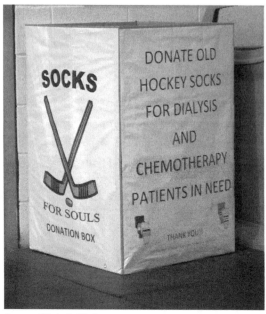

Courtesy of Kimberly Miloch.

Second, corporate social responsiveness (CSR_2) is regarded as more of a strategic aspect of the responsibility paradigm. As a result, CSR_2 has been discussed more in terms of how organizations respond to societal demands. In other words, sport organizations should take forward looking action to respond to and deal with stakeholders and public policy issues bringing them up to a level consistent with prevailing social norms. For example, responding to child obesity (e.g., the NFL's "Play 60 campaign"), diversity issues (e.g., NASCAR's "Drive for Diversity"), the environment (e.g., the Philadelphia Eagles "Go Green" initiative), poverty (e.g., Nike Foundation), and disease prevention (e.g., the NHL's "Hockey Fights Cancer" program) are all programs aimed at responding to various societal demands in and around these organizations' respective communities.

© Andrew Dieb/NewSport/Corbis.

Third, corporate citizenship (CC) means administering citizenship rights for individuals through compliance with ethical governance, endorsing global standards, and promoting philanthropic and volunteer activities (Matten and Crane, 2005). CC essentially implies that the organization itself becomes part of the public/social culture and can expand wherever business operations exist. Thus, CC is regarded as a cultural, legal, global, and embedded dimension of social involvement (Maignan, Ferrell, and Holt, 1999) and is

FIGURE 10.1

Geographical Focus of Social Involvement in Sport

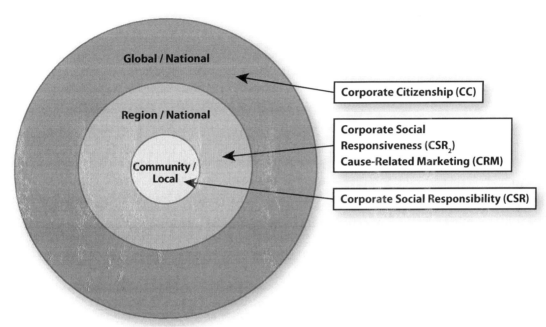

thought to be a more nationalistic and global framework rather than a localized and popular orientation. For example, Nike undertaking human rights initiatives in the countries where they conduct their manufacturing operations and the Adidas Group's "Adi Dassler Fund," which both enable global contributions to societies around the world.

Fourth, community involvement in sport is also grounded in the cause related marketing (CRM) paradigm, largely discussed as a partnership between the sport firm and a cause to attract consumers who want to make a difference through their purchasing. CRM involves cooperative marketing efforts between "for-profit" and "non-profit" organizations for mutual benefit. More broadly however, the term is sometimes used to refer to any social and other charitable marketing efforts. For example, since 1991, New Balance has been a national series sponsor of the Susan G. Komen Race for the Cure®, the world's largest and most successful education and fundraising event for breast cancer (New Balance, 2010). As well, the PGA TOUR has partnered with the Children's Miracle Network, which is a non-profit event that raises funds for more than 170 children's hospitals around the nation (PGA TOUR, 2010).

In a recent study that content analyzed the behaviors of a wide array of sport organizations (i.e., teams, leagues, businesses, and governing bodies), Walker and Parent (2010) found that geographic reach was one of the underpinning factors for the type of social involvement in which organizations engaged (see Figure 10.1). This strategic focus can benefit the organization by helping them garner significant assets that are discussed next.

Strategic Asset Generation from Social Involvement

Relational Assets

The increasing commitment to social involvement by modern business is spurred by the growing sense that consumers will reward "good" organizations through sustained relations. Both marketplace polls and a growing body of research on the topic has demonstrated that consumers are more likely to support organizations that engage in socially responsible actions, particularly in domains they deem appropriate and personally relevant (Du, Bhattacharya, and Sen, 2007). These findings are largely attributed to the manner in which ethics and social responsibilities humanize the organization, encouraging consumers to not just like, respect, or admire them, but actually identify and personally connect with what they are trying to accomplish. In turn, such well-discussed marketing benefits (for example increased sales) can materialize. Additional benefits go beyond purchasing the company's product to the rarer, longer-term relational benefits that manifest as loyalty (e.g., resilience to negative brand information) and advocacy (e.g., positive word-of-mouth,), which many scholars consider to be among the most salient paybacks of CSR engagement (Du, Bhattacharya, and Sen, 2007).

The inner ring of Figure 10.1 helps to illustrates how localized, community-based efforts can contribute to such relational capital. For example, collaborations and partnerships with local firms aimed at bettering the community in some way (e.g., community relations activities, philanthropic programs and strategies, and volunteer activities) can yield positive and immediate benefits (Waddock, 2004). Because of their central place in their respective communities, we clearly see that most sport teams' social efforts could be classified as localized and focused on social responsibility. Additionally, teams themselves are local businesses and CSR provides a strategic way for them to increase visibility, attract new stakeholders, and build their reputations.

Based on this commentary, organizations engaging in CSR activities focus primarily on relationship building in the community. Marquis, Glynn, and Davis (2007) noted that, "... the local geographic community as an immediate institutional environment thus serves both as a touchstone for legitimacy and as a target for social involvement" (928). Essentially, CSR attempts to build and foster (through extended efforts) relational assets. However, organizations operating in the broader industry context have the ability to garner similar relational assets as well.

Reputational Assets

Early social involvement work focused on firms' wrong-doings, how firms affect specific social groups, and how firms' actions might be controlled through regulation, public pressure, and judicial actions. Unfortunately, all too frequently the motives underlying most social involvement activities have centered on negating the effects that product and service offerings may have on society and as such, have traditionally been viewed as a "cost-item" to be encumbered by the company (Walker and Kent, 2009). Contrary to this idea, good corporate ethics is now said to contribute to a competitive organizational advantage. Such a competitive advantage is only gleaned from building a positive and consistent reputation among consumers. Consequently, a good reputation is regarded as one of the key outcomes of marketing and organizational positioning and may constitute the bulk of the worth for many organizations (Walker, et. al, 2010). Recently, sport marketers have become interested in how reputation relates to social policies because elements of involvement have been viewed as key drivers of a corporate reputation. Conversely, Hillenbrand and Money (2007) argued that rather than an antecedent of reputation, social responsibilities are key attributes in terms of how an organization's reputation is judged. Through an accumulation of marketing information that details the organization's social policies, consumers may generate lasting reputations because they translate the past social performance of an organization into expectative future behavior.

For example, CSR_2 and CC show the capacity of leagues and national/global organizations to respond to various social pressures placed on them by society. This orientation of social involvement allows for these organizations to create new contexts, new values, and new ways of thinking about social involvement, some of which can be seen today emerging in practice (e.g., MLB's partnerships with the Jackie Robinson Foundation, the Boys and Girls Clubs of America, the National Recreation and Park Association, and the National Urban League). The middle ring presented in Figure 10.1 classifies social involvement in a more regional and nationalistic light. This broader focus means that organizations adopting this strategy have the ability to be a change agent through their ability and capacity to respond to various societal demands and in turn increase their reputational assets.

Partnership Assets

Early social involvement discussions among sport marketers were grounded in the cause related marketing (CRM) paradigm, and were largely discussed as a partnership between the sport firm and a cause. As a result, many sport firms realized the strategic potential of partnerships when formulating a social involvement strategy. Increasingly, CRM was being used as a form of advertising by essentially promoting the company's image through an association with a specific cause. The success of these partnerships, in conjunction with general marketing communications, became important because marketers knew that responding to higher consumer expectations for social involvement was critical to sustain and attract new clients. Furthermore, the popularity of CRM programs was largely attributed to the integration of sport sponsorship into the overall marketing strategy. Among the most successful and recognizable examples of CRM sponsorships currently exist on the PGA TOUR with events that benefit children's charities. For example, The St. Jude Classic (formerly the FedEx St. Jude Classic), the Children's Miracle Network Classic, and the Shriner's Hospital for Children Open, all have various corporate sponsors seeking to align themselves with these causes that benefit society.

CRM provides a platform for examining consumers' interpretation of an event promotion strategy with an embedded social dimension by exploring behavioral and attitudinal responses to some level of corporate outreach (Lachowetz and Irwin, 2002). Presently, many public sentiments toward the actions and agendas of corporate America are at their lowest levels since the early 1980's, with most Americans disgusted over the immoral and unethical behavior of companies like Enron, Arthur Anderson, and Adelphia (to name a few).

Subsequently, research has suggested many consumers appreciate and support CRM programs. In fact, some marketplace polls have shown that an increasing number of consumers reward firms that are proactively engaged in environmental and other social issues; pointing to the ability to capitalize on strategic partnerships (Till and Nowak, 2000).

Summary

Strategic marketing management entails guiding an organization and its marketing efforts in a direction that optimizes the company strengths relative to its competitive environment in order to out-maneuver competitors, attract and sustain consumers, and ultimately achieve the purpose of the organization. Within this chapter, we discussed the role of strategy in the current sport marketplace and how to manage and implement a strategic marketing plan through process, change, and customer relationship management. In addition, the chapter covered how aspects of social responsibility have emerged as a new way for sport marketers to add "secondary value" to their brands beyond the traditional "on-field" sport product. In particular, we explored situations where marketers can strategically capitalize on their ability to foster reputational, relational, and partnership assets through social responsibility, social responsiveness, corporate citizenship, and cause-marketing efforts.

Discussion Questions

1. Why is strategy becoming increasingly prevalent in sport management education and practice?

2. How do strategy and purpose differ?

3. Give an example of a purpose or strategy of an athletic department, professional franchise, or community sport organization.

4. What can be the consequences of improper change management?

5. What are some ways to ensure that strategy remains in the forefront of all marketing efforts?

6. What are some examples of rewards programs or one-to-one marketing efforts in the sport industry?

7. How might you begin a customer relationship management program with an intercollegiate athletic department? Where might you draw the "picket fence"?

8. What are the fundamental differences between social responsibility, responsiveness, citizenship, and cause-marketing?

9. As a future sport marketer, how do you view the utility of integrating the aforementioned areas into the marketing mix?

10. In what ways can social involvement lead to a competitive advantage for the sport firm?

11. There were a few "assets" resulting from social involvement discussed in the chapter. Can you think of other "assets" that marketers can capitalize on through their social involvement?

12. Why do you think that geography plays a role in how and why sport firms engage in social involvement activities?

13. What are some examples of social involvement you have seen used in marketing and promotions activities of sport firms?

14. How do marketers ensure that their messages associated with social involvement aren't viewed by the consumer as overly strategic?

15. Given the high visibility of sport (e.g., teams, organizations, governing bodies), in what ways do you think that social involvement could be more (or less) impactful in sport than for mainstream businesses?

Critical Thinking Exercises

1. You have just been commissioned by the Mesquite Mosquitoes to create a strategic marketing plan for the business. The Mosquitoes are a new AA minor league baseball organization in a small city with a population of 15,000 located one hour from Las Vegas, NV. Without specifying details about the organization itself, create a list of the steps and strategic considerations you would include when completing this project.

2. Research an organization that you are interested in and/or familiar with. Conduct an audit of the marketing tactics being utilized. Based on what you see, describe the marketing strategy that you believe may be driving these efforts.

3. As the new CEO of the Woodland Hills YMCA, your charge is to take the organization from its current precarious financial situation to one that has a healthy bottom line. Paramount to this effort is a change in marketing strategy. Currently, there is no strategic direction, and marketing efforts have consisted of flyers to drive interest in new programs. Utilizing Kotter's change model, how will you implement a more sophisticated method of marketing management?

4. Calculate the lifetime value (LTV) of a 40-year-old football season-ticket holder who spends on average $60/game for each of the eight home games per season who plans on coming to the games for as long as he can (until he's 85). Based on this LTV, what strategies might you use to increase his level of consumption, reward him for being a loyal customer, and/or communicate marketing messages to him on a seemingly individual level?

5. In recent times there has been a surge in social involvement among sport firms. Think about a time when you have seen or experienced one these programs and talk about why it resonated with you.

6. Discuss why the strategic fit between a cause (in a CRM campaign) and the sport organization is essential for success. In this discussion, use some examples from the sport industry to illustrate.

7. You were recently hired by a sport organization to head up their social involvement campaign. You have little (working) knowledge of how these programs function. However, your boss has faith that you can handle the job and wants you to give a presentation to the board of directors in two weeks. What are the primary factors to consider when implementing a program (e.g., strategy, type of involvement, etc.)?

8. Stemming from the previous scenario, your boss has also hinted that he wants you to show some return on his investment in social involvement. Not being exactly sure what he means by "return," how would you describe the potential outcomes? Are these outcomes financial? If so, in what ways could the organization benefit financially? Are these outcomes non-financial? If so, in what ways can the organization benefit beyond the purely financial?

References

Algoe, S., J. Haidt. "Witnessing Excellence in Action: The other-praising emotions of elevation, admiration, and gratitude". *Journal of Positive Psychology* 4 (2009): 105–127.

Du, S., C. B. Bhattacharya, and S. Sen. "Reaping relational rewards from corporate social responsibility: The role of competitive positioning". *International Journal in Research Marketing* 24 (2007): 224–241.

Hillenbrand, C., and K. Money. "Corporate responsibility and corporate reputation: Two separate concepts or two sides of the same coin?" *Corporate Reputation Review* 10 (2007): 261–277.

Horwath, R. *The Origin of Strategy.* Strategic Thinking Institute, 2006.

Kotter, J. *Leading Change.* Cambridge, MA: Harvard Business School Press, 2005.

Lachowetz, T., and R. Irwin. "An application of a cause-related marketing program (CRMP)". *Sport Marketing Quarterly* 11(2) (2002): 114–116.

Marquis, C., M. A. Glynn, and G. F. Davis. "Community isomorphism and corporate social action". *Academy of Management Review* 32 (2007): 925–945.

Matten, D., & A. Crane. "Corporate citizenship: Toward and extended theoretical conceptualization". *Academy of Management Review* 30 (2005): 166–179.

Maignan, I., O. C. Ferrell, and G. T. M. Holt. "Corporate citizenship: Cultural antecedents and business benefits". *Journal of the Academy of Marketing Science.* 27 (1999): 455–469.

Morgan, R. M., and S. D. Hunt. "The commitment-trust theory of relationship marketing". *Journal of Marketing* 58 (July, 1994): 20–38.

New Balance. "Susan G. Komen race for the cure partnership". 2010. http://www.newbalance.com/komen/

PGA TOUR. "Children's Miracle Network Classic". 2010. http://www.pgatour.com/tournaments/r045/.

Porter, M. *Competitive Strategy* (revised ed.). The Free Press: New York, 1998.

Porter, M., and M. Kramer. "Strategy and society: The link between competitive advantage and corporate social responsibility". *Harvard Business Review* (December, 2006): 1–14.

Sport: John Wooden's simple strategy. *Time Magazine.* 1974. http://www.time.com/time/magazine/article/0,9171,879295,00

Sun-Tzu. *The Art of Warfare.* Tras. Roger T. Ames. Ballantine Books: New York, 1993.

Till, B. D., and L. I. Nowak. "Toward effective use of cause-related marketing alliance". *Journal of Product and Brand Management* 9(7) (2000): 472–484.

Waddock, S. "Parallel universes: Companies, academics, and the progress of corporate citizenship". *Business and Society Review* 109 (2004): 5–42.

Walker, M., B. Heere, M. M. Parent, and D. Drane. "Social responsibility and the Olympic Games: The mediating role of consumer attributions". *Journal of Business Ethics* 95(4) (2010): 659–680.

Walker, M., and M. M. Parent. "Toward an integrated framework of corporate social responsibility, responsiveness, and citizenship activities in sport". *Sport Management Review* 13(3) (2010): 198–213.

Walker, M., and A. Kent. "Do fans care? Assessing the influence of corporate social responsibility on consumer attitudes in the sport industry". *Journal of Sport Management* 23(6) (2009): 743–769.

CHAPTER 11

Sponsorship and Endorsement

Kimberly Miloch Texas Woman's University
Heidi Parker University of Southern Maine
Amanda Glenn Texas Woman's University
Jacquelyn Wilson Texas Woman's University

> *It is unlikely that consumers in general, or attendees of an event in particular, will feel any passion toward a product; they do, however, have strong feelings about causes, events, and sports teams with which they are affiliated. Companies that are able to successfully tap into a consumer's psychological connectedness to a property align themselves to something much more meaningful to that individual than a mere product. It would appear that, rather than creating mere awareness, the promise of sponsorship may lie in the opportunity to capture a consumer's 'share of the heart.'*
>
> (Madrigal, 2000, 22-23)

CHAPTER OBJECTIVES

After completing the chapter, the reader should be able to:

- Understand the role of sport sponsorship and athlete endorsement in sport marketing.
- Recognize and understand the steps in sponsorship acquisition.
- Identify the key concepts of sponsorship evaluation.
- Recognize the factors influencing selection of athlete endorsers.

Sponsorship

Sport sponsorship has evolved from simple signage at a ballpark to a driver of revenues for sport entities and a key focal point in the marketing strategy of many companies. Even in the midst of an economic recession, companies spent approximately $18 billion on sponsorship in 2011 and are projected to spend close to $18.87 billion in 2012 (IEG, 2012). Of those dollars, roughly 68%, or approximately $11.23 billion, are spent on sport sponsorship (IEG, 2010). For instance, Northeast Delta Dental recently signed a 10-year naming rights deal with the Toronto Blue Jays Double A affiliate team, the New Hampshire Fisher Cats; Safe Auto has signed on as a sponsor of Ultimate Fighting Championship (UFC); Farmers Insurance just agreed to $650 million, 30-year naming rights deal with the yet to be built Farmers Field in downtown Los Angeles; and for the first time in over a decade, the 2011 NHL All-Star game had a presenting sponsor—Discover Card. This chapter will outline the key concepts specific to sport sponsorship and athlete endorsement.

Sponsorship Defined

Sport sponsorship originally represented an uncluttered form of advertising which appealed to companies as a means to differentiate their products and brands from competitors. As sponsorship grew and became more cluttered, the need to strategically craft and develop unique sponsorships that connected with consumers became a central focus. Sponsorship is

Courtesy of Kimberly Miloch.

defined as "an investment, in cash or in kind, in an activity, in return for access to the exploitable commercial potential associated with that activity" (Meenaghan, 1991, 36). To become a sponsor, a company must purchase **rights** from a sport organization or event, after which, a company can use various marketing strategies to communicate their connection to the sport team or event. Sponsorship is based on the **exchange theory**, the idea that a successful exchange between two or more parties is dependent on both parties feeling what they receive for their services or goods is equal to their offerings (Crompton, 2004). In other words, *both* the sport organization and the sponsor must feel the relationship is beneficial to their respective organizational objectives.

Sponsorships originally started as an altruistic endeavor—organizations looking to support a cause deemed worthy or give back to their communities. However, sponsorship has grown into a complex marketing strategy with emphasis on increasing an organization's bottom line (Meenaghan, 2001). The purchasing and leveraging of sponsorships has become an integral part of the marketing mix and, and for many organizations, is the primary source of communication with consumers

(Howard and Crompton, 2005). As a result, the relationship between sport organizations and sponsoring businesses has become more complex with sport organizations dependent on sponsorship dollars and organizations looking to get the most from their investment (Burton and O'Reilly, 2011; Stotlar, 2004).

Sponsorship differs from traditional advertising in a number of ways. Recognizing the need to spend money in leveraging and activating sponsorships is one way in which sponsorship differs from traditional advertising. Additionally, the objectives of an organization are often different when marketing through sponsorship rather than more traditional methods. For instance, with traditional marketing efforts, and advertising in particular, it is somewhat evident a company is trying to promote or sell a product or service. Consumers may be guarded and skeptical and unconsciously block those advertising messages. However, sponsorship works differently as consumers see an organization providing money, goods, and/or services to a sport team or event and a sense of goodwill is created (Meenaghan, 1991). Consumers feel more positively about an organization that supports their favorite team or an event to which they have a personal connection. As Burton and O'Reilly (2011) note, sponsorships are associated with a particular sport entity, and this association may favorably drive consumer perceptions. For instance, consider how seeing a Gatorade commercial makes one feel compared to how knowing Gatorade is the sponsor of your favorite team. It may be that one feels more favorably about Gatorade when connecting to them positively with a favorite team, sport, or athlete.

Perhaps the main difference between traditional advertising and sponsorship involves the development of a relationship between sponsor and consumer. Sponsorship of a sporting event or team allows the sponsor to "establish an intimate and emotionally involved relationship(s) with a target audience" (Crompton, 2004, 270). This ability to connect emotionally with consumers is one of the main benefits of sponsorship. However, the key to this benefit is in understanding the consumer-team-sponsor relationship.

Consumer-Team-Sponsor Relationship

The consumer-team-sponsor relationship is best understood through Heider's (1958) **balance theory**. The balance theory suggests people try to maintain a sense of balance in their lives and their actions and judgments are often influenced by the need to preserve such balance. It is useful to discuss the balance theory using diagrams which represent the consumer-team-sponsor relationship (see Figure 11.1).

In general, the adages "your friends are my friends" and "the enemy of my enemy is my friend" summarize the balance theory. For example, consider the relationship shown between consumer, team, and sponsor in Figure 11.1. The first triangle shows a positive relationship between the consumer and the team as well as the sponsor and the team. The balance theory suggests, given the positive relationships between the team and consumer and the positive relationship between the team and sponsor, that the consumer and sponsor are also likely to have a positive relationship. In other words, the consumer, or fan, will feel better about the sponsor given their mutual relationship with the team, as this results in a balanced relationship. However, as shown in the third triangle of Figure 11.1, if a consumer has

FIGURE 11.1

Consumer-Team-Sponsor Relationships

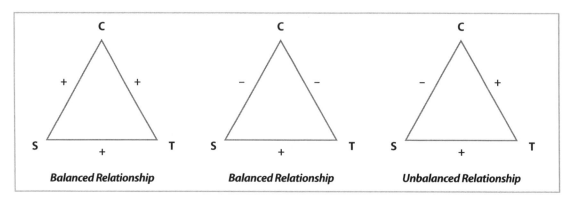

a negative relationship with a sponsor of their favorite team, the relationship is unbalanced and perhaps unsettling for the consumer.

For example, research which was conducted on NASCAR fans found that fans felt more favorably toward their favorite driver's sponsor than the sponsors of other drivers (Dalakis and Levin, 2005). Interestingly, the research also showed that fans felt more negatively toward the sponsor of a driver they strongly disliked than other team sponsors. This negative relationship is depicted in the second triangle in Figure 11.1—if the consumer (fan) does not like a team, they are also likely to have more negative feelings toward that team's sponsor.

However, the key to the relationship between the consumer and the sponsor is the *strength* of the relationship between the consumer and the team/event. Consumers that are not highly identified with, or feel strongly connected to, a particular team or sport event do not need to feel more positively about a sponsor in order to maintain a sense of balance. Yet, consumers who are highly identified with a team or sport event feel more favorably about the team/event sponsors and are more likely to purchase their products (Cornwell and-Coote, 2005; Gwinner and Swanson, 2003; Madrigal, 2000).

Therefore, a sport team or event provides an audience of consumers which sponsors can exploit by capitalizing on the consumer-team-sponsor relationship. If a sport organization or sporting event is a large part of a consumer's self-concept, by attaching a product or brand to the team or event, sponsors become intertwined in part of a "consumer's extended self" (Madrigal, 2000, 22).

Sponsorship Acquisition and Management

Several key steps are central in acquiring sport sponsorships. First, the sport entity must understand the typical goals and objectives of sponsors. Based on that understanding, sport entities must develop and refine their respective **sponsorship inventory**. A sponsorship inventory is a list of items that a sport entity has available to include as elements of a sponsorship. The inventory also includes the number of each item available and the market value of the item. Examples include season tickets, luxury suite, signage, community relations activities, in-arena or on-field promotions, public address announcements, website advertising, and so forth. Within an inventory, categories should be developed. Determining the categories for an inventory depends on the location or property, selecting the different levels of items that can be included in a sponsorship, and how it will be produced when sponsored. For tips on developing inventories and to view samples, log on to this text's companion website. After an inventory is developed or refined, sport entities must prospect for potential sponsors. In doing so, sport entities should segment their respective market for potential sponsors just as they would segment for target markets. Depending on the level of sport (i.e., major league, minor league, or interscholastic), the sponsorship inventory and market segmentation may differ. While prospecting, sport entities should identify viable target companies for sponsorship. Sport entities must research target companies and understand their marketing and brand management strategies and goals as well as identify key decision makers within the respective company. Once the key decision makers have been identified, they should be contacted with the goal of scheduling a face-to-face meeting so the sport entity and company can discuss the potential partnership. During this meeting, it is essential that the sport entity determine the objectives of the potential sponsor so that an appropriate sponsorship proposal may be designed and presented. Sponsorship proposals typically include a description of the sport organization or event; the proposed sponsorship, pricing for the sponsorship, important dates and terms, and first right of refusal. A sample sponsorship for a minor league franchise may be viewed in Table 11.1. For additional examples of sponsorship proposals, log on to this text's companion site. The sponsorship should also include strategies for leveraging and activation. The paragraphs below outline typical sponsor objectives.

TABLE 11.1

Minor League Franchise Sample Sponsorship
Doe's Food Stores **Sponsorship Agreement** **XYZ Athletics**

This sponsorship agreement expires July 31, 2013.

SIGNAGE

Scoreboard
One (1) 2' x 3' full color advertisement displayed on the bottom of the electronic scoreboard. Since every race concludes with the times being posted on the scoreboard, it will be the area in which the most fans are looking at the scoreboard.

Starting Block
Two (2) full color advertisements on the 1' x 1' area on top of starting blocks.
Four (4) full color advertisements on the 9" x 11" on sides of starting blocks. All races must begin from the starting blocks and this will allow fans and media to view the Doe's logo repeatedly.

Sectional Banner
Two (2) 5' x 7' full color advertisements in the primary viewing area for swimming. Banners will be hung above seating, where spectators on either side of the pool can view the banner across from their designated section.

CONCESSSIONS
Control of the concession stand will be awarded to Doe's upon agreement. This includes the ability to choose the menu or items sold. The concession stand will be staffed by XYZ Athletics Staff, but will be controlled by Doe's Food Stores.

TABLE 11.1 *continued*

GAME NIGHT SPONSOR

Two (2) event night sponsorships. Doe's will receive the role of title sponsor for two (2) nights of events throughout the season. Doe's will have the ability to distribute items or products consumers as they enter or exit the venue. Since distribution of promotional items and/or product sampling has been proven to increase brand loyalty among consumers, it is favorable for both the fans and the sponsor. Promotional items and/or products will be mutually determined by Doe's and XYZ.

DOE'S FIVE A DAY PROGRAM

Doe's will receive access to assist the Bus Brigade and will receive title sponsorship for local community schools transportation to and from XYZ Swimming Events. The Swimming Bus Brigade program will provide students throughout the community the chance to attend a Division I University campus and swimming events. This will be paired with the Doe's Five A Day program to help promote goal setting, working to achieve them, as well as healthy eating to Dallas youth.

GAME PROGRAM ADVERTISING

One (1) Permanent half page full color advertisement on the back of the official XYZ Swimming Program.
One (1) Full page, full color advertisement on the inside cover of Classic and special event printed materials.

SEASON TICKETS

Eight (8) season ticket passes for all home swimming events, including Classics and Special events. Doe's will also receive two (2) season passes for all XYZ athletic events.

PA ANNOUNCMENTS

Two (2) Public address announcements during each day of home events, Doe's will provide the materials for the public address announcement, however, XYZ announcing staff will perform announcement at appropriate times during the event.

USE OF XYZ LOGO

As a corporate partner for XYZ, Doe's has written permission to use the XYZ Athletics, and XYZ Mustang logo to leverage the sponsorship package. XYZ Athletic Corporate Relations officials will approve any promotional material developed by Doe's which includes the use of the XYZ, XYZ Swimming and Diving, XYZ Athletics, or XYZ Mustangs.

FIRST RIGHT OF REFUSAL

Doe's Food Stores, as a major corporate sponsor, is granted the first right of refusal for the time period of the 2011–2013 seasons.

COST OF PACKAGE: $18,000
$10,000 DUE AT SIGNING
$4,000 DUE APRIL 1, 2011
$4,000 DUE AUGUST 1, 2011

Sponsor Objectives

The growth of sponsorship has certainly changed the sport landscape in recent years. Sport organizations have become dependent on sponsorship dollars and some organizations have consistently utilized sponsorship as an important tool in the marketing mix. However, the growth of sport sponsorship has also led some consumers to feel like sport has become too commercialized and over saturated with company signage and brand logos. The "clutter," now commonplace in many venues, is ignored by many consumers and has been shown to be ineffective in terms of consumer sponsor brand recall tests. Additionally, some sport fans prefer the traditional feel of a venue, uncluttered with sponsor signage. This has led to some sport organizations, such as the University of Michigan, to forgo venue signage altogether.

Debates have also sprung up over the fit between a sponsor and a sporting event. For example, many American universities will not partner with alcoholic behavior companies. School officials feel that partnering with a company who sells alcohol sends the wrong message to the students of the school, who are predominately under the legal drinking age. Major League Baseball (MLB) and NASCAR have had similar decisions to make regarding the sponsorship of tobacco companies. Ultimately, sport managers must decide what products and brands are an appropriate match to the values of the organization.

Determining what organizations are a good fit to target for sponsorship is not a decision which should be taken lightly. In addition to fit, sport managers should consider company stability, company longevity, and company reputation.

The primary goal of any sponsorship and marketing strategy is to drive sales and revenues. Companies may have many objectives with sponsorship, and all of these objectives serve the ultimate goal of driving sales and revenue. Whether the objective is to increase awareness or to reinforce brand image, ultimately companies desire an increase in revenues and an increased market share. Thus, sponsorships should be designed based on sponsor objectives. In the past, sport entities developed standard sponsorship packages based on level of expenditures. This model is no longer appropriate in today's cluttered and return on

FIGURE 11.2

Steps in Sponsor Acquisition

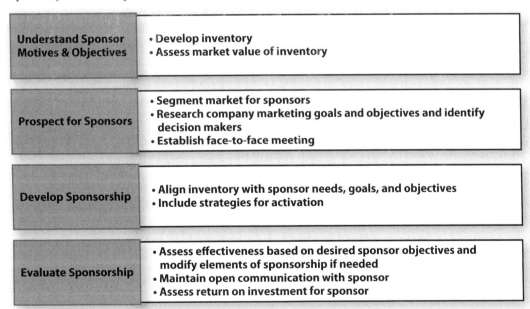

Developed from the framework of Irwin, Sutton, and McCarthy (2002), Mullin, Hardy, and Sutton (2007), and Stotlar (2009).

investment driven marketplace. Sport entities should match their sponsorship inventories with sponsor objectives, and be creative in designing sponsorships. Typical sponsor objectives include increasing awareness for a particular product or brand, increasing sales, maintaining a specific brand image, re-branding, increasing business-to-business partnerships, rewarding consumers or employees, gaining an increase in market share, gaining access to a desired target market, establishing a favorable rapport with target consumers, providing hospitality and entertainment opportunities, enhancing community relations, and differentiating from competing products or brands. Regardless of the objective, sport entities must strive to align objectives with the elements of the sponsorship. For example, as part of its desire to align itself with the U.S.G.A. and its consumer base, Polo engaged in a five-year partnership in which it will serve as the organization's official apparel partner. As part of this sponsorship, Polo will provide on-site retail shops at tournaments and promote its association with golf via various advertisements (Smith, 2011a). In efforts to enhance its fan experience, IndyCar designed the Izod IndyCar Fan Village at races. This piece of inventory not only adds value to the experience for fans, but it also provides a strategic avenue for sponsor activation. As part of the village, Verizon showcases its IndyCar content and phones. Honda is providing player autographs, and Izod is hosting a social media area, the Izod Social Cloud, in which fans are entertained with Twitter feeds, videos, and news (Mickle, 2011).

There are many ways an organization can sponsor a team or an event. For example, an organization may sign on as the title sponsor such as the Tostitos Fiesta Bowl or, in NASCAR, the Chase for the Sprint Cup. As a title sponsor, the sponsor name is incorporated into the name of the event. Likewise, organizations may also buy the naming rights to a building such as Lucas Oil Stadium or FedEx Field. Given the high visibility of the sponsorship, title sponsorships and naming rights are some of the most expensive and are often negotiated for extended periods of time.

Organizations can also become the official sponsor of a particular product category. For instance, Pepsi may sign on as the official beverage sponsor of an event. This type of sponsorship ensures that only Pepsi products are sold and consumed at the event. It is not uncommon for an event to have an official beverage sponsor, such as Coca-Cola or Pepsi, an official beer sponsor, such as Anheuser Busch, as well as official sponsors in a number of other product categories (i.e., apparel, equipment, etc.). For example, at Syracuse University, Pepsi is the official beverage sponsor, Budweiser is the official beer sponsor, and Nike is the official apparel and shoe sponsor.

Sport managers should understand the importance of building relationships with sponsors. This includes working to understand the desire of the sponsor and working together to create a customized sponsorship portfolio which meets the needs and expectations of both parties. For example, at Minute Maid Park, home of the Houston Astros, the sponsorship of the foul poles in the outfield was effective and a humorous play on words for the Chick-fil-a "Eat Mor Chikin®" use of the "Fowl Poles" for the MLB Games. This sponsorship was activated with a giveaway of free sandwiches to 30,000 fans at an Astros home stand during the summer of 2006 (CFA Houston, 2006). Chick-fil-a did not sponsor an entire event, just a small area that was able to be seen both on the field and on screen by at-home spectators.

After potential sponsors have been identified and research has been conducted, contact should be made with potential sponsors. Every encounter with a potential sponsor

TABLE 11.2

Sport Sponsorships	
NBA—American Express	Official title: "All-Star Entertainment Series Presented by American Express."
MLB—Houston Astros and Chick-Fil-A	Chick-Fil-A fowl poles at Minute Maid Park (if a ball hits a fowl pole in the outfield of Minute Maid Park, each spectator receives a coupon for a free Chick-Fil-A sandwich.)
MLB—Houston Astros and Marathon Oil	Marathon Oil Friday night fireworks; largest routine firework display in South Texas, that is designed to highlight downtown and Minute Maid Park on behalf of Marathon Oil.
NCAA—BCS Games	Examples: Tostitos Bowl, Meineke Car Care Bowl; the BCS games are sponsored and marketed on the sponsors packaging or main advertising materials.
2008—Olympics in Beijing and Coca-Cola	Coca-Cola Olympic torch relay; completely sponsored by Coca-Cola and expected to be a majorly watched part of the Olympic Opening Ceremony.
NFL—Coors Brewing and National Football League	Coors placed NFL logos on their cans and bottles during the season to promote the NFL.
NFL—Gatorade and National Football League	Gatorade is the official drink of the NFL on the field and it is routinely marketed during games and especially timeouts.
NASCAR—All Sponsorships	During each NASCAR race, drivers appear in commercials with their sponsors, it is important to both driver and sponsor to keep an open relationship. Often like Dale Earnhardt Jr. and the Budweiser sponsorship; or Clint Bowyer and Cheerios.
MLB—Ranger and Character Race by Ozarka	At the MLB Texas Rangers home games, Ozarka sponsors a race during the baseball game in which performers race across the field and the winner (1 or 3) will determine which card spectators received won the daily prize.
NFL—Snickers and NFL	"Snicker handles the hunger of the NFL"; where the Mars corporation handles the major hunger of the NFL players and fans with the Snickers candy bars.

Source: Choi, J. (2008). "Coca-Cola China's Virtual Olympic Torch Relay program at the 2008 Beijing Olympic Games: adding interactivity to a traditional offline Olympic activation." *International Journal of Sports Marketing & Sponsorship* 9(4), 246-255.

represents a key opportunity to build a relationship. In building the relationship, it is important to make sure the sponsor does not feel like every other cold call. When speaking to a potential sponsor in person or on the phone, as in sales, it is important to stay personable and understanding. If someone would like to reschedule a time to talk, politely and professionally schedule a time to call back. The more open the communication and the stronger the rapport that a sponsor and an organization can build, the easier it is for both parties to come to agreements and further the benefits of a full sponsorship. It is also common to offer sponsors **first right of refusal**. First right of refusal mandates the sport entity allow the sponsor to first rights to renew the sponsorship. In other words, the sport entity will not offer the sponsorship or any of its components to another potential sponsor unless the current company decides not to renew the sponsorship.

FIGURE 11.3
Sport Sponsor Objectives

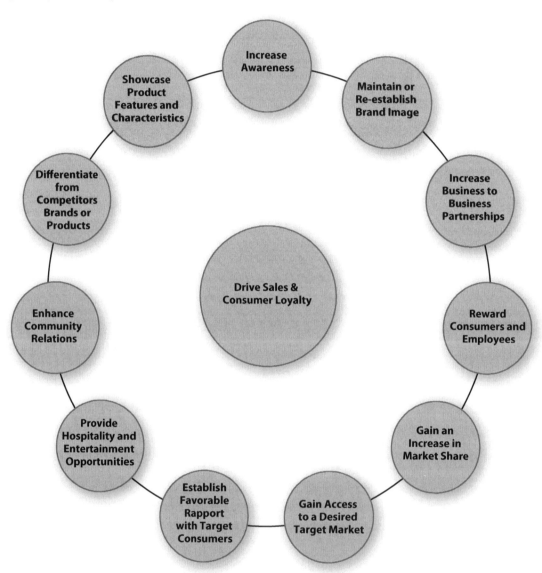

Developed from the framework of IEG (2012); Irwin, Sutton, and McCarthy (2002); Mullin, Hardy, and Sutton (2007); and Stotlar (2009).

Leveraging and Activation

In meeting the objectives of both parties, **leveraging** and **activation** of the sponsorship are key. Leveraging sponsorship should be a joint effort between the sport organization/event and the sponsor. Sport organizations should work with sponsors to assist them in finding ways to effectively leverage and communicate their relationship. In doing so, sport organizations help ensure sponsors maximize return on investment. If sponsors feel they are getting good return on their investment and view the sponsorship as beneficial, then they are more likely to renew their sponsorships and continue to build the relationship.

Leveraging is the process of communicating and marketing a sponsorship to consumers. In other words, when leveraging a sponsorship, companies desire to create an awareness of their association with the respective sport entity among the target consumer base. For example, Samsung, an official world-wide partner of the Olympic Games, pays for the right to communicate its affiliation with the Olympics through cash, goods, and/or services. Samsung must also find creative ways to leverage sponsorship and let the world know of its relationship with the Olympic Games.

Leveraging is essential for sponsorship effectiveness and the cost of leveraging sponsorship should be factored into the overall budget for sponsoring an event or team. It is common for companies to spend significant additional monies to both leverage and activate the sponsorship, and many often spend as much in leveraging as they spend on purchasing the initial sponsorship rights (Meenaghan, 1994).

Activation of the sponsorship is closely linked to leveraging, but focuses on creating a connection with consumers. While leveraging is intended to create awareness for the sponsorship, activation strategies focus on establishing a connection with consumers and meeting sponsor objectives through the components of the sponsorship. An activation strategy or plan ensures that the components and elements of the sponsorship are being utilized in a manner that meets sponsor objectives. Creating a connection with consumers and appropriately utilizing the elements of the sponsorship may occur through strategic use of media or promotions, social media, mobile technology such as text messaging, websites, and even business-to-business partnerships. Some common tools used for activation include print or television advertising, social media, mobile and web technologies, and public and community relations (IEG, 2005; Miloch and Lambrecht, 2006). Additional avenues for activation include hospitality events, retail outlets, and activities and promotions at the venue (It's all about, 2011).

Sport organizations and companies have recognized the importance of activation as a key driver of return on investment for sponsorships. For example, Major League Soccer sponsors activated their respective sponsorships with the league around its 2011 All-Star Game at Red Bull Arena in New Jersey. Anheuser-Busch designed its brand management campaign with the game as a focal point by using video advertising in Times Square. Pepsi advertised on subway trains. Allstate held a viewing party for fans, and Visa advertised on

Samsung as a World-Wide Olympic Partner

Samsung became a World-Wide Olympic Partner in 1997 after a successful relationship as a local sponsor of the 1988 Seoul Olympic Games. Samsung is currently committed to the Olympics through the 2016 Rio De Janeiro games.

As a World-Wide Partner in the wireless communication category, Samsung contributed 7,000 pieces of telecommunication equipment to the 2010 Vancouver Olympics. They also launched a software program, called Wireless Olympics Works (WOW), which allowed mobile phone users to receive real-time Olympic news and updates. Vice President and head of the Worldwide Sports Marketing section of Samsung Electronics, Gyehyun Kwon, had this to say about Samsung's relationship with the Olympics:

> *The Olympic Games are much more than sports and competition; they are about community, camaraderie, and individuals challenging themselves to find inspiration and achieve excellence. Samsung seeks to use mobile phone technology ... to unify people around the world and help them discover their own WOW moments during the Olympic Games.*

So how exactly did Samsung communicate its relationship with the Olympics? In addition to a series of commercials, advertisements, banners, and signage, Samsung found innovative and creative ways to leverage their Olympic Sponsorship. Among other things—

- Samsung secured prominent athletes, including Wayne Gretzky, Hayley Wickenheiser, Hannah Teeter, and Jarome Iginla, to serve on "Team Samsung" as brand ambassadors for their Samsung products and WOW mobile phone app.
- Samsung sold commemorative Vancouver 2010 Olympic Wrist Straps for cameras and cell phones.
- Samsung held a competition where ten "mobile explorers" were given $2000 of Samsung equipment and challenged to document, via online video blogs, the Vancouver Olympics by visiting venues, talking with spectators, and capturing the Olympic spirit on their Samsung Mythic mobile phones. Winners received $24,000 and were determined through on-line voting.
- Samsung hosted the Olympic Rendezvous @ Samsung Pavilion on site in Vancouver— an exceptional venue designed for hospitality, entertainment, experiential activity, Samsung product interaction, and spectator and athlete relaxation.

food trucks during the league's soccer expo. Castrol partnered with AutoZone to offer a sweepstakes in which the winners would win a trip to the game. MLS was strategic in its sponsorship offerings by holding numerous events in the days leading up to the game. This provided sponsors with numerous avenues to assist in activating their sponsorships (Dreier, 2011). Recognizing that many of its customers had an interest and identification with golf, JPMorgan Chase designed the reward program for its Chase Sapphire Card to include unique golfing experiences including a strategy session with a pro. The company activates its Sapphire Rewards at selected PGA Tour events (Chase delivers, 2011). Understanding its target consumer segment, Taco Bell partnered with ESPN and the BCS to market its $5 Touchdown Box value meal, in which the container converted into a finger football field. The meal was advertised on ESPN mobile applications, and allowed for consumers to easily locate a nearby Taco Bell restaurant or follow the chain's travelling truck. The truck is often utilized at BCS events or MLB games, and is also promoted via its own Twitter feed @tacobelltruck (Taco Bell Goes, 2011).

Sponsorship Pricing

Just as it is with the marketing mix, pricing is often the most difficult element of developing a sponsorship inventory and designing a sponsorship. Essentially, sponsorships should be priced on their respective market value within the respective geographic area of the sport entity and on the type of inventory utilized in the sponsorship. For example, exclusive inventory items such as naming rights or pouring rights mandate significant expenditures. Additionally, the ability of the sponsorship to reach consumers in a local market versus a national market will dramatically impact cost. While an assessment of market value is the primary means of pricing sponsorship, several other methods may prove useful. These are discussed in the following paragraphs.

The **cost-plus method** is determined by calculating the total actual expenses in providing a sponsorship package plus the organizations desired profit. The total expenses listed need to include labor, production, signage, souvenirs, and all other aspects of the event or package. This has been an effective way of determining pricing for several organizations including the USOC (Stotlar, 2009).

With **competitive market** pricing, sport organizations may examine other similar sponsorships either in the respective geographic market or in other similar markets to ascertain appropriate pricing. The *IEG Sponsorship Report,* or *sponsorship.com,* is one of the prominent publications on sponsorship. Published biweekly, the newsletter includes information, interviews, and activities all focused on sponsorship. Other publications like the *SportsBusiness Journal* and *Sport Marketing Quarterly* cover a wide array of industry and academic research focuses on marketing and will likely prove useful in improving sponsorship and assessing price.

Relative value pricing utilizes market research and published data to assess sponsorship value. In comparing pricing for a sponsorship, it is important to understand that a relative value can also be determined using research and a suggested relative value assigned. For example signage at a minor league baseball park could be compared to the cost of a billboard in the same geographic area. Additionally, one could compare the costs per impression of the billboard to that of average attendance at the venue. Similar determinations may be made utilizing public address at the venue and comparing those to radio advertisements (Stotlar, 2009).

Assessment and Evaluation of Sponsorships

Assessment of the sponsorship and the relationship between sponsor and organization must occur regularly. It is important to know if the sponsorship is effective, and that the sponsor is pleased with the results. The most common manner of evaluation for sponsorship is the measurement of return on investment. One particular way to determine the ROI for a sponsor at a major event is to survey spectators after they have left, and ask them about the sponsors' information that they noticed, and how they felt about it. O'Reilly and Madill (2009) highlighted several ways to assess sponsorship effectiveness including measuring sales, public relations efforts, media exposure, and brand perception. However, the researchers also noted a need for greater study and examination of appropriate sponsorship evaluation methods.

In preparing the results of a sponsorship assessment, it is important to provide the sponsor with data that illustrates the effectiveness of the sponsorship and with data that may also assist in enhancing the value of sponsorship. Reports should be customized for each sponsor and relate to the specific sponsor's objectives.

Endorsements

Similar to sponsorship, a well-selected athlete endorser combined with a strategic advertising campaign can resonate with audiences and distinguish products and brands. The use of celebrities and athletes as product endorsers is a well-established advertising technique, which is advantageous in assisting marketers in differentiating their respective products in a crowded and cluttered marketplace. Several theories and factors impact the selection of an athlete as an endorser.

The **associative learning theory** suggests consumers store information in association sets. Typically these association sets contain information that is similar or connected in a particular way. For example, when consumers think of a beach vacation, they may think of products such as sunscreen, swimsuits, and beach towels. These thoughts are part of consumers' "beach" association set. In matching athletes with product endorsements, the intent of the marketer is to connect a specific athlete with a product or brand so that over time the two become part of the same association set. For instance, the pairing of Michael Jordan and Tiger Woods with Nike was and often still is synonymous in the minds of consumers.

Based on the associative learning theory, the **match-up hypothesis** illustrates the importance of "fit" between the endorser and product. The more natural the fit between the endorser and the product (i.e., the more the relationship

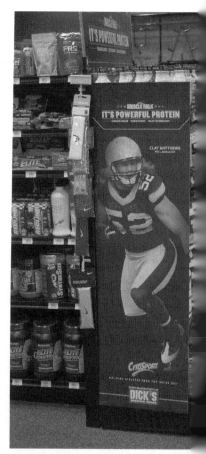

Courtesy of Kimberly Miloch.

between the two makes intuitive sense to consumers) the more effective the endorsement is likely to be. For example, athletes who endorse athletic products such as energy drinks, energy bars, or athletic apparel and equipment are more effective than non-athletes who endorse similar products. Likewise, athletes are perceived as more effective when they endorse athletic products than when endorsing non-athletic related products (i.e., cologne, watches, cars, etc.). It is imperative when selecting a celebrity endorser to consider carefully the fit of the celebrity and the brand. The stronger the perceived fit between the brand and the endorser, the more effective the endorsement.

© David Brabyn/Corbis.

However, it is not uncommon for products or brands not typically associated with sport to hire an athlete as spokesperson. For instance, Eli Manning is an endorser for Citizen Watches, Tiger Woods and Roger Federer were endorsers for Gillette, and Maria Sharapova is an endorser for Canon. In each of these cases, marketers strategically connected the attributes of the product to attributes of the athlete. Eli Manning and Citizen Watches were marketed as "unstoppable." The tag line for Woods and Federer with Gillette was "the best a man can get." The intent here was to associate success to the current number one player in golf and tennis to the Gillette products. Sharapova endorsed Canon's Power Shot camera with a tagline of "Make every shot a power shot." While the fit between these athletes and brands was not as intuitive, marketers strategically capitalized on the personal or professional attributes of the player in order to link the two in the minds of consumers.

Fit is not the only requirement for achieving an effective endorsement. Source credibility is also important. If consumers perceive an endorser is credible, they are more likely to have favorable perceptions of the product; thus making the endorsement more effective. Several characteristics impact endorser credibility. **Trustworthiness, expertise,** and **attractiveness** are considered to be the three most important characteristics in positively impacting endorser effectiveness (Amos, Holmes, and Strutton, 2008). Expertise was defined by Hovland, Janis, and Kelley (1953), as the extent to which an endorser is perceived to be a source of valid statements. For example, Nike did not need to prove it had great basketball shoes in the 1990's because Michael Jordan did it every time he played; furthermore he was viewed as an expert of the game of basketball. Trustworthiness is defined by, Hovland, Janis, and Kelley (1953), as the degree of confidence in the endorser's aim to communicate the statements he/she considers most valid. Trustworthiness can be demonstrated in the level of acceptance and the degree of confidence in the endorser and product. Kahle and Homer (1985) concluded that physical attractiveness is an essential signal in an individual's original

---

Is Using an Athlete Endorser Effective?

Past marketing and advertising strategies illustrate athletes and celebrities can and will continue to make a connection with consumers (Stotlar, 2005). In today's global marketplace, companies will consistently seek to make a genuine connection between their respective products and consumers. When using a celebrity or athlete as an endorser, companies want to know how a particular athlete will assist in driving sales and enhance or re-establish brand identity. Given the costs associated with endorsements, companies desire an appropriate return on investment and as outlined in this chapter consider numerous factors in the selection process. Using an endorser can be extremely effective when there is a direct connection between the endorser and the target market. In order to be impactful, companies must link the appropriate athlete to the desired target market. For example, Generation Y males seem to be more influenced by the action sports, while females tend to focus more on traditional sports, such as gymnastics and figure skating. When targeting Generation Y, companies should link specific athletes to their products because it will allow for strong relationships to form with brand loyal consumers. Athletes in the aforementioned sports as well as others can have an impact in reaching consumers as those in Generation Y will remember and consider them as role models. Given the factors and theories outlined in this chapter, discuss which athletes you perceive as ideal fits as endorsers for companies targeting consumers in Generation Y. Discuss the theories as they pertain to each specific athlete and discuss how the athletes you identified will be effective in reaching this target market.

---

judgment of a person. In other words, athletes who are viewed by consumers as trustworthy, as an expert at their sport, and as attractive make the most effective endorsers. In the examples above, Woods, Federer, Manning, and Sharapova are all considered as somewhat attractive, as experts in their respective sports, and as trustworthy brand ambassadors.

Endorsements and Controversies

Negative publicity involving a celebrity or an athlete can harshly impact an organization especially if it is a new organization where the endorser was used to establish a first impression to consumers. However, if the organization is more established, then the brand may not suffer; only the endorser's image and credibility will suffer. Hughes and Shank (2005) argue that if a well-liked athlete has a one-time violation it will carry less impact with the consumer than if the athlete has a history of repeated illegal or unethical events. Stock prices decline when there is negative publicity about the celebrity who endorses a company's brand (Louie, Kulik, and Jacobson, 2001). The amount of information known about the athlete and brand, timing of the negative information, and the strength of the link between the brand and athlete are factors that can predict the effect of negative information on the organizational brand (Till and Shimp, 1998).

Numerous athletes have been at the center of controversy. Pittsburgh Steeler quarterback Ben Roethlisberger, Olympian Michael Phelps, retired NFL quarterback Brett Favre, Tour de France champion Lance Armstrong, Tiger Woods, and Michael Vick are just a few of the athletes who have endured controversies and created uncertainty surrounding their respective endorsements. Tiger Woods was one of most recognizable faces in the sports world, especially in professional golf. Before his sex scandal allegations, Tiger Woods had been the perfect example and the gold standard of a great endorser. He was marketable, people loved him, and he was trusted as an expert in his sport. As soon as news broke about his sex scandal, his endorsements with Accenture and AT&T were dropped. Shortly thereafter, Gatorade followed suit and dropped the entire Tiger Woods drink line and his endorsements with the company. Swiss watch maker Tag Heuer and Gillette razor products stopped running his ad campaigns. Nike, NetJets, Upper Deck, TLC Vision, and Electronic Arts remained using Woods as an endorser despite his scandal. As an IMG client, Woods generated approximately $28 million for IMG golf prior to the scandal. This figure dropped to $15 million after the scandal (Smith, 2011b). Woods who earned $105,000,000 in endorsement money in 2008, saw his image tarnished by the multiple accounts of infidelity, which shed light onto a less than perfect personal life and shattered his carefully crafted "family man" image. In light of the accounts and fearing negative consequences, several of Woods' sponsors cut ties with the golfer and Woods lost an estimated $35 million dollars in endorsement revenue between 2008 and 2010.

Michael Vick had become known as the face of the NFL throughout his career. He was the star quarterback of the Atlanta Falcons, and the entire team's image was built around him. In 2007, he was convicted of dog fighting charges. Vick endorsed brands such as EA Sports, Kraft, Nike, and Coco-Cola (Lefton, 2010). After his conviction, a little more than 165,000 messages were sent to Nike convincing them to suspend Vick and two days after his indictment, Nike suspended him and vowed not to release his Air Zoom Vick V shoes. Needless to say Nike suspended Vick without pay, Reebok pulled his jerseys from retail shelves, and Upper Deck removed his autographed memorabilia from the online store.

Negative spillover effects can impact brand alliances. Since the image of the brand is composed of an accumulation of meanings, each time a brand associates with another brand, the experience impacts and contributes to its overall image (Rodrigue and Biswas, 2004). Once a celebrity's image is tainted, it is extremely difficult to restore their image to the public. Most companies will back out of an endorsement if the endorser is involved in negativity. Fear of negative consumer perceptions, and the impact of the controversy on revenue generation cause many companies to drop endorsers, as was the case with Vick and Woods. However, some companies will stand by the athlete during controversy. For example, to date Nike tried to repair its golf department after the Tiger Woods scandal by creating an ad featuring his late father in preparation for Woods' return to golf. The ad served to show the public that Woods continued to be focused and enthusiastic for the sport.

Discussion Questions

1. Discuss the role of sport sponsorship in marketing both the sport enterprise and a traditional company.

2. What, in your opinion, has contributed to the growth of sport sponsorship in the last decade?

3. What factors do you perceive are most important to potential sponsors when engaging in sponsorship?

4. How do athlete endorsers assist companies in connecting with consumers?

5. Who do you perceive as effective athlete endorsers? Why do you perceive these athletes are effective?

Critical Thinking Exercises

1. Consider you have been hired as the new Marketing Director for a minor league franchise in the Southwest. Outline how you will segment your market to target potential sponsors. What companies will you target and why? How might you develop a sponsorship to meet the needs of the company you have identified?

2. Working individually or as part of a group, select a sport team or event. Develop a sponsorship inventory for that organization. Include categories, items, and pricing.

3. You have recently accepted a position as the sport marketing director of a large company in the Northwest. The company desires to target young males. Detail how you will segment the market, and what athlete endorsers might you select to assist you in reaching that consumer segment.

References

Amato, C. H., C. Peters, and A. T. Shao. "An Exploratory Investigation into NASCAR Fan Culture." *Sport Marketing Quarterly,* 14(2) (2005): 71–83.

Burton, R. and N. O'Reilly. "Understanding why spnsorship continues to grow". *SportsBusiness Journal,* January 20, 2011.

CFA Houston. "CFA Houston", July 24, 2006, CHICK-FIL-A "FOWL POLES" TO MAKE DEBUT. http://www.cfahouston.com/pdfs/press_release.pdf

Chase delivers. "Chase delivers the rewards". *SportsBusiness Journal,* June 27, 2011: 14.

Choi, J., D. K. Stotlar, and S. Park. "Visual Ethnography of On-site Sport Sponsorship Activation: LG Action Sports Championship". *Sport Marketing Quarterly,* 15(2) (2006): 71–79.

Cornwell, T. B. and L. V. Coote. "Corporate sponsorship of a cause: the role of identification in purchase intent". *Journal of Business Research,* 58(3) (2005): 268–276.

Crompton, J. L. "Conceptualization and alternate operationalizations of the measurement of sponsorship effectiveness in sport". *Leisure Studies,* 23(3) (2004): 267–281.

Dalakas, V. and A. M. Levin. "The balance theory domino: How sponsorships may elicit negative consumer attitudes". *Advances in Consumer Research,* 32 (2005): 91–97.

Dreier, F. "MLS All-Star sees activation gain". *SportsBusiness Journal,* July 25, 2011: 10.

Gwinner, K., and S. Swanson. "A model of fan identification antecedents and sponsorship outcomes". *Journal of Services Marketing,* 17(3) (2003): 275–294.

Heider, F. *The psychology of interpersonal relations.* New York, NY: John Wiley & Sons, 1958.

Hovland, C. I., I. K. Janis, and H. H. Kelley. *Communication and persuasion.* New Haven, CT: Yale University Press, 1953.

Howard, D. R. & J. L. Crompton. *Financing sport.* Morgantown, WV: Fit Information Technologies, 2005.

Hughes, S., and M. Shank. "Defining scandal in sports: Media and corporate sponsor perspectives". *Sport Marketing Quarterly,* 14 (2005): 207–216.

IEG. "Performance research. Sponsors say return on investment is up and they are doing more to prove it". *IEG Sponsorship Report,* 24(4) (2005).

IEG. "Sponsorship spending", August 5, 2010, http://www.sponsorship.com

It's all about. "It's all about the activation". *SportsBusiness Journal,* 13, June 27, 2011.

Lefton, T. "Neither Vick's agent nor sponsors are in a rush to sign deals". *SportsBusiness Journal,* October 4, 2010.

Louie, T. A., R. L. Kulik, and R. Jacobson. "When bad things happen to the endorsers of good products". *Marketing Letters,* 12(1) (2001): 13–23.

Madrigal, R. "The influence of social alliances with sports teams on intentions to purchase corporate sponsors' products". *Journal of Advertising,* XXIX(4) (2000): 13–24.

Meenaghan, T. "Point of view: Ambush marketing: immoral or imaginative practice?" *Journal of Advertising Research,* September/October, 1994: 77–88.

Meenaghan, T. "Sponsorship—Legitimizing the medium". *European Journal of Marketing,* 25(11) (1991): 5–10.

Meenaghan, T. "Understanding sponsorship effects". *Psychology & Marketing,* 18(2) (2001): 95–122.

Mickle, T. "It takes a village, and IndyCar is planning one". *SportsBusiness Journal,* March 7, 2011: 6.

Miloch, K., and K. Lambrecht. "Consumer Awareness of Sponsorship at Grassroots Sport Events". *Sport Marketing Quarterly,* 15(3) (2006): 147–154.

O'Relly, N. and J. Madill. "Methods and metrics in sponsorship evaluation". *Journal of Sponsorship,* 2(3) (2009): 215–230.

Rodrigue, C. S., and A. Biswas. "Brand alliance dependency and exclusivity: An empirical investigation". *Journal of Product and Brand Management,* 13 (2004): 477–488.

Smith, M. "Drop in Woods' endorsement income made Steinberg too expensive to keep". *SportsBusiness Journal,* May 30, 2011b: 3.

Smith, M. "Polo dresses up U.S. Open merchandise sales". *SportsBusiness Journal,* June 13, 2011a: 6.

Stotlar, D. K. *Developing Successful Sport Sponsorship Plans.* 3rd ed., Morgantown, W.V.: Fitness Information Technology, 2009.

Stotlar, D. K. "Endorsements". *Berkshire Encyclopedia of World Sport,* 2 (2005): 506–510.

Stotlar, D.K. "Sponsorship evaluation: Moving from theory to practice". *Sport Marketing Quarterly,* 13 (2004): 61–64.

Taco Bell Goes. "Taco Bell goes mobile with truck, activation". *SportsBusiness Journal,* 19 (2011).

Till, B. D., and T. A. Shimp. "Endorsers in advertising: The case of negative celebrity information". *Journal of Advertising,* 27(1) (1998): 67–82.

© 2012, Shutterstock, Inc.

CHAPTER 12

Sport Brand Management and Licensing

Laci Wallace, M.S. East Texas Baptist University
Dr. Ryan Rodenberg Florida State University
Dr. Jason Lee University of North Florida
Dr. Kimberly Miloch Texas Woman's University

> *We have a clearly defined brand mission, vision, and values. Authenticity plays a vital role here. It builds trust and credibility with the consumer and provides the basis for identification with your brand, and it must never be jeopardized.*
>
> Eric Stamminger, Adidas group

CHAPTER OBJECTIVES

After completing the chapter, the reader should be able to:

- Acquire knowledge associated with key branding principles, concepts, and terminology.
- Recognize the role of effective branding efforts in the ever-evolving sport industry.
- Identify the importance of developing and maintaining strong brand identity and image.
- Appreciate the importance of brand loyalty.
- Recognize the benefits of effective brand management strategies.
- Relate aspects of branding to athlete endorsement.
- Recognize the role of effective licensing efforts in the sport industry.

Introduction to Sport Brand Management

Brands are products or services that communicate and interact with consumers through identifiable and unique experiences. **Brand management** is the strategic craft of developing an identity in the marketplace, creating valuable emotional connections through experiences, and determining characteristics that attract loyal customers. Ultimately, the goal of brand management is to simultaneously capture new customers, strengthen connections with loyal customers, and in some instances, establish innovative niches in a specific product category. Brand management involves both differentiating products and services from other competitive labels and developing appropriate two-way, interactive communication between consumers and products (Uggla and Filipsson, 2009). The evolving nature of the sport industry offers unique and challenging opportunities to build lasting impressions and relationships (Gladden, Irwin, and Sutton, 2001). Sport brands, over time and through proper management, will endure the evolving nature of the industry (i.e., globalization), the growing clutter of the marketplace (i.e., available products and services) and changes in technology (i.e., media communication tools and mobile technologies; Aaker and Keller, 1990; Richelieu and Desbordes, 2009).

Benefits of Branding

Regardless of the economic climate, a strong brand is essential in maintaining long-term financial viability. Given that sport presents both unique opportunities and challenges in developing appropriate brand management strategies, it should be a primary consideration in any sport organization's marketing plan. Sport marketing scholars, marketing scholars, and industry professionals have long noted the benefits of building strong brands (Aaker, 2007; Berry, 1999; Gladden and Funk, 2001; Gladden, Milne, and Sutton, 1998; Gladden and Milne, 1999; Gladden, Irwin, and Sutton, 2001; Keller, 1998; Miloch, 2010; Ross, 2006; Shocker, Srivastava, and Rueker, 1994; Walsh, Kim, and Ross, 2008). Developing and maintaining a strong **brand identity** and image provides the foundation for consumer loyalty and **brand equity**, which is of great benefit to sport entities. A strong brand presence benefits sustained revenue production for sport entities in several ways. Strong brands are well known among consumers in the marketplace, and typically are positioned favorably in the minds of consumers. This favorable awareness assists in differentiating products or services from competitors and serves as the foundation for establishing **brand loyalty** and equity in the marketplace.

Courtesy of Kimberly Miloch.

Brand loyal consumers are less likely than other consumers to switch brands due to changes in price or when new competition enters the marketplace. Loyal consumers are familiar and educated about the brand's products, and they also assist in marketing the brand's products by sharing their favorable experiences with other consumers. Loyal consumer bases often generate a certain level of sales, allowing the sport entity to better estimate and predict revenue streams (Bedbury, 2002; Gladden and Funk, 2001; Godin, 2002; Kuo, Chang, and Chen, 2004; Madrigal, 1995; and Shocker, Srivastave, and Ruekert, 1994). As illustrated by these advantages, consumers are often willing to spend more on brands with which they are familiar and for brands that have an established image within a specific product category (Miloch, 2010). As such, sport entities must focus on carefully and strategically communicating a strong brand image given the ability to favorably influence consumer perceptions, loyalty, and brand equity. The following sections outline the fundamental concepts and steps in strategic sport brand management.

Brands in Sport

The sport industry represents a long list of identifiable brand categories with many subcategories for each of the larger domains. Some of these major categories include professional athletes (i.e., Tiger Woods, David Beckham) teams (i.e., Yankees, Cowboys), leagues (i.e., National Football League, Major League Baseball), sport product companies (i.e., Nike, Adidas) and sport media (i.e., ESPN, *Sports Illustrated*). The large number of brand categories represents not only the diverse types of sport consumption and financial opportunities, but also the broad range of consumers needed for differentiation in the market.

Brand Theories

Much of Aaker's (1991) and Keller's (1993) work has contributed to the formation of sport-related brand management theories. These contributions resulted in the formation of the team association model (Gladden and Funk, 2002) and spectator-based brand equity (Ross, 2006). These theories have been applied to a variety of sport settings, including professional and collegiate settings (Bauer, Stokburger-Sauer, and Exler, 2008; Kaynak, Salmon, and Tatoglu, 2008).

The complexity of brand management exists in part because of the increased number of brands in the sport market, the variety of products and services offered, and the mass media surrounding the industry (Aaker, 2010; Aaker and Joachimsthaler, 2000). A brand that is distinctive and identifiable is fundamental to establishing stability in a technology-infused market (Kapfererm, 1992). The global reach of sporting events, such as the Olympics, has provided numerous sponsorship opportunities for companies to increase brand exposure and cultivate brand awareness (Dong-Hun, 2010). As the nature of the sport industry is continually changing, brand management has become an increasingly important aspect for sport brands to utilize and understand.

Theory provides a guideline to not only explain consumer behavior, but also is used by marketers to establish more effective promotions, create unique service opportunities, and to evaluate brands across a given standard. Theory attempts to explain the dynamics of brand management using applied and practical research approaches. Brand managers market specific aspects of the brand to increase the desired purchase and consumer behavior. The purpose of brand management techniques is to increase the brand's ability to not only develop products and services compatible with the consumer's current intentions, but also to communicate through marketing campaigns a message to targeted consumers.

Sport Celebrities

"Celebritydom" is prevalent in contemporary society. Sport's prominence has provided fertile ground building celebrity and ultimately establishing athlete's as visible "people brands." "Celebrity is one of those vexed terms that is easy to identify, yet hard to define. Celebrity is a cultural fabrication that is defined by characteristics such as fame, public perception, and awareness. Essentially, celebrity is being recognized as having fame in a society." (Lee and Laucella, 2011, 1428-1431).

Brand management is an essential element in the long-term sustainability and growth of the sport industry. As the industry expands, well-established products and services brands will account for the long-term resilience (Aaker, 1991; Aaker and Keller, 1990). To maintain competiveness, brand managers must carefully analyze competitors' qualities while also evaluating preferences of preferred consumers (McGlone and Martin, 2006; Stonehouse and Minocha, 2008). Businesses must stay relevant in the increasingly dynamic and complex market by "participating in the emerging market niches that represent future growth" (Aaker, 2004, 91). The investigation of consumers' preference, satisfaction, and purchase behavior guides brand-management (Keller, 2003). Eventually, the brand-building strategies cultivate long-term relationships and increase future involvement with consumption behaviors.

The celebrity athlete is not a new phenomenon, whether it was the sport stars of Golden Age of Sport (i.e., Babe Ruth, Jack Dempsey, Red Grange) or the host of contemporary sport stars (i.e., Tiger Woods, LeBron James, David Beckham, Serena Williams), visible sport personalities have great relation to the notion of branding. Athlete brands have been impacted through on-the-field exploits, corporate tie-ins (i.e., endorsements), and other forms of exposures. Athlete reach, notoriety, and likability are gauged by various resources (i.e., Sports Q scores, Forbes 100, Bloomberg Power 100). For example, Terry Lefton of the *SportsBusiness Journal* reported Marketing Evaluation's Top Sports Q Scores for 2010 included Michael Jordan with a Q score of 51 in the top spot with Shaun White and John Madden tied for the number 2 spot with Q scores of 41. Peyton Manning followed at number 4 with Q score of 40 (Lefton, 2010).

Celebrity is a multi-faceted notion. There are reluctant celebrities and celebrity hounds (those who seem willing to do whatever is needed to broaden their fame). Celebritydom may also be associated with negative occurrences (i.e., OJ Simpson and Mike Vick were celebrities whose public perception was greatly impacted by off-the-field scandal).

For additional information regarding sport celebrities read:

Lee, J.W., and P.C. Laucella. Sport Celebrities. *Encyclopedia of Sports Management and Marketing.* Thousand Oaks, CA: SAGE Publications, Inc., 2011.

Principles and Key Concepts of Branding

Strong brand elements are identifiable, enduring, and meaningful to consumers, and, as noted earlier, often have competitive advantages in the marketplace (Keller, 1999). For sport teams, this protection extends beyond some of these identifiable features (i.e., logo, phrases, colors, and names) and into unique experiences offered by sport teams (i.e., fan-identification and social status of attending events; Fink, et. al, 2009; Parent and Seguin, 2008). The brand-building strategies communicate what the brand is and what it is not, further reinforcing the competitive advantage.

Brand Awareness and Associations

Brand awareness describes consumer ability to recognize a given brand in a variety of settings and the identification of brand with a particular category. Brand recall and recognition is a valuable precursor to purchase decisions (Aaker, 1991; Keller 1998). Consumer ability to recognize the brand from memory and link previous experiences to current preferences determines possible consumption outcomes.

Increasing brand awareness is not simply accomplished by increasing the number of advertisements or money spent on advertisements. Awareness is developed through highly recognized sponsorship opportunities, athlete endorsements, product placements, and effective promotions. Through these activities, the brand image is established within a variety of settings and creates recognizable links to other brands.

Logos

"Logos are tangible representations that serve as distinct visual signatures that identify and differentiate brands, products, or organizations from others" (Lee, 2011, 778-780). Logos are used in branding by serving as totems used for image, awareness, personality, position, and identification. Logos are a form of intellectual property used to identify various marks, logotypes, and trademarks that can be used in different forms and fashions in association with sport brand management. As the concepts of branding and logos are heavily tied together, logos provide visual identity and representing for the sport entity.

Learning activity... Identify your "top ten" sport logos? Why did you select the ones that you selected? Odds are they either represent a sport organization or product that you have affinity for or perhaps there are other characteristics such as the color scheme or some other aesthetic characteristic.

Now think of 10 sport logos that you do not like. What were your motivating factors for selecting these? Do the selected images represent a rival team, is it an ugly image, or is there some other consideration?

For more information pertaining to logos, read:

Lee, J.W. Logo. *Encyclopedia of Sports Management and Marketing*. Thousand Oaks, CA: SAGE Publications, Inc., 2011.

Awareness is reinforced when the logo, slogan, or other identifiable components communicate the essences of the brand (Keller, 1999). Sport teams are at an advantage because the logo, mascot, colors, and location of a team are relatively stable. Because these factors do not change frequently, sport teams must cultivate renewed local awareness through activities such as community outreach, media coverage, and merchandise. However, the sport products and companies must rely heavily on the logo to communicate the brand awareness. Many times the logo is used to visually distinguish the brand, whereas the slogan provides additional brand communication.

Brands are associated with, identified by, and represented through various attributes. Brands may often be identified through various phrases such as slogans and taglines. Slogans are concise, memorable phrases that provide identity. Associated with the notation of slogans are the concepts of taglines, mottos, and jingles. Taglines and slogans are terms that are often used interchangeably. If a distinction is to be made, taglines generally have more sustainability, whereas slogans have a more limited shelf life. Slogans can be used for promotional purposes to describe motives and intentions. This, in turn, aids in the branding process as slogans are influential in constructing the brand identity of sport entities. Popular slogans associated with brands provide a variety of images for consumers. Sport teams can use slogans as well. On their way to the 2010 national championship run, the Auburn University program was noted for its use of the "All In" slogan. This is akin to the common use by teams to display team slogans on tee shirts and signage associated with the team (i.e., "No pain, no gain," or "Pain is temporary, pride is forever"). Taglines are quite prevalent as well and are often associated with noted sport brands (i.e., Nike—"Just Do It," EA Sports—"It's in the Game, "ESPN—"The Worldwide Sports Leader").

The awareness of a brand influences the consumer's identification and internalization of the brand's image (Ross, Russell, and Bang, 2008). Highly identified consumers demonstrate enduring purchasing behavior, promote their behavior to other consumers, and contribute to a community that further reinforces their identification (Foster and Hyatt, 2008). The internalization of a brand connects the individual's values, beliefs, and self-concept to consumption behavior. The outcome of brand awareness is for the brand to not only be recognized or recalled from memory, but also that the awareness of the brand creates an attraction (Funk and James, 2006).

Brand associations have been investigated in several sport domains as key factors influencing consumption behavior and describing preferences (Ross, Bang, and Lee, 2007; Ross, James, and Vargas, 2006). Gladden and Funk (2002) describe brand association factors as unique connections linking the individual to characteristics of the sport consumption. See Table 12.1 for a list of brand associations.

TABLE 12.1

Examples of Brand Associations	
Brand associations factors as defined by Ross, Russell, and Bang (2008).	1. **brand mark/logo:** logo, colors, distinctive symbols 2. **rivalry:** tough division, tough conference, team beats biggest opponent, team does well against major opponent 3. **concessions:** food or drink sold in stadium, specific foods in arena, eating atmosphere 4. **team history:** history of winning, rich history in the sport or community 5. **organizational attributes:** team committed to fans, team is loyal to fans, team gives back to the community 6. **non-player personnel:** coaches, front office, team management 7. **stadium community:** arena has unique qualities, design of the arena, arena improves experience 8. **team success:** performance of the team, team being successful, high quality players 9. **socialization:** place to spend time with friends, being a fan to meet other people, acquiring friends or seeing friends at the game 10. **commitment:** loyal fans, anything related to loyal fan behaviors, fans following the team for many generations or many years 11. **team characteristics:** team has distinctive characteristics, qualities and clear personality
Brand associations factors as defined by Gladden and Funk (2002).	**Benefits** identification, nostalgia, pride in place, escape, peer group acceptance **Attitudes** importance, knowledge, affect **Attributes** product delivery, start player, logo design, management, head coach, tradition, success, stadium/arena

Ross and colleagues (2008) link the factors of brand associations and awareness to measuring the brand equity of a team. Segmentation based on brand associations provides marketers the competitive advantage to strategically adapt marketing campaigns for these groups (Ross, 2007). Segmentation strategies provide marketers with valuable descriptive information related to the characteristics and behaviors specific to consumer groups, thus, increasing the brand's competitive advantage to deliver desired products and services relative to their consumer behavior. For example, loyal customers (i.e., season ticket holders) who spend more money and attend games more frequently, may have different expectations than new consumers. The marketing team must develop products and services within the brand that maximize the potential of both types of consumers, while also differentiating from other related experiences (Bowden, 2009).

Mascots

In sport team settings, various symbols are associated with brand's visual identity. Various symbols including team colors, uniforms, team names, and mascots are used to provide affiliation, identification, and differentiation. Such imagery serves as totems that allow for community through the association with representations, such as an animal, a person, or objects symbolizing entities. Consider the following sample mascots: Sparty the Spartan (Michigan State University), Uga (University of Georgia), or the Phoenix Suns' Gorilla. The preceding examples are ones that are well revered. There are negative associations that may be associated with potentially divisive mascots such as those associated with indigenous groups (Native American mascots controversy).

© Joy Feram, 2012. Under license from Shutterstock, Inc.

Brand Attributes

Brand attributes appeal to the emotional essence of the brand and the individual character-istics linked to the preferences of consumption. Brand attributes include product and non-product features offered through consumption (Bauer, Stokburger-Sauer, and Exler, 2008). The product and non-product related attributes, perceived benefits of consumption and an attitude towards consumption influences behavior (Kaynak, Salmon, and Tatoglu, 2008).

Keller (1993) described the non-product attributes to be factors associated with con-sumption, but not the actual product consumed. Gladden and Funk (2001) identified brand attributes as antecedents to brand equity factors and influence outcomes of brand-building efforts. Bauer and colleagues (2008) demonstrated that non-product related attributes, such as logo, stadium, and tradition, yielded stronger brand attitude and behavioral loyalty out-comes than product related attributes (i.e., success, players, management). For example, a ticket sales package for "Annual Father & Son Ballpark Event" would include particular brand associations (i.e., team history, commitment, organizational attributes, and social-ization) for the specific target market. By using these key phrases, this particular event will communicate effectively these associated experiences. Consumers within this target market would ideally be more attracted to this product, and may reinforce the emotional appeal the consumer originally had with this product.

Brand benefits are commonly described as functional (i.e., escape), symbolic (i.e., fan identification, peer group acceptance), and experiential (i.e., nostalgia, pride) consumption motives (Gladden and Funk, 2001; Kaynak, Salmon, and Tatoglu, 2008). The brand may provide benefits unique to individual consumers and may account for the formation of brand preferences. The tangible and intangible benefits of a brand further describe motives for consumption. The intangible features are associated with vicarious achievement, nostalgia for a team or player, performance of a star player, fan escape, team success, and peer group acceptance (Funk and James, 2006). The intangible qualities such as social status or identification create brand specific attributes and differentiation (Friedmann, 1986). This competitive advantage is harder to duplicate and unique to the given brand; thus valuable to maintain over time (Miloch, 2010).

Brand Loyalty

Loyal consumers generally believe the brand is superior, have expectations related to their experience, and often develop strong emotional connections to their consumption behavior (McQueen, Foley, and Deighton, 1993). The promotion and evaluation of various types of motives to consume sport reveal many benefits for sport marketers to establish brand loyalty (Ross, Russell, and Bang, 2008). Brand awareness and association factors contribute to loyal consumers with identifiable preferences in behaviors and attitudes (Ross, 2007). Through the process of engagement, consumers' experiences, either satisfying or dissatisfying, reinforce experiences that contribute to knowledge-based expectations and loyalty (Bowden, 2009). The loyalty characteristics are rooted in consumers' experience as well as the satisfaction, trust, and affective commitment. The established trust contributes to consumers' involvement with a particular brand (Bowden, 2009). This involvement represents a deeper dynamic of self-image, identification, and general interest or connection with consumption (Pritchard and Funk, 2010). Bowden (2009) summarizes involvement as a precursor to commitment and that the later commitment is linked to higher involvement.

Personal identification with organizations and with sport are linked to the many aspects of sport consumption behaviors (Woo, et al., 2009). Unique to the sport industry is the idea of fan group identity (Foster and Hyatt, 2008). This represents a group of people collectively linked to the sport entity through their participation and consumption (Fink et al., 2009). Satisfaction of these highly identified customers builds retention of consumers and maximizes the revenue generation through relationship marketing (Madrigal, 1995; McDaniel and Moore, 2005). Furthermore, the management of brands in sport connects consumers to expectations and identities related to consumption preferences (i.e., escape, eustress, entertainment) unique to different sports (i.e., individual vs. team, aggressive vs. non-aggressive; Wann, et al., 2008).

Although the brand may be identifiable by numerous target markets, sport consumers' experiences and interactions with the brand may vary based on the personal characteristics, service expectations and satisfaction, and emotional responses. Loyalty is further described in components of attitude and behavior (Kaynak, Salmon, and Tatoglu, 2008). Behavior is generally described as the consumers' direct purchase loyalty, while attitude is more subjective and indirect (Pritchard and Funk, 2010). Although the attitude toward a particular team may not generate direct revenue, Kaynak and colleagues (2008) determined that consumers' enduring attitude towards a team contributes to social aspects of interpersonal communication and identification with team as indicators of loyalty. Past game attendance and level of team commitment reveal a strong connection between attitude and ticket purchasing behavior (Funk, et al., 2009). Managing long-term relationships with consumers and cultivating new relationships is a constant process of engaging customers (Bowden, 2009). Sport provides many opportunities for brand extensions and strategic leveraging of brand image.

Brand Equity

A desired result of the implementation of any brand management strategy is to establish brand equity (Keller, 1999). **Brand equity** represents the actual or relative value of the company related to its ability to generate profit, and refers to the elevated price a consumer will pay for a well-established brand compared to its generic equivalent (Brewer and Pedersen, 2009; Keller, 1998). The perceived value is developed over time through a dynamic and strategic cultivation of experiences that reinforce consumer perception. The perceived value of a particular brand over another contributes to the consumption behavior of preferred brands' products and services over other similar offers from less identified brands. For example, the price of a plain white t-shirt is much less when compared to a white t-shirt with a Nike Swoosh. The Nike Swoosh logo increases the value of the item because of the perceived status associated with the Nike brand.

The elements of brand equity are primary factors contributing to brand loyalty, brand awareness, perceived quality, and brand associations (Aaker, 1991; Kaynak, Salmon, and Tatoglu, 2008). Brand equity provides brand stability through losing seasons, management changes, or economic downturns, when compared to other less-established brands. Some ways sport teams may cultivate brand equity are by establishing and reinforcing their identity through leveraging co-branded sponsorship, promoting rivalries with other teams, delivering the unique experience of attending a game, interactions with fans via social media, or designing popular logos (Richelieu and Pons, 2006). Nike, one of the largest sport apparel brands, cultivates a unique image through athlete endorsements and sponsorship opportunities (McGlone and Martin, 2006). Similarly, Under Armour has developed its brand through authentic and strategic associations as well as product placement (Miloch, et al., 2011).

Various sectors of the sport industry are leveraged with value-emphasizing co-brands (Keller, 2009; Frederick and Patil, 2010). The **brand architecture** represents a variety of products across a range of targeted customers to maximize potential growth (Keller, 2009). Building a portfolio with different brand attributes strengthens the possible attachments and identifications of consumers with the brand.

Brand endorsements by individual athletes influence sport consumption when the consumer identifies with an athlete and the respective sport product. The prior knowledge and experiences with a brand contribute to the influence and effectiveness of its advertising, and has also been noted to affect the positive or negative consumption outcomes (Carlson and Donavan, 2008). For instance, the athlete product-endorsement connects the combined brand image of the product and athlete to consumers with shared interest (Koernig and Boyd, 2009). David Beckham, one of the most recognized international athletes, represents a well-established multidimensional persona (Vincent, Hill, and Lee, 2009). Beckham's strategic endorsement history represents many subdivisions of his personality outside of professional sport in fashion, pop-culture, and entertainment. His brand portfolio is a unique example of how proper brand management can transcend the sport area and represent a larger brand-building initiative (Vincent, Hill, and Lee, 2009). Athlete endorsers are discussed in greater detail in Chapter 11.

Consumer-based brand equity is grounded in the concept that consumers' brand knowledge represents both the associations and awareness of the given product (Keller, 1993). Specific to sport, the effectiveness of brand-building activities contributes to the brand knowledge of a given athlete, team, or sport product (Koernig and Boyd, 2009). This knowledge is mediated by the awareness of such brand and the associations related to its consumption. **Brand image**, the perceptions about a brand formed by consumers' memory, is closely linked to the individual past experiences that contribute to brand equity (Keller, 1998). According to spectator-based brand equity, brand awareness leads to distinctive brand associations, and these associations contribute to loyalty behaviors (Ross, 2006; Ross, Russel, and Bang, 2008). Brand management is not only focused on promoting the positive components, but also on addressing the negative, less attractive aspects of a brand. Addressing both the positive and negative components of the brand increases the likelihood that positive brand association and attributes will endure the short-term turmoil of otherwise devastating situations (Aaker and Keller, 1990). Threats to brand management are discussed in more detail later in the chapter.

Role of Sport in Branding

Although the nature of sport is ever changing, the brands within those dynamics represent unique and distinguishable elements. The extension of brands to other markets through strategic sponsorship and endorsements are increasing as the use of technology, Internet, and media strengthen the global infrastructure of sport (Santomier, 2008; Richelieu and Desbordes, 2009). The positioning and leveraging of co-branding opportunities provide potential revenue generation outlets integral to the financial foundation of sport (Mueller and Roberts, 2008).

Communication is a key asset of sport over traditional marketing. As the popularity of sport sponsorship increases, the increase in value of TV rights, marketing during sporting events, and athlete endorsements offer profitable opportunities. These opportunities are not only connected to identifiable target markets (Fullerton and Merz, 2008), but offer exposure unique to events with high media exposure (Frederick and Patil, 2010).

Many teams utilize online communication to build interactive relationships with consumers (Galily, 2008) and manage brand image through relationship marketing (Girginov, et al., 2009). Although media consumption is classified as indirect consumer interactions

(Mullin, et al., 2007), the media plays a powerful and important role to control information and influence consumer perceptions (McCombs, 2005). The power of the media is apparent in the ability to frame events, people, and situations that influence the economic structure of the industry (Pedersen, et al., 2007; Fortunato, 2008; Zaharopoulos, 2007). The purchasing behaviors and fan identification with preferred athletes or teams may be influenced by the negative or positive media coverage (Carlson and Donavan 2008). The role of the traditional and social media in marketing the sport product is discussed in detail in Chapter 9.

© Jaggaf, 2012. Under license from Shutterstock, Inc.

The brand image of an athlete or team is an invaluable asset that must be cultivated through positive relationship-building marketing initiatives (Cunningham, Cornwell, and Coote, 2009). Sporting events provide a unique competitive advantage by offering exclusive sponsorships to corporations (Parent & Seguin, 2008). The brand connected-identities are paramount to the future brand extensions and purchase intentions, as it represents a connection to the consumers' perceived values. The increased use of sponsorship has resulted in the investigation of effectiveness of these communication tools, through measuring brand recall and recognition (Walsh, Kim, and Ross, 2008).

The sport industry provides many opportunities to cultivate and manage brand image through a variety of experiences. Video gaming, sponsorship, and TV viewership have been successfully used to enhance brand identification, affiliation, and points of attachment through repeated and satisfying experiences unique to identifiable segments (Fortunato, 2008; Kim and Ross 2006; Oates, 2009). These brand extensions fundamentally shape the perceived value of the core brand.

Threats to Brand Management

Brand management is not only promoting the positive components, but it is also addressing the negative, less attractive aspects of the respective brand. Addressing both the positive and negative components of the brand increases the likelihood that positive brand association and attributes will endure short-term turmoil of otherwise devastating situations (Aaker and Keller, 1990).

Brand-building efforts are a well-planned process that may be threatened by short-term unfavorable media coverage of athletes and teams. A brand's ability to effectively address negative media coverage in a timely manner is crucial to managing consumers' perceptions of a given brand and should be central to any brand management strategy.

Professional Athletes

Professional athletes are unique in that their brand value is dependent on both on-field performance and off-field behavior. Tiger Woods' brand recently experienced the consequences of negative media coverage. Tiger Woods took a short leave of absence from his athletic career when his previously unknown, alleged extramarital affairs and personal life were

---

People Brands

"Celebrities from a variety of genres have the potential to be personality brands. Serving as a popular source of entertainment, sport has the ability to present athletes as visible brands impacting society and commerce." (Lee and Miloch, 2011, XX.). People brands abound in different forms of entertainment. With regard to sport, various personalities can be viewed as brands. People brands in sport include athletes, coaches, and other people roles (i.e., media personalities). Sport people brands connection to the popularity of sport may provide advantages over non-sport people brands due to certain factors (sport's popularity, association factors, "fit" factors, etc.).

To illustrate the power of athletes as people brands, consider the following examples:

David Beckham

Davis Beckham is one of the most famous sport brands in the world. His brand has benefited from numerous factors associated with this celebrated figure. His on-field play, aesthetic appeal, celebrity spouse, fashion icon status, and other factors helped "Brand Beckham" take a global soccer and broaden his reach way beyond sport. Beckham's appeal has spawned a movie featuring his name (*Bend It Like Beckham*) and landed him an unprecedented deal in efforts to use his brand appeal to enhance Major League Soccer.

Brett Favre

What do you think of when you hear the name Brett Favre? Famed play caller, grizzled veteran, wishy-washy personality, good old boy, etc. Various connotations may come to mind. During his stellar playing career, the tractor riding country boy from Kiln, Mississippi, has enjoyed the spoils of being viewed as a carefree gunslinger, which has served as a visible pitchman for brands such as Wrangler, Snapper, Sears, and Prilosec. The various factors (both good and bad) have helped build the image "Brand Brett."

Danica Patrick

Danica Patrick has emerged as one of the most visible sport personalities in recent times. She is a highly commercialized woman who is an endorsement standout in the male-dominated world of motor sports. Her involvement in IndyCar racing and her subsequent foray into the world of NASCAR has allowed her to be a major player in the world of sport celebrity endorsers where she has also endorsed Motorola, Marquis Jet, Peak Antifreeze, Samsonite, Go Daddy, and Tissot.

Lee, J.W., and K. Miloch. Player as Brand. *Encyclopedia of Sports Management and Marketing.* Thousand Oaks, CA: SAGE Publications, Inc., 2011.

discussed on major media outlets in November 2009 (Gregory, 2010). Tiger Woods utilized social media to communicate directly with fans and generated fan support during a time of negative media coverage (Sanderson, 2010). Social media has become an increasingly popular tool to cultivate two-way communication with sport fans (Brody et al., 2010) and address situations in a timely manner (Shelton, 2009). Although the use of social media provided some immediate fan support, the aftermath of continual media coverage resulted in many endorsement deals withdrawing their affiliations.

The Tiger Woods situation impacted not only his current affiliation with the Professional Golfer's Association and current multi-million dollar endorsement contract with companies like Nike (Gregory, 2009), but it also threatened his ability to generate future lucrative relationships. Retrospectively, Tiger Woods ultimately did lose sponsors including Gillette, Accenture, AT&T, and PepsiCo, which estimated $35 million in annual income (Badenhausen, 2011). Slow to return to his previous brand-worthy endorsement status, Woods signed his first new endorsement deal in June 2011 with the Kowa Company endorsing heat rub cream that relieves muscle and joint pain (Badenhausen, 2011). Tiger Woods' endorsement deals may be on a long road to recovery, but the well-known athlete is still listed as one of the top 10 Celebrities by *Forbes* (Pomerantz, 2011). Time will eventually reveal if Tiger Woods' brand value will ever recover from the 2009 incident.

Sport Teams

Professional sport teams face many challenges to brand management in that it is comprised of many different components. A winning or losing season may impact the brand perception and affect short-term consumer behavior. Although a winning season may increase short-term revenue, team success has not been demonstrated as a strong predictor of long-term fan loyalty (Kaynak, Salmon, and Tatoglu, 2008). The vitality of the teams' brand image must rely on more than the outcome of the season (Gladden and Milne, 1999); the marketing team must cultivate the desired positive perceptions. Clavio and Miloch (2009) suggested that brand-building agenda setting strategies aid in the development and implementation of the preferred brand image. They suggest that brand managers must strategically build a favorable brand image around the broader aspects of attending the game, unique organizational attributes, and the fan experience.

Protection in Brand Management

A brand's ultimate goal is to increase the consumers' ability to recognize the brand, and provide basic characteristics that attract consumers to select the brand over other accessible options. A brand's competitive advantage encompasses not only the distinguishable services or unique products offered by a company, but brands must develop recognizable logos, phrases, or taglines that quickly communicate with consumers. One of the most valuable aspects of the brand is communicated within the first few seconds of interaction through brand recognition. The identifiable brand features (i.e., logo, colors, slogan, taglines) provide a vital consumer-to-brand link, offer distinction from other brands, and aid in the cultivation of unique consumer preferences. The identifiable aspects of the brand are valuable and protected by law, as they represent a symbolic relationship of the company. Licensing is discussed in the following section relative to brand management. With the proper cultivation and leveraging of meaningful brand names and logos, a company can increase the identification of its brand and further the unique associations with brand experience.

Sports Industry Licensing Overview

One of the major aspects of brand protection is focused on **licensing** of products. Greenberg and Gray (1998) found "the success of merchandise licensing though professional [and college] sports properties is growing almost exponentially" (697). Sports industry licensing has continued to grow over the course of the past decade. The non-profit International Licensing Industry Merchandisers' Association (LIMA) found that sports licensing has expanded in "scope and sophistication" over the course of the past ten years, with 2007 revenues estimated to be $815 million, making sports one of the top licensing revenue producers in the world. According to Greenberg and Gray (1998), three factors have primarily helped grow licensing in the sports industry: "(a) increased fan interest; (b) more pointed and sophisticated marketing; and (c) better quality products" (703).

Sports licensing involves a manufacturer of some commercial product, on one hand, and a professional athlete, labor union, professional team, or sports league, on the other hand. The two parties involved must agree to terms of a licensing agreement that allows the manufacturer (licensee) to use the name, likeness, logo, or symbol of the player, union, team, or league (licensor) in connection with a specific product. In granting such rights, the licensee has to pay the licensor a fee. This exchange of value between the licensor and the licensee creates a license. An example of a license is when the National Football League (NFL) allowed Reebok the exclusive right to place the logo of NFL teams on t-shirts and other clothing for resale. The "exclusivity" of the NFL-Reebok license led to a lawsuit that reached the US Supreme Court in 2010. Another example of licensing is sports video games.

Why is sports licensing so successful? Greenberg and Gray (2008) pointed towards the psychological aspect. Licensing allows sports fans to identify with certain players or teams. Licensing allows consumers to actually wear clothing that helps further ingratiate the fan with his or her favorite player or team. In fact, some officially licensed apparel is the exact replica of the uniform worn by college and professional athletes. LIMA described a number of other factors that help explain the usefulness of licensing from the licensees' perspective. These factors include the ability to open up new avenues of distribution and to help establish brand recognition in the marketplace.

Licensed products in the sports industry (and other industries) have certain legal protections. In addition to various state laws that differ by jurisdiction, the Lanham Act is a federal law frequently used to protect officially licensed products from infringement. In order to qualify for a remedy under the Lanham Act, two primary requirements must be met. First, the party claiming infringement, the plaintiff, must have an enforceable right that is valid. A valid trademark in the United States, for example, is evidenced by a current filing with the US Patent and Trademark Office. Second, proof must be offered that an actual infringement by the defendant occurred. To prove infringement, the defendant must have used the plaintiff's right in a recognizable way without permission. Second, such use must have damaged the plaintiff's commercial value.

Sample Sports Video Game Licensing Agreement

This sports video game licensing agreement ("Agreement") memorializes the understanding between _____ ("Company") and _____ ("Player") regarding the use of Player's name and likeness in a video game manufactured and sold by Company.

Company and Player agree as follows:

1. Definitions. The following terms shall be defined as follows:
   (a) "Licensee" shall mean Company.
   (b) "Licensor" shall mean Player.
   (c) "Territory" shall mean _____.
   (d) "Licensed Products" shall mean Company's video games featuring Player.
   (e) "Contract Period" shall commence _____, 20___ and conclude _____, 20___.
   (f) "Approved Formats" include game consoles manufactured by Sony, Microsoft, and Nintendo and IBM and IBM-compatible personal computers.

2. Grant of Rights. Licensor grants to Licensee the exclusive license to use Client's name and likeness in the Territory during the Contract Period solely in connection with the manufacture and sale of Licensed Products.

3. Guaranteed Compensation. Licensee shall pay Licensor _____ U.S. Dollars ($____) within ___ (___) days of execution of this Agreement.

4. Royalty Compensation. In addition to any other compensation, Licensee shall pay Licensor _____ percent (___%) of the wholesale price of each individual unit of Licensed Product sold. Payments for royalty compensation shall be made quarterly during the Contract Period and thereafter (if applicable).

5. Insurance. Licensee shall obtain and maintain product liability and advertising insurance for the Licensed Products in the amount of _____ U.S. Dollars ($____) during the Contract Period and for _____ (___) years thereafter.

6. Governing Law. Any dispute arising out of this Agreement shall be subject to the laws and courts of _____.

7. Indemnity. Licensee agrees to indemnify Licensor from and against any all expenses, damages, claims, or judgments, including attorneys' fees, arising out of any breach by Licensee of this Agreement. Licensor agrees to indemnify Licensee from and against any all expenses, damages, claims, or judgments, including attorneys' fees, arising out of any breach by Licensor of this Agreement.

8. Waiver. The failure of Licensee or Licensor at any time to demand strict performance with the terms of this Agreement shall not be construed as a continuing waiver of any legal rights that may arise.

9. Assignment. Neither Licensee nor Licensor shall have any right to grant sublicenses hereunder or otherwise assign any rights or obligations to one or more third parties.

10. Confidentiality. Neither party shall disclose any terms of this Agreement without pre-approval from the other party.

11. Entire Agreement. This Agreement constitutes the entire agreement between the parties and cannot be altered or modified except by a written agreement signed by both parties. Upon full execution, this Agreement will supersede all prior negotiations, understandings, or agreements between the parties.

ACCEPTED AND AGREED:

_____ ("Company")   _____ ("Player")

By: _____   Date: _____

Title: _____

Date: _____

Licensing and the Law—*American Needle v. NFL*

In 2010, issues involving sports industry licensing made it to the highest level of the United States judicial system in the case of *American Needle v. NFL*. At issue in the case was whether the NFL should be considered a "single entity," and thereby excluded from certain portions of antitrust law when it exclusively licenses league and team-specific intellectual property (e.g., names and logos). Plaintiff American Needle complained that the NFL's all-encompassing exclusive licensing contract with Reebok violated antitrust laws. Specifically, the plaintiff complained that the NFL-Reebok agreement represented an impermissible contract, combination, or conspiracy in restraint of trade. The NFL prevailed at the district court level and the grant of summary judgment was affirmed by the US Court of Appeals for the Seventh Circuit. The US Supreme Court agreed to hear the appeal and listened to oral arguments on January 13, 2010.

At the January 2010 oral argument session, both sides put forth their respective positions. American Needle contended that the concerted action of the NFL, its 32 teams, and Reebok should be subject to antitrust review. The NFL countered that its internal decision-making is analogous to a single entity, thereby distancing itself from antitrust scrutiny. The justices seemed generally skeptical of the NFL's position during oral argument. Such skepticism was reflected in the written opinion issued by the court on May 24, 2010.

Now-retired US Supreme Court Justice John Paul Stevens wrote a unanimous decision rejecting the NFL's claim. Justice Stevens concluded that the licensing activities of the NFL's 32 teams constitute concerted action and should be subject to lawsuits based on antitrust laws. As a result of the decision, the NFL will have to defend its licensing contract with Reebok. More generally, sports leagues will have to exercise caution in entering into exclusive licensing agreements. For example, individual NFL teams such as the Dallas Cowboys may move to negotiate individual licensing agreements if the NFL ultimately loses the case or the parties enter into a settlement agreement. At the time of this book's publication, American Needle and the NFL were preparing for trial.

In addition to the important intellectual property aspects, sports industry licensing results from the contractual agreement between the licensee and licensor. As illustrated in the sample contract included in the appendix to this chapter, there are a number of key provisions in any sports-related licensing agreement. First, the parties often negotiate an exclusivity clause whereby the licensee pays large sums of money to ensure that no competitor will have the same rights. Second, the parties to the contract are careful to include a definition of the product to which the license extends. For example, the recently completed NFL-Reebok licensing agreement granted Reebok the unfettered right to include NFL league and team logos on jerseys and other athletic-related pieces of clothing. However, the underlying licensing agreement did not grant Reebok the right to include such marks on posters, food, or a host of other product categories. Licenses in categories other than athletic attire were granted to other companies.

Learning Activity: Sports Video Games

Sports-related video games provide a good context for understanding how licensing agreements work. Each of the major North American team sports leagues (NFL, NBA, MLB, and NHL) has an officially licensed video game. The NCAA similarly markets college football and basketball through video games produced by EA Sports. Individual sports such as golf, tennis, and mixed martial arts also have officially licensed video games. For example, Tiger Woods lends his name and likeness to PGA Tour video game produced by EA Sports.

Review the video game licensing agreement and answer the following questions:

1. Why is a separate section for "Definitions" included? What other terms should be defined, if any?
2. How is the compensation structured?
3. Why is insurance important?
4. What does indemnity mean?
5. What is the purpose of the assignment section?

Third, almost all licensing agreements include specific language outlining the term and geographic scope. The term refers to the defined time period during which the license remains active. The geographic scope outlines the extent to which the license attaches in different markets. It is not unusual for a licensor to grant licenses covering the same subject matter to two or more companies who operate in different geographical regions. Together with certain legal protections afforded by intellectual property law, the terms of the licensing agreement memorialize the understanding between the two parties and help reduce counterfeiting, a growing sports industry licensing-related problem around the world.

Discussion Questions

1. Discuss the difference between brand awareness and brand association.

2. Discuss your favorite teams and the memories linked to your experiences. List how many brand associations you mention in your discussion.

3. Classroom discussion: Look around the room. How many brand names do you recognize? Are there any brands unfamiliar to you? Create groups of people that are familiar with the brand and those that are not. What are the common traits among those that are familiar (group 1) with the brand? Next, determine the traits that are similar with those that are familiar (group 1) and not familiar (group 2). Next, create an advertisement to reach the target market (familiar group 1) and the new market (unfamiliar group 2).

Critical Thinking Exercises

1. Do you have any negative associations with a sport brand? Discuss how the media shapes your experience and perceptions of the brand.

2. Did an athlete's behavior off the field influence your perceptions of a brand you prefer? Do athletes' images recover faster than a brand's image? Should brands evaluate the "risky" behavior of the athlete before using them as a spokesperson or endorser?

3. Do you think the brand image of the athlete is more valuable than a team's brand image? How can a team increase brand value? How can an individual athlete increase brand value?

4. Describe how you would target new customers and meet current customers' demands with advertisements. Give one example of a sport brand that consistently re-innovates and establishes a sound brand identity.

5. Consider you are the marketing director for an expansion franchise in one of the major professional leagues. What data would you need in order to develop sound brand management strategies? How would you establish brand awareness and brand identity?

References

Aaker, D. *Managing Brand Equity: Capitalizing on the Value of a Brand Name.* New York: The Free Press, 1991.

Aaker, D. *Brand Portfolio Strategy.* New York: Free Press, 2004.

Aaker, D. "Innovation: Brand it or lose it." *California Management Review,* 50 (2007): 8-24.

Aaker, D. "Marketing challenges in the next decade." *Journal of Brand Management,* 17 (2010): 315-316.

Aaker, D., and K. Keller. "Consumer Evaluations of Brand Extensions." *Journal of Marketing,* 54 (1990): 27-41.

Aaker, D., and E. Joachimsthaler. "The brand relationship spectrum: The key to brand architectire challenge." *California Managment Review,* 42 (2000): 8-23.

Badenhausen, K. "Tiger Woods adds first sponsor since scandal." *Forbes.* 2011. http://blogs.forbes.com/ kurtbadenhausen/2011/06/29/tiger-woods-adds-first-sponsor-since-scandal/

Bauer, H., N. Stokburger-Sauer, and S. Exler. "Brand image and fan loyalty in professional team sport: A refined model and emprical assessment." *Journal of Sport Management,* 22 (2008): 205-226.

Bedbury, S. *A new brand world.* New York: Free Press, 2002.

Berry, L. *Discovering the soul of service: The nine drivers of sustainable business success.* New York: Free Press, 1999.

Boone, L., C. Kochunny, and D. Wilkins. "Applying the brand equity concept to Major League Baseball." *Sport Marketing Quarterly,* 4 (1995): 33–42.

Bowden, J. "The process of customer engagement: A conceptual framework." *Journal of Marketing Theory and Practice,* 17 (2009): 63-74.

Brewer, R., and P. Pedersen. "Franchises, value drivers and the application of valuation analysis to sports sponsorship." *Journal of Sponsorship,* 3 (2010): 181-193.

Brody, J., V. Gregovits, N. Hill, M. McGee, P. McGee, S. O'Neil, et al. "Industry Insider: Sport Marketing Forecast." *Sport Marketing Quarterly,* 19 (2010): 4-7.

Carlson, B. , and D. Donavan. "Concerning the effect of athlete endorsement on brand and team-related intentions." *Sport Marketing Quarterly,* 17 (2008): 154-162.

Clavio, G., and K. Miloch. "Adgenda-setting in Minor League Hockey: A strategic justification adn practical guide." *International Journal of Sport Management and Marketing,* 5 (2009): 151-160.

Cunningham, S., T. Cornwell, and L. Coote. "Expressing identity and shaping image: The relationship between corporate mission and corporate sponsorship." *Journal of Sport Management,* 23 (2009): 65-86.

Dong-Hun, L. "Korean Consumer & Society: Attraction of sports marketing as means of communication." *Samsung Economic Research Institute Quarterly,* 3 (2010): 112-116.

Fink, J., H. Parker, M. Brett, and J. Higgins. "Off-Field Behavior of Athletes and Team Identification: Using Social Identity Theory and Balance Theory to Explain Fan Reactions." *Journal of Sport Management,* 23 (2009): 142-155.

Fortunato, J. "NFL Agenda-setting The NFL Programming Schedule: A Study of Agenda-setting." *Journal of Sports Media,* 3 (2008): 27-49.

Foster, W., and C. Hyatt, C. "Inventing team tradition: A conceptual model for the strategic development of fan nations." *European Sport Management Quarterly,* 8 (2008): 265-287.

Frederick, H., and S. Patil. "The dynamics of brand quity, co-branding adn sponsorship in professional sports." *International Journal of Sport Management and Marketing,* 7 (2010): 44-57.

Friedmann, R. "Psychological meaning of products: Identification and marketing applications." *Psychology & Marketing,* 3 (1986): 1-15.

Fullerton, S., and G. R. Merz. "The four domains of sports marketing: A conceptual framework." *Sport Marketing Quarterly,* 17 (2008): 90-108.

Funk, D., and J. James. "Consumer Loyalty: The meaning of attachment in the development of sport team allegiance." *Journal of Sport Management,* 20 (2006): 189–217.

Funk, D., K. Filo, A. Beaton, and M. Pritchard. "Measuring the motives of sport event attendance: Bridging the Academic-Practitioner divide to understanding behavior." *Sport Marketing Quarterly,* 18 (2009): 126–183.

Galily, Y. "The (Re)shaping of the Israeli sport media: The case of talk-back." *International Journal of Sport Communication,* 1 (2008): 273–285.

Girginov, V., M. Taks, B. Boucher, S. Martyn, M. Holman, and J. Dixon "Canadian national sport organizations' use of the web for relationship marketing in promoting sport participation." *International Journal of Sport Communication,* 2 (2009): 164–184.

Gladden, J., and D. Funk, "Developing an understanding of brand associations in team sport: Empirical evidence from consumers of professional sport." *Journal of Sport Management,* 16 (2002): 54–81.

Gladden, J., and D. Funk. "Understanding brand loyalty in professional sport: Examining the link between brand associations and brand loyalty." *International Journal of Sports Marketing and Sponsorship,* 3 (2001): 67–94.

Gladden, J., and G. Milne. "Examining the importance of brand equity in professional sports." *Sports Marketing Quarterly,* 8 (1999): 21–29.

Gladden, J., R. Irwin, W. Sutton. "Managing North American major professional sport teams in the new millennium A focus on building brand equity." *Journal of Sports Management,* 15 (2001): 297–317.

Gladden, J., G. Milne, and W. Sutton. "A conceptual framework for evaluating brand equity in Division I college athletics." *Journal of Sport Management,* 12 (1998): 1–19.

Godin, S. *Purple cow: Transform your business by being remarkable.* New York: Penguin Group, 2002.

Greenberg, M. J., and J. T. Gray. *Sports law practice.* 2nd ed., Charlottesville, VA:Lexis Law Publishing, 1998.

Gregory, S. "Tiger Woods's sponsors: Will any stick by him?" *Time: U.S.,* 2009., http://www.time.com/time/nation/article/0,8599,1948181,00.html

Gregory, S. "Why the Masters makes sense for Tiger." *Time: U.S.,* 2010., http://www.time.com/time/nation/article/0,8599,1972789,00.html

International Licensing Industry Merchandisers' Association. "Types of licensing." *Licensing.org,* March 20, 2010, http://www.licensing.org/education/licensing-types.php

Kapfererm, J. *Strategic brand management: New approaches to creating and evaluating brand equity.* New York: The Free Press, 1992.

Kaynak, E., G. Salmon, and E. Tatoglu. "An integrative framework lining brand associations and brand loyalty in professional sports." *Brand Managment,* 15 (2008): 336–357.

Kim, Y., and S. Ross. "An exploration of motives in sport video gaming." *International Journal of Sport Marketing & Sponsorship,* 8 (2006): 34–46.

Keller, K. "Brand Mantras: Rationale, criteria and examples." *Journal of Marketing Management,* 15 (1999): 43–51.

Keller, K. "Brand Synthesis: The multidemsion of brand knowledge." *Journal of Consumer Research,* 29 (2003): 595–600.

Keller, K. "Branding perspectives on Social Marketing." *Advances in Consumer Research,* 25 (1998): 299–302.

Keller, K. "Conceptualizing, Measuring, and Managing Customer-Based Brand Equity." *Journal of Marketing,* 57 (1993):1–22.

Keller, K. "Managing the growth tradeoff: Challenges and opportunities in luxury branding." *Brand Management,* 16 (2009): 290–301.

Koernig, S., and T. Boyd. "To Catch a Tiger or Let Him Go: The Match-up Effect and Athlete Endorsers for Sport and Non-Sport Brands." *Sport Marketing Quarterly,* 18 (2009): 25–37.

Kuo, T., C. Chang, and K. Chen. "Evolution of Scholars' approach to studying consumer loyality in recreation sport and fitness businesses." *The Sport Journal,* 7, 2004, http://www.thesportjournal.org/article/exploration-consumer-loyalty-recreational-sportfitness-programs

Lee, J. W. Logo. In Linda E. Swayne and Mark Dodds (Eds.). Vol. 2. *Encyclopedia of sports management and marketing.* Thousand Oaks, CA: Sage Reference, 2011a, 778–780.

Lee, J. W. Slogans. In Linda E. Swayne and Mark Dodds (Eds.). Vol. 3. *Encyclopedia of sports management and marketing.* Thousand Oaks, CA: Sage Reference, 2011b, 1378–1379.

Lee, J., and P. Laucella. Sport Celebrities. In Linda E. Swayne and Mark Dodds (Eds.). Vol. 4. *Encyclopedia of sports management and marketing.* Thousand Oaks, CA: Sage Reference, 2011, 1428–1431.

Lee, J. W., and K. Miloch. Player as Brand. In Linda E. Swayne and Mark Dodds (Eds.). Vol. 3. *Encyclopedia of Sports Management and Marketing.* Thousand Oaks, CA: Sage Reference, 2011b, 1126–1128.

Lee, J. W., and K. Miloch. Tagline. In Linda E. Swayne and Mark Dodds (Eds.). Vol. 4. *Encyclopedia of Sports Management and Marketing.* Thousand Oaks, CA: Sage Reference, 2011a, 1519–1520.

Lefton, T. "Penalty drop: Tiger Woods plummets on sports Q scores list." *SportsBusiness Journal,* June 7, 2010.

Madrigal, R. "Cognitive and affective determinants of fan satisfaction." *Journal of Leisure Research,* 27 (1995): 205–227.

McCombs, M. "A look at agenda-setting: Past, present and future." *Journalism Studies,* 6(4) (2005): 543–557. doi:10.1080/14616700500250438.

McDaniel, S., and S. Moore. "Pre-production relationship marketing: A lesson from sports marketing." *Journal of Relationship Marketing,* 4 (2005): 73–90. doi:10.1300/J366v04n01•06

McGlone, C., and N. Martin. "Nike's corporate interest lives strong: A case of cause-related marketing and leveraging." *Sport Marketing Quarterly,* 15 (2006): 184–189.

McQueen, J., C. Foley, and J. Deighton. "Decomposing a Brand's Consumer Francise into Buyer Types." In D. Aaker, and A. Biel (Eds.), *Brand equity & advertising: Advertising's role in building strong brands.* Hillsdale, NJ: Lawerence Erlbaum Associates, Inc., 1993, 235–245.

Miloch, K. "Introduction to Branding." In J. W. Lee (Ed.), *Branded: Branding in sport business.* Durham, NC: Carolina Academic Press, 2010, 3–9.

Miloch, K., J. Lee, V. Ratten, and P. Kraft, "Click clack: Examining the strategic and entrepreneurial brand vision of Under Armour." *International Journal of Entrepreneurial Venturing,* 4(1) (2012): 42–57.

Mueller, T., and M. S. Roberts. "The effective communication of attributes in sport-sponsorship branding." *International Journal of Sport Communication,* 1 (2008): 155–172.

Mullin, B., S. Hardy, and W. Sutton, *Sport marketing.* Champaign: Human Kinetics, 2007.

Oates, T. "New media and the repackaging of the NFL fandom." *Sociology of Sport Journal,* 26 (2009): 31–49.

Parent, M., and B. Sequin. "Toward a Model of Brand Creation for International Large Scale Sporting Events: The Impact of Leadership, Context, and Nature of the Event." *Journal of Sport Management,* 22 (2008): 526–549.

Pedersen, P., K. Miloch, and P. Laucella. *Strategic sport communication.* Champaign, IL: Human Kinetics, 2007.

Pomerantz, D. "Celebrity 100: Lady Gaga Tops Celebrity 100." *Forbes,* 2011, http://mobile.forbes.com/device/article.php?CALL_URL=http://www.forbes.com/2011/05/16/lady-gaga-tops-celebrity-100-11.html

Pritchard. M. and D. Funk. "The formation and effect of attitude importance in professional sport." *European Journal of Marketing,* 4(7/8) (2010): 1017–1036.

Richelieu, A., and M. Desbordes. "Football teams going international: The strategic leverage of branding." *Journal of Sponsorship,* 3 (2009): 10–22.

Richelieu, A., and F. Pons. "Tronto Maple Leafs Vs Football Club Barcelona: how two ledgendary sports built their brand equity." *International Journal of Sports Marketing & Sponsorship,* 7 (2006): 231–250.

Ross, S. "A conceptual framework for understanding spectator-based brand equity." *Journal of Sport Management,* 20 (2006): 22–38.

Ross, S. "Segmenting Sport Fans Using Brand Associations: A Cluster Analysis." *Sport Marketing Quarterly,* 16 (2007): 15–24.

Ross, S., H. Bang, and S. Lee. "Assessing Brand Associations for Intercollegiate Ice Hockey." *Sport Marketing Quarterly,* 16 (2007): 106–114.

Ross, S., J. James, and P. Vargas. "Developement of a scale to measure team brand associations in professional sport." *Journal of Sport Management,* 20 (2006): 260–279.

Ross, S., K. Russell, and H. Bang. "An empirical assessment of spectator-based brand equity." *Journal of Sport Management,* 22 (2008): 322–337.

Sanderson, J. "Framing Tiger's troubles: Comparing traditional and social media." *International Journal of Sport Communication,* 3 (2010): 438–453.

Santomier, J. "New media, branding and global sports sponsorship." *International Journal of Sports Marketing and Sponsorship,* 10 (2008): 15–28.

Shelton, K. "Using Facebook following tragedies: A lesson for community colleges." *Community & Junior College Libraries,* 15 (2009): 195–203.

Shocker, A., R. Srivastave, and R. Ruekert, R. "Challenges and opportunities facing brand management: An introduction to the special issue." *Journal of Marketing Research,* 31 (1994): 194–158.

Stonehouse, G., and S. Minocha. "Strategic process at Nike: Making and doing knowledge management." *Knowledge and Process Management,* 15 (2008): 24–31.

Uggla, H., and D. Filipsson. "Business and Brand Strategy: A framework for integration." *The Icfai University Journal of Business Strategy,* 6 (2009): 27–42.

Vincent, J., J. Hill, and J. Lee. "The multiple brand personalities of David Beckham: A case study of Beckham brand." *Sport Marketing Quarterly,* 18 (2009): 173–180.

Walsh, P., Y. Kim, and S. Ross. "Brand recall and recognition: A comparison of television and sport video games as presentation modes." *Sport Marketing Quarterly,* 17 (2008): 201–208.

Wann, D., F. Grieve, R. Zapalac, and D. Pease. "Motivational profiles of sport fans of different sports." *Sport Marketing Quarterly,* 17 (2008): 6–19.

Woo, B., G. Trail, H. Kwon, and D. Anderson. "Testing models of motives and points of attachment among spectators in college football." *Sport Marketing Quarterly,* 18 (2009): 38–53.

Zaharopoulos, T. "The news framing of the 2004 Olympic games." *Mass Communication & Society,* 10 (2007): 235–249. doi:10.1080/15205430701265752

Courtesy of Brian Turner

CHAPTER 13

Legal Issues in Sport Marketing

Christopher J. Cabott, Esq.
Lloyd Z. Remick, Esq.

So you think that all you need to know about sport marketing is four words ...
"Michael Jordan, Tiger Woods"... Guess again

CHAPTER OBJECTIVES

After completing the chapter, the reader should be able to:

- Identify and understand the legal concepts that are synonymous with sports marketing, such as intellectual property, contracts, and torts.
- Examine and evaluate the role of sport agents, and recognize the key regulations that govern their industry.
- Determine and discuss the impact of the increasing size of sports marketing in the global economy.
- Identify and assess the roles of individual, team, and league licensing rights in brand advertisements and marketing.

Introduction

In this chapter, you will become familiar with the following terms: sports marketing, intellectual property law, contract law, torts, patents, United States Patent and Trademark Office, trademarks, Lanham Act, domain names, the Anticybersquatting Protection Act, copyrights, the Copyright Act, ambush marketing, sponsorships, endorsements, venue naming rights agreements, incapacity, duress, misrepresentation, fraud, mistake, impossibility, unconscionability, the right of privacy, the right of publicity, fantasy sports, sports agent regulations, National College Athletic Association, the Uniform Athlete Agents Act, and the Sports Agent Responsibility and Trust Act amongst others.

© alexskopje, 2012. Under license from Shutterstock, Inc.

This chapter will further explore the interaction of the above concepts with sports marketing and how ambush marketing, venue naming rights, endorsements and sponsorships, social networking, event management, fantasy sports, agent regulation, and the right of publicity play a vital role in the expansion of the sports marketing industry. An illustration of how the dollars invested into sports marketing have increased over the years can be illustrated by the growth of the Olympics.

Contemporary sports marketing came into the limelight at the 1984 Summer Olympics in Los Angeles when McDonalds and Coca-Cola used the games as a platform to market their brands. Coca-Cola spent nearly $30 million—low in today's standards—to be the official sponsor of the games. This was the first time the world saw such an enormous tie-in between marketing and sports. The chart below further illustrates how Olympic marketing revenues have grown since the 1992 games, where the "Dream Team" was a sports marketing phenomena.

TABLE 13.1

Olympic Marketing Revenue: The Past Four Quadrenniums			
Source	1993–1996	1997–2000	2001–2004	2005–2008
Broadcast	$1,251,000,000	$1,845,000,000	$2,232,000,000	$2,570,000,000
Olympic Partner Sponsorships	$279,000,000	$579,000,000	$663,000,000	$866,000,000
Domestic U.S. Sponsorships	$534,000,000	$655,000,000	$796,000,000	$1,555,000,000
Ticketing	$451,000,000	$625,000,000	$411,000,000	$274,000,000
Licensing	$115,000,000	$66,000,000	$87,000,000	$185,000,000
Total	**$2,630,000,000**	**$3,770,000,000**	**$4,189,000,000**	**$5,450,000,000**

Note: All figures rounded to the nearest million USD. International Olympic Committee, 2010.

As one can see, sports marketing is a staple of modern popular culture; however, this staple is not all glitz and glamour. It is heavily regulated and governed by legal concepts. The most common of which is **intellectual property law**.

Intellectual Property Law

The laws of **patents, trademarks,** and **copyrights** are the primary three components of intellectual property law. A brief overview and examples of how they apply in the world of sports marketing follows.

Patents

A patent is essentially a limited monopoly that gives the patent holder the exclusive right to make, use, and sell the patented innovation, which in most cases is an invention, for a limited period of time. The United States Patent Act[1] governs patent law. Granting exclusive rights to the inventor is intended to encourage the investment of time and resources into the development of new and useful discoveries. In exchange for this exclusive right to create and invent, the patent holder must disclose to the United States Patent and Trademark Office (the "USPTO") all of the information behind how the invention, creation, or innovation came to be. Once the term of protection expires, the patented innovation enters into the public domain and is free for anyone to make, use, and/or sell. In order for an invention, creation, or innovation to be patentable, it must have patentable subject matter, utility, novelty, and enablement.

Patentable Subject Matter

The patentable subject matter requirement addresses the issue of which types of inventions can be considered for protection. The Patent Act defines the categories for patentable subject matter as any process, machine, manufacture, or composition of matter, or improvement thereof. The Supreme Court of the United States has found that Congress intended patentable subject matter to "include anything under the sun that is made by man."[2]

Utility is the second requirement for patentability. "Utility" means that the invention must be useful. The usefulness must be specific to the subject matter claimed, not a general use that could apply to a broad class of inventions. Substantial utility requires that the invention have a defined real-world use. A claimed use that requires or constitutes carrying out further research to identify or confirm a use in the context of the real world is not sufficient.

The novelty requirement consists of two distinct components: (1) that the invention is new, and (2) a statutory bar to patentability. The first component requires that the invention was not known or used by others in the United States, or patented or described in a printed publication, prior to invention by the patent applicant.[3] The statutory bar component applies to where the invention was in public use or on sale in the United States, or patented or described in a publication more than one year prior to the date of the application for a US patent.[4]

---

[1] 35 U.S. Const. §§ 1 *et seq.*

[2] *See Diamond v. Chakrabarty,* 447 U.S. Const. 303 (1980).

[3] *See* 35 U.S. Const. § 102(a)

[4] *See* 35 U.S. Const. § 102(b)

In other words, the right to a patent is lost if the inventor delays too long before seeking patent protection. The primary difference between the "new" component and the statutory bar component is that an inventor's own actions cannot destroy the novelty of his or her invention, but can create a statutory bar to patentability. In order for a patent to be novel, it must also be "non-obvious." The test for non-obviousness is whether the subject matter sought to be patented would have been obvious to a person having ordinary skill at the time the invention was made.[5]

The enablement requirement is directly related to the specification or disclosure, which must be included as a part of every patent application. "The specification shall contain a written description of the invention, and the process of making and using it, in full, clear, concise, and exact terms as to enable any person skilled in the [industry] to which it pertains ... to make and use the same, and shall set forth the best mode of carrying out the invention."[6]

Patent Application Process

The United States Patent and Trademark Office ("USPTO") issues patents. The process by which a patent is obtained from the USPTO is called "prosecution." Prosecution begins when a patent application is filed with the USPTO. Each patent application received is examined by a patent examiner. Once the examination is complete, the examiner may accept the application and issue a patent; issue a rejection of some or all of the claims made in the application; or issue an objection if there is a problem with the form of the application. If a claim is rejected as not patentable, or an objection as to the form of the application is issued, the examiner must notify the applicant, state the reasons for each rejection or objection and provide information and references to assist the applicant in judging the propriety of continuing the prosecution.[7]

Upon receiving notice of any objections or rejections issued by the USPTO, the applicant is entitled to a reexamination of the application regardless of whether the application has been amended to address the reasons stated by the examiner.[8] If the application is rejected a second time, or a final rejection is issued, the applicant may file an appeal of the decision with the Board of Patent Appeals and Interferences.[9] An applicant that is dissatisfied with the decision of the board has a choice between two further appeal options. The applicant can either appeal the board's decision to the United States Court of Appeals for the Federal Circuit, or pursue a civil action to obtain the patent by filing against the USPTO in the United States District Court for the District of Columbia. It often times takes up to seven years or more to have a patent application approved.

Term of Patent Protection

The term of protection for utility patents (the patent for actual inventions) is 20 years from the date of filing the application,[10] with extensions of up to five years for certain drugs,

---

[5] *See* 35 U.S. Const. § 103

[6] *See* 35 U.S. Const. § 112

[7] *See* 37 C.F.R. § 1.104; 35 U.S. Const. § 132

[8] *See* 35 U.S. Const. § 132

[9] *See* 35 U.S. Const. § 134

[10] 35 U.S. Const. § 154

medical devices, and additives.[11] The term of protection for design patents (the patent for a new design of something already in the market) is 14 years from the date of filing.[12] Despite these terms of ownership, if one is able to reverse engineer a patented invention (figure out how to create the invention on his or her own), such ingenuity permits that person to immediately market the reverse engineered item.

Examples of Patents in Sports and Sports Marketing

One of the most common and known patents in sports relates to golf balls. In fact, golf ball patents have been a highly contested matter. In 2006, Callaway sued Acushnet, the maker of the Titleist Pro V1 ball, alleging that Acushnet had infringed on a number of Callaway's patents that involved technological breakthroughs in producing multilayer, solid core balls that resulted in better performance for golfers.[13] In March of 2010, Acushnet won the suit and the four Callaway patents in question were found to be invalid.[14] Other patents in sports and sports marketing include TiVo (US Patent 7665111), baseball pitching backstops (US Patent 5573240), snow board bindings (US Patent 5820139), football helmets (US Patent 3751728), ice hockey pucks (US Patent 5695420), and basketballs (US Patent 4345759).

By way of contrast, one of the most iconic brands in sports marketing—Under Armour "wicking" apparel—is not patented. Under Armour founder Kevin Plank spent thousands of dollars in legal fees over seven years to prosecute the patent for the moisture "wicking" fabric before ultimately deciding that the opportunity cost was hurting his chances of capturing the market share. Immediately thereafter, Plank took the fabric to manufacturers to be made into shirts, pants, athletic under garments, etc. From there, the product went to retailers and the rest is history. Dozens of other companies compete with Under Armour's fabric when it comes to the performance apparel, but Under Armour has successfully won consumer confidence and the market share. It should be noted that Under Armour has not ignored the importance of securing and applying for patents for inventions more complicated than the traditional "wicking" apparel. Such complicated inventions include detachable athletic cleats (US Patent Application 20090077833). Under Armour and its famous logo are a great segue into the next form of intellectual property ... trademark law.

Trademark Law

A trademark is a word, symbol, or phrase, used to identify a particular manufacturer or seller's products and distinguish them from the products of another.[15] For example, the trademark in the name "Under Armour," along with its symbol, identify the company's apparel and distinguish it from other sports apparel. In like manner, the trademark "Pepsi" distinguishes the cola of one manufacturer from the cola of another (e.g., Coca-Cola). When names, symbols,

---

[11] 35 U.S. Const. § 156

[12] *See* 35 U.S. Const. § 173

[13] *See* Callaway Golf Co. v. Acushnet Co., 06cv91 (SLR), U.S. District Court, Delaware.

[14] http://www.businessweek.com/news/2010-03-29/callaway-golf-loses-bid-for-246-million-in-patent-damages.html

[15] 15 U.S. Const. §1127

distinguish it from other sports apparel. In like manner, the trademark "Pepsi" distinguishes the cola of one manufacturer from the cola of another (e.g., Coca-Cola). When names, symbols, logos, phrases, etc., are used to identify services (e.g., "Jiffy Lube") rather than products, they are called service marks. When a name is used to identify a company or entity (e.g., "H&R Block"), it is referred to as a trade name.

Trademarks make it easy for consumers to identify the source of products. Instead of asking a store clerk who makes certain athletic apparel in the store, consumers can look for identifying symbols, such as the Under Armour logo. By making goods easier to identify, trademarks give manufacturers an incentive to invest in the quality of their goods. After all, if a consumer tries an Under Armour product and finds it unsatisfactory, it is easy for her to avoid Under Armour in the future and instead buy a competing brand like Nike. Trademark law furthers these goals by regulating the use of trademarks, service marks, and trade names (collectively referred to hereafter as a "mark" or "marks").

Marks are governed by both state and federal law. Originally, state common law provided the main source of the protection. However, in the late 1800s, Congress enacted the first federal trademark law. Since that time, federal trademark law has expanded, taking over much of the ground initially covered by state common law. The main federal statute is the

© Natursports, 2012. Under license from Shutterstock, Inc.

Lanham Act, which was enacted in 1946 and most recently amended in 1996.[16] Today, federal law provides the most extensive source of protection for marks, although state common law actions are still available. Most of the discussion below focuses on federal law, as in today's digital world, even the most local product usually carries an online counterpart, which gives away to federal protection.

In order to qualify as a mark, the name, logo, symbol, etc., must be distinctive—that is, it must be capable of identifying the source of the particular good, service, and/or company. In determining whether a mark is distinctive, the courts group marks into four categories: (1) **arbitrary or fanciful**, (2) **suggestive**, (3) **descriptive,** or (4) **generic**. Because the marks in each of these categories vary with respect to their distinctiveness, the requirements for and degree of legal protection afforded a mark depends upon which category it falls within.

An arbitrary or fanciful mark is a mark that bears no logical relationship to the underlying product. "Xerox" is an example. Arbitrary or fanciful marks are inherently distinctive.

A suggestive mark is one that suggests a characteristic of the underlying good. For example, "Coppertone" is suggestive of sun-tan lotion, but does not specifically

---

[16]   15 U.S. Const. §§1051 *et seq.*

describe the underlying product. Like arbitrary or fanciful marks, suggestive marks are inherently distinctive.

A descriptive mark is one that describes a characteristic of the underlying product. For example, "Comfort Inn," describes the underlying product; a hotel room. The mark tells us something about the product. Unlike arbitrary or suggestive marks, descriptive marks are not inherently distinctive and are protected only if they have acquired "**secondary meaning**." Secondary meaning is acquired when the consuming public associates that mark with a particular source, rather than the underlying product. "Comfort Inn" has acquired secondary meaning because the consuming public associates that term with a particular provider of hotel services, and not with hotel services in general. When determining whether marks have acquired secondary meaning, courts look at: (1) the amount and manner of advertising; (2) the volume of sales; (3) the length and manner of the marks' use; and (4) results of consumer surveys.[17]

A generic mark is one that describes the general category to which the underlying product belongs. For example, the term "computer" is a generic term for computer equipment. Generic marks are not entitled to protection under trademark law. Accordingly, a manufacturer selling "Computer" brand computers would have no exclusive right to use that term with respect to that product, but the term "Apple" would work for computers, as it is arbitrary.

Assuming that a mark qualifies for protection, rights can be acquired in one of two ways: (1) by being the first to use the mark in commerce; or (2) by being the first to register the mark with the USPTO.[18] Although registration with the USPTO is not required for a trademark to be protected, registration confers a number of benefits to the registering party.[19] In most cases, registration gives a party the right to use the mark nationwide.[20] Registration constitutes nationwide notice to others that the mark is owned by a party. Registration also enables a party to bring an infringement suit in federal court.[21] It also allows a party to potentially recover treble damages (triple the amount of losses), attorneys' fees, and other remedies. One starts the registration process by filing an application with the USPTO. Some states also have their own registration systems, where the applicant only seeks protection in that state. When examiners review the applications, they will grant the application provided that the mark has qualified for protection as set forth above and the mark is not similarly confusing to another good, service, or company or entity already in use.

The rights to a trademark can be lost through abandonment, improper licensing, or assignment. A trademark is abandoned when its use is discontinued with an intent not to resume its use. Such intent can be inferred from the circumstances (e.g., non-use for three consecutive years constitutes abandonment). The basic idea is that trademark law only protects marks that are being used. So, for example, a recent case held that the Los Angeles

---

[17] Zatarain's, Inc. v. Oak Grove Smokehouse, Inc., 698 F.2d 786 (5th Cir. 1983).

[18] 15 U.S. Const. §1127(a)

[19] 15 U.S. Const. §1051

[20] 15 U.S. Const. §1072

[21] 15 U.S. Const. §1121

[22] MLB Properties, Inc. v. Sed Non Olet Denarius, Ltd., 817 F. Supp. 1103 (S.D.N.Y. 1993).

In terms of improper licensing, where the use of a mark is licensed (for example, to a franchisee) without any continued control by the mark's owner over the quality or use of the mark, the mark's registration will be canceled. Similarly, where the rights to a trademark are assigned to another party, without the corresponding sale of any assets, the mark's registration will be canceled. The rationale is that, under these situations, the mark no longer serves its purpose of identifying the goods, services, or name of a particular provider.[23]

Trademarks and the Internet/Domain Names

In view of the intersection of sports and the Internet, it is important to understand the legal aspects of domain names. The registration process for domain names is easy and inexpensive, so much so, that sometimes people seek to purchase the domain name of an existing mark in hopes of selling it to the owner of the mark for a handsome profit. Further, there is no governing body to determine whether the registration of a domain name has a likelihood of confusion, mistake, or deception with regards to existing domain names or marks. The domain name registrar (e.g., GoDaddy.com) is not liable for infringement if a third party registers and seeks to sell a domain name that illegally violates the right of a trademark owner.[24] These domain registration freedoms and incident concerns led Congress to pass the **Anticybersquatting Consumer Protection Act** (ACPA) in 1999.[25] The law was enacted to "protect consumers and American businesses, to promote the growth of online commerce, and to provide clarity in the law for trademark owners by prohibiting the bad-faith and abusive registration of distinctive marks as Internet domain names with the intent to profit from the goodwill associated with marks."[26] The statute created a specific federal remedy for such acts. It amends Section 43 of the Lanham Act by adding a new subsection, (d)(1)(A), which reads in part:

> "A person shall be liable in a civil action by the owner of a mark, including a personal name which is protected as a mark under this section, if, that person has a bad faith intent to profit from the mark, including a personal name which is protected as a mark under this section; and registers or uses a domain name that in the case of a mark that is distinctive at the same time of registration of the domain name, is identical or confusingly similar to that mark; or in the case of a famous mark that is famous at the time of registration of the domain name, is identical or confusing."

The ACPA allows for transfer of the domain name to the owner of the mark, if it was registered after the effective date of the act. The ACPA also allows the plaintiff to collect, in place of actual damages, statutory damages between $1,000 and $100,000 per domain name from violators of the ACPA.

---

[23] Dawn Donut Co., Inc. v. Hart's Food Stores, Inc., 267 F.2d 358 (2d Cir. 1959).

[24] Bird v. Parsons, 62 USPQ 2d 1905 (6th Cir. 2002).

[25] Pub. L. No. 106-113 199.

[26] Senate Report No. 106-140, at 4.

Copyright Law

Copyright law in the United States is based on the Copyright Act of 1976, a federal statute that went into effect on January 1, 1978. States cannot enact their own laws to protect the same rights as the rights provided by the Copyright Act or pass a law to extend copyright protection on works in the state beyond the term of protection afforded under the Copyright Act. Copyright law protects **works of authorship**. The Copyright Act states that works of authorship include the following types of works, amongst others: literary works, novels, nonfiction prose, poetry, newspapers, magazines, computer software, manuals, catalogs, brochures, musical works, songs, plays, operas, choreographic works, sculptural works, photographs, maps, paintings, drawings, graphic art, cartoon strips and cartoon characters, audiovisual works, movies, videos, television shows, interactive multimedia works, sound recordings, architectural works, and designs.[27]

To receive copyright protection, a work must be "original" and "fixed" in a tangible medium of expression.[28] Only minimal creativity is required to meet the originality requirement. No artistic merit or beauty is required. A work can incorporate pre-existing material and still be original. When preexisting material is incorporated into a new work, the copyright on the new work covers only the original material contributed by the author. According to Section 101 of the Copyright Act, a work is "fixed" when it is made sufficiently permanent to permit it to be perceived, reproduced, or otherwise communicated for a period of more than transitory duration. The form or medium does not make a difference. An author can "fix" words, for example, by writing them down, typing them on a typewriter, dictating them into a recorder, or entering them into a computer. A live television broadcast (e.g., an NFL game) is "fixed" if it is recorded simultaneously with the transmission of the content. Copyright protection arises automatically when an original work of authorship is fixed in a tangible form of expression. Registration with the Copyright Office by filing an application for the copyrightable work is optional (but you have to register before you file an infringement suit). Copyright applications are filed at the Copyright Office website.

The design of a useful article is protected by copyright only if, and to the extent that, the design "incorporates pictorial, graphic, or sculptural features that can be identified separately from, and are capable of existing independently of, the utilitarian aspects of the article."[29] For example, while a "normal" belt buckle is not protected, a three-dimensional belt-buckle design with a unique shape qualifies for limited protection. As one can imagine, this is where decorative and/or sports team or league themed sports apparel and equipment can fall into the realm of design copyrights.

The use of copyright notice is optional for works distributed after March 1, 1989, but creators of copyrightable content would certainly want to feature such notice for, if nothing else, their own credits. **Copyright notice** can take any of these three forms: (1) the "©" symbol followed by a date and name (e.g., © 2011 National Football League); (2) "Copyright"

---

[27] *See* 17 U.S. Const. §102

[28] *See* 17 U.S. Const. §102

[29] *See* 17 U.S. Const. §101

followed by a date and name (e.g., Copyright 2011 National Football League); (3) "Copr." followed by a date and name (e.g., Copr. 2011 National Football League).[30]

The Exclusive Rights

A copyright owner has five exclusive rights in the copyrighted work. They are (1) reproduction rights (the right to copy, transcribe, or imitate the work in fixed form); (2) modification rights (the right to modify the work to create a derivate work); (3) distribution rights (the right to distribute copies of the work by sale, rental, lease, or lending); (4) public performance rights (the right to recite, play, dance, act, or show the work for or to the public); and (5) public display rights (the right to show a copy of the work directly or by means of a film, slide, or television image at a public place or to transmit it to the public).[31] Anyone that violates any of the exclusive rights of a copyright owner is an infringer. A copyright owner can recover actual or, in some cases, statutory damages (up to $150,000 per act of infringement) from an infringer.[32] The federal courts have the power to issue injunctions (orders) to prevent or restrain copyright infringement and to order the impoundment and destruction of infringing materials.

Under current law, the copyright term for works created by individuals is the life of the author plus 70 years. The copyright term for **works made for hire** is 95 years from the date of first "publication" (distribution of copies to the general public) or 120 years from the date of creation, whichever expires first.[33] In today's modern world of everything being posted online, "publication" is virtually immediate. As a result, in a majority of cases, the copyright term for a "work made for hire" will be 95 years. Works made for hire are works created by employees for employers and certain types of specially commissioned works (e.g., a painted portrait).

Fair Use

The **fair use** of a copyrighted work, including use for purposes such as criticism, comment, news, education, parody, etc., is not an infringement of copyright. Copyright owners are, by law, deemed to consent to fair use of their works by others. The Copyright Act does not define "fair use."[34] Instead, whether a use is a fair use is determined by balancing (1) the purpose and character of the use; (2) the nature of the copyrighted work; (3) the amount and substantiality of the portion used in relation to the copyrighted work as a whole; and (4) the effect of the use on the potential market for, or value of, the copyrighted work.[35] As mentioned above, use of copyrighted material for criticism, comments, news, education, and parody is considered fair.

---

[30] *See* 17 U.S. Const. §401

[31] *See* 17 U.S. Const. §106

[32] *See* 17 U.S. Const. §504

[33] *See* 17 U.S. Const. §302

[34] *See* 17 U.S. Const. §107

[35] *See* 17 U.S. Const. §107

Intellectual Property Disputes and Ambush Marketing

From the above intellectual property summary, one can imagine various types of intellectual property disputes in sports marketing. Examples include, patent infringement with respect to patented sports equipment, counterfeit sales of merchandise featuring trademarked logos of NFL teams, and streaming copyrighted MLB Network content online without MLB's permission. These types of infringement all fall under the larger economic theory of unfair competition, which is something that intellectual property law seeks to prevent. One form of unfair competition that has become more prevalent in sports marketing is **ambush marketing**.

Ambush marketing is a marketing campaign that takes place around an event but does not involve payment of a sponsorship fee for such exposure. For most events of any significance, one brand will pay to become its exclusive and official sponsor of a given category (think McDonalds for food or Coca-Cola for pouring rights with the 1984 Olympics). Such exclusivity obviously prevents other brands from using the event to reach an audience that they would like to impact. In ambush marketing, the non-sponsoring, competing brands then find ways to promote themselves in connection with the same event and attempt to prevent the sponsoring brand from reaching its audience without paying a sponsorship fee or breaking the law.

The 1992 Summer Olympics in Barcelona is an example of ambush marketing. There, Nike contracted with NBC to sponsor the broadcast of press conferences and ceremonies featuring the USA basketball team (the "Dream Team"). In a completely separate deal, Reebok contracted with USA Basketball to be the team's official uniform and apparel sponsor. The Dream Team won the gold medal at the 1992 games and Reebok was poised to deepen its impact on the consumer audience when close-ups of the players wearing uniforms with the Reebok logo on them would be shown during the broadcast of the medal ceremony. Not so fast though. Nike, in its deal with NBC, had language in the contract that no other competing brand could show its name, logo, etc., during broadcasts of press conferences or ceremonies. As a result, the Dream Team players had to cover the Reebok logos on their uniforms during the medal ceremonies; essentially permitting Nike to overshadow Reebok's "moment in the sun."

Another example is the 1994 World Cup. MasterCard entered into an agreement with the Fédération Internationale de Football Association (FIFA) to be the "card-based payment and account access devices" sponsor for the tournament. Shortly thereafter, Sprint—the telecommunications sponsor for the World Cup—started manufacturing phone cards featuring the phrase "World Cup 94" on the front of the cards. MasterCard was upset because it believed that Sprint had overstepped its boundaries and entered into MasterCard's exclusive sponsorship category. MasterCard eventually sued Sprint for the alleged ambush marketing attempt and successfully enjoined Sprint from selling the phone cards when the court interpreted "card-based payment and account access devices," to include any telephone credit card. The court in its opinion explained that Section 43(a) of the Lanham Act bars consumer confusion and that the use of the Sprint "World Cup 94" phone cards could lead to consumer confusion as to who was the "card-based payment and account access devise" sponsor for the World Cup.[36]

On June 17, 2010, the US Soccer Federation obtained a preliminary injunction against retailer "The Sports Authority" (TSA) over the company's use of advertisements during the 2010 World Cup, which included official US Soccer trademarks in advertisements on Facebook and YouTube. In its complaint, US Soccer alleged that TSA's advertising campaign infringed on (ambushed) Dick's Sporting Goods' exclusive retail sponsorship relationship with US Soccer. While the advertisements had already aired once during the United States-England match, the injunction was filed to prevent TSA from running the advertisement a second time during the United States-Slovenia match on June 18th. The court granted the injunction and the advertisement did not run again.[37]

As stated above, the Lanham Act provides potential remedies for ambush marketing that result in consumer confusion or the likelihood of the same. It should be noted, however, that United States courts also recognize a company's First Amendment right to engage in commercial speech if consumer confusion is not threatened. Accordingly, organizations such as the USOC and FIFA, as well as their official sponsors, will no doubt continue to look for new and better methods of protecting their relationships and the benefits that sponsorship provide.

Contract Law

A **contract** is a legally binding agreement between two or more parties that is enforceable by law.[38] The elements of an enforceable express contract are (a) **offer**; (b) **acceptance**; (c) a **meeting of the minds;** and (d) **consideration**.[39] An offer is a demonstration of a desire to enter into an agreement and represents the first element of the formation process.[40] An offer is usually in writing, but can be oral. An acceptance is described as the manifestation of assent to the terms of an offer in the manner invited or required by the same.[41] The acceptance might be an action, abstaining from an action, or something else. For example, in an offer to pay someone $100 to mow her lawn, the acceptance would be the act of mowing the lawn. In an offer to pay an actor an additional $100,000 to not work on another film after the close of production of the film that the actor is currently working on in case the director needs the actor to come back for voiceovers during post-production, the acceptance would be the actor not working for another six months after the close of the current film.

---

[36] *See* MasterCard International, Inc. v. Sprint Communications Co., 1994 WL 97097 (S.D.N.Y. 1994), aff'd, 23 F.3d 397 (2d Cir. 1994).

[37] United States Soccer Federation Inc v. TSA Stores Inc., U.S. District Court, N. District of Illinois, No. 10-03755.

[38] Sheffrin O'Sullivan, *Economics: Principles in Action.* (Upper Saddle River: Pearson Prentice Hall, 2003), 523.

[39] Foundation Telecommunications, Inc. v. Moe Studio, Inc., 16 S.W.3d 531, 538 (Ark. 2000).

[40] RESTATEMENT (SECOND) OF CONTRACTS §24.

[41] RESTATEMENT (SECOND) OF CONTRACTS §24.

Consideration comes in two forms. The first is a benefit to the promisor, which is the party making the promise or offer.[42] The second comes in the form of a detriment to the offeree (the party accepting the offer).[43] The most common type of consideration is the payment of money. On the other side of coin (sometimes literally), the offeree does something that he or she is not obligated to do otherwise. Think about Lebron James's endorsement deal with Nike. Nike pays Lebron to wear and endorse its products exclusively for a period of years and he gives away his right to endorse other products or no product during the term of the endorsement agreement. The consideration is the payment that Nike remits to Lebron and him doing something that he is not obligated to do otherwise; endorsing Nike and surrendering his rights to endorse others or no one for a period of time.

The fourth and final element of a binding contract is a "meeting of the minds." Some refer to this as "agreeing to definite terms." Even if there is an offer, acceptance, and consideration, the agreement could be unenforceable if the agreement is indefinite with regards to the essential terms of the given arrangement.[44] In other words, a contract has to be more than an agreement to agree. Go back to the Lebron James/Nike endorsement contract. Nike offering Lebron money to endorse its products and him agreeing to do the same would constitute an offer and acceptance that is supported by consideration. However, if that is the extent of the arrangement, it is indefinite in a number of areas with regards to essential terms. For example, how much money is Lebron to receive? How will it be paid out (all at once, installments, etc.)? How long does the agreement last? What is the scope of the agreement (basketball sneakers and apparel only or does it expand to all apparel including sun glasses, hats, watches, etc., which would prevent Lebron from doing endorsements with other companies in those categories and significantly decrease his overall marketability)? Is the agreement for North America only? Can Lebron endorse Chinese basketball performance apparel in China? These important questions all need to be addressed with language, clauses, and terms. If they are not, a court could find that the agreement is an unenforceable contract.

Avoidance of Contract/Contract Defenses

Various circumstances and occurrences can make an otherwise enforceable contract "voidable." A **voidable contract** is one that potentially could be rescinded by one of the parties involved in the contract. The circumstances that most commonly make an otherwise enforceable sports marketing contract voidable are **incapacity, duress** or **undue influence, misrepresentation** or **fraud, mistake, unconscionability,** and **impossibility**. A brief discussion of each follows.

Incapacity

If a party attempting to enter into an agreement has not reached the age of majority (usually 18 years old, depending on the state) or is mentally infirm, then the contract will be voidable or, in certain circumstances, **void**, which means the agreement is rescinded as a matter

---

[42] *See* e.g., Hamer v. Sidway, 27 N.E. 256 (N.Y. 1891)

[43] *See* e.g., Hamer v. Sidway, 27 N.E. 256 (N.Y. 1891)

[44] RESTATEMENT (SECOND) OF CONTRACTS §33(2).

of law as though it was never entered into or enforced. Minors can rescind an enforceable contract with a non-minor party up until turning the age of majority or shortly thereafter.[45] When it comes to determining how long "shortly thereafter" is, that varies from jurisdiction to jurisdiction, but in most cases it will not exceed six months.[46]

The exception to avoidance of contract by means of incapacity is "necessaries." Common examples of necessaries are food, shelter, and clothing. The rationale is that regardless of age or mental capacity, these items are necessary for survival.[47] One should note that in some jurisdictions, particularly those that have produced a number of child entertainers and athletes, statutes have been enacted to curb a minor's ability to rescind a contract.[48] In almost every state, a party seeking to enter into a contract with a minor may have the contract ratified and approved by the Orphan's Court. Once the Orphan's Court ratifies and approves the contract, the minor or incapacitated person loses the right to rescind it based on incapacity grounds.

Duress or Undue Influence

If a party agrees to enter into a contract because that party has been induced to do so by an improper threat that leaves the party with no other choice than to enter into the contract, then the contract is voidable by the party that was subject to such inducement and/or improper threat.[49] The improper threat can take on many forms, including physical abuse, threats of criminal prosecution, and various types of economic duress characterized as "business compulsion."[50] It should be noted that once the threat has been removed or is over, the party subject to the undue influence must act quickly to rescind the contract based on the assertion of undue influence. If the party does not act quickly and continues to act under the contract without notifying the other party of the undue influence, such continuance shall be deemed a ratification of the contract.[51] In cases involving undue influence, courts examine the relationship between the parties (i.e., was the undue influence the result of some sort of relationship where there was a sense of confidence, trust, or dominance) and the degree of excessive persuasion exercised.[52]

The primary example of how undue influence intersects sports and sports marketing involves high school athletes seeking releases from their letters of commitment to play sports at a college or university. "Recruiting" usually involves relationships and pressures

---

[45] *See* McNaughton v. Granite City Auto Sales, 183 A. 340 (Vt. 1936).

[46] *See* Robinson v. Roquemore, 2 S.W. 2d 873 (Tex. Civ. App. 1928). *See also Forsyth v. Hastings,* 27 Vt. 646 (1855); and *Jones v. Jones,* 46 Iowa 466 (1877).

[47] *See* FARNSWORTH ON CONTRACTS §4.5, at 4.

[48] *See* Cal. Civ. Code §§3(a)(2)-(3) (West 1982); Cal.Lab. Code §1700.37 (West 1989); and N.Y. GEN. OBLIG. §3-101(2)(Consol. 1977).

[49] *See* RESTATEMENT (SECOND) OF CONTRACTS §175(1)

[50] *See* RESTATEMENT (SECOND) OF CONTRACTS §177

[51] *See* Gallon v. Lloyd Thomas Co., 264 F.2d 821 (8th Cir. 1959).

[52] *See* Kase v. French, 325 N.W. 2d 678 (S.D. 1982).

from high school coaches, college coaches, family, friends, alumni, etc. It is foreseeable that these types of scholarships and incident contracts to attend a school could be the product of undue influence.

Misrepresentation or Fraud

The Second Restatement of Contracts defines misrepresentation as "an assertion that is not in accord with the facts."[53] Misrepresentation will render a contract voidable if the misrepresentation was either fraudulent (knowingly false) or material (important) and induced the relying party's justifiable and reasonable reliance in entering into the particular contract.[54] One should note that concealing a material fact or non-disclosure of the same is equivalent to an assertion of a fact.[55] Accordingly, concealing or not-disclosing a material fact, which induces the other party into a contact is viewed in the same light as making a false statement or half-truth about that particular material fact. The assertion of misrepresentation and/or fraud for purposes of rescinding a sports marketing contract occurs when season ticket holders seek to cancel their contract with a professional sports team to purchase the requisite game plan for the following season. The season ticket holders usually make this assertion after a team refuses to offer them the first right to refuse purchasing additional season tickets or seat licensing rights, as guaranteed by the original season ticket purchase contract.[56]

Mistake

"Mistake" is a belief that is not in accord with the facts.[57] A mistake will render a contract voidable when, at the time the contract is formed, a basic erroneous assumption on which such agreement was based materially affects the exchange of performances.[58] Mutual mistakes, where both parties are mistaken about a material item or subject that induces the parties to enter into the contract, can assume many forms, including without limitation mistakes with regards to the year an item was made and/or its condition.[59] If the mistake is a conscious uncertainty on the part of both parties—a mutual mistake—then the risk of such mistake will have been assumed by both parties and, usually, the contract will not be voidable.[60]

Courts tend to be unwilling to permit a party to rescind a contract on the grounds of unilateral mistake, where only one party is mistaken about a material item of the contract,

---

[53] *See* RESTATEMENT (SECOND) OF CONTRACTS §159

[54] *See* Boston Mutual Ins. Co. v. New York Islanders Hockey Club, 165 F.3d 93 (1st Cir. 1999).

[55] *See* RESTATEMENT (SECOND) OF CONTRACTS §161

[56] *See* e.g., Charpentier v. Los Angeles Rams Football Club, 75 Cal. App. 4th 301 (Cal. Ct. App. 2000); Beder v. Cleveland Browns, Inc., 129 Ohio 3d 188 (Ohio App. 1998).

[57] *See* RESTATEMENT (SECOND) OF CONTRACTS §151

[58] Cozzillio et al., *Sports Law: Cases and Materials*, 2nd ed. (Durham: Carolina Academic Press, 1997), 131.

[59] Cozzillio et al., *Sports Law: Cases and Materials*, 2nd ed. (Durham: Carolina Academic Press, 1997), 131.

[60] *See* Gartner v. Eikill, 319 N.W. 2d 397 (Minn. 1982).

unless the other party knew of the mistake.[61] When analyzing whether a party can rescind a contract on the grounds of unilateral mistake, courts look at the following factors: (1) the materiality of the mistake; (2) how fair or unfair it would be to all parties to enforce the contract; (3) the "reasonableness" of the mistaken party's erred belief; (4) the prejudice to the non-mistaken party if the agreement is rescinded; and (5) the timing of notification that a mistake has been made.[62]

A recent matter that entered litigation, but was eventually settled, brought a unilateral mistake scenario to life in a sports marketing context. Years back an 11-year-old baseball card collector purchased a Nolan Ryan rookie card at an incredibly low price from a collectibles store when the part-time clerk did not realize that the advertised selling price on the card was incorrect. The astute collector—regardless of age—recognized the error and quickly purchased the card. When the owner of the store later learned of the error, he notified the collector that the store was rescinding the purchase based on grounds of unilateral mistake. The collector and his family refused to comply. The store owner later sued. Again, the matter eventually settled out of court, but one can see how the mistake can intersect sports marketing.[63]

Unconscionability

A contract may be deemed "unconscionable" if it involves unfair surprise or oppressive terms.[64] This type of assertion is usually made where a party was not represented by counsel and the terms of the contract that the party agreed to are so outrageous that it would be an injustice for the contract to be enforced with the agreed upon terms. Considering that most athletes and sports entities have counsel, agents, personal managers, business managers, etc., the assertion of unconscionability rarely arises in the context of sport marketing contracts. However, cases do arise occasionally where unconscionability is asserted to void a contract or a provision of a contract. A recent example occurred when the New Jersey Devils and Ilya Kovalchuk agreed to a 17-year contract. In order for a NHL player contract to be ratified, the National Hockey League Players Association (NHLPA)—the union for the players—must approve of the contract's terms. The NHLPA refused to approve this particular contract as the union believed that the term of the contract was too long and that in the later years the agreed upon compensation would be considerably lower considering inflation and the time value of money.

Impossibility

Every so often, a party may be rendered unable to fulfill contractual obligations because the promised performance has become impossible. In that event, the court will assess whether

---

[61] *See* Mutual of Enumclaw Ins. Co. v. Wood ByProducts Inc., 695 P.2d 409 (Idaho 1984).

[62] *See* MURRAY ON CONTRACTS §91

[63] Cozzillio et al., *Sports Law: Cases and Materials*, 2nd ed. (Durham: Carolina Academic Press, 1997), 132.

[64] *See* U.S. Const. §2-302

the inability to perform serves as an excuse for the other party's refusal to honor its obligations. The critical factors of asserting impossibility as the reason for why a party cannot fulfill its obligations under the contract and should not be held liable for the breach of the same are: (1) an unforeseen event rendering performance impossible or highly impracticable, and (2) that was beyond the control of the party claiming inability to perform.[65] If these factors are met, then the party unable to perform would be insulated from liability, with the obvious byproduct being the release of the other party's counter-obligations—assuming that the failed performance was substantial.[66]

An example of impossibility in a sports context might be where a sports event production and marketing company is producing a marathon for the first time in a new city. In order to produce the marathon, the production company needs to secure various sponsors, including title sponsors, finish line sponsors, official beverage sponsors, etc. The production company also seeks to secure broadcast rights through a local network. As a part of the production company's standard sponsorship contract, it requires that the sponsors pay half of the sponsorship fee upon signing and the other half 30 days prior to the marathon. The broadcast licensing contract for television coverage has the same clause. Much to the good fortune of the sports production and marketing company, it is able to secure a title sponsor and network for broadcasting nine months in advance and half of the respective fees under both contracts are paid immediately upon execution. Everything looks to be running fine, when a massive earthquake hits the host city for the marathon 45 days out from race day. There is a tremendous amount of damage to not only the route for the race but to the city in general. As a result, it is impossible for the host city to hold the marathon and too late to move it elsewhere. Despite that fact, the sports event production and marketing company requests that its title sponsor and broadcast rights licensee pay the balance of the respective sponsorship and licensing fee. Both the title sponsor and network refuse and claim that they are no longer obligated to remit further payment, as it is impossible for the event that was the subject of the contract to occur. Under this scenario, the title sponsor and network's assertion of impossibility would more than likely be legitimate grounds for rescinding their obligations and the contract as a whole.

Venue Naming Rights; Endorsements and Sponsorships

Two of the hottest topics in a contract sense that have a presence in sports marketing are venue naming rights agreements and endorsements and sponsorships. With regards to venue naming rights, they are the right to name a piece of property, either tangible property or an event, usually granted in exchange for compensation. Institutions like schools, places of worship, and hospitals have a tradition of granting donors the right to name facilities in exchange for contributions. Securing the naming rights for stadiums, theaters, and other public gathering places is seen by companies as a form of advertising and building goodwill in the community. As a result, naming rights deals worth millions of dollars have been made

---

[65] *See* Sunflower Electric Cooperative, Inc. v. Tomlinson, 638 P.2d 963 (Kan. Ct. App. 1981).

[66] *See* Shaw v. Mobil Oil Corp., 535 P.2d 756 (Ore. 1975).

throughout the world. Examples include Lincoln Financial Field ($139.6 million over 20 years) and Citizens Bank Park ($57.5 million over 25 years) in Philadelphia (Mediaventures, 2011).

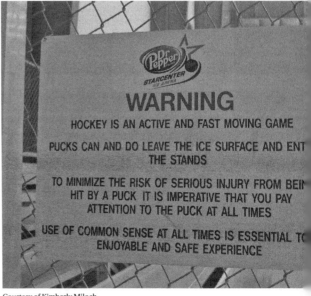

Courtesy of Kimberly Miloch.

In a few cases, naming rights contracts have been terminated prematurely. Such terminations may be the result of contractual options, sponsor bankruptcy, or scandals. For example, in 1986, Villanova University opened a new on-campus basketball arena called the "du Pont Pavilion." The facility was largely financed by John du Pont, a member of the influential du Pont family. When he was found guilty in the 1996 murder of Olympian Dave Schultz, Villanova stripped du Pont's name from the facility. It is now known simply as "The Pavilion." This is an illustration of one of the rights that the venue owner should seek in a naming rights agreement—the right to disassociate with the name sponsor in the event of an occurrence that brings a negative perception to the "name." In contract terminology, this is referred to as a morality clause. Often the name sponsor will also seek a morality clause so that it can terminate its affiliation with the venue and corresponding future payments of the licensing fee if the venue becomes tarnished in the eyes of the public. This is an important negotiation point as venues want the naming rights sponsor to commit to a long-term affiliation (often times up to 20 years or more) with guaranteed annual licensing fees. On the other hand, the sponsor wants the commitment to be short without licensing fee guarantees beyond a "year-to-year" basis.

In terms of endorsement and sponsorship agreements, numerous examples include Peyton Manning and Gatorade, Danica Patrick and Go Daddy, and Jimmy Rollins and Red Bull. Professor Heidi Parker's chapter in this book goes into detail about this topic, so there is no reason to be redundant about background and statistical information, but it would more than likely be helpful for the student that seeks to enter into sports marketing as an attorney, agent, or licensee to have a general sense of the types of clauses and terms that are usually associated with endorsement and sponsorship agreements. A partial breakdown/checklist is as follows.

Terms of Consideration for the Sponsor/Endorser

- Name and logo branding on-site, online, in press conference, and in broadcasts.
- If it is on the events side of sports marketing, visible "presented by" or "sponsored by" credits on and in the above mediums.
- Hospitality booths at any talent receptions, press conferences, charity events, etc.
- Guarantees that competing brands will not serve as co-sponsors or have any roles in the mediums in which the brand is featured to reduce the risk of ambush marketing.
- Division of revenues on sales of food, beverage, or merchandise of the sponsors' products.
- First and last rights of refusal to extend the existing sponsorship or endorsement.
- Non-disclosure and non-circumvention language to prevent against the communication or use of confidential or proprietary information.
- Indemnification in the event that the talent or event's failures or torts cause the brand to be named as a defendant in an action.
- A clause stating that the law of the state where the endorsing or sponsoring brand is located controls.
- A morality clause stating that if the talent or event's reputation becomes tarnished in the perception of the media and/or public that the brand has the right to terminate the relationship immediately and cancel the payment of any future endorsement or sponsorship fees.

Terms of Consideration for the Sponsee/Endorsee

- Term and duration of the relationship. (Talent wants the term to be as short as possible unless there is multi-year guaranteed compensation. Events want the term to be as long as possible.)
- Amount of the sponsorship/endorsement fee and how it will be paid out (e.g., lump sum, installments, etc.).
- Potential equity ownership in the brand (e.g., rapper 50-Cent receiving an equity interest in Vitamin Water and reaping the benefits when it was sold to Coca-Cola).
- Limiting the categories of sponsorship and endorsement so that the talent and/or event can bring in other brands with which to align. (For example, if a player receives an endorsement offer from Nike for apparel, perhaps it would make sense to exclude sunglasses, suits, swimsuits, non-athletic footwear, etc., so that additional endorsement deals could potentially be done with Oakley, BCBG, etc.)
- Ability to freely negotiate with other brands when an agreement expires without first right of refusal or last right of refusal restrictions.
- Indemnification in the event that the brand's failures or torts cause the talent or event to be named as a defendant in an action.
- A dispute resolution clause stating that despite the location of the governing law that the courts of the state in which the talent resides or event is located shall be a venue for litigation or arbitration proceedings.
- A morality clause stating that in the event that the brand's reputation becomes tarnished, the talent or event has the right to terminate the agreement immediately.

Torts

A **tort** is a civil harm committed between two parties. There are two types of torts: intentional torts and torts that arise from conduct that was not intentional, but nevertheless caused the harm in question. The latter usually falls into the categories of negligence, gross negligence, or recklessness. The tort that most often applies to sports marketing is the intentional tort of a violation of one's **right of publicity**, a right that evolves from the **right of privacy**.

The Rights of Privacy and Publicity

The modern law of invasion of privacy encompasses not one tort, but four. The four torts are: (1) intrusion upon one's seclusion, solitude, or private affairs; (2) public disclosure of embarrassing private facts about that person; (3) publicity which places him or her in a false light in the public eye; and (4) appropriation, for another party's advantage, of one's name, voice, likeness, identity, style, or persona.[67] The first three are variations of the right to be left alone. The fourth does not involve privacy at all, but the right of commercial exploitation of identity (in other words, a right of publicity). This right is the right of a person to be compensated for the use of his or her name, nickname, image, likeness, or other identifying characteristic for a commercial purpose, usually in an advertising or marketing campaign. This right protects the property interest in the publicity value of one's identity.[68]

Duration of the Right of Publicity

There is dispute among the states whether the right of publicity is a descendible property right. In other words, does it continue after the death of the person and descend to the deceased's heirs or estate? The majority of jurisdictions that have considered the question judicially or legislatively hold that the right of publicity is a property right and unconditionally descendible. The right descends to the heirs whether or not the celebrity exercises the right prior to death. For example, New York, Georgia, New Jersey, California, Kentucky, Tennessee, and Florida all provide for descendible rights of publicity.

Courts measure damages for right of publicity violations by a reasonable royalty or market value. This is a floor, not a ceiling, to damages. In *Waits v. Frito-Lav. Inc.,* 978 F.2d 1093, 1103 (9th Cir. 1992) cert, den., 506 US 1080, 113 S. Ct. 1047, 122 L.Ed.2d 355 (1993), the plaintiff, recording artist Tom Waits, who sued Frito Lay when it used a look-a-like of him in a commercial for the snack company without his permission, was awarded $100,000 for what was considered to be the fair market value of his services, had he chosen to do the commercial. The court also approved an award of $200,000 for injury to his "peace, happiness, and feelings," and $75,000 "for injury to his goodwill, professional standing, and future publicity value."

Courts may also award any profits earned by the infringer from its unauthorized use of the plaintiff's persona. In many states, a plaintiff can recover exemplary damages if he

---

[67]   *See* Prosser, Privacy. 48 Cal. L Rev. 383, 389 (1960).

[68]   Hirsch v. S.C. Johnson & Son. Inc., 90 Wise. 2d 379, 280 N.W.2d 129 (S. Ct. WI 1979).

can show that the defendant acted knowingly. In the *Waits* case, for example, the court also approved a $2 million punitive damage award against the defendants. Statutes in some states authorize the award of attorney's fees to prevailing plaintiffs, and in other states make attorney's fees awardable to any prevailing party, plaintiff, or defendant.[69]

Some of the most notable right of publicity actions, albeit not all of them successful for the plaintiffs, involve Kareem Abdul-Jabbar and General Motors for the use of his birth name Lew Alcindor in a commercial for the Oldsmobile 88 without his permission, Tiger Woods and Jireh Publishing, Inc., for the use of his image in lithographs without his permission, and Joe Namath suing *Sports Illustrated* for using his name and photograph without his permission.

Fantasy Sports

Fantasy Sports is one of the premiere examples of sports marketing. The Fantasy Sports Trade Association (FSTA) estimates that approximately 29.9 million individuals in the United States. and Canada participate in fantasy sports. Fantasy sports sites (e.g., Yahoo!, CBS Sports.com, Fox Sports, ESPN, etc.) provide gamers with the opportunity to organize private leagues and participate in public leagues for the fantasy sports of their choice. The contrast between private leagues and public leagues is stark. Friends organize private leagues, which are exclusive to those participants. Team owners in these leagues have the option of playing for bragging rights or for "winner takes all" payouts that are paid from the registration fees for the private league. Fantasy sports gamers participate in a public league by registering with a fantasy sports site and are assigned to a league with other random team owners. The FSTA estimates that fantasy sports have a $3 billion to $4 billion annual impact on the sports industry. Most of this revenue is generated from licensing and advertising on fantasy sites.

Fantasy sports are in many ways an application of trademark, copyright, licensing, and right of publicity law. Teams and leagues own trademarks, trade names, and service marks in and to their various names, logos, images, symbols, etc., and have the right to use them or prevent their use. Teams and leagues often times also own a copyright to the design of their logos or symbols. These organizations have the ability to license their properties and capitalize financially on the demand for the same. Professional football is an example. The words "National Football League," "National Football Conference," and "American Football Conference" are all registered trademarks owned by the NFL, as are the acronyms "NFL," "NFC," and "AFC," and their respective symbols. The NFL owns copyrights to the designs of these symbols. A fantasy sports site must receive a license from the NFL in order to use the foregoing properties to promote the site's fantasy football leagues.

The right of publicity is also very much involved with fantasy sports. When a fantasy sports site wants to use an image of a major league baseball player in uniform to promote its fantasy baseball leagues, which receive a great deal of revenue from banner ads and other advertisements, the site must receive permission from and compensate the featured player in order to use his name, image, and likeness. It doesn't end there though.

[69] *Compare* Wis.Stat.Ann. §895.50(1)(c) (West 1983) with Cal Civ.Code §§990(a), 3344(a) (West Supp.1988).

In order to feature the player's uniform and hat, the site must receive a license from the applicable team. In order to use the letters "MLB" and its red, white and blue "batter" symbol, the site must receive a license from the league. In the event that the site chooses to forego receiving the license from the player, there would most likely be an actionable right of publicity violation. If the team and league properties were used without permission, there would also most likely be actionable trademark and copyright infringement claims.

One should note that often, leagues and/or players' associations control the rights to license a player or players' likeness as shown with him/her/them in uniform. In the case of the NFL, the licensor of a player's likeness is not the player himself, but NFL Players, Inc., an organization that oversees the licensing and marketing of NFL players' names and likenesses. The Major League Baseball Players Association (MLBPA) has a similar scenario through its Group Licensing Agreement (GLA). Under that agreement, any company seeking to use the names or likenesses of two or more MLB players in connection with a commercial product, product line, or promotion must sign the GLA.

First Amendment Defenses to Intellectual Property Claims

The **First Amendment** is often asserted as a defense in fantasy sports actions involving trademark or copyright infringement or the right of publicity. A prime example is *NBA vs. STATS, Inc.,* 105 F.3d 841 (2nd Cir. 1997). During the 1990s tech-boom, many online fantasy sports sites signed licensing deals with various leagues and players associations (e.g., MLBPA), with the associations picking and choosing the licenses that they chose to issue, often times to the dismay of fantasy sites that were denied a license. In *NBA vs. STATS Inc.,* STATS, Inc., a major statistical provider to fantasy sports sites, along with Motorola, won the action against the NBA, which was trying to stop STATS from distributing game score information via a Motorola wireless device. STATS and Motorola argued that the reporting of individual, team, and league statistics was the reporting of news, which is protected under the First Amendment. The NBA unsuccessfully argued that Motorola disseminating this purely statistical information, and STATS providing the same, was an unauthorized use of the NBA's trademarked and copyrighted properties and a violation of the players' right of publicity.

Another renowned fantasy sports case is *CBC Distribution & Marketing, Inc. vs. MLBAM,* 505 F.3d 818 (8th Cir. 2007). There, CBC Distribution & Marketing, Inc., a fantasy sports data collection company, sued Major League Baseball Advanced Media (MLBAM, the MLB's Internet affiliate) when it would not issue CBC a new licensing agreement for fantasy baseball. CBC argued that it did not need a license as intellectual property laws do not apply to the actual game statistics that are tracked in fantasy sports. The FSTA filed an amicus curiae (friend of the court) brief in support of CBC arguing that if MLBAM won the lawsuit it would have a monopoly over the fantasy baseball industry. CBC won the suit. United States District Court Judge Mary Ann Medler ruled that statistics are a part of the public domain and can be used at no cost by fantasy companies. The MLBAM appealed. The 8th Circuit Court of Appeals upheld the decision in October 2007 and stated in its ruling that, "[I]t would be strange law that a person would not have a First Amendment right to use information that is available to everyone." One should note that the *STATS* and *CBC* cases do not stand for the proposition that players' images, photographs, and/or likenesses can be used by a fantasy sports site without a license. The same applies to team and league properties.

Gambling Concerns

Private fantasy sports leagues and their "winner takes all" or staggered payouts for first, second, or third place have drawn concern over whether they are forms of gambling. The greatest threat to date of shutting down these types of private leagues came with the introduction of the **Uniform Internet Gaming Enforcement Act of 2006** (UIGEA). The act's criminal provisions provide that no person engaged in the business of betting or wagering may knowingly accept directly or indirectly virtually any type of payment from a participant in unlawful Internet gambling (i.e., bets that are unlawful under other state or federal laws).

The major sports leagues became concerned that the UIGEA would cut down on fantasy sports licensing revenues, as registration fees paid in association with sports activity that is conducted online could be construed as "unlawful Internet gambling." Those fears were quelled when federal lobbyists were successful in arguing for a fantasy sports exemption. The UIGEA states that fantasy sports are exempt from the definition of "unlawful Internet gambling" provided that: (1) they are not based on the current membership of an actual sports team or on the score, point spread, or performance of teams; (2) all prizes and awards are established and made known before the start of the contest; and (3) winning outcomes are based on the skill of the participants and predominately by accumulated statistics of individual performance of athletes, but not solely on a single performance of an athlete.

Fantasy sports sites and major sports leagues recently received another victory against gambling concerns in *Humphrey v. Viacom, Inc. et al*, No. 06-276 (DMC) 2007 WL 1797648 (D.N.J. June 20, 2007). There, plaintiff Charles Humphrey, a Colorado attorney and professional poker player, brought a claim against Viacom, CBS Television Network, Sportsline.com, The Walt Disney Company, ESPN, The Hearst Corporation, Vulcan, Inc., Vulcan Sports Media, and *The Sporting News* for alleged violations of state gambling laws in New Jersey, the District of Columbia, Georgia, Illinois, Kentucky, Massachusetts, New Jersey, Ohio, and South Carolina. Humphrey claimed that the defendants operating fantasy sports sites that permitted private leagues to charge a registration fee was tantamount to unlawful gambling. The defendants filed a motion to dismiss the action. Judge Dennis M. Cavanaugh granted the motion and stated in his opinion that it would be "patently absurd to hold that the combination of an entry fee and a prize equals gambling." Judge Cavanaugh further stated that the UIGEA's fantasy sports exemption confirms that sites that operate private leagues with registration fees do not constitute gambling as a matter of law.

One should note that the UIGEA's fantasy sports exemption only means that fantasy sports leagues that meet the exemption criteria are not criminalized under the UIGEA. Conducting a fantasy contest for money could still violate other state or federal laws. It just seems less likely after *Humphrey*.

Sports Agent Regulations

We would be remiss if we did not discuss the legal aspects surrounding what is arguably the most famous—and infamous—sports marketing topic of all ... sports agents. Sports agents and the role that they play in the sports marketing industry are bigger than ever. From Arliss to Jerry McGuire to Scott Boras to Josh Luchs, the agent industry is on the tip of most sports fans' tongues. This is a highly competitive industry that is also heavily regulated. The two primary sports agent regulations are the **Uniform Athlete Agent Act** (the **UAAA**) and the **Sports Agent Responsibility and Trust Act** (**SPARTA**).

The UAAA

The National College Athletic Association (NCAA) sanctions academic institutions if they permit a student-athlete that becomes ineligible academically or for NCAA violations to participate in a game. Unfortunately, one of the most common NCAA violations is athletes accepting money or other items of value from sports agents. In order to crackdown on agent induced ineligibility, in 1998, several universities and the NCAA (which cannot punish agents because it does not have jurisdiction over them) asked the National Conference of Commissioners on Uniform State Laws (NCCUSL) to draft a model uniform agent regulation. In response, NCCUSL drafted the UAAA in the fall of 2000.

The purpose of the UAAA is to regulate agents, reduce student-athlete ineligibility, and protect academic institutions from sanctions. The UAAA requires that agents register with the state prior to contacting a student-athlete. Additionally, agents must disclose their professional and criminal history to the Secretary of State for the state in which the athlete attends college and/or resides. The UAAA also requires agents to grant the Secretary of State the authority to issue subpoenas if compliance information is needed. Further, the UAAA prohibits agents from funneling money or tangible benefits to student-athletes and their families. Agents that violate these regulations are subject to criminal and administrative penalties.

For purposes of reducing ineligibility, the UAAA requires that agents provide student-athletes with an ineligibility warning at the bottom of every agency contract. Once an agency contract is signed, the agent and the student-athlete must forward written notice of the contractual relationship to the athletic director at the student-athlete's school or to any school that the agent believes that the student-athlete will attend. Such notice must be given within the lesser of 72 hours or the student-athlete's next scheduled athletic event. Simultaneously, the UAAA gives student-athletes the right to cancel agency contracts within 14 days of execution.

The UAAA protects academic institutions by affording them the opportunity to seek civil remedies from agents and/or student-athletes if they are sanctioned due to an agent's or a student-athlete's failure to notify their athletic director regarding a signed agency contract within the appropriate period of time. Ironically, the UAAA does not provide student-athletes with a right to seek civil remedies from agents if they are rendered ineligible due to an agent's failure to abide by UAAA regulations. Additionally, UAAA safeguards do not apply to student-athletes that have exhausted their eligibility. The UAAA also does not establish a uniform registration fee. As a result, registration fees vary from $30 annually to $2,500 every two years among the member states. As this chapter goes to print, 40 of the 50 states have adopted the UAAA.

SPARTA

The House of Representatives passed SPARTA on June 4, 2003. Soon thereafter, Senator Ron Wyden (D-Ore) filed an identical bill in the Senate. It passed there on September 4, 2004. SPARTA serves as a federal backstop to the UAAA. Its primary focus is on regulation and enforcement. SPARTA makes it unlawful for an agent to provide student-athletes with false or misleading information, false or misleading promises or representations, or anything of value. Additionally, SPARTA requires that agents warn student-athletes in a disclosure form that they may lose their eligibility if they sign an agency contract or falsify its date. Before entering into the agency contract, student-athletes must sign the disclosure form. Once the agency contract is signed, both the agent and the athlete must contact the institution's athletic department within the lesser of 72 hours or the student-athlete's next schedule athletic event.

Seeking strict enforcement, SPARTA has the Federal Trade Commission (FTC) enforce its agency contract regulations. Specifically, SPARTA gives the FTC the authority to "enforce [SPARTA] in the same manner, by the same means, and with the same jurisdiction, powers, and duties, as though all applicable terms and provisions of the FTC Act were incorporated into and made a part of this Act." The FTC fines agents $11,000 per incident of unfair or deceptive acts or practices that violate SPARTA. It also permits state attorney generals to act in federal court on behalf of the FTC. In these cases, all damages, restitution, and other compensation go to the state. A state also has a cause of action on behalf of its residents if it has reason to believe that an agent has threatened or adversely affected a resident's interest.

Academic institutions may also seek remedial damages from student-athletes or agents, if their behavior causes the schools to incur expenses. These expenses include losses resulting from penalties, disqualification, suspension, and/or restitution for losses suffered due to self-imposed compliance actions. Remedies for such suits include enjoinder, enforcement, damages, and restitution. SPARTA does not, however, address registration fees or provide student-athletes with a cause of action if they are injured due to an agent's misconduct.

As one can see, despite the perceived thrill of "SHOW ME THE MONEY" and other materialistic perceptions, state and federal sports agent regulations provide serious consequences. One should also note that the NFL, MLB, NBA, and NHL, have their own agent compliance guidelines, which must be followed carefully. Penalties for violations include a loss of licensure, fines, and possible criminal ramifications.

Summary

On the surface, the legal and business concepts of intellectual property, contracts, tort law, and those associated with fantasy sports and sports agent regulation seem completely opposite of the creative aspects of ball games, events, websites, Twitter pages, athletes wearing brand laden apparel, the marketing of logos at the Olympics and the World Cup, and the names of stadiums. As one can see though, the legal and business sides of sports marketing are linked to its glamour. As with all things in life, the law lives where you least expect it.

Discussion Questions

1. How do intellectual property laws impact sport marketers?

2. How do copyright and trademark laws assist in protecting brand image?

3. What are the specific laws governing sport agents? How might the sport agent impact the marketability of a specific athlete?

4. What are the legal issues pertinent to fantasy sports?

5. What is meant by an athlete's right of publicity? How do courts balance right of publicity with privacy rights?

6. What is the role of contract law in sponsorship and endorsement? What constitutes a contract? How do the parameters of contract law impact sponsorship and endorsements?

7. Discuss the use of the First Amendment in fantasy sport cases. How has it been utilized as a legal defense? What are the outcomes of such a defense?

Critical Thinking Exercises

Below are a number of discussion questions and critical thinking exercises that will help students absorb and expand upon the above concepts.

1. A client comes to you and says that she has designed and manufactured a new training cleat that has an electronic timer built into the shoe. This cleat provides athletes with accurate times, distances, and speeds on their performance. Essentially, the product eliminates human error in hand timing and allows any running surface to become an electronically timed track, similar to what is featured at the NFL Combine. This cleat is the first of its kind. Your client wants to know how to protect this creation. What advice would you give her?

2. You are general counsel for Nike. The director of marketing has created the following slogan for Nike's new ice hockey apparel: "It's only cold … when you lose." You are asked to draft a memorandum on whether the slogan is eligible for copyright and/or trademark protection. What would you advise?

3. You have a client that is a leading Internet marketing company that specializes in designing athlete websites, integrating social media, and creating real-time content that viewers can subscribe to through new software that your client has developed. Your client has had the good fortune of securing a meeting with Derek Jeter. Prior to having the meeting, Jeter's agent has required that your client provide a breakdown as to how the software works and why it is different from the client's competitors. What advice would you give your client as to how to protect the software but still have the meeting?

4. You are counsel to the career money list leader on the PGA tour. Red Bull wants to enter into an endorsement relationship with your client. What elements would need to be in place in order for this arrangement between your client and Red Bull to be an enforceable contract? What are some of the key negotiation points that you would want to make sure are addressed in the agreement?

5. Citizens Bank—the naming rights sponsor of the baseball stadium in Philadelphia, Citizens Bank Park—has decided to discontinue its sponsorship of the venue and not renew the naming rights agreement when it expires. After the agreement expires, the Phillies approach Bank of America about being the new naming rights sponsor. Bank of America agrees and asks the Phillies to prepare the contract. What specific clause would Bank of America want in the contract to prevent any potential abandonment of its trademark or trade name rights in the name "Bank of America?" What other restrictions would Bank of America want in place in terms of ATM machines and other banking devices, branding, signage, etc., used in and around the ballpark?

6. You are a multi-time all-star baseball player that is very vocal about his political affiliation as an Independent. One night after you hit a walk-off homerun to win the game, you are asked in the post-game interview, "what could make this moment better?" You respond, "Independent candidate Jane Smith winning the upcoming Presidential election." Smith's campaign manager hears of your statement and has t-shirts made featuring your image on the front and beneath it the words: "ENDORSES JANE SMITH FOR PRESIDENT OF THE UNITED STATES." Smith starts selling these shirts at rallies to raise money for her campaign. You are disturbed by this because, although you support her, you never intended for your statement to turn into a fundraiser and you are not receiving any portion of the funds raised. What potential claims would you have against Smith and her campaign manager? What defenses would they most likely assert? Do you think you would be successful if you filed a complaint to start a lawsuit based on your potential claims?

References

International Olympic Committee. "Olympic marketing fact file", 2010, http://www.olympic.org/Documents/fact_file_2010.pdf

Mediaventures. "Revenues from sport venues", 2011, http://www.sportsvenues.com/pdf/names.pdf

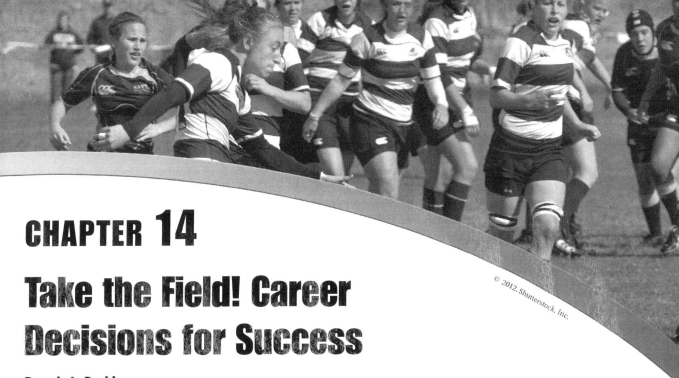

CHAPTER 14

Take the Field! Career Decisions for Success

Bonnie L. Parkhouse
Brian A. Turner Ohio State University

If you don't know where you are going, you will wind up somewhere else.

Yogi Berra

CHAPTER OBJECTIVES

After completing the chapter, the reader should be able to:

- Construct a cover letter and resume.
- Develop a 30 second "elevator interview."
- Understand the importance of networking, including social networking.
- Establish and outline clear and measurable career goals and objectives.
- Identify the skills necessary for entry and advancement in the sport industry.

The adage, "Today is the first day of the rest of your life," starts right now! An impressive job title, a six-figure salary and a glamorous job description are not the keys to a successful career. The right career path is the one that's right for you—one in which you feel challenged, fulfilled, respected, and appreciated. There's no specific formula or clear-cut path to a successful career. It's a combination of doing your **H**omework, getting **I**n the door, being in the **R**ight place at the right time, **E**xperience, and **D**edication. This combination gets you **HIRED**!

Because the job market continues to be saturated with college graduates, prospective employers can be selective in who they hire. This chapter provides insight into how you can be competitive in the marketplace.

Homework

All of the National Football League (NFL) teams started receiving Howie Roseman's job inquiries while he was still in high school. He studied the bios of NFL front-office personnel and called administrative assistants, getting to know them by name. Howie is currently the General Manager of the Philadelphia Eagles.

Golf legend Bobby Jones often said that the game of golf is played on a 5½ inch course... the space between your ears. Obtaining a job in sport is not a matter of luck. It involves a thought process that requires the following: 1) self-examination of your strengths and weaknesses; 2) planning a career path and a list of specific objectives to attain these goals; 3) studying organizations to determine how they would benefit from your specific attributes and special skills; 4) researching organizational or depth charts to determine specific areas of interest and fit; and 5) interviewing sport management/marketing professionals to identify specific job opportunities and determining your market value for successful salary negotiations. The job will go to the person with this competitive edge. Specifics on this thought process will be addressed in following sections of this chapter.

There are no shortcuts in the career search process. "With very few exceptions, most of those who struggle in their job search do so because they haven't prepared. They don't really know who they are, what they want to do, why they'd be good at it, what a potential employer is looking for, or how they might add value to a particular organization" (Sullivan, 2002, 4).

Getting in the Door

"Getting your foot in the door" and then "putting your best foot forward" are not clichés to be taken lightly when considering a career in this industry. These jobs are rarely found in the classified ads. Persistence is a major key in opening the corporate door. Remember the unpaid intern, Howie Roseman, who became the general manager of the Philadelphia Eagles. His tireless job hunt paid off. "Was this guy the most persistent guy in the history of America or was he crazy?" Joe Banner, the Eagles' president, asked (Jensen, 2010, E1).

The "Take any job to get in the door" mentality is often not the most appropriate because it could force one to make a commitment difficult to get out of for both personal and professional reasons (e.g., a contract that cannot be broken, geographical ties, and comfort levels). Life is too short not to take time initially to pursue job opportunities in areas of real interest or passion.

The adage, "You don't get a second chance to make a first impression" is so important once one has an opportunity. Does this mean that you have to do it right the first time? Yes, especially if it's a middle- or upper-level management position which requires previous experience. However, most readers of this chapter will probably be inexperienced students embarking on their first position in the sport industry. Therefore, it is reasonable to expect mistakes. More important is demonstrating the ability to quickly learn from them without repetition. In this endeavor, mentors are essential. Being surrounded by and listening to knowledgeable people is a major plus. In retrospect, and rightfully so, successful people usually give credit to others who have influenced their success. It's impossible to do it alone!

"Putting your best foot forward" should not be limited by a job description or the ceiling on a depth or organizational chart. Going "beyond the call of duty" voluntarily and creating a unique niche of expertise which is beneficial to the organization's success is characteristic of individuals who have excelled in this industry.

Marketing oneself effectively requires the ability to match personal skills with the needs of a prospective employer. Further, it requires such job-related skills as **cover letter/resume** construction, **interview** techniques, **portfolio** development, and **salary negotiation** strategies. In the interest of brevity, self-help or how-to information on these topics is available on websites and in published books. In their book *Introduction to Sport Management: Theory and Practice,* Nagel and Southall (2011) list resources for starting your career, securing your first sport management opportunity, and career advancement tips. Additionally, they include several websites for jobs in sports. Some of those resources are listed at the end of this chapter. The following sections give a brief synopsis of these job-related skills.

Cover Letter and Resume Construction

The cover letter should be specifically tailored (customized) for each organization that is sent the resume. It is meant to separate you from the "rest of the pack" of applicants. Always address it to a specific person in charge of the job search. "To Whom It May Concern" is not acceptable (see the sidebar for other common mistakes with cover letters). Take the opportunity to specifically inform the prospective employer of why you should be hired for the position advertised. How can the business benefit from your knowledge, experience, and special skills? The cover letter should be powerful and compelling, yet brief (one page in length).

© Tony Northrup, 2012. Under license from Shutterstock, Inc.

Cover Letters: Top 7 Problems Applicants Have with Cover Letters
By Buffy Fileppell, Founder of TeamWork Online

1. **No cover letter.** Make sure you have a cover letter for every job application you submit. This is your chance to pitch for the job. Use it.

2. **Cover letter template.** If your cover letter sounds "canned" employers can tell. Customize it to their needs, or your application will go in the can ... the trash can.

3. **"Have Done" versus "Can Do."** Except for internships, employers want someone who "has done" the skill rather than "can do" the skill. That's where internships are helpful. The difference is how many years have you done the skill.

4. **Boy Scout Law.** Everyone says they are "trustworthy, loyal, and helpful." Employers first want to know proven results in business skills, such as sales, marketing, event management, customer service, etc., that specifically meet their job needs. The Boy Scout law skills are deciphered at the interview.

5. **Extensive experience.** A 40-year-old has extensive experience; a recent or to-be college graduate does not. If the job is junior level, don't worry. Employers want to know you have had at least "some" experience, but in exactly the area they need. Go strong in one area, not weak broadly.

6. **Mis-spellings or bad grammar.** Check your spelling before you paste or type in your cover letter. With so many candidates to choose from, employers will turn away a candidate who does not spell words correctly or has grammatical errors.

7. **You love the team.** Employers don't want to hire fans. That is nice, but a big turn off for employment. They want someone who can build their businesses, not yearn for autographs.

In conjunction with cover letter issues, employers tend to pass on applicants who apply for a job but their resumes or applications do not support they have the skills to do those jobs. It would be similar to a swimmer applying for a football scholarship. One could say I am an athlete, but one has skills in swimming, not football. So, if you don't show you have had sales experience, you probably should not apply for a sales job.

And lastly, most resumes list the applicant's job responsibilities, not their accomplishments. This makes it hard for the employer to determine the strengths and knowledge base of the potential hire. Make it easy for them. Tell the employer what accomplishments you had, things you did that made a positive impact in each job you held. Employers like to hire the best at something. They like to think they have hired the #1 pick in the draft.

What is TeamWork Online? We are a recruiting software provider that networks 700+ sports employment pages into a single system to better match employers to candidates—91% of the time in the last 12 months. http://www.teamworkonline.com.

FIGURE 14.1
Example Cover Letter

Kendra Lee
123 Main St.
Springfield, AL 12345
January 1, 2011

The Ohio State University
1010 Fawcett Center
2400 Oletangy River Road
Columbus, OH 43201

Mr. John Smith:

I am interested in working as an Assistant Director of Athletics Communications at The Ohio State University working with the women's hockey team. Overall, I have nine years of working experience in the sports information field at four different universities and at the Olympic level.

For four years, I worked in the sports information office at Concordia College in Moorhead, Minn. I gained knowledge in website and athletic program design as well as familiarity with The Automated Scorebook. I am proficient in the Stat Crew in-game statistical program for a variety of sports including hockey, basketball, football, volleyball, soccer, and baseball.

After earning my bachelor's degree, I spent one year as an intern at the University of North Carolina at Greensboro in the sports information office. While serving as an intern, I had the opportunity to work with an assortment of varsity teams, including both the men and women's soccer teams that participated in the 2006 NCAA tournaments.

During the summer of 2008, I served as the communications intern for U.S. Figure Skating in Colorado Springs, Colo. There, I gained valuable insight into the Olympic world and was a major part in creating the U.S. Figure Skating media guide as well as aiding in the media planning for upcoming U.S. Figure Skating events.

I was the graduate assistant in the Athletics Communication office at The Ohio State University for two years where I acted as the secondary contact for the men and women's swimming and diving teams and the baseball team and aided when needed in other sports. Currently, I am the Assistant Director of Media Relations at Auburn University and act as the primary contact for volleyball, men and women's swimming and diving and men's tennis.

I have a strong passion for athletics, especially at the collegiate level, and would greatly appreciate this opportunity to work for a university that exemplifies greatness in the world of college sports. Please consider my application and I look forward to meeting you for an interview.

Sincerely,

Kendra Lee
Enclosure

FIGURE 14.2
Example Resumes

BRUCE A. WIMBISH II

1000 Main Street, Gahanna, OH 43230 • 614-555-5555 (cell) • bruce_wimbish@12345.com

OBJECTIVE   To utilize and build eight years of sports marketing and media relations experience towards the pursuit of the lead executive and administrative role for an organization.

SKILLS   Marketing and Promotions, Branding, Media Relations, Sports Information & Writing, Athlete Relations, Sports Statistics & Analysis, Sports Business Communications, Pitching Stories for Media Coverage, Preparing Talking Points, Key Messages and Organizational Highlights, Team & Business Interviews, Media Administration & Internal Communications, Web Content Creation, Event Photography, Marketing & Branding, Community & Civic Relations, Urban Marketing, Diversity Initiatives

EXPERIENCE   **Greater Columbus Sports Commission**   **Columbus, OH**

Dec 2010–present   *Senior Marketing & Communications Manager*

- Responsible for generating positive exposure for the GCSC and Columbus as a premier national destination for sporting events.
- Developing marketing and publicity plans to promote designated hosted events.

Major Points of Impact: *1.) Led rebranding efforts for GCSC with new logo and full collateral materials 2.) In collaboration with 15 sports organizations, directed a $50K, 10-page advertorial in SportsBusiness Journal to promote destination nationally 3.) Led collaborative efforts for 200Columbus: the Bicentennial sports committee 4.) Led collaborative efforts for Blue Jackets, Clippers and Crew for special marketing project 5.) Pitched front page feature in Columbus Dispatch on city's March "Money Month".*

Aug 2008–Nov 2010   **Cleveland Cavaliers (NBA)**   **Cleveland, OH**

Basketball Communications Manager

- Supported the basketball communications team's efforts to coordinate the team's relationship with the media while helping to develop and distribute team information to key internal and external stakeholders and fans.
- Covered practice and assisting with day-to-day media availability.
- Issued media credentials and scouting requests; preparing game seating charts.
- Assisted in writing press releases and player bios, was lead author of team's game notes distributed daily media along with statistics and authored press releases, player bios and team pages for season/playoff media guides.
- Searching for, compiling, and distributing daily news clips on a rotating basis.

Major Points of Impact: *1.) Led efforts for game notes being considered one of top versions in the league, redesigned game administrative documents (game notes, starter-inactive sheet, injury reports, postgame notes, photo lanes chart) 2.) Increased team and player statistical depth including discovery, organization and distribution 3.)Merged business areas into game notes (attendance, television ratings, web stats, community relations 4.) Enhanced credentialing process including organizing, design and printing 5.) Improved media administration including organizing all levels of contacts and distribution lists organization; creating larger photo archives.*

Aug 2007–Jul 2008   **Cleveland Cavaliers (NBA) & Quicken Loans Arena**   **Cleveland, OH**

Corporate Communications Manager

- Maintained high profile for organizational business activities and achievements in marketing, corporate sales, ticket sales, and community relations within local and national trade publications and media outlets; created talking.
- Facilitated media exposure supporting corporate and marketing partnerships including $25M state-of-the-art practice facility, Cleveland Clinic Courts.
- Built relationships with media in the areas of sports, business, entertainment, metro, arts & life, community relations, and tracked media exposure to measure added value.

FIGURE 14.2
Example Resumes (continued)

Major Points of Impact: *1.) Transformed newly created position of corporate communications into one of the best departments in NBA 2.) Greatly enhanced organizational profile with consistent placement in industry-leading publication, SportsBusiness Journal 3.) Increased amount of coverage for our community relations initiatives (avg. two TV cameras per event) 4.) BHC helped increase African-American fan base percentage and organizational profile in specific segment's community.*

Oct 2004–Jul 2007	**Cleveland Cavaliers (NBA) & Quicken Loans Arena**	**Cleveland, OH**

Corporate Communications Coordinator
- Proactively collaborated with internal teams (marketing, corporate and ticket sales and community relations) to develop business media opportunities.
- Analyzed business data and statistics to create organizational growth messages.
- Coordinated and tracked event publicity, interviews, and TV/radio appearances.
- Created Black Heritage Celebration (BHC) for team's African-American fan base.

Jun–Aug 2004	**Cleveland Cavaliers (NBA) & Quicken Loans Arena**	**Cleveland, OH**

Marketing Intern
- Coordinated the Cavaliers Caravan summer schedule including event planning, structure, setup, layout, and staffing coordination.
- Participated on the department's ethnic audience segmentation (African-American and Latino), marketing matrix and external idea network task forces.
- Coordinated with all departments to create a unified photo database by compiling respective photos throughout organization.
- Managing team fan mail including cataloguing entries into database.

Feb 2003–May 2004	**Columbus Blue Jackets (NHL) & Columbus Destroyers (AFL)**	**Columbus, OH**

Corporate Sales/Client Services Intern
- Developed and revising partnership proposals for prospective partners; managing layout templates and element structures through league research.
- Updated corporate partnership recaps, contracts, photos radio/television affidavits and ratings for the 2003-2004 seasons.

EDUCATION	**The Ohio State University – College of Education**	**Columbus, OH**

Master of Arts – School of Physical Activity & Education Sciences
Sport Management–June 2008

	The Ohio State University – Max M. Fisher College of Business	**Columbus, OH**

Master of Business Administration
Marketing Management–June 2002

	The University of Cincinnati	**Cincinnati, OH**

Bachelor of Business Administration
Operations Management–June 2000

COMMUNITY INVOLVEMENT
The Ohio State University Alumni Association, member
The University of Cincinnati Alumni Association, member

HONORS AND ACHIEVEMENTS
Who's Who in Black Columbus, 2011 | Who's Who in Black Cleveland, 2006-2010
2008 Alltel Four-Pillar Tribute Award for Community Service
Kaleidoscope Magazine - 40 Under 40 Achievement, Class of 2005
College of Business Graduation Ceremony Speaker, Class of 2000

REFERENCES   Provided upon request.

FIGURE 14.2
Example Resumes (continued)

Contact Information:
St. John Arena
Columbus, Ohio 43210
555-555-5555 (cell)
XXXX@osu.edu

Kendra A. Lee

EDUCATION

The Ohio State University – Columbus, Ohio   Graduated June 2009
Masters – Sport Management

Concordia College – Moorhead, Minn.   Graduated April 2006
B.A. in Communication – Mass Media   Minor: Religion

SUMMARY

» Nine years experience working with media and collegiate sports.
» Sports writing skills developed through website and media guide composition.
» Writing ability acquired through publication of athletic game and feature stories.
» Organizational skills advanced through compilation of statistical data.
» Leadership qualities obtained through work-related positions and positions in extracurricular activities.

WORK EXPERIENCE

Assistant Director of Media Relations   July 2009 – Present
Auburn University – Auburn, Ala.
» Served as primary contact for volleyball, men and women's swimming and diving and men's tennis.
» Produced the 2009-10 and 2010-11 media guides for volleyball, men and women's swimming and diving and men's tennis.
» Created and maintained volleyball, men's and women's swimming and diving and men's tennis Facebook and Twitter pages.
» Operated Stat Crew in-game statistical program for volleyball, tennis and other sports when needed.
» Maintained and updated the website for assigned sports.
» Wrote and published game day stories, as well as athlete and coach biographies.

Athletic Communications Graduate Assistant   Aug. 2007 – June 2009
The Ohio State University – Columbus, Ohio
» Served as primary statistician for women's and men's volleyball teams, as well as for men's and women's basketball teams.
» Acted as primary media contact for the 2008 Big Ten and 2008 NCAA Women's Swimming and Diving Championships held in Columbus.
» Coordinated, assigned and managed the men and women's basketball stats group.
» Provided media with up-to-date basketball statistics after every home game.
» Operated Stat Crew in-game statistical program for all sports when needed.
» Served as secondary media contact for men's and women's swimming and diving programs and baseball team.
» Assisted in production of the 2007-08 and 2008-09 media guides.
» Wrote and published game day stories, as well as athlete and coach biographies.
» Updated and maintained team websites.
» Traveled with women's basketball team to 2009 NCAA Sweet 16 and assisted with media requests.

Communications Intern   June 2008 – Aug. 2008
U.S. Figure Skating – Colorado Springs, Colo.
» Gathered needed information for 2008-2009 U.S. Figure Skating media guide and aided in its production.
» Assembled and updated athletes' online biographies.
» Wrote and published news releases to the organization's website.
» Subsequent to internship, performed media relations duties for the 2009 U.S. Figure Skating Championships as requested by U.S. Figure Skating.

FIGURE 14.2
Example Resumes (continued)

Sports Information Intern   Aug. 2006 – June 2007
University of North Carolina at Greensboro – Greensboro, N.C.
» Served as primary media contact for women's soccer, wrestling and baseball.
» Assisted in the production of 2006 women's soccer media guide.
» Produced 2006-07 wrestling and 2007 baseball media guide.
» Wrote and published game day programs and game stories.
» Assisted in production of fall and winter sports' media guides.
» Acted as interim volleyball and women's basketball sports information director.
» Operated Stat Crew in-game statistical program for all sports when needed.
» Served as men's and women's soccer contact during 2006 NCAA tournament.
» Operated Stat Crew for basketball at Southern Conference Basketball Tournament.
» Volunteered at Division I Women's Basketball Greensboro Regional.

Sports Information Assistant   Sept. 2002 – May 2006
Concordia College Athletics Department – Moorhead, Minn.
» Performed following tasks for volleyball, football, basketball, hockey, soccer, track, baseball, softball and tennis regular seasons and for the NCAA Division III National football playoffs:
    » Maintained and updated schedules and rosters on athletic website.
    » Wrote and published individual athlete biography pages for website.
    » Assisted in publication of the 2005 football preseason media guide.
    » Served as media liaison for football and basketball games.
    » Utilized the Stat Crew in-game statistical program for all sports listed and provided media with game statistical recaps.

COMPUTER EXPERIENCE

Microsoft Office Suite: Microsoft Word, Microsoft Excel, Microsoft Power Point, Microsoft Outlook, Microsoft Access.
Also: Adobe InDesign, Adobe Photoshop, Adobe Acrobat, JumpTV web publisher, Netitor web publisher

The resume is a precursor to the interview, and a well-constructed resume is essential in securing an interview. It is typically scanned rather than read; therefore, format, brevity, and organization are extremely important. A cluttered resume padded with meaningless detail is distracting. There are many sample resumes online. A good site for sample resumes for a variety of fields and professions is Monster.com. Find a template that is both visually appealing and "fits" your experience.

Equally important are such communication skills as grammar, spelling, punctuation, and appropriate word choice. A misspelled word or poor grammar might lead a potential employer to believe the candidate does not pay attention to details and could eliminate him/her immediately. Be sure to have several other individuals review your resume before sending it out with your application materials. A well-organized, visually appealing, and concisely informative (more is not better) resume must also be truthful.

Falsifying or misrepresenting yourself on a resume is extremely dangerous and a quick way to the unemployment line. Such an unacceptable practice will invariably come back to haunt those who are dishonest. A classic example is the December, 2001 resignation of George O'Leary as head coach of the Notre Dame football program, arguably one of the most prestigious positions in college football. Five days after being hired, further background checks revealed that he had falsified his resume, claiming he had played football at the University of New Hampshire and that he had a master's degree in education from New York University (Fountain and Wong, 2001). He was quickly fired by Notre Dame.

References are important to include in the resume. Select three to five individuals (non-relatives) who can speak to your qualifications and include them on your reference list. Be sure to include their full name, current position and organization, address, phone number, and email address.

© Andrey_Popov, 2012. Under license from Shutterstock, Inc.

Interview Techniques

Almost all jobs or internships require some kind of interview. It is also a two-way conversation. The employer and candidate both ask questions. The employer is looking for information not available on the resume (e.g., verbal communication skills, problem solving ability, personal interests, people skills, and personality traits) that determine if the candidate is a good fit. The candidate also has the obligation to ask meaningful questions that will determine whether the organization is suitable for him/her.

An important suggestion for those inexperienced in the interview

Interview Preparation and Typical Questions

One should prepare for an interview by researching the organization and gaining as much knowledge as possible about those who will be conducting the interview. The more knowledge one acquires about the organization and those conducting the interview, the better prepared one will be to answer questions and leave a favorable impression.

After researching the organization and individuals conducting the interview, one should brainstorm in anticipation for the various questions that may be asked at the interview. Typical interview questions include:

- Tell us about yourself.
- Tell us why you want this position.
- Why do you believe you are the best fit for this position?
- What are your strengths and weaknesses?
- Tell us about a difficult situation you faced and how you handled it.

Potential employers may provide you with a specific scenario and ask you to respond to that scenario. If this is not your first position into the field, a typical question may include why you want to leave your current position. Also depending on the position, one may be asked their level of experience in a specific area such as sales, sponsorship, or event operations.

It is equally important to identify two to three key points you want the interviewers to remember about you and your fit for the position. Once you've identified those key points and have brainstormed about the questions that may be asked, determine how you will consistently respond and make those points as you answer questions.

During most interviews, potential employers will ask you if you have any questions for them. It is important to have always prepared one or two questions to ask. Having questions for the potential employer shows forethought on your behalf and can yield additional insights about the organization and the position. It also allows you an opportunity as a potential hire to set yourself apart from other interviewees. Some questions you may consider asking include:

- If hired for the position, what would you want me to accomplish within the first month, three months, and six months?
- How does this position fit into the overall mission of the organization?

Asking questions also provides an opportunity for your to clarify anything previously asked or relayed to you earlier in the interview.

After the interview has concluded, it is appropriate and recommended that you write a thank you to those conducting the interview. This should be received by those conducting the interview within 24 hours. This thank you should be short, simple, and to the point. This also provides you with an opportunity to briefly and eloquently emphasize one or two key points about your fit for the position or about strengths you possess that would benefit the organization.

process is to take the time to participate and observe yourself in mock interviews. A video camera will more objectively tell the truth about such vocalized pauses as "ahs" and "ums," irritating habits and gestures, and overused words.

Nagel and Southall (2011) provide interviews with a number of sport management professionals from various segments of the industry. The advice is very helpful; so is the insight gained from the types of questions asked (again, additional resources are also included at the end of this chapter).

Portfolio Development

The portfolio is a great tool to showcase one's ability and experience and to become competitive in the hiring process. Basically, it's a collection of a person's professional work over time; individuals new to the job market should use their student portfolios. This information provides insight not included in the resume. It is an important and effective marketing tool often underutilized because it is developed over time and, therefore, is time consuming. **Electronic portfolios** (or e-portfolios) are growing in popularity. A personal website may be developed that includes a resume, industry related volunteer or work experience, educational background, and any special skills you may want to showcase. One should utilize the e-portfolio to showcase completed projects that have relevance to positions desired in the industry and that illustrate your skills. For example, you may have been required to develop a sponsorship proposal or give a sales presentation in one of your courses. These are projects that should be included in the e-portfolio to highlight your strengths as a potential hire. Essentially, an e-portfolio serves as a central point of reference for your work related materials. You may even include the link to it on your resume or refer to it in a cover letter. Doing so may allow potential employers to review your work and compare your work with that of other job candidates.

Salary Negotiation Strategies

Typically, salaries are negotiated in this industry and are based on the type of position, skill sets of individuals, and duties and responsibilities of the position. Salaries obviously vary based on these and other factors. The salary discussion should only be negotiable and discussed towards the end of the interview process. It is important that candidates know their market value and how to negotiate for the most appropriate salary possible. In order to be paid the maximum salary for a specific position, individuals must be able to articulate and communicate their value to the organization. It is based on such factors as experience, skills, competition, and geographical location. Understanding how to communicate this value and knowledge of the most appropriate survey for your value requires research. However, because this field is so specialized, current information is more reliable from people who are in similar positions or professors who have graduates in the field. Since salary figures are sensitive, it may be difficult to obtain this information. Knowing someone who is in the industry and willing to share this information may be advantageous and effective.

Being in the Right Place at the Right Time

In February 1987, a month after starting a non-paid internship for academic credit to network, gain experience, and establish a reputation as a dedicated "employee," Zack Hill was determined to get to work on time in a blizzard. His destination then was the Philadelphia 76ers' offices at Veterans Stadium. Only one other person in that organization made it to work that morning. He was John Nash, General Manager of the 76ers organization. After breakfast together, the general manager sent Zack home for the rest of the day, having had the opportunity to listen to the young intern's ambitious plans for the future. Had Zack not been determined to get to work that morning under such inclement conditions, perhaps he wouldn't be where he is today—the Senior Director of Communications for the Philadelphia Flyers.

Networking is an opportunity to make yourself known. More importantly, it is a time for others, especially in influential positions, to get to know you. Recommendations by network contacts often have greater credibility and influence in a job search (Young, 1990). Joining professional organizations and attending conferences are a great way to meet and network with individuals in specific fields (even as a student). For example, those interested in collegiate sports marketing should consider becoming members of the National Association of Collegiate Marketing Administrators (NACMA) and attending their annual conference. Organizations like NACMA typically offer significant discounts on membership and conference registration fees to current students.

Sometimes overlooked with regard to networking is the "elevator interview" or "elevator pitch." As previously mentioned, you only have one chance to make a first impression. Suppose you have a chance encounter in an elevator, in a hotel lobby, or even your local grocery store with someone who works for an organization where you would like to work. You have approximately 30 seconds to "sell yourself" and let this individual know why you would be an outstanding asset to his/her organization. Practicing and perfecting your elevator interview should be a top priority; you never know when you may run into someone in the field who can help you land a job. Finally, be sure to follow up with a short thank-you note within the week after meeting that person.

Social networks are discussed in more detail in Chapter 9, but social networking is also relevant to professional networking. With over 750 million active users (Facebook Statistics, n.d.), Facebook has become a tool for meeting individuals, and just as important, maintaining relationships. Similarly, Twitter is a great way to connect and interact with individuals in a given field. However, with the ease of Internet searches, everyone should understand that pictures or comments posted on social network sites might be seen by potential employers. An unflattering picture on Facebook or a comment criticizing an organization on Twitter may eliminate you from being considered for a position with a company.

Finally, LinkedIn is a site that claims to be the world's largest professional network. With over 120 million members, "LinkedIn connects you to your trusted contacts and helps you exchange knowledge, ideas, and opportunities with a broader network of professionals" (LinkedIn, n.d.). The site makes it easy to keep up with former classmates, colleagues, and business contacts; they update their profile, so you will not lose that connection when they move or change jobs. The profile portion of the site is like an online resume and allows you to include a photo, an executive summary and skill set, education, three recent positions, and three recommendations from your connections. LinkedIn also allows you to search for open jobs based on keywords, titles, location, functions, experience, and industries (LinkedIn, n.d.). Google Profiles is another site where you can post your bio and links to sites about you.

Experience

According to New York City Mayor Michael Bloomberg, "Eighty percent of success is showing up … early." (Couric, 2011, 37). Being early is necessary in one's career experiences, as well as in the workplace. **Volunteering** (working for free) for hands-on experience and to learn job-related skills allows you to gain valuable real-world experience and increase your network base.

Being in such a competitive industry, the more experience you can get, the more marketable you will be in the future. Therefore, it is important to volunteer early in your college career. Through the guidance of academic advisors and other professors, freshmen and sophomores can start this process earlier. It's never too early! Volunteering is also a great way to become visible at the national level by serving on regional and national professional association committees. Chairs of committees especially at the national level have important contacts. Their recommendations are valuable because of their visibility and credibility.

Graduate School

One way to gain more experience and to separate you from others is to attend graduate school. Many job openings in sports now list a master's degree as a preferred requirement. According to the North American Society for Sport Management website, there are over 150 master's programs in sport management in theUnited States (to see the list, go to http://www.nassm.com/InfoAbout/SportMgmtPrograms/United_States). You may also investigate pursuing a Master of Business Administration (MBA) degree. While the focus of most MBA programs is not specifically on sport, they do give you a solid business background. A recent trend, however, is to offer an MBA in sport management (or an MBA with a concentration in sport management). Several schools now offer this type of degree.

A graduate degree can give you the additional knowledge to succeed in the sport industry, but just as important, it allows you to gain more experience. Most graduate programs require a full-time internship as part of the curriculum, with many also requiring/ encouraging practicum experiences. The internship or practicum provide students with an ideal culminating experience to bridge the theories and concepts learned in their curriculum with the real-world challenges and demands of the sport industry. They often also assist students in determining which area of the field most appeals to them. For example, students may select an internship in sales, event operations, or social media. These experiences, combined with students' academic backgrounds, often lay the foundation for entry and advancement of a career in sport.

Internships in the sports industry, probably more than in most other industries, are critical to young professionals beginning their careers. As forementioned, they are academic accredited work experiences obtained by students before graduating from a sport management academic program. They provide practical on-the-job experience in a sport organization (the "real world"), rather than a classroom, where problem solving opportunities are more prevalent and realistic.

Besides invaluable work experience, they provide networking opportunities and an advantage over the competition for future employment in the organization. This is why it is important to take advantage of the situation by outperforming and proving yourself different and more valuable than other interns.

Dedication

According to retired college football coach Lou Holtz, "No one has ever drowned in sweat" (Benson, 2008, 217). Also, "There are no traffic jams along the extra miles," claimed football hall of famer Roger Staubach (Benson, 2008, 62). Working in the entry-level sport industry is hard work. It is not glamorous; the hours are long, the pay is low and no task is beneath you. No job is too small. You must pay your dues because you're not entitled to anything.

To be successful:

- Follow your passion. If you love what you're doing, you'll do it very well.

- Never stop learning. Staying current on everything sports-related is a necessary life-long endeavor in this industry. Read newspapers, Facebook, Twitter feeds, and blogs about the industry.

- Following a comfortable linear career path on the organization's depth chart may not always be the solution. The challenge is knowing when to go nonlinear, such as relocating geographically for a promotion or invaluable experience. Going out of your comfort zone may be frightening but it should not be ignored.

- Get to work first and leave last. In between, never say, "I can't," "That's impossible," or "There isn't enough time."

Jobs in Sport Management

Just like contests on the field, finding a job in the sport industry is highly competitive. It is not uncommon for sport organizations to receive several hundred (or even several thousand) applications for a single open position or internship. For example, an executive from ESPN claimed they had more than 10,000 applications in one year for around 60 internships (Miller and Shales, 2011). TeamWork Online averages 135 applications for each of its job postings (B. Filippell, personal communication to author, August 15, 2011).

A comprehensive list of jobs in sport management would be impossible to include in the limited space we have in this chapter. According to the United States Department of Labor (n.d.), as of May 2010, there were 131,180 individuals working in the spectator sport industry. This figure was down over 5% from 2008 (not surprising because of the economic downturn). Over three times as many individuals (477,820) worked in fitness and recreation sports centers. This sector was down only 3% from 2008. The average salary for those in the spectator sport industry was $41,560. However for those categorized in management positions (CEO's, GM's, and various other manager positions), the average salary was $112,860. Individuals working in fitness and recreation sports centers make about $10,000 less ($30,390) than those in the spectator sport industry.

Courtesy of Kimberly Miloch.

Individuals seeking employment in the sport industry usually have a preference for jobs based on context (e.g., professional sports, intercollegiate sports, campus recreation, etc.) or function (marketing, event management, public relations, etc.). In professional sports, teams have a multitude of positions. The Green Bay Packers from the National Football League (NFL) list 209 positions on their staff directory (see Figure 14.3), while the Dallas Mavericks of the National Basketball Association (NBA) list 144 positions (see Figure 14.4). A major difference between these two teams can be found in ticket sales. Since the Packers sell out every home game and have a season ticket waiting list of over 80,000, they only have 4 positions in ticketing. The Mavericks, on the other hand, have 25 employees in ticket sales and another 4 in ticket administration. Overall, there are more jobs in ticketing for NBA, Major League Baseball (MLB), and National Hockey League (NHL) teams than any other area. According to Washo (2004), ticketing is the best way to break into the sport industry. He also believes "students with no desire to be salespeople have no business being in the sports business."

Large university athletic departments also employ many individuals. For example, The Ohio State University lists almost 500 employees on its website (The Ohio State University Athletic Department, n.d.). Even the smallest school in the Big 10 Conference, Northwestern University, has just under 200 employees (Northwestern University Athletic Department, n.d.). Colleges and universities have areas such as academic support and compliance that are not seen at the professional level.

Typically, sport organizations with openings post a position announcement, otherwise known as a job posting. These postings usually include the minimum educational requirements and experience for the position (e.g., bachelor's degree required; 3 years working in the field), a summary of the duties and responsibilities for the position, and a salary range, among others. The postings will also include information on how to apply for the position and what to include in your application materials. Many organizations will now only accept applications electronically. This process cuts down on paper and allows the organization to screen out applicants who do not meet the minimum requirements of the job.

There are numerous websites that list job openings in sports. Some are free, while others charge a premium to view the openings. You should explore several of these sites to see if they have jobs that interest you (especially before paying for access to a site). For those interested in intercollegiate athletic positions, the National Collegiate Athletic Association (NCAA) lists openings on their website. (no charge to search).

FIGURE 14.3
Green Bay Packers Staff Directory

Administration
President & Chief Executive Officer (CEO)
Vice President of Finance
Vice President of Sales & Marketing
Vice President of Organizational/Staff Development
Vice President of Administration/General Counsel
Staff Counsel
Senior Legal Assistant
Executive Assistant to the President
Administrative Assistant – Finance/Organizational & Staff Development
Administrative Assistant – Sales & Marketing
Chairman Emeritus

Finance
Accounting Manager
Assistant Accounting Manager
Senior Accountant
Accountant
Accounting Assistant
Accounts Payable Assistant (2)
Payroll Coordinator

Human Resources
Human Resources Manager
Human Resources Coordinator

Public Relations
Director of Public Relations
Assistant Director of Public Relations/Corporate Communications
Assistant Director of Public Relations
Public Relations Coordinator
Communications Manager
Public Relations Intern (2)
Team Photographer

Packers Media Group
Director of Packers Media Group
Internet Coordinator
Marketing Analyst – Packers Media Group
Editor/Producer – Packers Media Group
Staff Writer
Internet/Packers Media Group Intern

Marketing
Director of Marketing & Corporate Sales
Manager of Corporate Sales
Corporate Sales Executive (3)
Manager of Partnership Services
Senior Partnership Services Coordinator
Partnership Services Coordinator (2)
Manager of Premium Seating Sales and Service
Premium Seating Coordinator (2)

Marketing Manager
Graphic Designer
Marketing Assistant
Game and Fan Development Manager
Marketing Intern (5)

Information Technology
Director of Information Technology
Assistant Director of Information Technology
Computer Systems Administrator
Business Services Analyst
Computer Services Analyst
Data Warehouse Analyst
Computer Systems Technician
IT Support Specialist
Help Desk/Administrative Assistant

Community Outreach
Manager of Community Outreach & Player/Alumni Relations
Corporate Donations Supervisor
Community Outreach Coordinator
Youth Football Coordinator
Community Outreach Assistant (2)
Community Outreach Intern

Packers Hall of Fame
Hall of Fame and Stadium Tour Manager
Hall of Fame Group Sales Coordinator
Hall of Fame Assistant/Educational Coordinator

Ticketing
Director of Ticket Operations
Box Office Manager
Ticket Office Coordinator (2)

Packers Pro Shop
Director of Retail Operations
Packers Pro Shop Buyer
Manager of Warehouse & Concessions Operations
Packers Pro Shop Store Manager
Customer Service & Training Coordinator
Direct Marketing Campaign Coordinator
Assistant Buyer
Assistant Manager-Team Stores (3)
Warehouse Coordinator (2)
Warehouse Assistant
Purchasing Administrative Assistant

Premium Sales and Guest Services
Director of Premium Sales and Guest Services
Special Events Corporate Sales Manager
Special Events Account Executive
Special Events Coordinator (2)
Special Events Assistant
Administrative Assistant, Special Events
Guest Services Supervisor
Guest Services Assistant/Switchboard
Guest Services Assistant/Reception
Guest Services Assistant/Atrium Concierge (5)

Facilities And Fields
Director of Facility Operations
Facilities Manager
Fields Manager
HVAC Manager
Electrical Manager
Maintenance Supervisor (2)
Manager of Atrium Operations
Plumber/Beverage Systems Technician
Janitorial Coordinator
Electrical Assistant
HVAC Assistant (2)
Fields Assistant (3)
Maintenance Assistant
Atrium Operations Lead (3)
Administrative Assistant-Facilities

Security
Director of Security/Risk Management
Building Security Supervisor
Security Officer (11)
Loading Dock Assistant
Security/Risk Management Assistant
Mail Clerk (2)

Football Operations
Executive Vice President, General Manager &
Director of Football Operations
Vice President of Football Administration/Player
Finance
Director of Research and Development
Director of Player Development
Football Administration Coordinator
Coaching Administrator
Executive Assistant—General Manager
Salary Cap Analyst
Corporate Travel Manager
Manager of Family Programs
Executive Assistant—Head Coach
Administrative Assistant-Coaching Staff

Coaching
Head Coach
Assistant Head Coach/Inside Linebackers
Offensive Coordinator
Defensive Coordinator
Special Teams Coordinator
Strength & Conditioning Coordinator
Wide Receivers
Offensive Line
Quarterbacks
Running Backs
Offensive Quality Control
Tight Ends
Special Teams Assistant
Assistant Wide Receivers/Special Teams
Outside Linebackers
Defensive Quality Control
Secondary—Safeties
Defensive Line
Secondary—Cornerbacks
Strength & Conditioning Assistant (2)

Player Personnel
Director—Football Operations
Director of College Scouting
Assistant Director of College Scouting (Midwest)
College Scout (Northeast)
College Scout (Southeast)
College Scout (Southwest)
College Scout (West Coast)
College Scout (Midlands)
College Scouting (National Football Scouting)
Assistant Director of Pro Personnel
Assistant Director of Player Personnel
Scouting Assistant
College Scouting Coordinator
Pro Personnel Coordinator

Video
Video Director
Assistant Video Director
Video Assistant (2)

Equipment
Equipment Manager
Assistant Equipment Manager (2)
Equipment Assistant (2)

Medical
Head Athletic Trainer
Team Physician
Associate Team Physician
Assistant Athletic Trainer (3)
Intern Athletic Trainer

From http://www.packers.com/team/front-office.html

FIGURE 14.4
Dallas Mavericks Staff Directory

OWNER

PRESIDENT'S OFFICE
President and Chief Executive Officer
Senior Executive Assistant

HUMAN RESOURCES
Senior Vice President of Human Resources
Receptionists (2)

BASKETBALL OPERATIONS
President of Basketball Operations/General Manager
Head Coach
Assistant General Manager
Assistant Coaches (2)
Player Development/Game Prep
Special Assistant to Head Coach
Director of Basketball Analytics
Travel Manager/Coaches Assistant
Director of Basketball Development
Player Development Coach
Free Throw Coach
Head Athletic Trainer
Assistant Athletic Trainer
Team Physician
Team Internist
Assistant Coach/Strength and Conditioning
Equipment Manager
Scouts (4)
Director of International Scouting
Advance Scouts (2)
Head Video Coordinator/Scout
Video Scouts (2)
Director of Player Personnel
Director of Sports Psychology
Massage Therapist

ACCOUNTING
Vice President & Chief Financial Officer
Financial Analyst/Ticket Systems Manager
Senior Accountant & Payroll Manager
Senior Accountant
Senior Financial Supervisor
Accounting Associate (2)
Controller

Information Systems
Director of Technology & Information Systems
Systems Analyst
Email Coordinator

Ticket Administration
Director of Ticket Administration
Ticket Administrators (3)

MARKETING, COMMUNICATIONS & COMMUNITY RELATIONS
Vice President Marketing and Communications

Basketball Communications
Director of Basketball Communications
Basketball Communications Manager
Basketball Communications Coordinator

Corporate Communications/ Community Relations
Corporate Communications/Community Relations Manager
Corporate Communications/Community Relations Coordinator

Marketing
Marketing Manager
Creative Producer
Marketing Operations Manager
Marketing Coordinator
Player Relations Manager
Creative Editor/Producer Designer
Interactive Database Manager
Interactive Web Manager
Interactive Content Manager
Graphic Designer
Manager of Publishing
Community Basketball Manager
Mascot Manager

MERCHANDISE
Vice President of Merchandising
Merchandise Manager/ Buyer
Ultimate Fan Shop Store Manager—North Park
Ultimate Fan Shop Assistant Manager—North Park
Merchandise Operations Manager
MavGear Manager/Merchandise Inventory Controller

TICKET SALES & CUSTOMER SERVICE
Vice President of Ticket Sales & Services
Director of Ticket Sales & Services
Group Sales Manager
Ticket Sales Service Consultant
Director of Service and Retention
Ticket Sales Account Executives (20)

CORPORATE SPONSORSHIPS
Senior Vice President of Corporate Sponsorships
Sponsor Services Coordinator
Broadcast/Trafficking Coordinator
Corporate Sponsorship Activation Manager
Senior Director of Corporate Sponsorships
Director of Corporate Sponsorships (4)
Corporate Account Executives (4)

OPERATIONS
Vice President of Operations & Arena Development
Operations Manager
Director of Security

DALLAS MAVERICKS BROADCASTING
Director of Production

GAMEDAY STAFF
Public Address Announcer
Stats Crew (24)

From http://www.nba.com/mavericks/mavs_front_office_2011.html

FIGURE 14.5
Example Job Postings

PROJECT ASSISTANT
REQUISITION # 59815

Persons with disabilities may contact the recruiting department if accommodations are needed.

POSITION BASICS

Position Title:	Assistant Director of Marketing-Athletics
Advertising Ends on:	March 1, 2011
Advertising Started on:	April 1, 2012
Organization:	Athletics
Department:	Intercollegiate Athletics

SALARY

Salary:	$27,345.00 to Commensurate
Pay Grade:	03

JOB DETAILS

Percent Time:	100%
Type of Position:	Regular: A position which is considered essential for the effective long-term operation of the university. Persons appointed to this position will receive the privileges and benefits associated with regular employment status, including all health benefits.
Duties:	Middle State University, a NCAA Division I FBS institution and a member of the Big State Conference, is currently seeking a self-motivated, goal-oriented individual who possesses the skills and creativity required to successfully assist in directing the marketing efforts on behalf of the University's 29 intercollegiate athletics sports programs.

Responsibilities

Responsibilities include, but are not limited to, create and implement marketing plans that aggressively enhance the outreach efforts of the Department and maximize the opportunities to generate revenue through the sale of season, mini-plan, and single-event tickets; create, develop and implement crowd interactive promotions at all home events;

FIGURE 14.5
Example Job Postings (continued)

<table>
<tr><td></td><td>assists in the production and scheduling of all print, electronic, and new media advertising (including social media); assists in the production of all printed materials used in support of the marketing efforts; assists in the programming and event-day operation of the dasher boards, courtside displays, and digital message centers inside University venues; assists in the management of student, intern and volunteer employees; serve as one of the department's liaison to the Athletics Ticket Office; serve as one of the department's liaisons to the Middies, the official student support organization of the Department of Intercollegiate Athletics; perform other duties as assigned by the Director of Marketing.</td></tr>
<tr><td>**Education Required:**</td><td>Bachelor's degree in marketing, business, sports marketing, sports management/administration or another related field, or equivalent combination of education and experience is required.</td></tr>
<tr><td>**Education Preferred:**</td><td>Master's degree in sports marketing, sports management/administration or another related field.</td></tr>
<tr><td>**Experience Required:**</td><td>Some (1 year) administrative, supervisory and program experience, which includes full-time professional experience in sports marketing at the intercollegiate level or professional sports; knowledge of NCAA rules and regulations as they pertain to marketing at the intercollegiate athletics level; superior interpersonal, organizational, and communication skills; demonstrated ability to manage multiple tasks and projects simultaneously; demonstrated ability to meet established goals and deadlines; demonstrated understanding and appreciation of new and social media as part of the marketing mix; proficient with Word and Excel computer software applications.</td></tr>
<tr><td>**Desirable Qualifications:**</td><td>Five years of full-time professional experience in sports marketing at the NCAA Division I level; proficient with Adobe InDesign computer software application; a minimum of two years of experience working with the base operating system used for message centers built by Daktronics; preference will be given to the candidate that best meets the programmatic needs of the External Affairs unit of the Middle State University Department of Intercollegiate Athletics.</td></tr>
</table>

ONLINE APPLICATION OPTIONS

Application Type:	This job requires basic applicant information, plus a resume. Your resume should not be sent to the contact below. The resume will be attached during the Online Application Process.

FIGURE 14.5
Example Job Postings (continued)

Cover Letter:	A plain text cover letter is required.
References:	Must have at least three references. References must be filled out online during the application process, however, only professional references will be allowed.
Driving License Required:	In order to be hired for this job, you must have a valid US driving license.

CONTACT INFORMATION

For further information about this position, please contact:

Contact: Jane Smith
Middle State University Department of Athletics
Middies Arena
1 University Drive
Middle City, OH 55555

Please Note: Your resume should not be sent to the contact above. The resume should be attached during the Online Application Process.

Summary

Despite being in a field with long hours and (typically) low starting salaries, a job in the sport industry can be extremely rewarding. To be a competitive candidate for a job in sports, individuals must be able to promote themselves in ways that separate them from others. Gaining as much experience in the field, by volunteering and/or interning, to build your resume is a must. Expanding your network with contacts in the industry is also something that you have to develop. Interview preparation is also essential in securing a position. Regardless of career goals, one must strategically enhance the set of skills necessary to gain entry and to advance a career in the sport industry. This chapter has outlined key areas of focus for career development and entry into the profession.

Critical Thinking Exercises

1. Search the Internet for sample resumes (if possible, from individuals in the sport industry). Choose a style/template that is suitable for you, then develop your own resume.

2. Prepare a set of questions (8–10), then interview (preferably in person, but over the phone is acceptable) an individual in the sport industry. When choosing your interviewee, think about individuals who are in positions that you could see yourself working in the future.

3. With a classmate (or two), take turns conducting mock interviews with each other for a job in the sport industry.

4. Develop your 30-second elevator interview, and then videotape yourself presenting it. Write a critique of your presentation. As an added activity, show it to someone else and get feedback on your performance.

5. Secure 3–5 job postings for a position (e.g., intercollegiate athletics marketing assistant) in which you may be interested. Summarize the qualifications and skills needed for this position.

References

Benson, M. *Winning words: Classic quotes from the world of sports.* New York, NY: Taylor Trade Publishing, 2008.

Brzezinski, M. *Knowing your value.* New York, NY: Weinstein Books, 2010.

Couric, K. *The best advice I ever got: Lessons from extraordinary lives.* New York, NY: Random House, Inc., 2011.

Fountain, J. W., and E. Wong. "Notre Dame coach resigns after 5 days and a few lies." *New York Times,* December 15, 2001, http://www.nytimes.com/2001/12/15/ sports/notre-dame-coach-resigns-after-5-days-and-a-few-lies.html

Jensen, M. His perseverance paid off. *Philadelphia Inquirer,* 182, July 19, 2010: E6., 2010 Facebook Statistics. (n.d.) https://www.facebook.com/press/info.php?statistics

LindedIn. (n.d.) LinkedIn Learning Center. http://learn.linkedin.com

Miller, J. A., and T. Shales. *These guys have all the fun: Inside the world of ESPN.* New York, NY: Little, Brown and Co., 2011.

Nagel, M. and S. Southall. *Introduction to sport management: Theory and practice.* Dubuque, IA: Kendall Hunt Publishing Company, 2011.

Northwestern University Athletic Department. (n.d.) Staff directory. http://nusports.cstv.com/school-bio/ nw-athdept.html

Sullivan, R. *Getting your feet in the door when you don't have a leg to stand on.* New York, NY: The McGraw-Hill Companies, 2002.

The Ohio State University Athletic Department. (n.d.) Staff directory. http://www.ohiostatebuckeyes.com/ staffdir/osu-staffdir.html

United States Department of Labor Bureau of Labor Statistics. *Occupational employment statistics.* 2010. http://www.bls.gov/oes/

Washo, M. *Break into sports through ticket sales.* Rutherford, NJ: MMW Marketing, 2004.

Young, D. Mentoring and networking: Perceptions by athletic administrators. *Journal of Sport Management,* 4 (1990): 71–79.

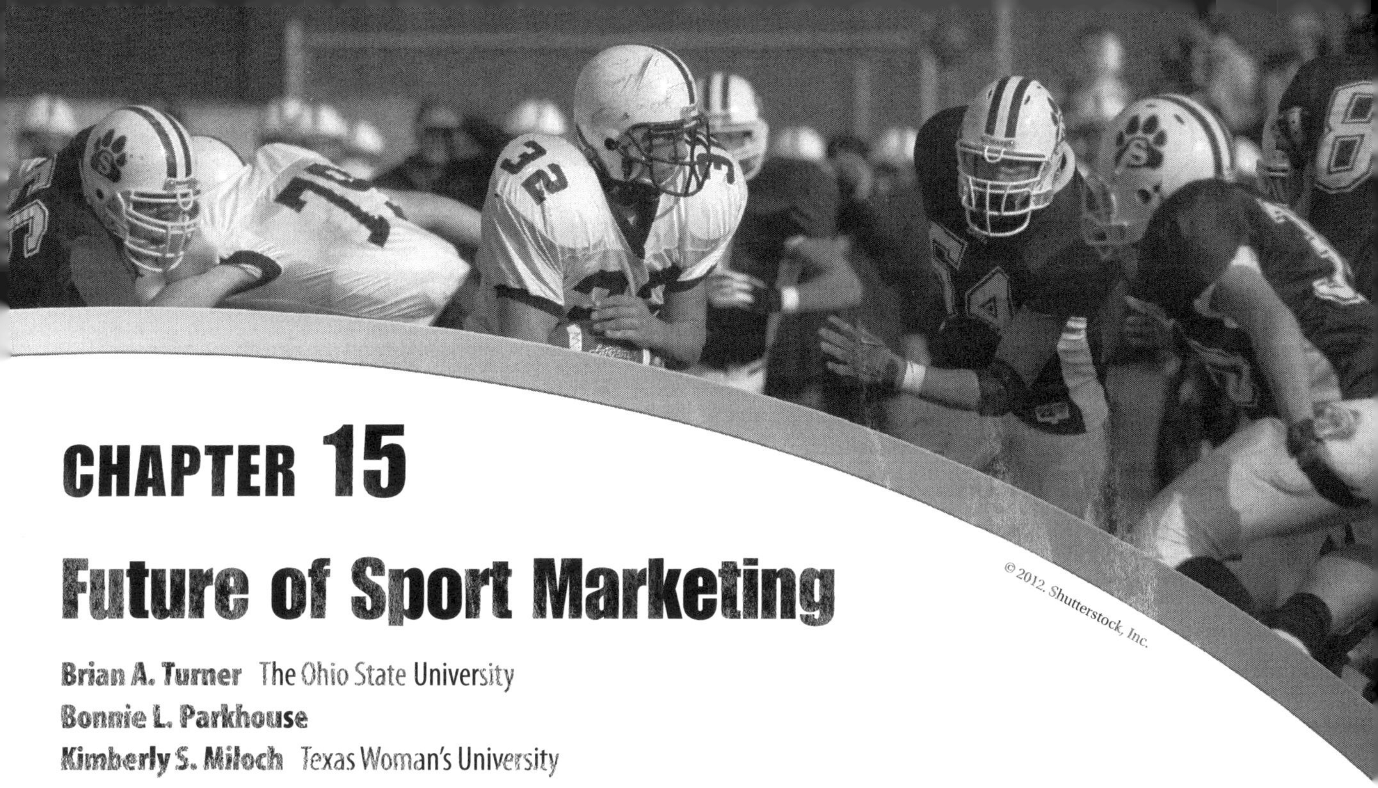
© 2012, Shutterstock, Inc.

CHAPTER 15

Future of Sport Marketing

Brian A. Turner The Ohio State University
Bonnie L. Parkhouse
Kimberly S. Miloch Texas Woman's University

The best thing about the future is that it comes only one day at a time.
Abraham Lincoln

CHAPTER OBJECTIVES

After completing the chapter, the reader should be able to:

- Identify the current curricular trends in the academic discipline of sport marketing.
- Identify and outline future industry trends and challenges facing sport marketers.
- Recognize the role of technology and social media in impacting sport consumption and the future positions in sport marketing and management.

As outlined in the previous chapters, the field of sport marketing has experienced tremendous growth and continues to evolve and change. As with any industry, professionals and academicians must adapt and respond to trends and challenges. Innovations like increased mobile and digital technology and trends such as social media consumption will impact how sport marketers communicate to target audiences and position their respective products. Consumer demand will continue to vary and consumer preferences for consumption and products will continue to impact how products are developed and marketed. These challenges and trends will require additional research and study among academicians and sport industry professionals. This also will likely impact the type of curriculum offered in higher education as well as the type of positions and job skills and requirements of sport industry professionals. This chapter highlights current and future challenges and trends facing professionals in academia and in the sport marketing industry.

Academic Trends

It might be hard to believe, but sport management is still a relatively new academic field. There was tremendous growth in the number of sport management programs in the 1990's and early 2000's, but this growth has slowed considerably the last several years. Many of the early programs developed out of physical education or kinesiology departments. It was not uncommon to have sport management students take traditional courses in these areas (e.g., anatomy and physiology). The coursework and curriculum in sport management and marketing has evolved and many programs now have a business-focused curriculum. Additionally, it is possible in the future for programs to separate themselves from other units and create their own schools or departments (such as the Mark H. McCormack Department of Sport Management at the University of Massachusetts).

A degree in sport management or a related field will continue to be a prerequisite for entry into the sport industry. While an undergraduate degree is necessary, advanced education in the form of a graduate degree combined with field experience in the industry is important to gaining entry and advancing in the industry. There are numerous colleges and universities that offer master's degrees in sport management, with a growing number offering Master of Business Administration (MBA) degrees in sport management or MBAs with a concentration in sport management. Both of these are viable options that help students gain the knowledge, skills, and experience to be successful in the sport industry. Additionally, in the future we see programs allowing students to focus their degree plan on specific areas of sport management (e.g., marketing, sales, event management, etc.) as opposed to more general degrees in sport management. These programs will allow students to gain much more knowledge in areas where they want to focus their careers.

Early sport management faculty, due to attrition in physical education, had a background and credentials in such areas as coaching and teaching methods. Just as the curriculum has evolved, so, too, has the experience and background of faculty in sport management. Current faculty with degrees and experience in marketing, management, and communication related fields have become the norm. In the future, we see this continuing, with faculty becoming even more specialized in areas of sport management. With the rate of change in the sport industry, faculty will need to focus on a specific area (or two) in order to give students the most current information. The era of sport management "generalists" will continue to decline.

In the years in which the first issues of the *Journal of Sport Management* were published, it was recommended that two or more specializations should be offered in the curriculum to address the unique competencies of a variety of sport management areas (Parkhouse, 1987). At that time, the Internet and cell phones did not exist; technology was extremely limited. VCRs were in their infancy. Today, the World Wide Web, mobile media, and social media have become some of the primary modes for disseminating information. Given the advancement of sport marketing and technology in the past twenty-five years, academic research and curriculum require an emphasis on technology-based sport marketing and communication.

Textbooks are becoming more affordable to students because they can now be rented. Wireless reading devices will also play a role in the future of textbooks, and many publishers offer electronic and digital versions of textbooks. These versions are often less expensive than hard copy textbooks, and it is anticipated that digital textbooks will represent a significant portion of textbook sales in the coming years (Reynolds, 2011).

Technology will continue to influence the manner in which products are marketed and impact consumers' experiences. As new technologies emerge, so, too, will more creative marketing strategies. This is particularly true of virtual and mobile technology.

In the past decade, virtual signage was used to electronically insert an image onto a playing surface for advertising purposes. Earlier technologies to enhance viewer interest also included instant replay and slow motion. Today, virtual technology is being used in other ways. For example, to facilitate home viewer interest, the strike zone is projected in Major League Baseball (MLB). It's the "yellow line" indicating yardage needed for a first down in the National Football League (NFL) and in major professional tennis tournaments, such as the US Open and Wimbledon, it is the Hawkeye Sensors that assist officials in determining if close shots are within the lines on the court. Fans watch a replay of the shot on the big screen and see if the balls were "in" or "out" based on the results from the Hawkeye sensors.

Since there are over 5 billion cell phone subscriptions worldwide (Whitney, 2010), mobile technology takes convenience and accessibility to another level. It continues to challenge marketers, but it also provides unique ways to reach and communicate with consumers that may be more impactful than general advertising. The ability of consumers to customize their technologies will also impact how marketers deliver messages and communicate with them in the future.

Online and Hybrid Learning

Distance education or online learning are terms used in reference to online courses. **Hybrid** or **blended courses** refer to courses that include a mix of online and face-to-face course components. Student demand for online courses, and flexibility to accommodate busy schedules and other time constraints combined with infrastructure demands have acted as a catalyst for the growth of online learning. As noted by Allen and Seaman (2011), approximately 31%

of college students are enrolled in at least one online course (2011, 4), and more than 6.1 million students were enrolled in an online course in Fall 2010 (2011, 4). Additionally, the researchers reported that 65% of universities in their study on distance education indicated that online course offerings were a component of long-term strategic planning (2011, 4). Just as technology impacts the manner in which consumers desire, seek, and acquire information, it also impacts the manner in which students learn and obtain information. Consequently, this influences the manner in which instructors and professors teach as well as structure courses. To respond to technological advances and appropriately address the role of technology in learning, the Association for American State Colleges and Universities commissioned a Red Balloon Project with one of the primary goals focused on best practices in educational technology use to most appropriately align with how students gain and disseminate knowledge. Various technologies also now offer instructors a means to engage students and provide a mentoring relationship. Course management systems such as Blackboard and E-college provide tools like video, online chat, archived videos, and discussion forums to enhance and encourage student interaction and engagement. Instant messaging devices and video chat services such as Skype and Oovoo also provide instructors with a means to interact with students face-to-face in a virtual environment. While a physical space should always be maintained for scholarly discourse and learning, it is apparent that a curricular focus on distance education will continue to maintain a presence in higher education.

As the curriculum and academic environment in sport marketing and management responds to trends and challenges, so, too, will professionals in the industry. Some of the aforementioned trends are also highlighted in the trends and challenges facing industry professionals. We asked experts in the areas of college sports, facility management, high school sports, minor league baseball, social media, sponsorships, and ticketing to give their opinions on the future of sports. Here is what they had to say:

College Sports
David Brown
College Sport Marketing Consultant

College athletics is a business and making money is part of it. Every year it costs more and more revenue to run an athletic program. An increase in scholarships and building and/or updating new facilities headline expense reports. Most schools have already outsourced their multi-media marketing rights and are thus receiving guaranteed revenue. And with fund raising efforts flat over the last couple of years, the only real area for major revenue growth is ticket sales. Athletic departments have already started focusing on filling empty seats in their arenas/stadiums. They will either outsource their ticket sales or create an in-house sales group. This follows along exactly what the professional teams have already done for quite some time.

The entertainment dollar has become more competitive than in previous years, so athletic departments are focusing on creating value for their customers. They now spend more time on the fan experience. In fact, more and more athletic marketing departments are changing their name to fan experience and promotions. There will be less focus on marketing the sports that will generate little or no revenue to the department. More resources will be given primarily to those sports that have the biggest upside in revenue through ticket sales, concessions, and merchandise sales. Remember college athletics is a business.

The way marketing departments communicate to their target audiences will continue to change every year. Hiring specific individuals to handle digital and social media is becoming a popular thing to do. Funds within the marketing budget are now being shifted away from traditional advertising buys (television, newspaper, and radio) to a more targeted way to reach their audience (email, Facebook, Twitter, websites, etc.).

In the future you will see a consolidation of services from outsourced companies. IMG College's acquisition of ISP was just the start. These companies will continue to try and gain more market share in college athletics. They will do this primarily through adding more services like ticketing, chair backs, licensing, personal seat license sales, suite sales, and possibly even development work to what they have to offer schools. This will allow schools to have a one-stop-shop for outsourcing their areas of need by putting their product in the hands of the experts in the field.

Facility Management
Bredan Buckley
Director of Booking, Jerome Schottenstein Center and Nationwide Arena

Courtesy of Kimberly Miloch.

Facility management is a career option that most of my peers, including myself, never planned on pursuing. People come to facility management for different reasons; sometimes it is for a class requirement and sometimes it is because they are interested in sports as a potential career option. It is a profession that has been around for as long as there have been buildings, such as the Coliseum in Rome. It is also a profession that almost every local community, regardless of size, find themselves responsible for.

It is hard to imagine how an industry that has been around for as long as facility management could possibly change. People have been purchasing tickets for admission to live events seemingly since the beginning of time. Even the events have not changed all that much. We have gone from gladiators competing against each other in feats of strength to modern sporting exhibitions.

Many forms of entertainment come and go. There was a time in American history when the family would gather around the radio and listen to programming together. That was quickly replaced by the home television which has evolved in recent years with cable programming, shows available on demand, and high definition images. Movie theaters are losing business because the home experience has improved so much in recent years. Theaters are now offering premium experiences with exclusive showings, stadium seating, and improved food and beverage offerings just to compete with the home experience.

Fortunately for facility managers, the only thing that cannot be replaced by technology and comfort is the ability to experience a live event. It would seem that there is something in the human psyche that craves the opportunity to experience something in person, with their fellow human beings, especially something that cannot be duplicated like a sporting competition or even a concert where no two can possibly be exactly the same.

So where is this taking the facility management industry in the future? To understand that, at least in the near future, we must understand what has happened to the industry in the recent past. During the boom of the last part of the twentieth century and beginning of the twenty-first century, professional sports franchises, major universities, and local municipalities decided that they did not need to coordinate their facility efforts together in order to design a successful business model. There was enough money in the local community to sell tickets to their events, enough marketing money in the market to fill all their needs as it relates to sponsorship, and enough prospering businesses to buy long-term leases in their luxury suites.

The result of the building boom of yesteryear is that today we are dealing with a surplus of facilities, and those formerly abundant revenue streams have severely diminished due to the recent recession. Businesses are being more selective with their marketing dollars and the general public is being more selective with their personal entertainment dollars. Unfortunately, much like a home mortgage, most facilities have a thirty-year plan for addressing the debt service related to their original construction costs as well as their annual operating budgets. Many of these facilities used the assumption that the bull market would last forever and that they could count on consistent revenue streams for those thirty years.

Looking at the future of facility management I expect to see a need for bright, hardworking, entrepreneurial minded individuals who can think outside of the box and create opportunities out of the current state of the industry. The old model of "build it and they will come" no longer holds true. The successful facility manager will know how to deliver what the customer wants as far as programming and overall experience are concerned. Most importantly the facility manager of tomorrow will be on the cutting edge of marketing; knowing how to deliver a message to the customer on their terms. Customers are no longer willing to be bombarded with messages they do not feel are relevant to them. Customers know how to receive messages about only products they are already interested. We are all going to have to meet that need without betraying the trust of the customer by sending them messages they do not want to hear; shutting them out from our message forever. It is a challenge that all industries are going to struggle with in the coming years, and one that I am not entirely sure has a correct answer. This is going to take work.

High School Sports
Ananka Allen
Associate Athletic Director, Irving Independent School District

Today's high school sportscape is increasingly changing with the continuous creation of new technologies and the frequent implementations of program modifications due to current economic conditions. Athletic administrators and coaches must be flexible and willing to adapt to their changing environment, which often means researching and applying new methods to remain up-to-date with current trends. Some of the more contemporary trends in high school sport are the allowance of corporate sponsorship of high school venues and events, the presence of corporate sponsorship on high school team web pages, and the branding and marketing of high school team merchandise on a national level.

As state and federal funding of public education declines, a deficit estimated at $140 billion across 40 states (Howard, 2011) must be accounted for, which often comes in the form of decreased funding for extracurricular programs. The existing budget crisis has caused many high schools to cut back on sports across the country, which can be detrimental for the 7.6 million high

© Larry St. Pierre, 2012. Under license from Shutterstock, Inc.

school athletes who currently benefit from athletic competition. For example, many schools are eliminating purchases of new equipment, transportation to and from games, lower-level or non-revenue producing teams, and in the worst-case scenarios, entire athletic programs. Some programs have had to reduce or eliminate coaching stipends and decrease the number of coaches serving on the athletic staff altogether.

This financial deficit leaves high school athletic administrators with the difficult task of reconfiguring their budgets with the goal of saving their districts money that will support academic programs. Though the idea has been shied away from in the past, many of these athletic programs are now turning to corporate sponsorship of venues and events to generate revenue to keep their programs afloat (Pierce and Clavio, 2009). Corporations are eager to display their name on stadiums, post signage within the venues, and promote their products during games because the teenage demographic is a potential pool of new consumers. Examples of these sponsorships are as follows:

- Vernon Hills High School in Illinois sold the naming rights of its stadium for $100,000, which is now called Rust-Oleum Stadium.
- Naperville High School in Chicago agreed to name Under Armour as their official equipment sponsor which allowed banners to be hung in the school's stadium.
- Southern California's regional high school basketball championships are officially named the Toyota basketball championships because of the company's $165,000 donation.

In addition to sponsorship of high school venues, advertisements of sponsors' products and services are being made on high school sport web pages. Kentucky recently broadcasted its Boys and Girls Sweet 16 Tournaments on iHigh.com and received 254,000 views. The site allows games to be viewed on iPad, iPhone, Android, Windows, or Blackberry smartphones (Peek, 2011) and displays sponsors such as Adidas offering sport specific merchandise on its homepage. Arizona and Michigan are two states that are also moving toward incorporating this trend on their web pages (Frushour and Schmidt, 2011). Michigan's state athletic page, mhsaa.com, had 22 million page views last year, while the program has 5,400 Facebook fans and 1,200 Twitter followers that are possible targets for marketers. Arizona recently began using social media to communicate with fans and plans to create sponsor activation programs on Facebook and Twitter this year. Corporations are currently allowed to sponsor individual Arizona high schools and advertise on aia365.com, which has received over 2 million views by the end of July, 2011.

High schools are also marketing and distributing branded merchandise with their logos for purchase by consumers beyond their home towns. This allows alumni and other interested customers to purchase t-shirts, sweat shirts, hats, and other merchandise locally and through online retailers while supporting the athletic departments. A newly launched initiative by the National Federation of State High School Associations allows schools to license and distribute team merchandise for the purpose of ensuring the receipt of funds since stores may currently use high school logos without paying royalties. In its first year, the program was able to allocate $820,000 to just over 6,300 schools through local, regional, and national distribution (National Federation of State High School Associations, 2011).

When choosing to seek corporate sponsorship or to market high school merchandise, athletic directors must choose the path that will work best for their organization. Forsythe (2000) suggested high school athletic administrators should clearly spell out the benefits that involved parties will receive through any sponsorship opportunities and focus on image enhancement and increased brand awareness when participating in new forms of revenue generation for their athletic programs.

Minor League Baseball
Becky Kremer
CFO, Gary (IN) Southshore Railcats

Welcome to the world of Minor League baseball where teams live by the motto of fun, affordable, family entertainment. Between the crack of the bat to the between inning contests and mascot entertainment, baseball fans, non-baseball fans, and people of all ages can find something to enjoy. A Minor League baseball game is an overall experience, not just a game of hits, runs, and outs. Unfortunately, teams lack the help of big name players and fancy Major League stadiums, so to generate the experience and draw fans, Minor League office executives are forced to be creative and properly execute a number of trends common in Minor League

© Bill Florence, 2012. Under license from Shutterstock, Inc.

baseball. A few of these trends include group nights, promotions and giveaways, and marketing through social media.

Revenue streams in Minor Leagues are vitally important. They typically include corporate sponsorships, season tickets, mini plans, group ticket sales, and individual ticket sales. Of these five categories, group sales have become the life blood of any organization. A group sale helps guarantee two things: money paid in advance and higher attendance. A group individual who has a pre-purchased ticket is more likely to attend a baseball game when there is a chance of rain, as opposed to the individual or family who waits to buy their ticket(s) the day of the game. To increase group sales, teams have targeted corporations, businesses, and previous groups from past years. However, going above and beyond, teams have begun focusing on fundraisers and awareness days with examples such as Strike Out Lupus or Asthma Awareness Day. Not only do these days generate awareness and revenue for the purpose, but they show community support and increase attendance and revenue for the organization.

Drawing fans to a game is one element, making sure the fans have a good time to want to attend another game is a second element. This falls under the component of promotions and giveaways. Once a fan enters the ticket gate, the experience begins. A giveaway to the first specific number of fans is one attraction. Popular giveaways drawing fans include bobble heads, baseball gloves, chest protector backpacks, baseball bats, t-shirts, and hats. Another attraction and additional value to a purchased ticket is a fireworks show after the game. Trends for these two events have become Friday Fireworks and Souvenir Saturday games, although that's not always the case. In between the giveaways and fireworks, fans enjoy watching between-inning promotions such as the classic dizzy bat race, kids running across the outfield, potato sack race, and other creative promotions bringing laughter and entertainment to everyone participating and watching. Finally, the face of any Minor League team, the mascot, mingles throughout the crowd signing autographs, taking pictures, and helping create lasting memories for every fan. Many children may not know a single player's name, but they remember the furry mascot.

Marketing the team schedule is another factor imperative to the success of a Minor League organization. In the past years, trends in marketing have seen a decline in expensive television, newspaper, and radio advertisements to an increase in free e-mail newsletters, Facebook posts, Twitter tweets, YouTube videos, and other social media outlets. They are a great way to share information (press releases, team updates, game scores, and mascot appearances), to have competitions for tickets, and most importantly, to keep the team in the forefront of people's minds. Another trend in the media world is iPhone and Android applications. The benefit of having a free team application available to fans far outweighs the cost of having an application created. With up-to-date information at the touch of a finger, fans feel more involvement in the team which creates more excitement at the games. Finally, one of the newest options is advertising the team and ticket sales over Groupon. Groupon is a great way to reach thousands of fans and selling tickets to fans who may have never bought tickets before by offering a discounted deal.

The best thing about Minor League baseball is the fun never stops. Outside the box ideas are always encouraged whether they deal with new group nights, funnier promotions, or a new Facebook fan competition. Drawing the fans to the stadium and keeping the fans entertained is the goal. Making sure the fans want and know when to come back is the ultimate goal.

Social Media
Tariq Ahmad
Sports and Social Media Researcher

Social media continues to grow exponentially. Along with networking, keeping up with family and friends, and posting pictures and comments, users can also support their favorite sports teams, leagues, and athletes. With the intersection of social media and sports continuing to expand, trends and themes will emerge. Outlined below are the three trends to look out for in the future:

Engage

Social media has created a new way for fans and teams to connect with each other. Instead of reading about your favorite team or athlete in newspapers, watching TV, on the Internet, etc., social media has now broken down this medium and allows fans, teams, and athletes to directly contact each other. However, teams and leagues need to actively engage with fans. There are quite a few teams that have over a million Facebook fans, but do very little in actively communicating with fans. Instead, it is just used as a news broadcast. Talking to fans, engaging them in conversation, listening to their ideas and concerns, and making them feel valued will be the key to success through social media.

Location-based services

Location-based services (LBS) will be a major trend in the coming years. With the growth and popularity of Facebook Places, Foursquare, and SCVNGR, among other LBS sites, it is inevitable these social media tools will gain increased usage. The ability to check-in to a location to let people know where you are and what you are doing is great. I feel that more professional sports leagues and teams (as well as colleges and universities) will follow the NBA's lead and start creating applications that allow fans to show their spirit and pride more than just attending the game or wearing your favorite team's merchandise. However, the key is that these services have to provide *tangible* AND *intangible* benefits to the fans. Instead of just offering badges, offer discounts in-arena for merchandise and concessions (similar to the NBA Turnstile application). And for those who cannot make it to the arena but who check-in from home? Offer them discounts from local retailers and the official online team store, as well as discounts for tickets so they can attend future games. As for intangible benefits, offer fans a chance to meet players after the game, give them locker room access, or have the chance to sit with the media during post-game interviews.

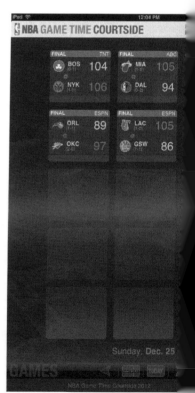

Courtesy of Brian Turner.

Mobile

With over half of the world's population owning a mobile device, it is critical to capitalize on this opportunity. As more social media sites are available to use on mobile devices, it is important to bring services to the fingertips of people. Give fans discounts for checking-in to arenas and stadiums through their mobile devices. Also, when fans are looking down at their phones (checking emails, sending text messages, etc.) during the course of a game, is a perfect time to capitalize. Let fans send tweets to the team that may be featured on the scoreboard at halftime. Let fans email pictures from their seats that will be uploaded to the team's Facebook page. People are using mobile devices: give the fan a good reason to use them for social media purposes in relation to sport.

Sponsorships

J. W. Cannon

Veteran Marketer and Sponsorship Professional

It's absolutely amazing that we've passed through what many feel is the "golden age" of the sponsorship industry, hit rock bottom, and slowly picked ourselves up off the ground as an industry all in the span of ten years. Sponsorship rights fees continued to go higher, the fees media paid for the carriage rights to sports programming went higher, and sponsorships became a larger percentage of organizations' marketing budgets. Sponsorships used to be the Teflon part of a company's marketing mix—no matter what you threw against it, somehow none of it was able to stick.

Those days, as they say, are over.

The recent collapse in the world economy has forced the industry to right-size itself. No longer are properties able to command and justify the types of rates they once received—at least not without drastically changing the ways they do business. And no longer are we as marketers able to justify spending millions of dollars on expenditures that may or may not provide an adequate value to the company.

I see three major shifts in the industry, some of which are already under way:

1. Companies will stop chasing the mythical ROI (Return on Investment) and start focusing more on ROO (Return on Objectives).

    Several years ago, some thought it was a good idea to devise a way to standardize the many intricacies of the sponsorship industry by placing a dollar value on everything. X-value for your sign. X-value in media exposure for your brand. Folks used these figures to show infinitely larger dollar returns on the amount of money that was spent on sponsorship. It caused properties to continue to drive the price tag up to unsustainable levels, and companies to continue to write large checks.

    Then one day, someone had the thought to pull back the curtain and reveal that we really hadn't accomplished anything at all. That sign in the outfield sure was pretty, but what did it do to my company's bottom line? What did it do to shift consumers' perception of my brand? All along, we had been measuring just for the sake of measuring, and not measuring what was important to us as individual sponsors.

    ROI is not what we will be chasing any more. ROO is what the smart sponsors will be focusing on, and many companies have started to realize this. Clearly defining what you expect to accomplish from a sponsorship and building in research and measurement methodology to support those objectives will be the preferred way of doing business. Every company is different and every objective is different, but when the results are strung together, they tell a story of how that sponsorship impacted your unique situation.

2. The overall sponsorship pie will continue to get bigger, but the slices will get much smaller.

The industry will continue to grow and thrive based on the fact that sponsors will get smarter about their investments, how they measure them, and how they go to market with their programming. Sports, as it often has, will continue to be the driving force behind the sponsorship industry, and will continue to get the lion's share on sponsorship investment.

However, shifts in consumer behavior have already caused investments to shift into other areas of sponsorship such as entertainment or cause-related partnerships. The more traditional sports (football, etc.) will continue to get their dollars because of their mass appeal. But more and more we'll see some of that spending shift into non-traditional sports (such as lacrosse or running)—ones where sponsors will reach fewer consumers, but will be able to connect with them more deeply and more intimately.

3. Personalization will officially replace mass appeal.

We've become a society that expects the world to revolve around us as individuals and cater to our whims. The advances in Internet and mobile technology have not just made us more connected as a society, but have allowed us to better personalize our sports and entertainment consumption. We've gone from one ESPN channel to several. DIRECTV allows you to watch any NFL game on Sunday, rather than just the ones you are forced to watch in your geographic area. Additionally, you can watch it on your PC, smart phone, or tablet. And so on, and so on.

Smart sponsorship marketers are realizing this trend, and starting to develop programming that no longer just caters to the masses. Using the advances in technology and social media, they're leveraging these new tools to better connect with individual consumers. Mass appeal mediums such as TV and radio will always play an important role, but slowly more and more dollars will shift to support niche initiatives.

Ticketing
Jeff Kline
President, Veritix
I Know You Intimately and You Have No Idea Who I Am!
It's not just about the game anymore, it's about who's attending the game, how many games they have attended, what they did when they got to the game, and will they do it again. This is all very valuable information that most teams and venues have no idea how to obtain. Ticketing used to be all about how fast you could sell tickets; mostly about distribution. Whoever had the most outlets and largest call center would sell thousands of tickets very quickly. Today, however, the world and expectations have changed. It's not just about how many tickets were sold but rather who bought them, who used them, how much they paid for them, do they have similar interests, and what else can I sell them?

Technology and innovation have come a long way to help teams understand this information. Data capture and outreach is as important, if not more so than how many tickets were sold. The power for teams to extend the fan relationship and interact directly with their fans is better now than ever before. How, you may ask? By the innovation and rapid acceptance of paperless or digital tickets. Specifically, Flash Seats. Flash Seats is a patented digital platform that allows customers to conveniently and securely buy, sell, and transfer tickets. Before I go too far, in the interest of full disclosure, I am the president of the company that developed such technology. That said, it helps to clearly illustrate my point. Data is king. Flash Seats allows consumers the ability to buy tickets and have them electronically sent to them. The ticket is tied to a unique form of identification (credit card or driver's license), something unique and intrinsically valuable to the consumer. When one purchases a ticket, they need only to register that identification and go to the gate for entry. The usher swipes that card and they are in the game. No lost, stolen or counterfeit tickets. In fact, no tickets. Just your identification and you are in. It is safe, secure, and team endorsed. By way of example you can buy seats from The Cleveland Cavaliers at Flash Seats.com. From the beginning to the end of the transaction you are on the team's website, interacting with the brand and team you love and they are doing the same. The secret sauce though is yet to come.

Because the ticket is tied to your unique form of identification and is electronic, you can easily and securely buy, sell, or transfer that seat to anyone. Each and every time the seats change hands, the team is capturing valuable data and profile information on consumers. This trend is new and exciting for sports teams everywhere. For a traditional NBA game sold with paper tickets, the team may know 4–5% of the people that are in the building. With digital tickets the team knows not only who is in each and every seat, but how often they are, what they paid for the seats, who sent them the seats, and when, and what they did once they arrived at the game. Said another way, what retail or entertainment entity can succeed by not knowing 95% of their customers? Digital technology has cast a new and very bright light on what teams are able to do with their customers. For example, if I transfer all my November and December games to my cousin, the team can and should call me and make sure everything is all right. At the same time they can and should call my cousin to see if they want to buy season tickets. The driver to delivering a deeper more meaningful relationship with the fan is DATA.

Sports is an industry that has long depended on loyalty, customer interaction, and appreciation. Until recently it had no tools to facilitate such activities. Sure you can give away t-shirts, or have a fan appreciation night, but once they walk out those doors, you have no idea who came in those doors. Data capture, security, and convenience have become staples that teams live and die by. Teams, now more than ever, understand the competition for the entertainment dollar. Consumers have many choices and priorities. You must keep them engaged and make sure they feel appreciated and valued. You can only do that if you know who they are and what they like.

The moral of the story here is that teams understand and know they have to work harder and smarter to keep fans engaged and happy. Innovation and technology have come a long way to accomplish this. Fans want to feel a part of the team. They want the same loyalty they bring to the event each and every night, reciprocated and acknowledged. In short, they expect more and teams need to deliver. Teams are working hard to develop new ways to make sure fans understand and appreciate their efforts. Both on and off the field, the court, the ice, etc. ... Yes, sports is about wins and losses. The team wins and so does the fan.

Summary

It is apparent that technology, specifically mobile, on-demand, and digital technologies will impact how students learn and also impact the manner in which consumers gather and acquire information. This will impact consumer demand and likely lead to increased specialized areas of study within sport marketing and management curriculums and specialized positions within the sport industry. This chapter highlighted the current and future challenges facing professionals in academia and in the sport marketing and management industry.

Critical Thinking Exercises

1. Consider tracking your media usage and consumption for 48 hours. Track the manner in which you communicate and acquire information. Determine your primary means of gathering and acquiring information. What are the primary purposes of your communication, and how often do you communicate via mobile or social media? Considering your own media usage and consumption, what strategies would you develop and utilize to disseminate messages about a specific sport product to a specific consumer segment?

2. After reading the trends and challenges facing industry professionals above, evaluate your skill set and experience. What skills and experience should you acquire to best prepare yourself for entry into the industry?

3. Consider the academic and industry trends and challenges outlined above. What types of specialized skills and coursework do you perceive will be needed to best prepare students for entry into the field in the next 5–10 years? Develop an activity that you believe should be included as part of a course or training for students.

Discussion Questions

1. What are the key trends facing sport marketers in the future?

2. What are the key challenges facing academics and sport industry professionals in the next several years?

3. Should the sport management curriculum be modified to better address trends and challenges facing industry professionals? If so, how do you recommend it be modified?

4. What specialized skill sets are needed among professionals desiring a career in sport marketing?

5. How will mobile and digital technology impact the manner in which students learn and consume information in the future?

6. How will mobile and digital technology impact consumer demand for sport in the next 5–10 years?

7. What role will social media play in the marketing mix?

References

Allen, I. E. and J. Seaman. *Going the distance: Online education in the United States.* Babson Park, MA: Babson Survey Research Group & Quahog Research Group, 2011.

American Association of State Colleges and Universities. "Red Balloon Project." http://www.aascu.org/Red_Balloons_Project.aspx?LangType=1033 (Para 7, 2011)

Forsythe, E. "Tackling sponsorships: Interscholastic sports administrators hoping to strike sponsorship pay dirt must learn to hone their approach strategies." *Athletic Business,* 24(12) (2000): 89–96.

Frushour, A., and C. Schmidt, Sponsors on websites: Good, bad, necessary? "Presented at the 2011 Annual National Federation of High Schools Summer Meeting, Philadelphia, PA, July.

Howard, B. "Education funding crisis affects activity programs." *High School Today,* 4(8) (2011): 10–12.

National Federation of State High School Associations. "Game stats." *High School Today,* 4(7) (2011): 22.

Parkhouse, B.L. "Sport management curricula: Current status and design implications for future development." *Journal of Sport Management,* 1(2) (1987): 93–115.

Peek, S. "Kentucky 'smartly' broadcast basketball games." *High School Today,* 4(8) (May, 2011): 38.

Pierce, D. and G. Clavio. "Examining the use of corporate sponsorship in Indiana high school football." *Indiana AHPERD Journal,* 38(1) (2009) 4–9.

Reynolds, R. "Trends influencing the growth of digital textbooks in US Higher Education." *Publishing Research Quarterly,* 27(2) (2011): 178–187.

Whitney, L. "Cell phone subscriptions to hit 5 billion globally." *CNET Reviews*, February 16, 2010, http://reviews.cnet.com/8301-13970_7-10454065-78.html

Glossary

Acceptance the manifestation of assent to the terms of an offer in the manner invited or required by the same. The acceptance might be an action, abstaining from an action, or something else.

Accessibility one of the key criteria for investing in segmentation initiatives. The organization must determine whether or not the consumer segment could be reached through traditional communication mediums (e.g., advertisements, cold calls).

Achievement Motivation motive driven by the need to win, to compete, and to be the best. Sport participants motivated by these needs require social comparison. It is not enough to improve; they must be better than their competitors.

Activation creating a connection with consumers. An activation strategy or plan ensures that the components and elements of the sponsorship are being utilized in a manner that meets sponsor objectives.

Advertising form of communication used to persuade consumers to purchase an organization's products and/or services.

Ambush Marketing a marketing campaign that takes place around an event but does not involve payment of a sponsorship fee for such exposure.

Americans with Disabilities Act a federal law enacted to protect and insure equal rights and treatment for Americans with disabilities.

Anticybersquatting Consumer Protection Act (ACPA) law enacted to "protect consumers and American businesses, to promote the growth of online commerce, and to provide clarity in the law for trademark owners by prohibiting the bad-faith and abusive registration of distinctive marks as Internet domain names with the intent to profit from the goodwill associated with Marks." (Senate Report No. 106-140, at 4).

Arbitrary Mark also known as fanciful mark; it is a mark that bears no logical relationship to the underlying product. "Xerox" is an example. Arbitrary or fanciful marks are inherently distinctive.

Aspirational Reference Groups groups (e.g., teams, individual players on a team, etc.) that consumers aspire to be like. Marketers use sport teams and athletes as spokespersons or in advertisements to take advantage of their position as an aspirational reference group.

Associative Learning Theory suggests consumers store information in association sets. Typically these association sets contain information that is similar or connected in a particular way. In matching athletes with product endorsements, the intent of the marketer is to connect a specific athlete with a product or brand so that over time, the two become part of the same association set.

Asymmetrical Communication Model two-way public relations model that is imbalanced in that information leaves the organization and attempts to persuade/change public behavior.

Attachment a feeling that binds an individual to an entity. In sports, this could be to a team, player, coach, or event.

Attitudes a general evaluation of something. Attitudes can be thought of as liking or disliking and include the strength of feelings toward an object. A large part of sport marketing efforts are designed to change people's attitudes in order to create positive thoughts, feelings, and intentions toward our products and services. Attitudes consist of three components: (1) beliefs, the cognitive aspect of attitudes; (2) feelings, the affective aspect of attitudes; and (3) experiences, the behavioral aspect of attitudes.

Attractiveness an essential signal in an individual's original judgment of a person. One of the three most important characteristics in positively impacting endorser effectiveness (the others being **trustworthiness** and **expertise**).

Balance Theory people try to maintain a sense of balance in their lives and their actions and judgments are often influenced by the need to preserve such balance. In general, the adages "your friends are my friends" and "the enemy of my enemy is my friend" summarize the balance theory.

Bases for Segmentation the consumer characteristics that sport organizations consider when developing specific marketing plans. Could include demographics, psychographics, and behavioral.

BIRGing basking in reflected glory. When a fan's team wins, fans extend the win (and achievement) to themselves. A BIRGing fan would say "we won" in this instance.

Blended Courses See **Hybrid Courses**.

Blog or web log, is an internet-based journal used to communicate unique, consumer-friendly material which promotes the organization's agenda. It provides an avenue for consumers' interest in hearing directly from current and former players, coaches, and front office personnel.

Brand a verbal or visual way of identifying the sport product as distinguished from other sport product, such as a name, design, symbol, or some combination of the three. Products or services that communicate and interact with consumers through identifiable and unique experiences.

Brand Architecture represents a variety of products across a range of targeted customers to maximize potential growth (Keller, 2009).

Brand Associations unique connections linking the individual to characteristics of the sport consumption (Gladden & Funk, 2002).

Brand Attributes appeal to the emotional essence of the brand and the individual characteristics linked to the preferences of consumption.

Brand Awareness consumer ability to recognize a given brand in a variety of settings and the identification of brand with a particular category (Aaker, 1991; Keller 1998).

Brand Endorsements See **Endorsements**.

Brand Equity the actual or relative value of the company related to its ability to generate a profit, and refers to the elevated price a consumer will pay for a well-established brand compared to its generic equivalent (Brewer & Pedersen, 2009; Keller, 1998).

Brand Identity the personality of the brand (Shank, 2004, 228). See also **Brand Image**.

Brand Image perceptions about a brand formed by the consumers' memory (Ross, 2006; Ross et al., 2008). The consumers' set of beliefs about a brand (Shank, 2004, 228).

Brand Loyalty consumer loyalty by consistent and continuous repeat purchasing of a specific sport product or brand.

Brand Management the strategic craft of developing an identity in the marketplace, creating valuable emotional connections through experiences, and determining characteristics that attract loyal customers.

Brand Positioning "a relatively stable set of consumer perceptions (or meanings) of a brand in relation to competitive alternatives" (Kates & Goh, 2003, 59).

Break-Even Analysis the point at which total costs (i.e., fixed costs + variable costs) equals total revenue. This is calculated by dividing the fixed costs by the contribution margin, which is price minus the variable cost per unit (i.e., fan).

Bundled the practice of combining and selling multiple items for one price (e.g., season ticket packages will often be bundled with ancillary items such as parking or other specialty products or service).

Causal Designs useful in examining if changes in one variable develop changes in the outcome or behavior of another variable being measured.

Cause-Related Marketing (CRM) typically considered a partnership between the sport entity and a cause to attract consumers who want to make a difference through their purchasing.

Competitive Marketing sponsorship pricing strategy in which sport organizations examine other similar sponsorships, either in the respective geographic market or in other similar markets, to ascertain appropriate pricing.

Consideration one of the elements of an enforceable express contract. It comes in two forms: a benefit to the promisor (i.e., the party making the promise or offer) and a detriment to the offeree (the party accepting the offer). The most common type of consideration is the payment of money.

Contract an enforceable, legally binding agreement between two or more parties.

Copyright Law protects "works of authorship." The Copyright Act states that works of authorship include the following types of works, amongst others: literary works, novels, nonfiction prose, poetry, newspapers, magazines, computer software, manuals, catalogs, brochures, musical works, songs, plays, operas, choreographic works, sculptural works, photographs, maps, paintings, drawings, graphic art, cartoon strips and cartoon characters, audiovisual works, movies, videos, television shows, interactive multimedia works, sound recordings, architectural works, and designs (17 U.S. Const. §102).

Copyright Notice optional for works distributed after March 1, 1989, but creators of copy-rightable content would certainly want to feature such notice for, if nothing else, their own credits. Copyright notice can take any of these three forms: (1) the "©" Symbol followed by a date and name (e.g., © 2011 National Football League); (2) "Copyright" followed by a date and name (e.g., Copyright 2011 National Football League); (3) "Copr." followed by a date and name (e.g., Copr. 2011 National Football League; 17 U.S. Const. §401).

CORFing cutting off reflected failure. Opposite of **BIRGing** where fans tend to distance themselves from a loss in order to protect their self-esteem. A CORFing fan would say "they lost" after their team loses a game.

Corporate Citizenship (CC) administering citizenship rights for individuals through compliance with ethical governance, endorsing global standards, and promoting philanthropic and volunteer activities (Matten & Crane, 2005).

Corporate Social Responsibility (CSR) organizational practice that manifests itself in a variety of forms such as event programming, environmental sustainability, and corporate citizenry. Sport organizations which engage in CSR are frequently considered to be involved in "cause-related marketing."

Corporate Social Responsiveness (CSR2) typically refers to how organizations respond to societal demands.

Cost-Plus Method sponsorship pricing strategy that is determined by calculating the total actual expenses in providing a sponsorship package plus the organizations desired profit. The total expenses listed need to include labor, production, signage, souvenirs, and all other aspects of the event or package.

Cost-Plus Pricing pricing method where a fixed percentage mark-up is added to the cost of a product. This is more common with tangible sport products, such as equipment or souvenirs.

Cover Letter a letter outlining a job applicant's credentials and accomplishments typically used in conjunction with a resume.

Culture an external factor that affects customer consumption behaviors. It exerts a powerful influence on our norms, values, attitudes, beliefs, and consequently, on the decisions we make.

Customary Pricing pricing method in which customers expect a certain traditional price (e.g., $5 "cheap seats"). Customary pricing is especially strong where consumers are used to consuming their sports for free.

Customer Relationship Management (CRM) a business strategy designed to maximize profitability and customer satisfaction through the coordination of initiatives to build, nurture, and sustain fan identify and/or consumer loyalty.

Descriptive Mark one that describes a characteristic of the underlying product (e.g., "Comfort Inn," describes the underlying product; a hotel room). The mark tells us something about the product.

Descriptive Research appropriate for targeted group study, and the examination of relationships between two or more variables connected to a target group.

Direct Reference Groups family and friends; they are likely to interact with you directly.

Distance Education a term used to describe courses and education offered partially or fully online.

Distribution the place from which the product can be purchased. See also **Place**.

Diversification offering a new product to a new market.

Duress also known as undue influence; occurs when a party agrees to enter into a contract because that party has been induced to do so by an improper threat that leaves the party with no other choice than to enter into the contract. The contract is voidable by the party that was subject to such inducement and/or improper threat.

Dynamic Pricing method where prices can change daily based on a set of variables (Muret & Lombardo, 2010).

80/20 Principle principle outlining that 80% of a company's revenue is generated from 20% of its customers.

Electronic Portfolios an electronic version of a portfolio. See also **Portfolio**.

Emotions an internal factor that affects customers' consumption behaviors. It is an affective state of having joy, sadness, love, hate, etc.

Endorsements well-established advertising technique where a celebrity is used to try to sell an organization's products and services.

Eustress the positive stress associated with high levels of arousal and excitement, drives many to watch sport competitions.

Exchange Theory idea that a successful exchange between two or more parties is dependent on both parties feeling what they receive for their services or goods is equal to their offerings (Crompton, 2004).

Experimental Research appropriate research to employ for causal-comparative research because it utilizes the manipulation of variables against constants.

Expertise the extent to which an endorser is perceived to be a source of valid statements (Hovland et al., 1953). One of the three most important characteristics in positively impacting endorser effectiveness (the others being **trustworthiness** and **attractiveness**).

Explanatory Research attempts to answer the critical questions of how and why, associated with sport consumption, to help predict future trends, behaviors, and preferences. Expands on descriptive research.

Exploratory Research flexible and dynamic type of research aimed to gain a deeper understanding about a particular problem, idea, and/or issue that has not been clearly identified.

Fair Use not an infringement of copyright; includes use for purposes such as criticism, comment, news, education, parody, etc. Determined by balancing (1) the purpose and character of the use; (2) the nature of the copyrighted work; (3) the amount and substantiality of the portion used in relation to the copyrighted work as a whole; and (4) the effect of the use on the potential market for, or value of, the copyrighted work (17 U.S. Const. §107).

Fanciful Mark See **Arbitrary Mark**.

First Amendment part of the Bill of Rights. It prohibits Congress from interfering with citizens' freedom of religion, speech, assembly, or petition. In sports, it is often asserted as a defense in fantasy sports actions involving trademark or copyright infringement or the right of publicity since the reporting of news is protected under this amendment.

First Right of Refusal mandates that the sport entity allow the sponsor to first rights to renew the sponsorship. In other words, the sport entity will not offer the sponsorship or any of its components to another potential sponsor unless the current company decides not to renew the sponsorship.

Fraud See **Misrepresentation**.

Generic mark one that describes the general category to which the underlying product belongs. For example, the term "Computer" is a generic term for computer equipment. Generic marks are not entitled to protection under trademark law.

Goals broad-based or general statements designed to provide programmatic direction and typically focus on ends rather than means (Allison & Kaye, 2005; Le Blanc, 2008).

Goods tangible products with physical features that offer benefits to customers.

Historical methods trace the various aspects of culture and change in society within narrative and analytical forms to promote the sequential understanding of events/activities through the cultural products people create such as architecture, art, and literature (Seifried, 2010).

Hybrid Courses courses that include a mix of online and face to face course components.

Identifiability one of the key criteria for investing in segmentation initiatives. The organization must be able to recognize a specific, targeted market.

Identification the extent to which an individual feels psychologically connected to an entity. In sports it could be to a player or coach, but more often it is **team identification**.

Impossibility when a party is rendered unable to fulfill contractual obligations because the promised performance has become impossible.

Incapacity If a party attempting to enter into an agreement has not reached the age of majority (usually 18 years old, depending on the state) or is mentally infirm, then the contract will be voidable or, in certain circumstances, "void," which means the agreement is rescinded as a matter of law as though it was never entered into or enforced. Minors can rescind an enforceable contract with a non-minor party up until turning the age of majority or shortly thereafter.

Indirect Reference Groups include groups to which you aspire, subcultures, social institutions such as media, religion, and political and educational systems, and even ethnic and national cultures.

Intellectual Property Law See **patents**, **trademarks**, and **copyrights**.

Internships academic accredited work experiences obtained by students before graduating from an academic program which provide practical on-the-job experience.

Interview a formal interaction between an employer and a job applicant.

Lanham Act the federal law governing trademarks. It was enacted in 1946 and most recently amended in 1996.

Leveraging process of communicating and marketing a sponsorship to consumers. In other words, when leveraging a sponsorship, companies desire to create an awareness of their association with the respective sport entity among the target consumer base.

Licensing a legal process in which two parties agree to terms specific to the use of a name, likeness, logo, or symbol of a player, union, team, league, or licensor in connection with a specific product.

Marketing the activity focusing on satisfying needs and wants through exchange processes.

Marketing Goals provide direction for marketing programs, and assist in defining the purpose of the plan, guide the planning process, and define what is to be accomplished.

Marketing Management Philosophy in the sport industry, this is generally one of market orientation where the organization strives to focus on customer wants and needs in an effort to satisfy them.

Marketing Mix the strategic integration and utilization of the five P's of marketing, product, price, place, promotion, and public relations.

Marketing Objectives marketing specific performance targets necessary to achieve each designated marketing goal. See also **Objectives**.

Marketing Plan a written document outlining an organization's strategy and the course of action necessary to implement that strategy.

Marketing Research a systematic process approach involving the collection, organization, examination, and presentation of information on a defined area of study to enhance decisions throughout the strategic marketing process.

Market Development offering existing products to a new market by presenting existing products in a way that will attract new consumer groups.

Market Penetration development of strategies that cause an organization's existing consumers to consume more of its product(s) or gain customers from the competition.

Market Segmentation the process of dividing a large, heterogeneous market into smaller groups of more homogeneous groups with similar wants, needs, and/or demands.

Mastery Motivation a more intrinsic motivation often represented as competition with one's self. It does not require social comparison. Challenge and learning play a big role in motivating mastery-oriented sports participants.

Match-Up Hypothesis illustrates the importance of "fit" between the endorser and product. The more natural the fit between the endorser and the product (i.e., the more the relationship between the two makes intuitive sense to consumers) the more effective the endorsement is likely to be. Based on the **Associative Learning Theory**.

Media Relations primarily concerned with maintaining strong relationships with the media at a local, regional, and sometimes national or international level.

Meeting of the Minds one of the elements of an enforceable express contract. Some refer to this as "agreeing to definite terms." Even if there is an offer, acceptance, and consideration, the agreement could be unenforceable if the agreement is indefinite with regards to the essential terms of the given arrangement. In other words, a contract has to be more than an agreement to agree.

Meta-Personal Connection concept that states consumers are increasingly interested in electronically mediated personal engagement from their sources of sports entertainment, in addition to (or as opposed to) face-to-face personal engagement.

Misrepresentation "an assertion that is not in accord with the facts."(RESTATEMENT (SECOND) OF CONTRACTS §159). Misrepresentation will render a contract voidable if the misrepresentation was either fraudulent (knowingly false) or material (important) and induced the relying party's justifiable and reasonable reliance in entering into the particular contract.

Mission Statement an organizational statement that differentiates the organization from other organizations by declaring what business the organization performs and whom the organization serves.

Mistake a belief that is not in accord with the facts. A mistake will render a contract voidable when, at the time the contract is formed, a basic erroneous assumption on which such agreement was based materially affects the exchange of performances.

Motivation driving force behind our actions. In sport marketing, it can be characterized as the needs and desires of potential fans, participants, and other sport consumers. Sport marketers are successful when they can identify the core needs of their target markets, and design and promote products that meet those needs.

New Media a merging of traditional media forms (such as audio, video, and written word) with interactive digital technology, frequently through the moderating factor of the Internet. New media's focus is on interactivity and individual consumer focus, as opposed to the broader audience approach of traditional media.

Objectives represent specific performance targets necessary to achieve each designated goal. Objectives are specific, measurable, achievable, relevant, and timely statements that support each marketing goal.

Odd-Even Pricing prices that are just below a whole number (e.g., $49.95 instead of $50). Consumers perceive the lower price as a greater value despite the small difference.

Offer a demonstration of a desire to enter into an agreement and represents the first element of the formation process. An offer is usually in writing, but can be oral.

One-to-one Marketing a practice in which sport marketers strive to cater to individualized products, promotions, and avenues of communication unique to each buyer.

Organizational Culture the shared values, beliefs, and assumptions of organizational members that guide and establish preferred behaviors within an organization (Shein, 1991).

Outcome Objectives an objective that identifies the end result or outcome for users of the organization's products and services as a result of their participation.

Partnership Assets representative of early social involvement by sport entities and characterized by partnerships between sport entities and causes.

Patents essentially a limited monopoly that gives the patent holder the exclusive right to make, use and sell the patented innovation, which in most cases is an invention, for a limited period of time.

Perceptions customer interpretations of messages they receive based on their personal knowledge and experiences.

Personal Selling a form of promotion involving any face-to-face communication between the seller and a potential consumer.

Place refers to the location from which the product can be purchased. See also **Distribution**.

Podcasts an audio or video content package which is distributed through digital means. In most cases, the term podcast is synonymous with audio content, and this audio content is normally distributed as an MP3, which is generally a small, compressed audio format that is playable on a variety of hardware, including home computers, smartphones, and personal music players.

Porter's 5 Forces Model developed by Michael Porter (1989), this analysis model focuses on internal and external factors influencing marketing success.

Portfolio a collection of materials used to showcase a job applicant's skills, credentials, and appropriate samples of work pertinent to specific jobs or positions within the workforce.

Positioning refers to the process in which marketers try to create an image for their organization, goods, or services in the mind of their target markets (Reis & Trout, 1981).

Post-Purchase Evaluation the act of consumers continuing to evaluate their purchase decisions after the purchase has been made.

Press-Agency Model one-way public relations model that involves seeking attention in almost any form. These are among the most traditional in sport, usually relying on the mass media to aid in the dissemination process.

Prestige Pricing charging unusually high prices for a product to help maintain an exclusive image (e.g., courtside seats at an NBA game).

Price the amount a customer pays for a product.

Primary Data sources of data emerging directly from those involved with events or activities associated with the specific research question related to the study.

Process Management the process of aligning organizational marketing strategy with staffing and financial resources.

Process Objectives objectives that serve to specify a tactic, action, or means to achieve outcome objectives. Also known as **action objectives**.

Product typically refers to the sport contest or game itself. Also refers to that which is being marketed.

Product Development offering a new product to an existing market.

Product Extensions items or additional products helping to make the product more tangible for the consumer. Examples include game programs and souvenirs.

Product Life Cycle (PLC) tool to evaluate the various stages that products pass through during their life. Includes four stages: introduction, growth, maturity, and decline.

Promotion method used by the sport marketer to create awareness of the sport product in the minds of consumers.

Promotional Mix "the combination of tools available for sport marketers to communicate with the public" (Shank, 2010, 277).

Psychographics process of segmentation where marketers make their decisions based on the psychological preferences of the consumers being targeted. Described as an innovative marketing strategy, this method is characterized by the use of an individual's "mindset" to make business decisions.

Psychological Involvement an internal factor that affects customers' consumption behaviors. It is a function of one's interest in a player, team, sport, brand, or sport organization and their importance in one's life.

Public Information Model one-way public relations model that focuses on the dissemination of accurate and favorable information about the organization.

Publicity media exposure for the sport organization that the organization does not actually pay for.

Public Relations "managerial communication-based function designed to identify a sport organization's key publics, evaluate its relationships with those publics, and foster desirable relationships between the sport organization and those key publics" (Stoldt et al., 2012, 2).

Qualitative Research data research and analysis measures that provide rich descriptions of reality, but are difficult to generalize due to the special attention to specific environments.

Quality Reference Point point that consumers use to gauge their consumption decisions. When consumers are constantly provided with products that exceed their expectations, they then have a new quality reference point.

Quantitative Research data research and analysis measures offering tightness of control (e.g., how many people attend sporting events and venues as live or remote spectators).

Reference Group serve as a point of comparison or a sounding board for the choices we make. They influence our values, attitudes, perceptions, and even our sense of who we are. Reference groups can be either **direct** or **indirect** in their influence.

Reference Pricing a price someone expects based on previous experience or value judgment. This can be a competitor's price, a stated "regular" price, or value judgment.

Relational Assets the concept that consumers will reward "good" organizations through sustained relations when organizations engage in social involvement.

Relative Value sponsorship pricing strategy which utilizes market research and published data to assess sponsorship value. In comparing pricing for a sponsorship, it is important to understand that a relative value can also be determined using research and a suggested relative value assigned (e.g., signage at a minor league baseball park could be compared to the cost of a billboard in the same geographic area).

Reposition a strategy where an organization attempts to change the image or perception of a product or service in the minds of consumers.

Reputational Assets building a positive and consistent reputation among consumers through social involvement.

Responsiveness one of the key criteria for investing in segmentation initiatives. This is the most important segmentation criterion because it determines whether a potential target market will be interested in your product.

Resume a document outlining a job applicant's contact information, qualifications, education, employment history, and other pertinent details submitted for consideration of employment.

Retention Potential one of the key criteria for investing in segmentation initiatives. It relates to whether or not the consumer segment can become repeat purchasers. While retention is not necessarily a mandatory segmentation criterion, it is at least important to consider because it provides sport organizations with an understanding of the working environment they are facing as they move forward with their marketing initiatives.

Right of Privacy comprised of four torts: (1) intrusion upon one's seclusion, solitude or private affairs; (2) public disclosure of embarrassing private facts about that person; (3) publicity which places him or her in a false light in the public eye; and (4) appropriation, for another party's advantage, of one's name, voice, likeness, identity, style, or persona. The first three are variations of the right to be let alone. The fourth does not involve privacy at all, but the right of commercial exploitation of identity (in other words, a **Right of Publicity**).

Right of Publicity the right of a person to be compensated for the use of his or her name, nickname, image, likeness, or other identifying characteristic for a commercial purpose, usually in an advertising or marketing campaign. This right protects the property interest in the publicity value of one's identify.

Rights companies purchase "rights" from sport entities in order to engage in sponsorship with the sport entity and use its images in promoting the sponsorship.

Salary Negotiation negotiations focused on monetary compensation for work performed based on type of position, skill sets, and duties and responsibilities associated with a specific position.

Sales Promotions "short term incentives, usually designed to stimulate immediate demand for sports products or services" (Shank, 2005, 277).

Secondary Data data existing in a variety of forms, but generally has been collected at a previous point in time.

Secondary Meaning acquired when the consuming public associates that mark with a particular source, rather than the underlying product (e.g., "Comfort Inn" has acquired secondary meaning because the consuming public associates that term with a particular provider of hotel services, and not with hotel services in general). When determining whether Marks have acquired secondary meaning, courts look at: (1) the amount and manner of advertising; (2) the volume of sales; (3) the length and manner of the Marks' use; and (4) results of consumer surveys.

Self-Esteem a more general need or motivation that can also drive sports spectating. Being a fan of a sports team can enhance one's self-esteem and maintain one's self-concept.

Service Quality a consumer's comparison of expectations with actual performance. The key to defining quality is to view it from the customer's (fan's) perspective. Different customers will seek different dimensions of quality, including product performance, features, reliability, conformity, durability, serviceability, aesthetics, and perceived quality.

Services intangible, less standardized, perishable from a time perspective, heterogeneous and often inseparable from the provider.

Social Media a form of digital, interactive communication that for sport organizations can be both public relations and marketing. Social media creates dialogue, that it is two-way. It engages individuals in conversations and creates relationships.

Social Motivation the participation motive most linked to spectator motives. Sport participants with a need for social interaction can clearly find that in team sports and also through the social life surrounding sport competitions.

Social Networking a collection of individuals who share connections, and through those connections are able to exchange information and opinion.

Sponsorship "an investment, in cash or in kind, in an activity, in return for access to the exploitable commercial potential associated with that activity" (Meenaghan, 1991, 36).

Sponsorship Inventory a list of items that a sport entity has available to include as elements of a sponsorship. The inventory also includes the number of each item available and the market value of the item. Examples include season tickets, luxury suite, signage, community relations activities, in-arena or on-field promotions, public address announcements, website advertising, and so forth.

Sport Marketing the activities of product and service marketers using sport as a promotional vehicle or sponsorship platform (Gray & McEvoy, 2005).

Sport Promotional Mix the strategic utilization and integration of communication channels designed to achieve sport marketing objectives and reinforce brand image. Traditional elements of the promotional mix include advertising, public and community relations, and sales strategy and promotion.

Sports Agent Responsibility and Trust Act (SPARTA) made it unlawful for an agent to provide student-athletes with false or misleading information, false or misleading promises or representations, or anything of value. Additionally, SPARTA requires that agents warn student-athletes in a disclosure form that they may lose their eligibility if they sign an agency contract or falsify its date. Serves as a federal backstop to the **Uniform Athlete Agent Act (UAAA)** and has a primary focus on regulation and enforcement.

Subculture an external factor that affects customers' consumption behaviors. It is a subset of a larger culture and operates in ways similar to aspirational groups.

Substantiality one of the key criteria for investing in segmentation initiatives. It is primarily concerned with determining if a potential segment is large enough (and/or with enough resources) to justify the investment in a segmentation process.

Suggestive Mark one that suggests a characteristic of the underlying good (e.g., "Coppertone" is suggestive of sun tan lotion, but does not specifically describe the underlying product).

SWOT Analysis an analysis by which organizations identify internal and external factors to capitalize on (strengths and opportunities) and factors needing to be controlled or eliminated (weaknesses and threats).

Symmetrical Communication Model two-way public relations model that is balanced and uses both research and dialogue to adjust the relationship between an organization and its publics. Understanding, rather than persuasion, is the principal objective of two-way symmetrical public relations.

Target Markets the segments for which marketers feel they will have the most success pursuing. Target markets are selected based on a thorough analysis of consumer data, and choices should be consistent with marketing objectives.

Team Identification the extent to which an individual feels psychologically connected to a sports team. It is an important consumer behavior variable because the more a fan sees himself as a fan of the team, the more he/she supports the team.

Theoretical Research use of various techniques and methods to create conclusions about a topic of investigation through deductive reasoning and the use of data explored.

Tort a civil harm committed between two parties. There are two types of torts: intentional torts and torts that arise from conduct that was not intentional, but nevertheless caused the harm in question. The latter usually falls into the categories of negligence, gross negligence or recklessness.

Trademarks distinctive identifiers that make it easy for consumers to identify the source of products. It could be a name, word, symbol, etc. that distinguishes an organization's products from those of competitors.

Trustworthiness the degree of confidence in the endorser's aim to communicate the statements he/she considers most valid (Hovland et al., 1953). One of the three most important characteristics in positively impacting endorser effectiveness (the others being **expertise** and **attractiveness**).

Unconscionability unfair surprise or oppressive terms in a contract. This type of assertion is usually made where a party was not represented by counsel and the terms of the contract that the party agreed to are so outrageous that it would be an injustice for the contract to be enforced with the agreed upon terms.

Undue Influence See **Duress**.

Uniform Athlete Agent Act (UAAA) regulates agents, reduce student-athlete ineligibility, and protect academic institutions from sanctions. The UAAA requires that agents register with the state prior to contacting a student-athlete. Additionally, agents must disclose their professional and criminal history to the Secretary of State for the state in which the athlete attends college and/or resides. The UAAA also requires agents to grant the Secretary of State the authority to issue subpoenas if compliance information is needed. Further, the UAAA prohibits agents from funneling money or tangible benefits to student-athletes and their families. Agents that violate these regulations are subject to criminal and administrative penalties.

Uniform Internet Gaming Enforcement Act of 2006 (UIGEA) states that no person engaged in the business of betting or wagering may knowingly accept directly or indirectly virtually any type of payment from a participant in unlawful internet gambling (i.e., bets that are unlawful under other state or federal laws).

Value Chain Analysis an analysis and model developed by Michael Porter (1985) which focuses on activities that enhance organizational marketing.

Variable Ticket Pricing involves setting multiple price points. This idea of "smoothing" or variable pricing is where two different prices are changed based on prime and non-prime schedules. This has been most noticed within the sport product category with seat location within a stadium or venue.

Vision Statement a statement that incorporates the primary vision of how the organization activates its mission statement.

Void when an agreement is rescinded as a matter of law as though it was never entered into or enforced.

Voidable Contract a contract that potentially could be rescinded by one of the parties involved. The circumstances that most commonly make an otherwise enforceable sports marketing contract voidable are **incapacity, duress** or **undue influence, misrepresentation** or **fraud, mistake, unconscionability,** and **impossibility**.

Volunteering the act of working for non-financial compensation.

Works Made for Hire works created by employees for employers and certain types of specially commissioned works (e.g., a painted portrait). The copyright term for "works made for hire" is 95 years from the date of first "publication" (distribution of copies to the general public) or 120 years from the date of creation, whichever expires first.

Works of Authorship include the following types of works, amongst others: literary works, novels, nonfiction prose, poetry, newspapers, magazines, computer software, manuals, catalogs, brochures, musical works, songs, plays, operas, choreographic works, sculptural works, photographs, maps, paintings, drawings, graphic art, cartoon strips and cartoon characters, audiovisual works, movies, videos, television shows, interactive multimedia works, sound recordings, architectural works, and designs.

Index